BEGINNING
IPHONE® SDK PROGRAMMING with OBJECT...

▶ PART V APPENDICES

BEGINNING

iPhone® SDK Programming
with Objective-C®

BEGINNING

iPhone® SDK Programming with Objective-C®

Wei-Meng Lee

Wiley Publishing, Inc.

Beginning iPhone® SDK Programming with Objective-C®

Published by
Wiley Publishing, Inc.
10475 Crosspoint Boulevard
Indianapolis, IN 46256
www.wiley.com

Published simultaneously in Canada

ISBN: 978-0-470-50097-2

Manufactured in the United States of America

10 9 8 7 6 5 4 3 2 1

For general information on our other products and services please contact our Customer Care Department within the United States at (877) 762-2974, outside the United States at (317) 572-3993 or fax (317) 572-4002.

Wiley also publishes its books in a variety of electronic formats. Some content that appears in print may not be available in electronic books.

Library of Congress Control Number: 2009940280

To my family:
Thanks for the understanding and support while I
worked on getting this book ready! I love you all!

ABOUT THE AUTHOR

WEI-MENG LEE is a technologist and founder of Developer Learning Solutions (www.learn2develop.net), a technology company specializing in hands-on training for the latest Microsoft and Mac OS X technologies. He is also an established author with Wrox and O'Reilly.

Wei-Meng first started the iPhone programming course in Singapore and it has since received much positive feedback. His hands-on approach to iPhone programming makes understanding the subject much easier than reading books, tutorials, and documentation from Apple.

Contact Wei-Meng at weimenglee@learn2develop.net.

CREDITS

ACQUISITIONS EDITOR
Scott Meyers

PROJECT EDITOR
Ami Frank Sullivan

TECHNICAL EDITOR
Trenton Shumay

PRODUCTION EDITOR
Eric Charbonneau

COPY EDITOR
Susan Christopherson

EDITORIAL DIRECTOR
Robyn B. Siesky

EDITORIAL MANAGER
Mary Beth Wakefield

MARKETING MANAGER
Ashley Zurcher

PRODUCTION MANAGER
Tim Tate

VICE PRESIDENT AND EXECUTIVE GROUP PUBLISHER
Richard Swadley

VICE PRESIDENT AND EXECUTIVE PUBLISHER
Barry Pruett

ASSOCIATE PUBLISHER
Jim Minatel

PROJECT COORDINATOR, COVER
Lynsey Stanford

PROOFREADER
Jen Larsen, Word One

INDEXER
Johnna VanHoose Dinse

COVER DESIGNER
Michael E. Trent

COVER IMAGE
© JamesBrey/istockphoto

ACKNOWLEDGMENTS

WRITING A BOOK IS A HUGE COMMITMENT, and writing a book on iPhone programming is an even larger commitment. Now that this book is finally done, I would like to take this chance to thank the many people who made this a reality.

First, I want to thank Scott Meyers, who had faith in me when he signed me up for this book. I hope I have not disappointed him. Thank you, Scott!

Next, a huge thanks to Ami Sullivan, my editor, who is the real hero who got this book done. During the writing process, I was very involved in running iPhone courses and when I was off course in the writing road, Ami pulled me up and gently gave me a nudge. She was firm in having me adhere to the strict deadlines, but was very understanding when things slipped. I deeply appreciate her patience with me, for without her, this book would not be in your hands now. For that, please accept my sincere thanks, Ami!

Last, but not least, I want to thank my parents, and my wife, Sze Wa, for all the support they have give me. They have selflessly adjusted their schedules to accommodate my busy schedule when I was working on this book. My wife has also stayed up with me on numerous nights as I was furiously working to meet the deadlines, and for this I would like to say this to her and my parents: "I love you all!" Finally, to our lovely dog, Ookii, thanks for staying by my side, even though you may not understand why I was always pounding on my keyboard!

CONTENTS

PART V: APPENDICES

INTRODUCTION

The iPhone SDK was officially announced by Apple on March 6, 2008, at an Apple Town Hall meeting. In the early days of the SDK, iPhone development was shrouded in secrecy because Apple has imposed a Non-Disclosure Agreement (NDA) on developers who downloaded the SDK. No one was allowed to publicly discuss the SDK and the various APIs shipped with it. Apple had presumably done this to ensure the stability of the SDK. This move caused an uproar from developers because it prevented them from posting questions on public forums and getting help quickly. Nor could books be written about it or training courses developed. The adoption of Objective-C as the programming language for the iPhone SDK did not help. In fact, that language has a steep learning curve for developers, who for the most part are coming from more mainstream languages such as Java, C++, C#, and VB.NET.

With pressure from the public, Apple finally lifted the NDA in late 2008. This was welcome news to developers, albeit a little late. Overnight, discussion forums appeared and Web sites dedicated to iPhone development mushroomed.

Although Web sites and discussion forums talking about iPhone development are numerous, one obstacle remains — the learning curve for getting started is simply too great. Many developers are struggling to get started with Xcode and Interface Builder. At the same time, they have to grapple with the arcane syntax of Objective-C and to constantly remember which objects to free up and which ones not to.

This book was written to bridge the gap.

When I first started learning about iPhone development, I went through the same journey that most iPhone developers go through: Write a Hello World application, mess with Interface Builder, try to understand what the code is doing, and repeat that process. I was also overwhelmed by the concept of a View Controller and wondered why it is needed if I simply want to display a view. My background in developing for Windows Mobile and Android did not help much, and I had to start working with this concept from scratch.

This book is written to make the life of a beginning iPhone developer as easy as possible. It covers the various topics in such a manner that you will progressively learn without being overwhelmed by the details. I adopt the philosophy that the best way to learn is by doing, hence the numerous Try It Out sections in all the chapters, which first show you how to build something and then explain how things work.

Although iPhone programming is a huge topic, my aim for this book is to get you started with the fundamentals, understand the underlying architecture of the SDK, and appreciate why things are done certain ways. It is beyond the scope of this book to cover everything under the sun related to iPhone programming, but I am confident that after reading this book (and doing the exercises), you will be well equipped to tackle your next iPhone programming challenge.

WHO THIS BOOK IS FOR

This book is for the beginning iPhone developer who wants to start developing iPhone applications using the Apple iPhone SDK. To truly benefit from this book, you should have some background in programming and at least be familiar with object-oriented programming concepts. If you are totally new to the Objective-C language, you might want to jump straight to Appendix D, which provides an overview of the language. Alternatively, you can use Appendix D as a quick reference while you tackle the various chapters, checking out the syntax as you try the exercises. Depending on your learning pattern, one of those approaches may work best for you.

WHAT THIS BOOK COVERS

This book covers the fundamentals of iPhone programming using the iPhone SDK. It is divided into 17 chapters and five appendices.

Chapter 1: Getting Started with iPhone Programming covers the various tools found in the iPhone SDK and explains their uses in iPhone development.

Chapter 2: Write Your First Hello World! Application gets you started with Xcode and Interface Builder to build a Hello World application. The focus is on getting your hands dirty, and more details on the various parts and components are covered in subsequent chapters.

Chapter 3: Outlets, Actions, and View Controllers covers the fundamental concepts of iPhone programming: outlets and actions. You learn how outlets and actions allow your code to interact with the visual elements in Interface Builder and why they are an integral part of every iPhone application.

Chapter 4: Exploring the Views describes the use of the various views that make up the user interface (UI) of your iPhone applications. You learn the techniques to manipulate the UI of your application, as well as how views are stored internally.

Chapter 5: Keyboard Inputs shows you how to deal with the virtual keyboard in your iPhone. You see how to hide the keyboard on demand and how to ensure that your views are not blocked by the keyboard when it is displayed.

Chapter 6: Screen Rotations demonstrates how you can reorient your application's UI when the device is rotated. You learn about the various events that are fired when the device is rotated. You also learn how to force your application to display in a certain display orientation.

Chapter 7: View Controllers shows how you can create an application with multiple views. You learn how to build an iPhone application using the Window-based Application template.

Chapter 8: Tab Bar and Navigation Applications shows you how to build Tab Bar applications and Navigation applications using the templates provided by the SDK. Using these two application templates, you can create sophisticated multiview applications.

Chapter 9: Utility Applications shows you how to build yet another type of application in the iPhone — utility applications.

Chapter 10: Using the Table View explores one of the most powerful views in the iPhone SDK — the Table view. The Table view is commonly used to display rows of data. In this chapter, you also learn how to implement search capabilities in your Table view.

Chapter 11: Application Preferences discusses the use of application settings to persist application preferences. Using application settings, you can access preferences related to your application through the Settings application available on the iPhone and iPod Touch.

Chapter 12: Database Storage Using SQLLite3 covers the use of the embedded SQLite3 database library to store your data.

Chapter 13: File Handling shows how you can persist your application data by saving the data to files in your application's sandbox directory. You also learn how to access the various folders available in your application sandbox.

Chapter 14: Programming Multi-touch Applications shows how you can implement multi-touch capability in your iPhone application. You learn how to implement gestures such as the famous "pinching" gesture.

Chapter 15: Simple Animations provides an overview of the various techniques you can use to implement simple animations on the iPhone. You also learn about the various affine transformations supported by the iPhone SDK.

Chapter 16: Accessing Built-in Applications describes the various ways you can access the iPhone's built-in applications, such as the Photo Library, Contacts, and others. You also learn how you can invoke built-in applications such as Mail and Safari from within your applications.

Chapter 17: Accessing the Hardware shows you how you can access the hardware of your iPhone, such as the accelerometer, as well as how to obtain your geographical information through Core Location.

Appendix A: Answers to Exercises contains the solutions to the end of chapter exercises found in every chapter except Chapter 1.

Appendix B: Getting around in Xcode provides a quick run-through of the many features in Xcode.

Appendix C: Getting around in Interface Builder provides an overview of the many features of Interface Builder.

Appendix D: Crash Course in Objective-C provides a crash course in Objective-C. Readers who are new to this language should read this chapter before getting started.

Appendix E: Testing on an Actual iPhone or iPod Touch shows how you can test your application on a real device.

HOW THIS BOOK IS STRUCTURED

This book breaks down the task of learning iPhone programming into several smaller chunks, allowing you to digest each topic before delving into another more advanced topic. In addition, there are a few chapters that cover topics already discussed in the previous chapter. This is because there is usually more than one way of doing things in Xcode and Interface Builder, and hence this approach allows you to learn the different techniques in developing iPhone applications.

If you are a total beginner to iPhone programming, it would be motivational for you to start with Chapters 1 and 2. Once you have gotten things moving, head on to the Appendices to read more about the tools and language you are using. Once you are ready, you can now continue with Chapter 3 and gradually move into more advanced topics.

A feature of this book is that all the code samples in each chapter are independent of those discussed in previous chapters. That way, you have the flexibility to dive into the topics that interest you and start working on the Try It Out labs.

WHAT YOU NEED TO USE THIS BOOK

Most of the examples in this book run on the iPhone Simulator (which comes as part of the iPhone SDK). For exercises that access the hardware (such as the camera and accelerometer), you need a real iPhone or iPod Touch. Appendix E shows how you can test your application on a real device. For applications that access the phone function, you need an actual iPhone (the iPod Touch has no built-in phone).

In general, to get the most out of this book, having a real iPhone or iPod Touch is not necessary (although it is definitely required for testing if you plan to deploy your application on the AppStore).

CONVENTIONS

To help you get the most from the text and keep track of what's happening, we've used a number of conventions throughout the book.

TRY IT OUT   **These Are Exercises or Examples For You to Follow**

The Try It Out exercises appear once or more per chapter as exercises to work through as you follow the text in the book.

1. They usually consist of a set of numbered steps.

2. Follow the steps through with your copy of project files.

How It Works

After each Try It Out, the code you've typed is explained in detail.

> **WARNING** *Boxes like this one hold important, not-to-be forgotten information that is directly relevant to the surrounding text.*

> **NOTE** *Notes, tips, hints, tricks, and asides to the current discussion look like this.*

As for other conventions in the text:

➤ New terms and important words are *highlighted* in italics when first introduced.

➤ Keyboard combinations are treated like this: Control-R.

➤ Filenames, URLs, and code within the text are treated like so: `persistence.properties`.

➤ Code is presented in two different ways:

```
We use a monofont type with no highlighting for most code examples.
We use bolding to emphasize code that is of particular importance in the
present context.
```

SOURCE CODE

As you work through the examples in this book, you may choose either to type in all the code manually or to use the source code files that accompany the book. All the source code used in this book is available for download at `www.wrox.com`. When at the site, simply locate the book's title (use the Search box or one of the title lists) and click the Download Code link on the book's detail page to obtain all the source code for the book. Code that is included on the Web site is highlighted by the following icon.

Available for download on Wrox.com

Listings include the filename in the title. If it is just a code snippet, you'll find the filename in a code note such as this.

> **NOTE** *Because many books have similar titles, you may find it easiest to search by ISBN; this book's ISBN is 978-0-470-50097-2.*

After you download the code, just decompress it with your favorite compression tool. Alternatively, go to the main Wrox code download page at `www.wrox.com/dynamic/books/download.aspx` to see the code available for this book and all other Wrox books.

ERRATA

We make every effort to ensure that there are no errors in the text or in the code. However, no one is perfect, and mistakes do occur. If you find an error in one of our books, such as a spelling mistake or faulty piece of code, we would be very grateful for your feedback. By sending in errata, you may save another reader hours of frustration and at the same time help us provide even higher-quality information.

To find the errata page for this book, go to www.wrox.com and locate the title using the Search box or one of the title lists. Then, on the book details page, click the Book Errata link. On this page, you can view all errata that has been submitted for this book and posted by Wrox editors. A complete book list including links to each book's errata is also available at www.wrox.com/misc-pages/ booklist.shtml.

If you don't spot "your" error on the Book Errata page, go to www.wrox.com/contact/ techsupport.shtml and complete the form there to send us the error you have found. We'll check the information and, if appropriate, post a message to the book's errata page and fix the problem in subsequent editions of the book.

P2P.WROX.COM

For author and peer discussion, join the P2P forums at p2p.wrox.com. The forums are a Web-based system for you to post messages relating to Wrox books and related technologies and interact with other readers and technology users. The forums offer a subscription feature to e-mail you topics of interest of your choosing when new posts are made to the forums. Wrox authors, editors, other industry experts, and your fellow readers are present on these forums.

At http://p2p.wrox.com, you will find a number of different forums that will help you not only as you read this book but also as you develop your own applications. To join the forums, just follow these steps:

1. Go to p2p.wrox.com and click the Register link.

2. Read the terms of use and click Agree.

3. Complete the required information to join as well as any optional information you want to provide and click Submit.

4. You will receive an e-mail with information describing how to verify your account and complete the joining process.

 NOTE *You can read messages in the forums without joining P2P, but to post your own messages, you must join.*

After you join, you can post new messages and respond to messages that other users post. You can read messages at any time on the Web. If you want to have new messages from a particular forum e-mailed to you, click the Subscribe to This Forum icon by the forum name in the forum listing.

For more information about how to use the Wrox P2P, be sure to read the P2P FAQs for answers to questions about how the forum software works as well as for many common questions specific to P2P and Wrox books. To read the FAQs, click the FAQ link on any P2P page.

PART I
Getting Started

Getting Started with iPhone Programming

➤ How to obtain the iPhone SDK

➤ The components included in the iPhone SDK

➤ The Features of the development tools — Xcode, Interface Builder, iPhone Simulator

➤ The Capabilities of the iPhone Simulator

➤ The Architecture of the iPhone OS

➤ The Frameworks of the iPhone SDK

➤ The Limitations and characteristics of the iPhone

Welcome to the world of iPhone programming! That you are now holding this book shows that you are fascinated with the idea of developing your iPhone applications and want to join the ranks of those tens of thousands of developers whose applications are already deployed in the AppStore.

As the old Chinese adage says, "To accomplish your mission, first sharpen your tools." Successful programming requires you first of all to know your tools well. Indeed, this couldn't be more true for iPhone programming — you need to know quite a few tools before you can even get started. Hence, the goal of this chapter is to show you the various relevant tools and information you need to jump on the iPhone development bandwagon.

Without further ado, it's time to get down to work.

OBTAINING THE IPHONE SDK

To develop for the iPhone or iPod Touch, you first need to sign up as a Registered iPhone Developer at http://developer.apple.com/iphone/program/start/register/. The registration is free and provides you with access to the iPhone SDK and other resources that are useful for getting started.

After signing up, you can download the iPhone SDK (see Figure 1-1).

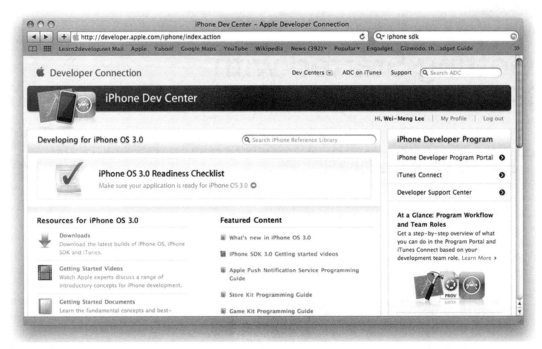

FIGURE 1-1

Before you install the iPhone SDK, make sure you satisfy the following system requirements:

➤ Only Intel Macs are supported, so if you have another processor type (such as the older G4 or G5 Macs), you're out of luck.

➤ You have updated your system with the latest Mac OS X release.

An iPhone/iPod Touch device is highly recommended, though not strictly necessary. To test your application, you can use the included iPhone Simulator. However, if you want to test certain hardware features like the camera, accelerometer, and such, you would need to use a real device.

When the SDK is downloaded, proceed with installing it (see Figure 1-2). You will be asked to accept a few licensing agreements and then select the destination folder in which to install the SDK.

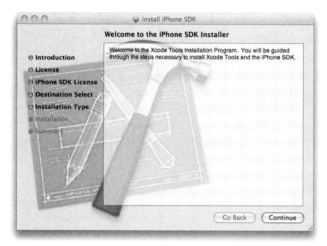

FIGURE 1-2

If you have selected the default settings during the installation phase, after the installation you should be able to find the various tools installed in the /Developer/Applications folder (see Figure 1-3).

FIGURE 1-3

COMPONENTS OF THE IPHONE SDK

The iPhone SDK includes a suite of development tools to help you develop applications for your iPhone and iPod Touch. It includes:

➤ Xcode — the Integrated Development Environment (IDE) that allows you to manage, edit, and debug your projects.

➤ Dashcode — the Integrated Development Environment (IDE) that allows you to develop web-based iPhone applications and Dashboard Widgets. Dashcode is beyond the scope of this book.

➤   iPhone Simulator — provides a software simulator to simulate an iPhone on your Mac.

➤   Interface Builder — provides a visual editor for designing your user interfaces for your iPhone applications.

➤   Instruments — analysis tool to help you optimize your application in real-time.

The following sections discuss each tool in more detail.

Xcode

As mentioned, all the tools in the iPhone SDK are installed in the `/Developer/Applications` folder (when using the default settings). One of those tools is Xcode.

To launch Xcode, double-click the Xcode icon (refer to Figure 1-3). Alternatively, go the quicker route and use Spotlight: Simply type **Xcode** into the search box and Xcode should be in the Top Hit position.

After Xcode is launched, you see the Welcome screen, shown in Figure 1-4.

FIGURE 1-4

Using Xcode, you can develop different types of iPhone and Mac OS X applications (see Figure 1-5).

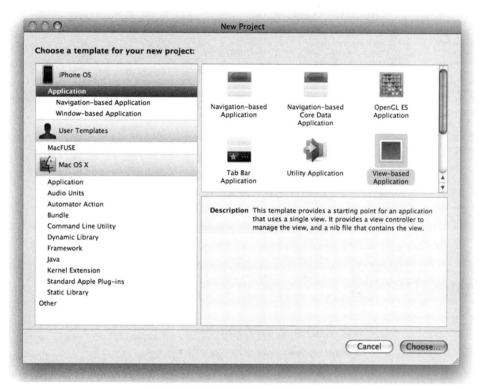

FIGURE 1-5

The IDE in Xcode provides many tools and features that make your development life much easier. One such feature is Code Completion (see Figure 1-6), which displays a pop-up list showing the available classes and members (such as methods, properties, and so on).

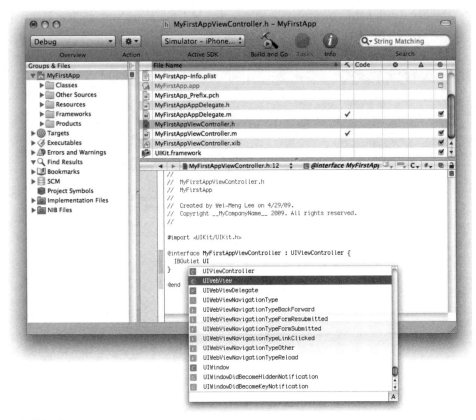

FIGURE 1-6

 NOTE *For a more comprehensive description of some of the most commonly used features in Xcode, refer to Appendix B.*

iPhone Simulator

The iPhone Simulator (see Figure 1-7) is a very useful tool included in the iPhone SDK that you can use to test your application without using your actual iPhone/iPod Touch. The iPhone Simulator is located in the `/Developer/iPhone OS <version>/Platforms/iPhoneSimulator.platform/Developer/Applications/` folder. Most of the time, you don't need to launch the iPhone Simulator directly — running (or debugging) your application in Xcode automatically brings up the iPhone Simulator. Xcode installs the application on the iPhone Simulator automatically.

THE IPHONE SIMULATOR IS NOT AN EMULATOR

The iPhone Simulator is a simulator, not an emulator. So what is the difference? Well, a simulator tries to mimic the behavior of a real device. In the case of the iPhone Simulator, it simulates the real behavior of an actual iPhone device. However, the simulator itself uses the various libraries installed on the Mac (such as QuickTime) to perform its rendering so that the effect looks the same as an actual iPhone. Also, applications tested on the simulator are compiled into x86 code, which is the byte-code understood by the simulator.

In contrast, an emulator emulates the working of a real device. Applications tested on an emulator are compiled into the actual byte-code used by the real device. The emulator executes the application by translating the byte-code into a form that can be executed by the host computer running the emulator.

A good way to understand the subtle difference between simulation and emulation is this: Imagine you are trying to convince a child that playing with knives is dangerous. To *simulate* this, you pretend to cut yourself with a knife and groan in pain. To *emulate* this, you hold a knife and actually cut yourself.

The iPhone Simulator can simulate different versions of the iPhone OS (see Figure 1-8). This capability is very useful if you need to support older versions of the platform as well as testing and debugging errors reported in the application on specific versions of the OS.

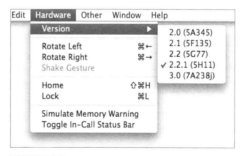

FIGURE 1-8

FIGURE 1-7

Features of the iPhone Simulator

The iPhone Simulator simulates various features of a real iPhone or iPod touch device. Features you can test on the iPhone Simulator include:

➤ Screen rotation — left, top, and right

➤ Support for gestures:

  ➤ Tap

  ➤ Touch and Hold

  ➤ Double Tap

  ➤ Swipe

  ➤ Flick

  ➤ Drag

  ➤ Pinch

➤ Low-memory warning simulations

However, the iPhone Simulator, being a software simulator for the real device, does have its limitations. Features not available on the iPhone Simulator include:

➤ Obtaining location data — it returns only a fixed coordinate, such as Latitude 37.3317 North and Longitude 122.0307 West

➤ Making phone calls

➤ Accessing the Accelerometer

➤ Sending and receiving SMS messages

➤ Installing applications from the App Store

➤ Camera

➤ Microphone

➤ Several features of OpenGL ES

It is worth noting that the speed of the iPhone Simulator is more tightly coupled to the performance of your Mac, as opposed to how the actual device performs. Hence, it is important that you test your application on a real device rather than rely exclusively on the iPhone Simulator for testing.

Although you have limitations with the iPhone Simulator, it is definitely a useful tool to get your applications tested. That said, testing your application on a real iPhone or iPod touch device is imperative before you deploy it on the AppStore.

NOTE *For a more detailed look at how you can test your application on a real device, refer to Appendix E.*

Uninstalling Applications from the iPhone Simulator

The user domain of the iPhone OS file system for the iPhone Simulator is stored in the `~/Library/ Application Support/iPhone Simulator/User/` folder.

 NOTE *The* `~/Library/Application Support/iPhone Simulator/User/` *folder is also known as the* `<iPhoneUserDomain>`.

All third-party applications are stored in the `<iPhoneUserDomain>/Applications/` folder. When an application is deployed onto the iPhone Simulator, an icon is created on the Home screen (shown on the left in Figure 1-9) and a file and a folder are created within the `Applications` folder (shown on the right in Figure 1-9).

FIGURE 1-9

To uninstall (delete) an application, execute the following steps:

1. Click and hold the icon of the application in the Home screen until all the icons start wriggling. Observe that all the icons now have an "x" button displayed on their top left corners.

2. Click the x button (see Figure 1-10) next to the icon of the application you want to uninstall.

3. An alert window appears asking if you are sure you want to delete the icon. Click Delete to confirm the deletion.

FIGURE 1-10

WARNING *When the application is uninstalled, the corresponding file and folder in the Applications folder are deleted automatically.*

To reset the iPhone Simulator to its original state, the easiest way is to select the iPhone Simulator ⇨ Reset Content and Settings menu item.

Interface Builder

Interface Builder is a visual tool that allows you to design your user interfaces for your iPhone applications. Using Interface Builder, you drag and drop views on windows and then connect the various views with outlets and actions so that they can programmatically interact with your code.

 NOTE *Outlets and actions are discussed in more detail in Chapter 3.*

Figure 1-11 shows the various windows in Interface Builder.

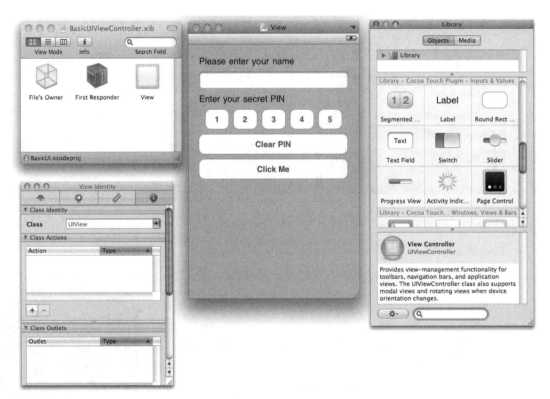

FIGURE 1-11

Appendix C discusses Interface Builder in more detail.

Instruments

The Instruments (see Figure 1-12) application allows you to dynamically trace and profile the performance of your Mac OS X and iPhone applications.

FIGURE 1-12

Using Instruments, you can:

➤ Stress test your applications

➤ Trace your applications for memory leaks

➤ Gain a deep understanding of the executing behavior of your applications

➤ Track difficult-to-reproduce problems in your applications

NOTE *Covering the Instruments application is beyond the scope of this book. For more information, refer to Apple's documentation.*

ARCHITECTURE OF THE IPHONE OS

Although this book doesn't explore the innards of the iPhone OS, understanding some of the important points of the iPhone OS is useful. Figure 1-13 shows the different abstraction layers that make up the Mac OS X and the iPhone OS.

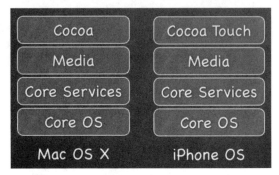

FIGURE 1-13

 NOTE *The iPhone OS is architecturally very similar to the Mac OS X except that the topmost layer is the Cocoa Touch for iPhone instead of the Cocoa Framework.*

The bottom layer is the Core OS, which is the foundation of the operating system. It is in charge of memory management, the file system, networking, and other OS tasks, and it interacts directly with the hardware. The Core OS layer consists of components such as:

➤ OS X Kernel

➤ Mach 3.0

➤ BSD

➤ Sockets

➤ Security

➤ Power Management

➤ Keychain

➤ Certificates

➤ File System

➤ Bonjour

The Core Services layer provides fundamental access to iPhone OS services. It provides an abstraction over the services provided in the Core OS layer. The Core Services layer consists of the following components:

➤ Collections

➤ Address Book

➤ Networking

➤ File Access

➤ SQLite

➤ Core Location

➤ Net Services

➤ Threading

➤ Preferences

➤ URL Utilities

The Media layer provides multimedia services that you can use in your iPhone applications. The Media layer consists of the following components:

➤ Core Audio

➤ OpenGL

➤ Audio Mixing

➤ Audio Recording

➤ Video Playback

➤ JPG, PNG, TIFF

➤ PDF

➤ Quartz

➤ Core Animation

➤ OpenGL ES

The Cocoa Touch layer provides an abstraction layer to expose the various libraries for programming the iPhone and iPod Touch, such as:

➤ Multi-Touch events

➤ Multi-Touch controls

➤ Accelerometer

➤ View Hierarchy

➤ Localization

➤ Alerts

➤ Web Views

➤ People Picker

➤ Image Picker

➤ Controllers

The iPhone SDK consists of the following frameworks shown in Table 1-1, grouped by functionalities.

 NOTE *A framework is a software library that provides specific functionalities.*

TABLE 1-1: The Frameworks in the iPhone SDK

FRAMEWORK NAME	DESCRIPTION
AddressBook.framework	Provides access to the centralized database for storing a user's contacts.
AddressBookUI.framework	Provides the UI to display the contacts stored in the Address Book database.
AudioToolbox.framework	Provides low-level C APIs for audio recording and playback, as well as managing the audio hardware.
AudioUnit.framework	Provides the interface for iPhone OS-supplied audio processing plug-ins in your application.
AVFoundation.framework	Provides low-level C APIs for audio recording and playback, as well as for managing the audio hardware.
CFNetwork.framework	Provides access to network services and configurations, such as HTTP, FTP, and Bonjour services.
CoreAudio.framework	Declares data types and constants used by other Core Audio interfaces.
CoreData.framework	Provides a generalized solution for object graph management in your application.
CoreFoundation.framework	Provides abstraction for common data types, Unicode strings, XML, URL resource, and so on.
CoreGraphics.framework	Provides C-based APIs for 2D rendering; based on the Quartz drawing engine.

FRAMEWORK NAME	DESCRIPTION
CoreLocation.framework	Provides location-based information using a combination of GPS, cell ID, and Wi-Fi networks.
ExternalAccessory.framework	Provides a way to communicate with accessories.
Foundation.framework	Provides the foundation classes for Objective C, such as `NSObject`, basic data types, operating system services, and so on.
GameKit.framework	Provides networking capabilities to games; commonly used for peer-to-peer connectivity and in-game voice feature.
IOKit.framework	Provides capabilities for driver development.
MapKit.framework	Provides an embedded map interface for your application.
MediaPlayer.framework	Provides facilities for playing movies and audio files.
MessageUI.framework	Provides a view-controller–based interface for composing e-mail messages.
MobileCoreServices.framework	Provides access to standard types and constants.
OpenAL.framework	Provides an implementation of the OpenAL specification.
OpenGLES.framework	Provides a compact and efficient subset of the OpenGL API for 2D and 3D drawing.
QuartzCore.framework	Provides ability to configure animations and effects and then render those effects in hardware.
Security.framework	Provides the ability to secure your data and control access to software.
StoreKit.framework	Provides in-app purchase support for applications.
SystemConfiguration. framework	Provides the ability to determine network availability and state on device.
UIKit.framework	Provides the fundamental objects for managing an application's UI.

SOME USEFUL INFORMATION BEFORE YOU GET STARTED

You now have a very good idea of the tools involved in iPhone application development. Before you go ahead and take the plunge, the following sections discuss some useful information that can make your journey a more pleasant one.

Versions of iPhone OS

At the time of writing, the iPhone OS is in its third revision — that is, version 3.0. The iPhone OS has gone through several revisions, and the major versions are as follows:

➤   1.0 — initial release of iPhone

➤   1.1 — additional features and bug fixes for 1.0

➤   2.0 — released with iPhone 3G; comes with App Store

➤   2.1 — additional features and bug fixes for 2.0

➤   2.2 — additional features and bug fixes for 2.1

➤   3.0 — third major release of the iPhone OS; see the next section for what is new in iPhone OS 3.0

For a detailed description of the features in each release, check out `http://en.wikipedia` `.org/wiki/IPhone_OS_version_history`.

WHAT'S NEW IN IPHONE OS 3.0

In June 2009, Apple released the third major revision of the iPhone OS with an updated device — the iPhone 3GS. The *S* stands for *speed:* The new device has a faster processor (600 MHz), and the reoptimized OS makes the iPhone run faster in all aspects.

Some of the important new features of iPhone OS 3.0 include:

➤   Voice activation.

➤   Improved camera (3 megapixel and autofocus) and support for video capturing.

➤   Ability to locate your iPhone through the Find My iPhone feature (requires a subscription to a MobileMe account).

➤   Support for MMS and tethering (requires provider support).

➤   Cut, Copy and Paste support.

➤   New developer APIs:

  ➤   Push notifications for third-party applications.

  ➤   Bluetooth services: A2DP, LDAP, P2P, and Bonjour.

  ➤   Mapping of the API.

  ➤   Sending e-mails from within applications.

Testing on Real Devices

One of the most common complaints that beginning iPhone programmers made was about the inability to test iPhone applications they have developed on their actual devices. It seems odd that as the owner of the device, they can't even test their applications on it. Turns out that for security reasons, Apple requires all applications to be signed with a valid certificate, and for testing purposes, a developer certificate is required.

To test your applications on a device, you must sign up for the iPhone Developer program and request that a developer certificate be installed onto your device. This is a lengthy process, but I give you detailed help with it in Appendix E.

Screen Resolution

The iPhone is a beautiful device with a high-resolution screen. At 3.5 inches (diagonally), the iPhone screen supports multitouch operation and allows a pixel resolution of 480 x 320 at 163 ppi (see Figure 1-14). When designing your application, note that despite the 480 x 320 resolution, most of the time you're limited to 460 x 320 pixels because of the status bar. Of course, you can turn off the status bar programmatically and gain access to the full 480 x 320 resolution.

Also, be mindful that users may rotate the device to display your application in Landscape mode. In that case, you have to make provisions to your user interface so that the applications can still work properly in Landscape mode should you decide to support the new orientation.

FIGURE 1-14

 NOTE *Chapter 6 discusses how to handle screen rotations.*

Single-Window Applications

If you are new to mobile programming, you need to be aware that the limited screen real estate means that most mobile platforms support only single-window applications — that is, your application window occupies the entire screen. The iPhone is no exception to this platform limitation. Overlapping windows that are so common in desktop operating systems (such as Mac OS X and Windows) are not supported on the iPhone.

No Background Applications

One of the major challenges in programming mobile devices is power management. A badly written application can be a resource hog and will drain the battery of the device very quickly. Apple acknowledges this issue, and from reviewing experiences obtained from other platforms, decided that major culprits in hurting battery life and performance are background applications. On other platforms (such as Windows Mobile), when an application goes out of view (because of an incoming call, for example), the application remains in memory, and each background application retained in memory continues to takes its toll on the device's performance and battery life.

Apple's solution to this problem is simple: Disallow applications to run in the background. Although this is an effective solution, it has irked a lot of developers. Many useful applications require background operation to function correctly. For example, a chatting application needs to be running to receive messages from other users. To overcome this limitation, Apple has developed its Push Notification Service, which feeds applications with data even when they are not running. This service was released with iPhone 3.0. Using push technology, a device is constantly connected to Apple's server through an IP connection. When a device needs attention, a notification is sent from Apple's server to the device, thereby alerting the specific application that needs to service that notification.

 NOTE *Push notification is beyond the scope of this book. For more information, visit Apple's iPhone Dev Center at* `http://developer.apple.com/iphone/ index.action.`

Restrictions on Calling Third-Party Applications

Another restriction that Apple places on iPhone developers is that you are not allowed to call third-party applications from within your application. In addition, you can't run interpreted code from within your application. A good example involves writing a Web browser application for the iPhone. Because Web applications typically use JavaScript for client-side interactivity, this restriction by Apple means that you can't run JavaScript code from within your application.

SUMMARY

This chapter offered a quick tour of the tools used for iPhone application development. You also learned some of the characteristics of iPhone, such as the one-application limit and inability to call third-party applications. In the next chapter, you develop your first iPhone application, and you will soon be on your way to iPhone nirvana!

▶ WHAT YOU HAVE LEARNED IN THIS CHAPTER

TOPIC	KEY CONCEPTS
Obtaining the iPhone SDK	Register as an iPhone Developer at http://developer.apple.com first and download the free SDK.
iPhone Simulator	Most of the testing can be done on the iPhone Simulator. However, it is strongly recommended that you have a real device for actual testing.
Limitations of the iPhone Simulator	Access to hardware is generally not supported by the simulator. For example, the camera, accelerometer, voice recording, and so on are not supported.
Frameworks in the iPhone SDK	The iPhone SDK provides several frameworks that perform specific functionalities on the iPhone. You program your iPhone applications using all these frameworks.
Background applications	The iPhone does not support third-party background applications.
Screen resolution	480 x 320 pixels (with status bar hidden). 460 x 320 pixels (with status bar visible).
Single window applications	All iPhone applications are single-windowed — that is, all windows fill the entire screen and overlapping windows are not allowed.

Write Your First Hello World! Application

WHAT YOU WILL LEARN IN THIS CHAPTER

➤ Create a new iPhone project

➤ Build your first iPhone application using Xcode

➤ Design the user interface (UI) of your iPhone application using Interface Builder

➤ Write some simple code to allow the application to rotate its content based on the orientation of the device.

➤ Add an icon to your iPhone application

Now that you have set up all the tools and SDK, you are ready to start developing for the iPhone and iPod Touch! For programming books, it is customary to start the chapter by showing you how to develop a "Hello World!" application. This approach allows you to use the various tools very quickly without getting bogged down in the details. It also provides you with instant gratification: You see for yourself that things really work, which can be a morale booster that inspires you to learn more.

GETTING STARTED WITH XCODE

Power up Xcode and you should see the Welcome screen, as shown in Figure 2-1.

NOTE *The easiest way to start Xcode is to type **Xcode** in Spotlight and then press the Enter key to launch it.*

FIGURE 2-1

To create a new iPhone project, choose File ⇨ New Project. Figure 2-2 shows the different types of projects you can create using Xcode. There are two primary categories: iPhone OS applications and Mac OS X applications. This book covers, obviously, iPhone applications. Hence, click the Application item listed under iPhone OS to view the different templates available for developing your iPhone application.

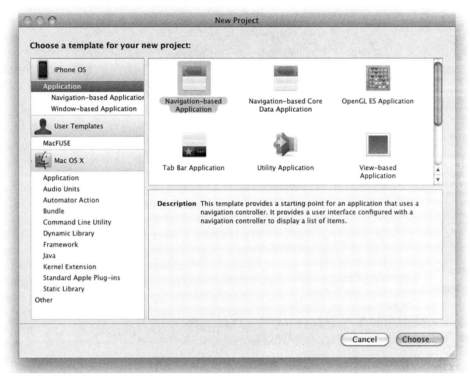

FIGURE 2-2

Although there are quite a few types of iPhone applications you can create, for this chapter, select the View-Based Application template and click the Choose button.

> **NOTE** *Subsequent chapters show you how to develop some of the other types of iPhone applications, such as Utility Application, Tab Bar Application, and Navigation Application.*

Select the View-Based Application template and click Choose. Name the project `HelloWorld` and click Save. Xcode then proceeds to create the project for the template you have selected. Figure 2-3 shows the various files and folders in your project.

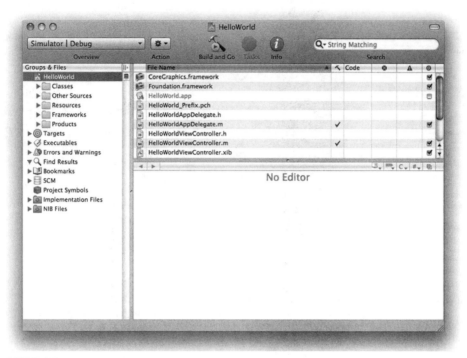

FIGURE 2-3

The left panel of Xcode shows the groupings in the project. You can expand on each group to reveal the files contained in each group (and folders). The right panel of Xcode shows the files contained within the group (or folder) you have selected on the left panel. To edit a particular file, select that file, and the editor at the bottom of the right panel opens the file for editing. If you want a separate window for editing, simply double-click a file to edit it in a new window.

In the following Try It Out, you will learn how to customize the Xcode toolbar area to add commonly used items.

TRY IT OUT   Customizing the Xcode Toolbar Area

Codefile [HelloWorld.zip] is available for download from Wrox.com

The top part of Xcode is the toolbar area. This area contains all the toolbar menu items that are commonly used in the development process. You can customize the toolbar area to add such items.

1.   Give this a try by choosing View ➪ Customize Toolbar. A drop-down window appears (see Figure 2-4).

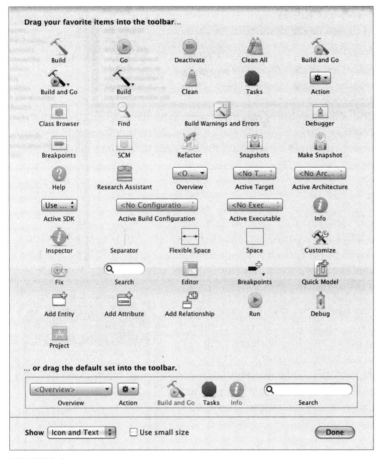

FIGURE 2-4

2. To add an item to the toolbar, simply drag and drop the item onto the toolbar. Figure 2-5 shows the Active SDK item added to the toolbar.

FIGURE 2-5

3. The Active SDK item allows you to select whether to deploy your application to a real device or the iPhone Simulator (see Figure 2-6).

How It Works

FIGURE 2-6

By adding commonly used items to the Xcode toolbar area, you can improve the efficiency of your development process. In this case, you have added the Active SDK toolbar item to the toolbar area so that you can quickly switch between testing your application on the iPhone Simulator and on a real device simply by selecting the active SDK on the toolbar.

Using Interface Builder

Until now, this project has had no UI. To prove this fact, simply press Command-R (or select Run ⇨ Run), and your application is deployed to the included iPhone Simulator. Figure 2-7 shows the blank screen displayed on the iPhone Simulator. It's good to see this now, because as you go through the chapter you will see what changes occur based on your actions.

Obviously, a blank screen is not very useful. So, it's time to try adding some controls to the UI of your application. If you examine the list of files in your project, you notice two files with the .xib extension — MainWindow.xib and HelloWorldViewController. xib. Files with .xib extensions are basically XML files containing the UI definitions of an application. You can edit .xib files by either modifying their XML content, or more easily (and more sanely), edit them using Interface Builder.

Interface Builder comes as part of the iPhone SDK and allows you to build the UI of an iPhone (and Mac) applications by using drag-and-drop.

Double-click the HelloWorldViewController.xib file to launch Interface Builder. Figure 2-8 shows Interface Builder displaying the content of HelloWorldViewController.xib (which is really empty at this moment). As you can see, the Library window shows all the various controls that you can add to the UI of your iPhone application. The View window shows the graphical layout of your UI. You will see the use of the other windows shortly.

FIGURE 2-7

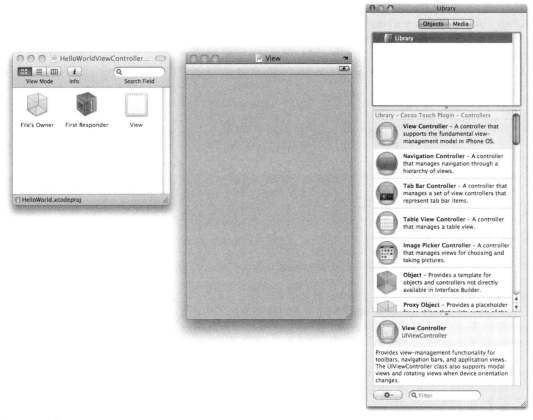

FIGURE 2-8

Now, scroll down to the Label control in the Library pane and drag and drop a `Label` view onto the View window. After the `Label` view is added, select the `Label` view and choose the Tools ⇨ Attributes Inspector. Enter **Hello World!** in the Text field. Also, next to Layout, click the center Alignment type (see Figure 2-9).

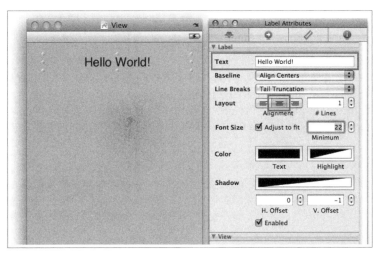

FIGURE 2-9

Next, from the Library window drag and drop a Text Field view to the View window, followed by a Round Rect Button view. Modify the attribute of the Round Rect Button view by entering Click Me! in the Title field (see Figure 2-10).

FIGURE 2-10

NOTE *Rather than specify the* `Title` *property of a view to make the text display in the view (for example, the Label and the Round Rect Button views), you can also simply double-click the view itself and type the text directly. After you've done this, you can rearrange the controls and resize them to suit your needs. Note that Interface Builder provides you with alignment guidelines to help you arrange your controls in a visually pleasing layout.*

Save the `HelloWorldViewController.xib` file by pressing Command-S. Then, return to Xcode and run the application again by pressing `Command-R`. The iPhone Simulator now displays the modified UI (see Figure 2-11).

Tap the Text Field view and watch the keyboard automatically appear (see Figure 2-12).

If you press the Home button on the iPhone Simulator, you will notice that your application has been installed on the simulator (you need to flick to the next page on the right after the Home screen is displayed). To go back to the application, simply tap the HelloWorld icon again (see Figure 2-13).

FIGURE 2-11

FIGURE 2-12

FIGURE 2-13

 NOTE *Only one application can run on the iPhone at any time (except for some built-in applications by Apple). Hence, when you press the Home button on your iPhone, your application exits. Tapping an application icon starts the application all over again.*

Changing Screen Orientations

The iPhone Simulator also supports changes in view orientation. To change the view to Landscape mode, press the Command-→ key combination. Figure 2-14 shows how your application looks in Landscape mode. Press Command-← to change back to Portrait mode.

FIGURE 2-14

Notice that your application does not respond to changes in view orientations. To make your application respond appropriately when the view orientation changes, you need to modify your code.

In Xcode, edit the `HelloWorldViewController.m` file and look for the following code segment (this block of code is commented out by default):

```
- (BOOL)shouldAutorotateToInterfaceOrientation:(UIInterfaceOrientation)
interfaceOrientation {
    // Return YES for supported orientations
    return (interfaceOrientation == UIInterfaceOrientationPortrait);
}
```

 NOTE *At this juncture, do not worry about the other files such as* `HelloWorldAppDelegate.h` *and* `HelloWorldAppDelegate.m`. *You learn more about them in later chapters.*

Modify the preceding code to return YES, as shown in the following snippet:

```
- (BOOL)shouldAutorotateToInterfaceOrientation:(UIInterfaceOrientation)
interfaceOrientation {
    // Return YES for supported orientations
    return YES;
}
```

Run the application again. This time, notice that your application rotates as the view orientation changes (see Figure 2-15).

FIGURE 2-15

Views Repositioning

In the previous section, you saw that as the orientation changes, the size and positioning of the views remain. In the real world, this scenario is not desirable because it doesn't give the user a good experience while using your application. Ideally, you should reposition your views on the screen so that they change with the view orientation.

To reposition your views, go to the Interface Builder, select the Label view, and choose Tools ⇨ Size Inspector. Modify the `Autosizing` attribute of the view as shown in Figure 2-16 (observe carefully the various anchors that are set in the Autosizing section). This will cause the Label view to expand/contract as the view orientation changes. At the same time, the view will anchor to the left, top, and right of the screen.

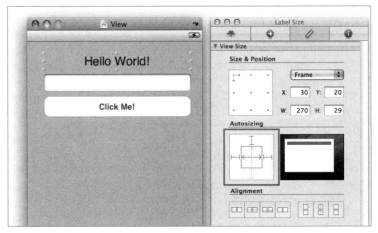

FIGURE 2-16

Likewise, modify the `Autosizing` attribute of the Text Field view as shown in Figure 2-17. Note the different pixel sizes.

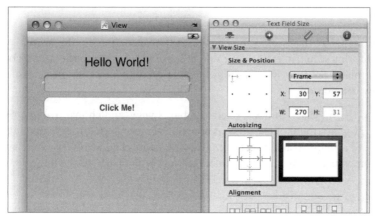

FIGURE 2-17

Finally, modify the `Autosizing` attribute for the `Round Rect Button` control as shown in Figure 2-18. This time, you are not resizing the view when the view orientation changes. Instead, you are only anchoring it to the top of the screen.

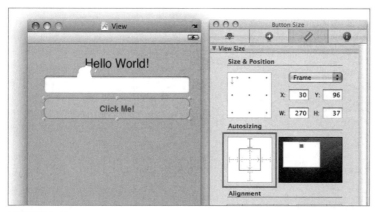

FIGURE 2-18

That's it! Within Interface Builder, you can click the arrow located at the top-right corner (see Figure 2-19) of the screen to rotate the screen so that you can view the effect of the changes you have made immediately.

FIGURE 2-19

Go back to Xcode and run the application again. This time, notice that the controls reposition and resize themselves as you rotate the screen (see Figure 2-20).

FIGURE 2-20

Writing Some Code

So far, you have not written any code, because you should be comfortable with Xcode and Interface Builder before embarking on coding. Nevertheless, it's now time to write some code to give you a flavor of programming with iPhone.

Recall that in the section about the Interface Builder, earlier in this chapter, I show a window labeled `HelloWorldViewController.xib`. Within this window are three components: File's Owner, First Responder, and View.

Select File's Owner and then choose Tools ➪ Identity Inspector from the menu.

In the Identity Inspector window, click the + (plus) button shown under Class Actions (see Figure 2-21). Enter **btnClicked:** in the action name field. (Remember to include the colon because it is part of an action name.) Doing so creates an action (also known as an event handler) named `btnClicked:`.

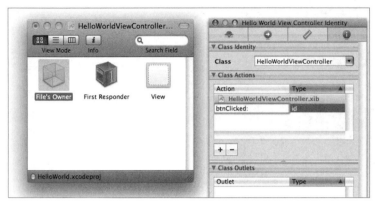

FIGURE 2-21

Control-click the Round Rect Button view in the View window and drag it to the File's Owner item in the `HelloWorldViewController.xib` window (see Figure 2-22). A small pop-up containing the `btnClicked:` action appears. Select the `btnClicked:` action. Basically, what you are doing here is linking the `Round Rect Button` view with the action (`btnClicked:`) so that when the user clicks the button, the action is invoked.

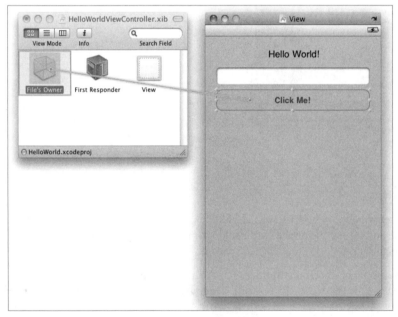

FIGURE 2-22

In the `HelloWorldViewController.h` file, add a header declaration for the `btnClicked:` action:

```
//
//  HelloWorldViewController.h
//  HelloWorld
//
//  Created by Wei-Meng Lee on 3/30/09.
//  Copyright __MyCompanyName__ 2009. All rights reserved.
//

#import <UIKit/UIKit.h>

@interface HelloWorldViewController : UIViewController {

}

//---declaration for the btnClicked: action---
-(IBAction) btnClicked:(id)sender;

@end
```

In the `HelloWorldViewController.m` file, add the code that provides the implementation for the `btnClicked:` action:

```
- (void)dealloc {
    [super dealloc];
}

//---implementation for the btnClicked: action---
-(IBAction) btnClicked:(id)sender {
    //---display an alert view---
    UIAlertView *alert = [[UIAlertView alloc]
                          initWithTitle:@"Hello World!"
                          message: @"iPhone, here I come!"
                          delegate:self
                          cancelButtonTitle:@"OK"
                          otherButtonTitles:nil, nil];
    [alert show];
    [alert release];
}

@end
```

FIGURE 2-23

The preceding code displays an alert containing the sentence "`iPhone, here I come!`"

That's it! Go back to Xcode and run the application again. This time, when you tap the button view, an alert view displays (see Figure 2-23).

CUSTOMIZING YOUR APPLICATION ICON

As you have observed earlier in Figure 2-13, the application installed on your iPhone Simulator uses a default white image as your application icon. It is possible, however, to customize this icon. When designing icons for your iPhone applications, bear the following in mind:

➤ Design your icon to be 57 x 57 pixels. Larger size is all right because iPhone automatically sizes it for you. In fact, you should design your icons in a larger size in the event Apple releases new devices that are larger than the current size/form factor.

➤ For distribution through the App Store, you need to prepare a 512 x 512 pixel image.

➤ Use square corners for your icon image, because iPhone will automatically round them and add a glossy surface (you can turn off this feature, though).

In the following Try It Out, you will learn how to add an icon to your application so that the iPhone Simulator will use it instead of the default white image.

TRY IT OUT   Adding an Icon to the Application

1.   To make your application more interesting, you should specify your own icon. Before you do so, note that icons for the iPhone come in two sizes: 57 x 57 pixels (for the main screen) and 29 x 29 pixels (as shown in the Settings application). Figure 2-24 shows the two possible sizes for the icon.

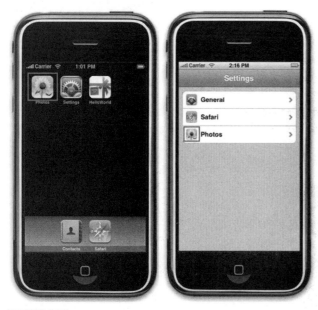

FIGURE 2-24

2. To add an icon to your application, drag and drop an image onto the Resources folder of your project (see Figure 2-25). You will be asked if you want to make a copy of the image you are dropping. Check this option so that a copy of the image will now be stored in your project folder.

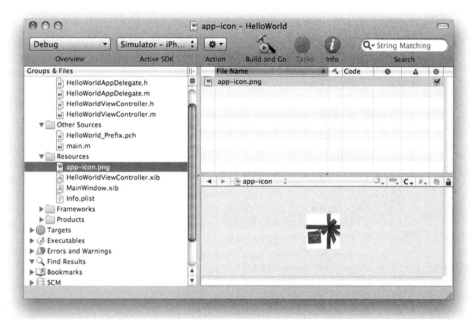

FIGURE 2-25

3. Select the `Info.plist` item (also located under the Resources folder). Select the Icon file item and set its value to the name of the icon (`app-icon.png`; see Figure 2-26). This specifies the name of the image to be used as the application icon.

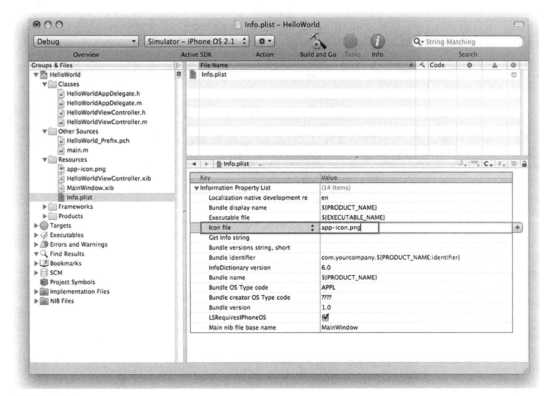

FIGURE 2-26

Run the application and test it on the iPhone Simulator. Press the Home button to return to the main screen of the iPhone. You should now see the newly added icon (see Figure 2-27).

SUMMARY

This chapter was a whirlwind journey of developing your first iPhone application. Although you may still have many questions, the aim of this chapter was to get you started. The next few chapters dive deeper into the finer details of iPhone programming, and the secret of all those mysterious items working in tandem are gradually revealed.

FIGURE 2-27

EXERCISES

1. You tried to add an icon to your iPhone project in Xcode. What is the size of the image that you should provide?

2. If your application needs to support a different display orientation, what should you do?

▶ **WHAT YOU HAVE LEARNED IN THIS CHAPTER**

TOPIC	KEY CONCEPTS
Xcode	Create your iPhone application project and write code that manipulates your application.
Interface Builder	Build your iPhone UI using the various views located in the Library.
Repositioning views	Use the Autosizing feature in Interface Builder to ensure that the views resize even when there is an orientation change.
Adding application icon	Add an image to the project and then specify the image name in Icon file property of the `info.plist` file.
Creating icons for your iPhone applications	Icon size is 57 x 57 pixels (Home screen) and 29 x 29 pixels (Settings). For AppStore hosting, size is 512 x 512 pixels.

3

Outlets, Actions, and View Controllers

WHAT YOU WILL LEARN IN THIS CHAPTER

➤ How to declare and define outlets

➤ How to declare and define actions

➤ How to connect outlets and actions to the views in your
View window

➤ How to add a new View Controller to your application

In the previous chapter, you built a simple Hello World! iPhone application without understanding much of the underlying details of how things work together. In fact, one of the greatest hurdles in learning iPhone programming is the large number of details you need to learn before you can get an application up and running. This book aims to make the iPhone programming experience both fun and bearable. Hence, this chapter starts with the basics of creating an iPhone application. You learn about the various files that make up an iPhone application project, as well as how your code is connected with the graphical widgets you see on an iPhone application.

BASIC CODE AND UI INTERACTIONS

A View-based Application project is a good starting point for developing a single-view application and provides an excellent opportunity for you to understand some of the important concepts in iPhone programming, so that's what you'll work with in this section. You will need to download the code.

To start, launch Xcode and create a new View-based Application project (see Figure 3-1) and name it `BasicUI`.

Codefile [BasicUI.zip] available for download at Wrox.com

FIGURE 3-1

Xcode displays the list of files in the project (see Figure 3-2).

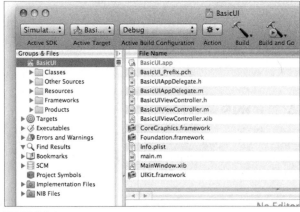

FIGURE 3-2

As you can see, many files are created for you by default when you create a new project. The iPhone SDK tries to make your life simple by creating some of the items that you will use most often when you develop an iPhone application. Table 3-1 describes the use of the various files created in the project.

TABLE 3-1: The Various Files Created in the Project

FILE	DESCRIPTION
BasicUI.app	The application bundle (executable), which contains the executable as well as the data that is bundled with the application.
BasicUI_Prefix.pch	Contains the prefix header for all files in the project. The prefix header is included by default in the other files in the project.
BasicUIAppDelegate.h	Headers file for the application delegate.
BasicUIAppDelegate.m	Implementations file for the application delegate.
BasicUIViewController.h	Headers file for a View Controller.
BasicUIViewController.m	Implementations file for a View Controller.
BasicUIViewController.xib	The XIB file containing the UI of a view.
CoreGraphics.framework	C-based APIS for low-level 2D rendering.
Foundation.framework	APIs for foundational system services such as data types, XML, URL, and so on.
Info.plist	A dictionary file that contains information about your project, such as icon, application name, and others; information is stored in key/value pairs.
main.m	The main file that bootstraps your iPhone application.
MainWindow.xib	The XIB file for the main window of the application.
UIKit.framework	Provides fundamental objects for constructing and managing your application's UI.

 NOTE *The numbers and types of files created are dependent on the type of project you have selected. The View-based Application template is a good starting point to understanding the various files involved.*

The `main.m` file contains code that bootstraps your application. It contains the following code, and you rarely need to modify it:

```
#import <UIKit/UIKit.h>

int main(int argc, char *argv[]) {
    NSAutoreleasePool * pool = [[NSAutoreleasePool alloc] init];
    int retVal = UIApplicationMain(argc, argv, nil, nil);
    [pool release];
    return retVal;
}
```

Most of the hard work is done by the `UIApplicationMain()` function, which examines the `Info` `.plist` file to obtain more information about the project. In particular, it looks at the main nib file you will use for your project. Figure 3-3 shows the content of the `Info.plist` file. Notice that the `Main nib file base name` key is pointing to `MainWindow`, which is the name of the NIB file to load when the application is started.

WHAT DO XIB AND NIB STAND FOR?

In your journey of iPhone application development, you will always come across files with the .xib extension (sometimes also known as NIB files). So, what do the NIB and .xib stand for, exactly? To understand this, a little history lesson is in order. Turns out that the current Mac OS X was built upon an operating system called NeXTSTEP, from a company known as NeXT (founded by Apple's cofounder, Steve Jobs, in 1985). The *N* in NIB stands for NeXTSTEP. As for .xib, the *x* in presumably stands for XML, because its content is saved as an XML file. The IB stands for Interface Builder, the application that allows you to visually construct the UI for your application.

Key	Value
▼ Information Property List	(12 items)
Localization native development region	English
Bundle display name	${PRODUCT_NAME}
Executable file	${EXECUTABLE_NAME}
Icon file	
Bundle identifier	com.yourcompany.${PRODUCT_NAME:identifier}
InfoDictionary version	6.0
Bundle name	${PRODUCT_NAME}
Bundle OS Type code	APPL
Bundle creator OS Type code	????
Bundle version	1.0
LSRequiresIPhoneOS	☑
Main nib file base name	MainWindow

FIGURE 3-3

Editing XIB Files

Double-click the `MainWindow.xib` file to edit it using Interface Builder. As mentioned, the XIB file represents the UI of your application, and it is used almost exclusively by Interface Builder.

NOTE *An XIB file is actually an XML file. You can view and edit it using applications such as TextEdit. However, most of the time, you use Interface Builder to visually modify the UI of your applications.*

When the `MinWindow.xib` file is opened by Interface Builder, you see a window with the same title as the name of the file (see Figure 3-4).

This window contains five items:

➤   The `File's Owner` item represents the object that is set to the owner of the user interface (i.e., the class that is responsible for managing the content of the XIB file).

➤   The `First Responder` item represents the object that the user is currently interacting with. Chapter 4 discusses first responder objects in more detail.

➤   The `BasicUI App Delegate` item points to the `BasicUIAppDelegate` class. (More on this topic shortly.)

FIGURE 3-4

➤   The `BasicUI View Controller` item points to a View Controller that you will be using to display your UI.

➤   The `Window` item is the screen that you will see when the application is launched.

Delegates

The `BasicUIAppDelegate.m` file contains code that is typically executed after the application has finished loading, or just before it is being terminated. For this example, the content of it is as follows:

```
#import "BasicUIAppDelegate.h"
#import "BasicUIViewController.h"

@implementation BasicUIAppDelegate

@synthesize window;
@synthesize viewController;

- (void)applicationDidFinishLaunching:(UIApplication *)application {
    // Override point for customization after app launch
    [window addSubview:viewController.view];
    [window makeKeyAndVisible];
}
```

When the application has finished launching, it sends its delegate the `applicationDidFinishLaunching:` message. In the preceding case, it uses a View Controller to obtain its view and then adds it to the current window so that it can be displayed.

The `BasicUIAppDelegate.h` file contains the declaration of the members of the `BasicUIAppDelegate` class:

```
#import <UIKit/UIKit.h>

@class BasicUIViewController;

@interface BasicUIAppDelegate : NSObject <UIApplicationDelegate> {
    UIWindow *window;
    BasicUIViewController *viewController;
}

@property (nonatomic, retain) IBOutlet UIWindow *window;
@property (nonatomic, retain) IBOutlet BasicUIViewController *viewController;

@end
```

Of particular interest is this line:

`@interface BasicUIAppDelegate : NSObject <UIApplicationDelegate> {`

The `<UIApplicationDelegate>` statement specifies that the class implement the `UIApplicationDelegate` protocol. Put simply, it means that you can now handle events (or messages) defined in the `UIApplicationDelegate` protocol. Examples of events in the `UIApplicationDelegate` protocol are the following:

➤ `applicationDidFinishLaunching:` (You saw this implemented in the `BasicUIAppDelegate.m` file.)

➤ `applicationWillTerminate:`

➤ `applicationDidDidReceiveMemoryWarning:`

> **NOTE** Protocols are discussed in more detail in Appendix D.

View Controllers

In iPhone programming, you typically use a View Controller to manage a view as well as perform navigation and memory management. In the project template for a View-based Application, Xcode automatically uses a View Controller to help you manage your *view*. Think of a view as a screen (or window) you see on your iPhone.

> **NOTE** This section is an introduction to the basics of View Controllers; Chapter 7 covers more advanced View Controller topics and includes multi-view application instructions.

Earlier in this chapter, you saw that the `MainWindow.xib` window contains the BasicUI View Controller item. When you double-click it, it shows a window of the same name (see Figure 3-5).

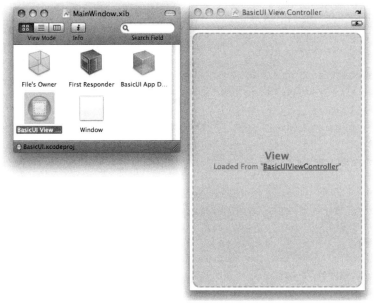

FIGURE 3-5

As you can see from the window, the view says that it is loaded from `BasicUIViewController`. The `BasicUIViewController` refers to the name of the `BasicUIViewController.xib` file, which is also within your project.

Now, double-click the `BasicUIViewController.xib` file to edit it in Interface Builder (see Figure 3-6).

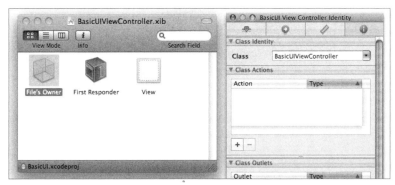

FIGURE 3-6

As with the `MainWindow.xib` file, a few objects are contained inside the `BasicUIViewController.xib` window. In this case, the window contains three items: `File's Owner`, `First Responder`, and `View`.

You can right-click (or Control-Click) the File's Owner item to view its outlets (see Figure 3-7). For now, note that the `view` outlet is connected to the `View` item.

The `View` item represents the screen that appears on your application. Double-click View to display it (see Figure 3-8).

FIGURE 3-7

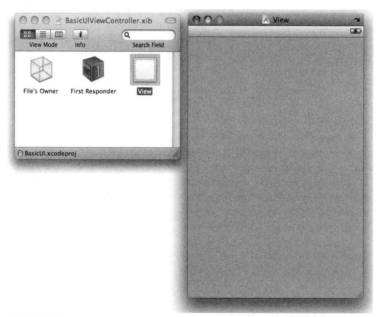

FIGURE 3-8

Designing the View Window

To design your View window, you can drag and drop views from the Library window (choose Tools ⇨ Library). Figure 3-9 shows the Library window containing all the various views you can add to your View window.

If you are new to iPhone development, you may not know that it is better to display the various views in the Library window as icons and labels. To do so, click the asterisk/star-like icon located at the bottom on the Library window and select View Icons and Labels (see Figure 3-10).

Doing so displays the view names together with the icons (see Figure 3-11).

FIGURE 3-9

FIGURE 3-10

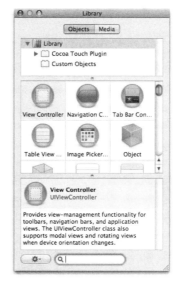

FIGURE 3-11

Populate the View window as shown in Figure 3-12. The following views are used:

➤ Label

➤ Text Field

➤ Round Rect Button

FIGURE 3-12

What your application will do is simple: When the user enters his or her name in the Text field and clicks the Round Rect button, the application displays an alert view showing the user's name.

Creating Outlets and Actions

In order for your application to interact with views on the View window, you need a mechanism to reference your views on the window and at the same time provide methods to be invoked when some events happen on the window. In iPhone programming, these two mechanisms are known as *outlets* and *actions*, respectively.

In the `BasicUIViewController.xib` window (see Figure 3-13), select the File's Owner item and view its Identity Inspector window (choose Tool ⇨ Identity Inspector). Under the Class Actions section, click the plus (+) button to add an action named `btnClicked:`. Under the Class Outlets section, click the plus button to add an outlet named `nameTextField`. Set its Type to `UITextField`.

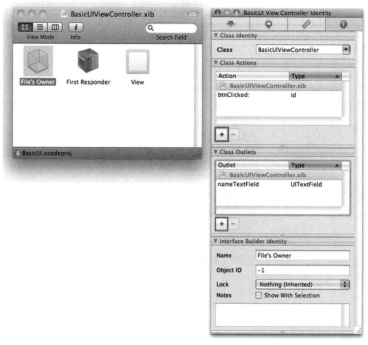

FIGURE 3-13

An *action* is a method that can handle events raised by views (for example, when a button is clicked) in the View window. An outlet, on the other hand, allows your code to programmatically reference a view on the View window.

With the File's Owner item selected, choose the File ⇨ Write Class File menu item. Interface Builder generates the code necessary to represent the outlets and actions that you have just added. Because the project template already includes class files that are used by the View Controller, you see the prompt as shown in Figure 3-14.

 NOTE *You can also manually modify the View Controller files (the .h and .m files). But the Interface Builder has this nice little feature that helps you generate code for your outlets and actions.*

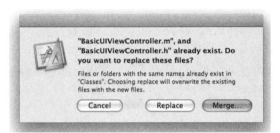

FIGURE 3-14

At this juncture, you have two options:

➤ Replace the existing class files in your project. Doing so overwrites all the changes that you might have made to your existing class files.

➤ Merge the newly generated code with the existing class files. I recommend this option because it allows you to selectively choose the statements to insert into your existing class files.

Click the Merge button. You should now see the window as shown in Figure 3-15, displaying the content of BasicViewController.h.

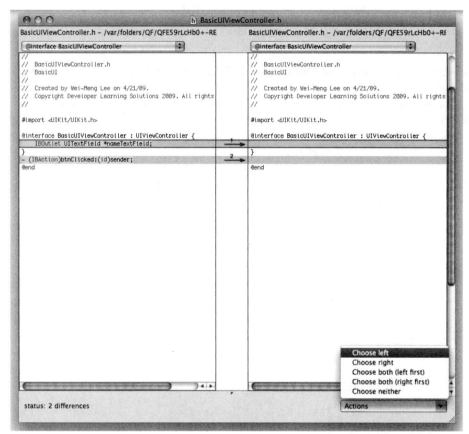

FIGURE 3-15

The left of the window shows the code that Interface Builder has generated for you, whereas the right side shows the content of the original file. The gray sections show the code to be inserted. Because you want the two statements to be inserted into the original file, select each section, and at the bottom-right corner of the screen, click the Actions list and select Choose Left. Repeat the same step for the second block of code.

The window should now look like Figure 3-16. Note the direction of the two arrows.

```
#import <UIKit/UIKit.h>                              #import <UIKit/UIKit.h>

@interface BasicUIViewController : UIViewController {   @interface BasicUIViewController : UIViewController {
    IBOutlet UITextField *nameTextField;
}                                                    }
- (IBAction)btnClicked:(id)sender;
@end                                                 @end
```

FIGURE 3-16

Save the file by pressing Command-S. To close the window, press Command-W.

You now see the window for the next file — `BasicViewController.m`. Repeat the same steps outlined previously (though the second block of code does not seem to include anything; see Figure 3-17). Save and close the window.

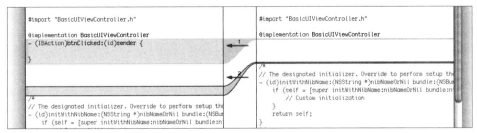

FIGURE 3-17

Back in Xcode, you see the following in the `BasicViewController.h` file:

```
#import <UIKit/UIKit.h>

@interface BasicUIViewController : UIViewController {
    IBOutlet UITextField *nameTextField;

}

- (IBAction)btnClicked:(id)sender;

@end
```

The `IBOutlet` identifier is used to prefix variables so that Interface Builder can synchronize the display and connection of outlets with Xcode. The `IBAction` identifier is used to synchronize action methods.

In the `BasicViewController.m` file, you see the following statements inserted:

```
#import "BasicUIViewController.h"

@implementation BasicUIViewController

- (IBAction)btnClicked:(id)sender {
}

//...
```

Now that you know what an outlet is and does, it's time to practice adding outlets in the following Try It Out.

TRY IT OUT   Adding Outlets Using Code

To add outlets or actions to a View Controller, you can either use Interface Builder to add them and then generate the class file, or write the code yourself. To see how this is done, execute the following steps.

1.   Manually add another IBOutlet object to the class (BasicUIViewController.h), as follows:

```
#import <UIKit/UIKit.h>

@interface BasicUIViewController : UIViewController {
    IBOutlet UITextField *nameTextField;
    IBOutlet UITextField *ageTextField;
}

- (IBAction)btnClicked:(id)sender;

@end
```

2.   In this case, you are manually adding an outlet (named ageTextField) to the View Controller.

Save the file and select the File's Owner item in the BasicUIViewController.xib file. Note its Identity Inspector window — it's the one on the right in Figure 3-18.

 NOTE *Note that the outlets are now listed under* BasicUIViewController.h. *If you refer to Figure 3-13, you will notice that when you create your outlets using the Identity Inspector window, the outlets are listed under* BasicUIViewController.xib. *This is because at that time the outlets have not been declared to the* .h *file yet.*

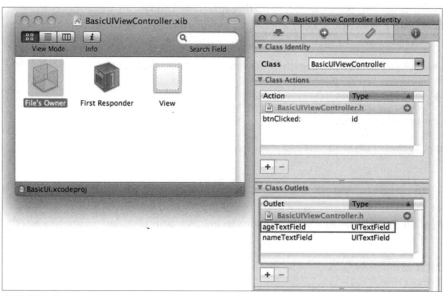

FIGURE 3-18

The `ageTextField` outlet appears in the Class Outlets section, proving that coding directly in the .h file works as well.

 NOTE *If you want to remove any of the outlets listed under* `BasicUIViewcontroller.h`, *you have to remove them manually in the* .h *file. This is evident when you see that the minus (-) button is grayed out.*

If, at this point, you add another outlet using the Identity Inspector window, the outlet you added will be listed under `BasicUIViewController.xib` (see Figure 3-19). After the outlet is declared in the .h file, the outlet then appears under `BasicUIViewController.xib`.

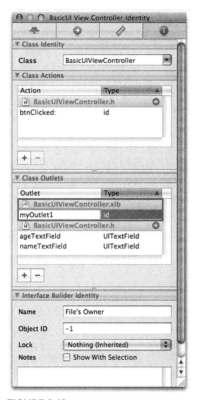

FIGURE 3-19

WHERE DO YOU DECLARE YOUR OUTLETS AND ACTIONS?

In Apple's demos and many other getting started tutorials, the actions and outlets are often declared directly in the .h file and then linked to the views in Interface Builder because it's probably the fastest and most common way for programmers to integrate their code with their UI. The process of adding the actions and outlets in Interface Builder and then declaring them in the .h file is a bit more tedious.

However, adding your actions and outlets directly in Interface Builder does have its advantages. It allows the UI to be designed by a non-programmer. The designer can focus on the UI design, and create the actions and outlets and connect them to the views without worrying about the code. After the design is completed, the programmers can then take over and define the actions and outlets declared in Interface Builder.

Linking View Controller to Outlets and Actions

After actions and outlets are defined in the View Controller, you must have a way to connect them to the views in the View window. To link the events of the views in the View window to the actions defined in the View Controller, you need to Control-click and drag the view to the File's Owner item.

For this example, Control-click and drag the Click Me button and drop it on the File's Owner item. As you drag, notice that an elastic band appears. As your mouse hovers over the File's Owner item, it is highlighted (see Figure 3-20). When you release the mouse button, a pop-up appears. The btnClicked: action is now shown under the Events section.

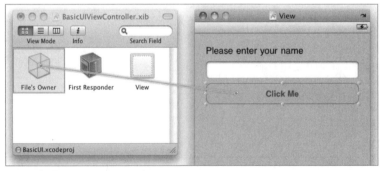

FIGURE 3-20

WARNING *Remember that to link actions, you always drag from the view in the View window onto the File's Owner item.*

To link the outlets defined in the View Controller onto the views on the View window, Control-click and drag the File's Owner item onto the view you want to connect to (see Figure 3-21). You now see the list of outlets that you have defined in your View Controller under the Outlets group. Select the `nameTextField` outlet.

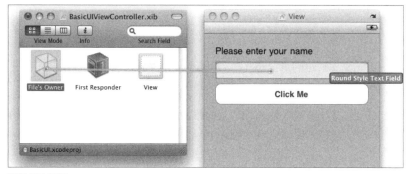

FIGURE 3-21

 NOTE *The `ageTextField` outlet is not used in this example and is there for illustration purposes only.*

 WARNING *Remember that to link outlets, you always drag from the File's Owner item onto the required view in the View window. This is the direct opposite of linking actions.*

With the actions and outlets connected, you can right-click (or Control-click) the File's Owner item to view its connections (see Figure 3-22). As you can observe, the `nameTextField` outlet is connected to a Round Style Text Field view, and the `btnClicked:` action is connected to a Round Rect Button's `Touch Up Inside` event.

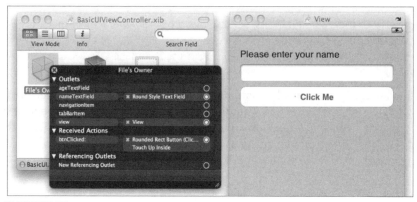

FIGURE 3-22

Because pressing the button is such a common activity in iPhone applications, when you connect a button with an action, the `Touched Up Inside` event of the button is automatically linked with the action. If you want to link some other events with an action defined in the View Controller, right-click the button view and click and drag the event (represented as a circle). Then connect it with the File's Owner item (see Figure 3-23).

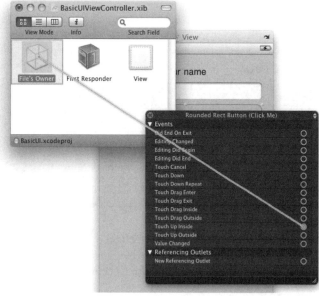

FIGURE 3-23

If the action is connected properly, you should see the action listed next to the event name (see Figure 3-24).

FIGURE 3-24

Exposing Outlets as Properties

Recall that earlier, in the BasicUIViewController.h file, an outlet and an action were generated for you:

```
#import <UIKit/UIKit.h>

@interface BasicUIViewController : UIViewController {
    IBOutlet UITextField *nameTextField;
}

- (IBAction)btnClicked:(id)sender;
@end
```

The nameTextField is an IBOutlet instance member of type UITextField. A good practice in iPhone programming is to expose the member variable as a property using the @property identifier:

```
#import <UIKit/UIKit.h>

@interface BasicUIViewController : UIViewController {
    IBOutlet UITextField *nameTextField;
}

@property (nonatomic, retain) UITextField *nameTextField;

- (IBAction)btnClicked:(id)sender;
@end
```

> **NOTE** *The IBOutlet tag can also be added to the* @property *identifier. This syntax is common in the Apple documentation:*
>
> ```
> @property (nonatomic, retain) IBOutlet UITextField *nameTextField;
> ```

> **NOTE** *For the use of the* nonatomic *and* retain *identifiers, refer to Appendix D, where you can find an introduction to Objective-C. Also, the* @synthesize *keyword, discussed shortly, is explained in more detail there as well.*

When the outlet is now exposed as a property, you need to define the getters and setters for the property. A quick and easy way is to use the @synthesize keyword in the BasicUIViewController.m file, like this:

```
#import "BasicUIViewController.h"

@implementation BasicUIViewController

@synthesize nameTextField;
```

Coding the Action

As shown earlier, you connected the Touch Up Inside event of the Round Rect Button view with the btnClick: action defined in the View Controller. To implement the btnClick: method, code the following in the BasicUIViewController.m file:

```
#import "BasicUIViewController.h"

@implementation BasicUIViewController

@synthesize nameTextField;
```

```objectivec
- (IBAction)btnClicked:(id)sender {

    NSString *str = [[NSString alloc]
            initWithFormat:@"Hello, %@", nameTextField.text ];
    UIAlertView *alert=[[UIAlertView alloc]
                            initWithTitle:@"Hello"
                            message: str
                            delegate:self
                            cancelButtonTitle:@"OK"
                            otherButtonTitles:nil, nil];
    [alert show];
    [alert release];
    [str release];
}

- (void)dealloc {
    [nameTextField release];
    [super dealloc];
}

@end
```

You use the `@synthesize` identifier to get the compiler to generate the *accessor* and *mutator* (also commonly known as *getters* and *setters*) for the `nameTextField` property. The `UIAlertView` class displays an alert window with the content specified.

That's it! To test the application, press Command-R in Xcode. If the current active SDK selected is the iPhone Simulator (3.0) (see Figure 3-25), the iPhone Simulator is launched.

FIGURE 3-25

Enter your name and click the Click Me button. Figure 3-26 shows the alert view displaying the name you have entered.

A More Complex Example

Now that you have seen the detailed walkthrough of how to define outlets and actions and then link them with the View Controller, it is time for a more complex example. Using the same project you created, modify the program so that the user needs to enter a secret PIN before an alert view can be displayed. Figure 3-27 shows the additional views needed to add to the View window.

As shown in Figure 3-27, the additional views are

➤ Label

➤ Round Rect Button

FIGURE 3-26

Defining the Outlets and Actions

In the `BasicUIViewController.h` file, add the following object and actions:

```
#import <UIKit/UIKit.h>

@interface BasicUIViewController : UIViewController {
    IBOutlet UITextField *nameTextField;
    NSMutableString *secretPin;
}

@property (nonatomic, retain) UITextField *nameTextField;

- (IBAction)btnClicked:(id)sender;
- (IBAction)clearPinBtnClicked:(id)sender;
- (IBAction)pinBtnClicked:(id)sender;

@end
```

FIGURE 3-27

The `NSMutableString` class represents a mutable string (that is, its content can be changed after it has been initialized). In contrast, the `NSString` class represents an immutable string (that is, its content cannot be changed after it has been initialized).

Connecting the Outlets and Actions

In Interface Builder, connect the five Round Rect buttons to the `pinBtnClicked:` action. This means that one single action will handle the five buttons' `TouchUp Inside` event. In addition, connect the Clear PIN button to the `clearPinBtnClicked:` action. The connections for the File's Owner item should now look like those shown in Figure 3-28.

FIGURE 3-28

Implementing the Actions

In the `BasicUIViewController.m` file, provide the following implementations:

```
#import "BasicUIViewController.h"

@implementation BasicUIViewController

@synthesize nameTextField;

- (IBAction)clearPinBtnClicked:(id)sender {
    //---clears the secret pin---
    [secretPin setString:@""];
}
```

```
- (IBAction)pinBtnClicked:(id)sender {
    //---append the pin entered to the string---
    [secretPin appendString:[sender titleForState:UIControlStateNormal]];
}

- (IBAction)btnClicked:(id)sender {
    //---if the user has entered the pin correctly---
    if ([secretPin isEqualToString: @"2345"]) {
        NSString *str = [[NSString alloc]
            initWithFormat:@"Hello, %@", nameTextField.text ];
        UIAlertView *alert = [[UIAlertView alloc]
                              initWithTitle:@"Hello"
                              message: str
                              delegate:self
                              cancelButtonTitle:@"OK"
                              otherButtonTitles:nil, nil];
        [alert show];
        [alert release];
        [str release];
    }
}

- (void)viewDidLoad {
    //---init the string with an initial capacity of 1---
    secretPin = [[NSMutableString alloc] initWithCapacity:1];
    [super viewDidLoad];
}

- (void)dealloc {
    [nameTextField release];
    [secretPin release];
    [super dealloc];
}
```

In the preceding code, when the View is loaded, you initialize the mutable string secretPin with an initial capacity of one. A mutable string is a string whose content can be edited. In this case, you initialize it by setting its initial length to one. Whenever the user presses the buttons labeled 1 to 5, the pinBtnClicked: method is called. You use the titleForState: method together with the UIControlStateNormal constant to extract the text displayed on the button and then append it to the secretPin string:

```
[secretPin appendString:[sender titleForState:UIControlStateNormal]];
```

> **WARNING** The UIControlStateNormal constant represents the normal state of a view (control). Some other possible states are UIControlStateHighlighted (when the view is highlighted) and UIControlStateDisabled (when the view is disabled).

That's it! Press Command-R to debug the application on the iPhone
Simulator. The alert view is displayed only after the user has entered
the correct pin number (see Figure 3-29).

VIEW CONTROLLERS

The previous section discusses the View-based Application project,
which by default contains a View Controller already configured for
your application use. In this section, you learn how to manually add
a View Controller to your application and set it to an XIB file. The
best way to see this is to create a Window-based Application project.
The Window-based Application project template provides a skeleton
project containing a delegate and a window. This template provides
a starting point for developing any type of iPhone applications.

Let's now create a new Window-based Application project using
Xcode (see Figure 3-30).

FIGURE 3-29

FIGURE 3-30

Name the new project as `BasicUI2`. When the project is created, you see the list of files, as shown in Figure 3-31. The main difference between a View-based application and a Window-based application is that for a Window-based application project, no default View Controller is created for you — the application just creates an application delegate and a main window for you.

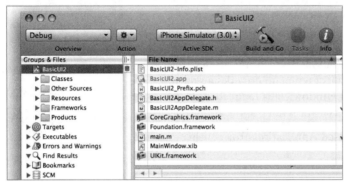

FIGURE 3-31

Adding a View Controller

To manually add a View Controller class to the project, right-click the project name (`BasicUI2`) in Xcode and choose Add ⇨ New File. You'll need to download the code to do this.

You see the New File window, as shown in Figure 3-32. Under the iPhone OS section on the left, select Cocoa Touch Class and then select the `UIViewController` subclass template on the right. Select the With XIB for User Interface option so that in addition to adding a View Controller class, it will also add an XIB file. Click Next.

FIGURE 3-32

In the next window, you are asked to name your new View Controller class. Name it
MyViewController.m (see Figure 3-33). A corresponding .h file is then created for you.
Click Finish.

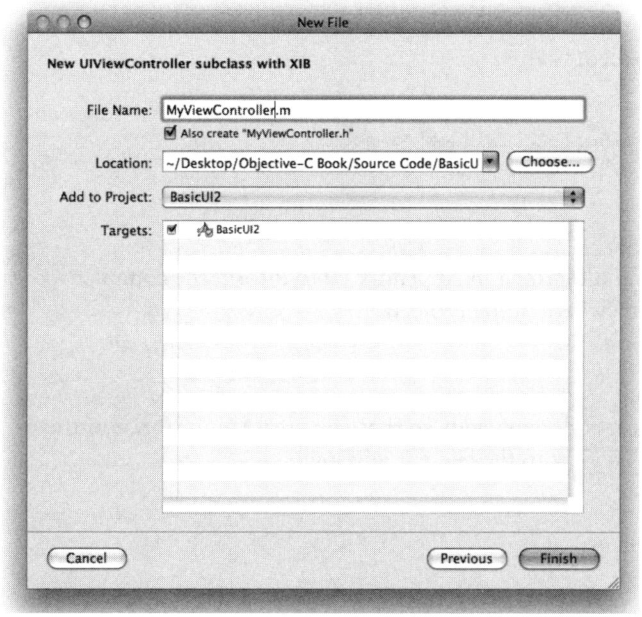

FIGURE 3-33

Three files are now created for you (see Figure 3-34):

➤   MyViewController.h

➤   MyViewController.m

➤   MyViewController.xib

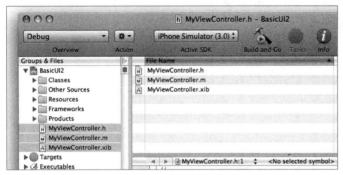

FIGURE 3-34

In the `BasicUI2Delegate.h` file, create an instance of the View Controller that you have just created and expose it as a property so that it can be used throughout the entire application:

```
#import <UIKit/UIKit.h>

@class MyViewController;

@interface BasicUI2AppDelegate : NSObject <UIApplicationDelegate> {
    UIWindow *window;
    MyViewController *myViewController;
}

@property (nonatomic, retain) IBOutlet UIWindow *window;
@property (nonatomic, retain) MyViewController *myViewController;

@end
```

Note that you use a forward declaration (described in Appendix D) to inform the compiler that the `MyViewController` class is defined somewhere in the project:

```
@class MyViewController;
```

In the `BasicUI2Delegate.m` file, add the following code so that you create an instance of the `MyViewController` class and then set its view to the current window:

```objc
#import "BasicUI2AppDelegate.h"
#import "MyViewController.h"

@implementation BasicUI2AppDelegate

@synthesize window;
@synthesize myViewController;

- (void)applicationDidFinishLaunching:(UIApplication *)application {

    //---create an instance of the MyViewController---
    MyViewController *viewController = [[MyViewController alloc]
                                  initWithNibName:@"MyViewController"
                                  bundle:[NSBundle mainBundle]];

    //---set the instance to the property---
    self.myViewController = viewController;
    [viewController release];

    //---add the view of the view controller---
    [window addSubview:[myViewController view]];

    // Override point for customization after application launch
    [window makeKeyAndVisible];
}

- (void)dealloc {
    [myViewController release];
    [window release];
    [super dealloc];
}

@end
```

Codefile [BasicUI2.zip]

The result of the preceding code is that when the application runs, the newly added View Controller will be loaded.

Customizing the View

With the View Controller properly wired up, it is now time to customize the new view so that it can do something useful. To make things interesting, double-click the MyViewController.xib file and add a Web view to the View window (see Figure 3-35). A Web view is a Web browser view and is used for displaying Web content.

FIGURE 3-35

In `MyViewController.h`, create an outlet for the Web view and expose it as a property:

```
#import <UIKit/UIKit.h>

@interface MyViewController : UIViewController {
    IBOutlet UIWebView *webView;
}

@property (retain, nonatomic) UIWebView *webView;

@end
```

Back in the `MyViewController.xib` file, connect the outlet to the Web view. To verify that the connection is made correctly, right-click the File's Owner item. You should see the connection shown in Figure 3-36.

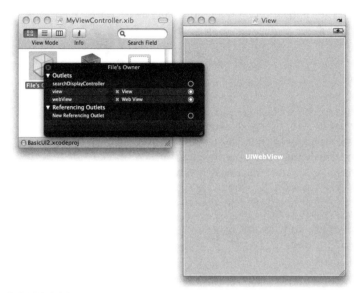

FIGURE 3-36

In the `MyViewController.m` file, code the following so that when the view is loaded, it displays the Web page of Apple.com in the Web view:

```
#import "MyViewController.h"

@implementation MyViewController

@synthesize webView;

// Implement viewDidLoad to do additional setup after loading the view,
// typically from a nib.
- (void)viewDidLoad {
    NSString *strUrl = @"http://www.apple.com";

    //---create an URL object---
    NSURL *url = [NSURL URLWithString:strUrl];

    //---create an URL Request Object---
    NSURLRequest *request = [NSURLRequest requestWithURL:url];

    //---load the request in the UIWebView---
    [webView loadRequest:request];

    [super viewDidLoad];
}

- (void)dealloc {
    [webView release];
    [super dealloc];
}

@end
```

That's it! Press Command-R to test the application on the iPhone Simulator. Figure 3-37 shows the simulator displaying Apple's home page.

SUMMARY

In this chapter, you have seen the use of XIB files as well as the role played by View Controllers in an iPhone application. Understanding the use of outlets and actions is extremely important because it is the cornerstone of iPhone development. Throughout this book, you will come across them frequently.

In the next chapter, you learn how you can control the virtual keyboard that automatically pops up when the user tries to enter some data into your application.

FIGURE 3-37

EXERCISES

1.   Declare and define an outlet for a UITextField view using code.

2.   Declare and define an action using code.

▶ WHAT YOU HAVE LEARNED IN THIS CHAPTER

TOPIC	KEY CONCEPTS
Delegate files	The delegate files contain code that is typically executed during the loading/unloading of the application.
View Controllers	View Controllers manage views as well as perform navigation and memory management.
Action	An action is a method that can handle events raised by views (for example, when a button is clicked, etc.) in the View window.
Outlet	An outlet allows your code to programmatically reference a view on the View window.
Adding outlet using code	Use the `IBOutlet` keyword: `IBOutlet UITextField *nameTextField;`
Adding action using code	Use the `IBAction` keyword: `- (IBAction)btnClicked:(id)sender;`
Connecting actions	To link actions, you always drag from the view in the View window onto the File's Owner item.
Connection outlets	To link outlets, you always drag from the File's Owner item onto the required view in the View window.

Exploring the Views

WHAT YOU WILL LEARN IN THIS CHAPTER

➤ How to use the `UIAlertView` to display an alert view to the user

➤ How to use the `UIActionSheet` to display some options to the user

➤ How to use the `UIPageControl` to control paging

➤ How to use the `UIImageView` to display images

➤ How to use the `UISegmentedControl` to display a set of buttons for the user to choose among

➤ How to use the `UIWebView` to display Web content in your application

➤ How to add views dynamically to your application during runtime

➤ How to wire a view to a View Controller

➤ How to switch between views

Up to this point, you should already have some ideas of how to use Xcode and Interface Builder to build iPhone applications. In this chapter, you dive into the various views that you can use to spice up your applications. You learn how you can add views using Interface Builder, as well as how to create views dynamically during runtime.

USING THE VIEWS

So far, you have seen quite a number of views in action in the previous few chapters — Round Rect Button, TextField, and Label. All these views are quite straightforward, but they give you a good opportunity to understand how to apply the concepts behind outlets and actions.

To use more views, you can locate them from the Library window in Interface Builder (see Figure 4-1).

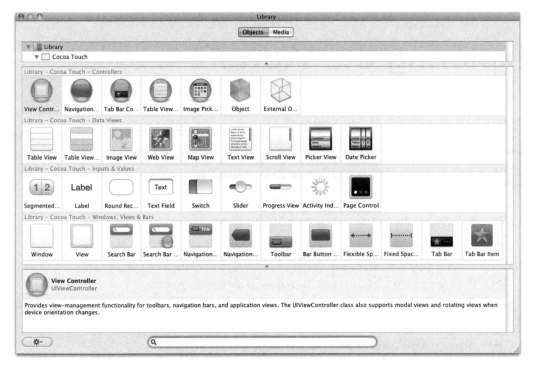

FIGURE 4-1

As you can see, the Library is divided into sections:

➤ Controllers — contains views that control other views, such as the View Controller, Tab Bar Controller, Navigation Controller, and so on

➤ Data Views — contains views that display data, such as the Image View, Table View, Data Picker, Picker View, and so on

➤ Inputs and Values — contains views that accept inputs from users, such as the Label, Round Rect Button, Text Field, and so on

➤ Windows, Views & Bars — contains views that display other, miscellaneous views, such as View, Search Bar, Toolbar, and so on

In the following sections, you learn how to use some of the views available in the Library. Although it is beyond the scope of this book to show the use of each view, you have the opportunity to see a number of views in action throughout the book. In this chapter, you learn some of the fundamental concepts of dealing with views so that you can use other views without problems.

Using the Alert View

One of the views that is not listed in the Library is the UIAlertView. The UIAlertView displays an alert view to the user and is usually created during runtime. Hence, to use it you have to create it using code.

 NOTE *You have actually seen the* UIAlertView *in the previous chapter. In this section, you see how it actually works.*

The UIAlertView is useful for cases in which you have to display a message to the user. In addition, it can serve as a quick debugging tool when you want to observe the value of a variable during runtime.

The following Try It Out explores the UIAlertView in more detail. You need to download the code as indicated here.

TRY IT OUT **Using the Alert View**

Codefile [UsingViews.zip] available for download at Wrox.com

1. Using Xcode, create a new View-based Application project and name it UsingViews.

2. In the UsingViewsViewController.m file, add the following code that appears in bold to the viewDidLoad method:

```
- (void)viewDidLoad {

    UIAlertView *alert = [[UIAlertView alloc] initWithTitle:@"Hello"
                            message:@"This is an alert view"
                            delegate:self
                            cancelButtonTitle:@"OK"
                            otherButtonTitles:nil];
    [alert show];
    [alert release];
    [super viewDidLoad];

}
```

3. Press Command-R to test the application on the iPhone Simulator. When the application is loaded, you see the alert view as shown in Figure 4-2.

4. Back in Xcode, modify the `otherButtonTitles` parameter by setting it with the value shown in bold:

```
UIAlertView *alert = [[UIAlertView alloc]
                    initWithTitle:@"Hello"
                    message:@"This is an alert view"
                    delegate:self
                    cancelButtonTitle:@"OK"
                    otherButtonTitles:@"Option 1",
                    @"Option 2", nil];
```

5. In the `UsingViewsViewController.h` file, add the following line that appears in bold:

```
#import <UIKit/UIKit.h>

@interface UsingViewsViewController : UIViewController
    <UIAlertViewDelegate> {

}

@end
```

FIGURE 4-2

6. In the `UsingViewsViewController.m` file, add the following method:

```
- (void)alertView:(UIAlertView *)alertView clickedButtonAtIndex:
    (NSInteger)buttonIndex {

    NSLog([NSString stringWithFormat:@"%d", buttonIndex]);

}
```

7. Press Command-R to test the application in the iPhone Simulator. Notice that there are now two additional buttons besides the OK button (see Figure 4-3).

8. Click any one of the buttons — Option 1, Option 2, or OK.

9. In Xcode, press Command-Shift-R to view the Debugger Console window. Observe the values printed. You can rerun the application a number of times and click the different buttons to observe the values printed.

10. You should observe the values printed for each button clicked:

➤ OK button — 0

➤ Option 1 — 1

➤ Option 2 — 2

FIGURE 4-3

How It Works

To use UIAlertView, you first instantiate it and initialize it with the various arguments:

```
UIAlertView *alert = [[UIAlertView alloc] initWithTitle:@"Hello"
                          message:@"This is an alert view"
                          delegate:self
                          cancelButtonTitle:@"OK"
                          otherButtonTitles:nil];
```

The first parameter is the title of the alert view, which you set to "Hello". The second is the message, which you set to "This is an alert view". The third is the delegate, which you need to set to an object that will handle the events fired by the UIAlertView object. In this case, you set it to self, which means that the event handler will be implemented in the current class, that is, the View Controller. The cancelButtonTitle parameter displays a button to dismiss your alert view. Last, the otherButtonTitles parameter allows you to display additional buttons if needed. If no additional buttons are needed, simply set this to nil.

To show the alert view modally, use the show method:

```
[alert show];
```

For simple use of the alert view, you don't really need to handle the events fired by it. Tapping the OK button (as set in the cancelButtonTitle parameter) simply dismisses the alert view.

If you want more than one button, you need to set the otherButtonTitles parameter, like this:

```
UIAlertView *alert = [[UIAlertView alloc] initWithTitle:@"Hello"
                          message:@"This is an alert view"
                          delegate:self
                          cancelButtonTitle:@"OK"
                          otherButtonTitles:@"Option 1", @"Option 2", nil];
```

Note that you need to end the otherButtonTitles parameter with a nil or a runtime error will occur.

Now that you have three buttons, you need to be able to know which button the user pressed —in particular, whether Option 1 or Option 2 was pressed. To do so, you need to handle the event raised by the UIAlertView class. You do so by ensuring that your View Controller conforms to the UIAlertViewDelegate protocol:

```
@interface UsingViewsViewController : UIViewController
    <UIAlertViewDelegate> {
    //...
```

The UIAlertViewDelegate protocol contains several methods associated with the alert view. To know which button the user tapped, you need to implement the alertView:clickedButtonAtIndex: method:

```
- (void)alertView:(UIAlertView *)alertView clickedButtonAtIndex:
    (NSInteger)buttonIndex {

    NSLog([NSString stringWithFormat:@"%d", buttonIndex]);

}
```

The index of the button clicked will be passed in via the clickedButtonAtIndex: parameter.

NOTE *Refer to Appendix D for a discussion of the concept of protocols in Objective-C.*

Using the Action Sheet

Although the Alert view can display multiple buttons, its primary use is still as a tool to alert users when something happens. If you need to display a message with multiple choices for the user to select, you should use an action sheet rather than the Alert view. An *action sheet* displays a collection of buttons among which the user can select one. It always emerges from the bottom of the screen and is anchored to the sides of the screen, giving the cue to the user that the action sheet's details are connected to the current application. A good example of the use of an action sheet is when you tap on the "+" button in Safari. Tapping on the "+" button displays an action sheet where you add a bookmark, add the current page to the Home Screen, or mail the link of the current page. The following Try It Out puts you to work with an action sheet.

TRY IT OUT **Using an Action Sheet**

1. Using the same project created in the previous section, modify the viewDidLoad method (in the UsingViewsViewController.m file) as follows:

```
- (void)viewDidLoad {

    UIActionSheet *action = [[UIActionSheet alloc]
                        initWithTitle:@"Title of Action Sheet"
                        delegate:self
                        cancelButtonTitle:@"OK"
                        destructiveButtonTitle:@"Delete Message"
                        otherButtonTitles:@"Option 1", @"Option 2", nil];
    [action showInView:self.view];
    [action release];
    [super viewDidLoad];

}
```

2. In the UsingViewsViewController.h file, add the following statement that appears in bold:

```
#import <UIKit/UIKit.h>

@interface UsingViewsViewController : UIViewController
    <UIActionSheetDelegate> {

}

@end
```

3. In the `UsingViewsViewController.m` file, add the following statement that appears in bold:

```
- (void)actionSheet:(UIActionSheet *)actionSheet
clickedButtonAtIndex:(NSInteger)buttonIndex{

    NSLog([NSString stringWithFormat:@"%d", buttonIndex]);

}
```

4. Press Command-R to test the application using the iPhone Simulator. Figure 4-4 shows the action sheet in action.

5. Click any one of the buttons: Delete Message, Option 1, Option 2, or OK.

6. In Xcode, press Command-Shift-R to view the Debugger Console window. Observe the values printed. You can rerun the application a number of times and click the different buttons to observe the values printed.

7. You should observe the values that printed for each button clicked:

➤ Delete Message — 0

➤ Option 1 — 1

➤ Option 2 — 2

➤ OK — 3

FIGURE 4-4

How It Works

The action sheet works very similarly to the Alert view but is visually different. To show the action sheet, you need to specify the view that the action sheet is originating from:

```
UIActionSheet *action = [[UIActionSheet alloc]
                          initWithTitle:@"Title of Action Sheet"
                          delegate:self
                          cancelButtonTitle:@"OK"
                          destructiveButtonTitle:@"Delete Message"
                          otherButtonTitles:@"Option 1", @"Option 2", nil];
[action showInView:self.view];
```

Note that the button as specified in the `destructiveButtonTitle:` parameter is displayed in red.

To handle the events fired by the action sheet, you need the View Controller to conform to the `UIActionSheetDelegate` protocol:

```
@interface UsingViewsViewController : UIViewController
    <UIActionSheetDelegate> {
    //...
```

To know which button was tapped, you need to implement the `actionSheet:clickedButtonAtIndex:` method:

```
- (void)actionSheet:(UIActionSheet *)actionSheet
clickedButtonAtIndex:(NSInteger)buttonIndex{

    NSLog([NSString stringWithFormat:@"%d", buttonIndex]);

}
```

The index of the button clicked will be passed in via the `clickedButtonAtIndex:` parameter.

Page Control and Image View

On the Home screen of the iPhone, you see a series of dots at the bottom of the screen. A lighted dot represents the currently selected page. As you swipe the page to the next page, the next dot will be lighted. In the iPhone SDK, the series of dots is represented by the `UIPageControl` class. Figure 4-5 shows the page control in action on the Home screen of the iPhone.

In the following exercise, you learn how to use the page control view within your own application to switch between images displayed in the ImageView view.

FIGURE 4-5

TRY IT OUT Using the Page Control and the Image View

1. Using the same project created in the previous two sections, add five images to the Resources folder by dragging and dropping them from the Finder. Figure 4-6 shows the five images added to the project.

2. Double-click the `UsingViewsViewController.xib file` to edit it using Interface Builder.

3. Drag and drop two ImageView views onto the View window. (see Figure 4-7). At this point, overlap them (but not entirely) as shown in the figure.

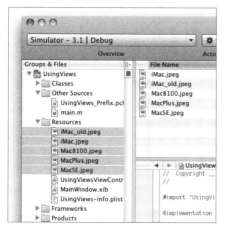

FIGURE 4-6

FIGURE 4-7

4. With one of the ImageView views selected, open the Attributes Inspector window and set the `Tag` property to 0. Select the second ImageView and set the `Tag` property to 1 (see Figure 4-8).

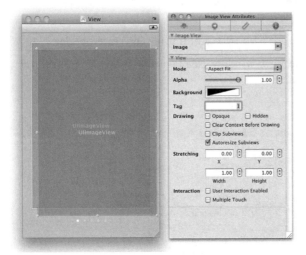

FIGURE 4-8

5. Drag and drop the Page Control view onto the View window and set its number of pages to five (see Figure 4-9).

 NOTE *Ensure that you increase the width of the Page Control view so that all five dots are now visible.*

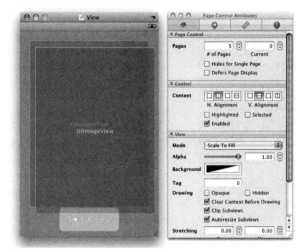

FIGURE 4-9

6. Back in Xcode, in the `UsingViewsViewController.h` file, define three outlets and two `UIImageView` objects:

```
#import <UIKit/UIKit.h>

@interface UsingViewsViewController : UIViewController {
    IBOutlet UIPageControl *pageControl;
    IBOutlet UIImageView *imageView1;
    IBOutlet UIImageView *imageView2;

    UIImageView *tempImageView, *bgImageView;
}

@property (nonatomic, retain) UIPageControl *pageControl;
@property (nonatomic, retain) UIImageView *imageView1;
@property (nonatomic, retain) UIImageView *imageView2;

@end
```

7. In Interface Builder, connect the three outlets to the views on the View window. Figure 4-10 shows the connections made for the `imageView1`, `imageView2`, and `pageControl` outlets.

FIGURE 4-10

8. You can now rearrange the ImageView views on the View window so that they overlap each other.

9. In Xcode, add the following statements that appear in bold to the
UsingViewsViewController.m file:

```
#import "UsingViewsViewController.h"

@implementation UsingViewsViewController

@synthesize pageControl;
@synthesize imageView1, imageView2;

- (void)viewDidLoad {

    //---initialize the first imageview to display an image---
    [imageView1 setImage:[UIImage imageNamed:@"iMac_old.jpeg"]];
    tempImageView = imageView2;

    //---make the first imageview visible and hide the second---
    [imageView1 setHidden:NO];
    [imageView2 setHidden:YES];

    //---add the event handler for the page control---
    [pageControl addTarget:self action:@selector(pageTurning:)
        forControlEvents:UIControlEventValueChanged];
```

```objc
    [super viewDidLoad];

}

//---when the page control's value is changed---
- (void) pageTurning: (UIPageControl *) pageController
{
    //---get the page number you can turning to---
    NSInteger nextPage = [pageController currentPage];
    switch (nextPage) {
        case 0:
            [tempImageView setImage:[UIImage imageNamed:@"iMac_old.jpeg"]];
            break;
        case 1:
            [tempImageView setImage:[UIImage imageNamed:@"iMac.jpeg"]];
            break;
        case 2:
            [tempImageView setImage:[UIImage imageNamed:@"Mac8100.jpeg"]];
            break;
        case 3:
            [tempImageView setImage:[UIImage imageNamed:@"MacPlus.jpeg"]];
            break;
        case 4:
            [tempImageView setImage:[UIImage imageNamed:@"MacSE.jpeg"]];
            break;
        default:
            break;
    }

    //---switch the two imageview views---
    if (tempImageView.tag==0) { //---imageView1---
        tempImageView = imageView2;
        bgImageView = imageView1;
    }
    else {    //---imageView2---
        tempImageView = imageView1;
        bgImageView = imageView2;
    }

    //---animate the two views flipping---
    [UIView beginAnimations:@"flipping view" context:nil];
    [UIView setAnimationDuration:0.5];
    [UIView setAnimationCurve:UIViewAnimationCurveEaseInOut];
    [UIView setAnimationTransition: UIViewAnimationTransitionFlipFromLeft
        forView:tempImageView cache:YES];
    [tempImageView setHidden:YES];
    [UIView commitAnimations];

    [UIView beginAnimations:@"flipping view" context:nil];
    [UIView setAnimationDuration:0.5];
    [UIView setAnimationCurve:UIViewAnimationCurveEaseInOut];
    [UIView setAnimationTransition: UIViewAnimationTransitionFlipFromRight
        forView:bgImageView cache:YES];
    [bgImageView setHidden:NO];
```

```
        [UIView commitAnimations];

}

- (void)dealloc {
    [pageControl release];
    [imageView1 release];
    [imageView2 release];
    [super dealloc];
}

- (void)didReceiveMemoryWarning {
    // Releases the view if it doesn't have a superview.
    [super didReceiveMemoryWarning];
}

- (void)viewDidUnload {
}

@end
```

FIGURE 4-11

10. Press Command-R to test the application on the iPhone Simulator. When you tap the Page Control located at the bottom of the screen, the image view flips to display the next one (see Figure 4-11).

How It Works

When the View is first loaded, you get one of the ImageView views to display an image and then hide the other:

```
//---initialize the first imageview to display an image---
[imageView1 setImage:[UIImage imageNamed:@"iMac_old.jpeg"]];
tempImageView = imageView2;

//---make the first imageview visible and hide the second---
[imageView1 setHidden:NO];
[imageView2 setHidden:YES];
```

You then wire the Page Control so that when the user taps it, an event is fired and triggers a method. In this case, the pageTurning: method is called:

```
//---add the event handler for the page control---
[pageControl addTarget:self action:@selector(pageTurning:)
    forControlEvents:UIControlEventValueChanged];
    [super viewDidLoad];
```

In the pageTurning: method, you determine which image you should load based on the value of the Page Control:

```
//---when the page control's value is changed---
- (void) pageTurning: (UIPageControl *) pageController
{
    //---get the page number you can turning to---
    NSInteger nextPage = [pageController currentPage];
```

```
        switch (nextPage) {
            case 0:
                [tempImageView setImage:[UIImage imageNamed:@"iMac_old.jpeg"]];
                break;
            case 1:
                [tempImageView setImage:[UIImage imageNamed:@"iMac.jpeg"]];
                break;
            case 2:
                [tempImageView setImage:[UIImage imageNamed:@"Mac8100.jpeg"]];
                break;
            case 3:
                [tempImageView setImage:[UIImage imageNamed:@"MacPlus.jpeg"]];
                break;
            case 4:
                [tempImageView setImage:[UIImage imageNamed:@"MacSE.jpeg"]];
                break;
            default:
                break;
        }
        //...
    }
```

You then switch the two ImageView views and animate them by using the various methods in the UIView class:

```
        //---switch the two imageview views---
        if (tempImageView.tag==0) { //---imageView1---
            tempImageView = imageView2;
            bgImageView = imageView1;
        }
        else {      //---imageView2---
            tempImageView = imageView1;
            bgImageView = imageView2;
        }

        //---animate the two views flipping---
        [UIView beginAnimations:@"flipping view" context:nil];
        [UIView setAnimationDuration:0.5];
        [UIView setAnimationCurve:UIViewAnimationCurveEaseInOut];
        [UIView setAnimationTransition: UIViewAnimationTransitionFlipFromLeft
            forView:tempImageView cache:YES];
        [tempImageView setHidden:YES];
        [UIView commitAnimations];

        [UIView beginAnimations:@"flipping view" context:nil];
        [UIView setAnimationDuration:0.5];
        [UIView setAnimationCurve:UIViewAnimationCurveEaseInOut];
        [UIView setAnimationTransition: UIViewAnimationTransitionFlipFromRight
            forView:bgImageView cache:YES];
        [bgImageView setHidden:NO];
        [UIView commitAnimations];
```

Specifically, you apply the flipping transitions to the ImageView views:

```
    [UIView setAnimationTransition: UIViewAnimationTransitionFlipFromLeft
        forView:tempImageView cache:YES];
```

Grouping Views Using the Segmented Control

A segmented control is a horizontal view that contains a series of buttons. Using a segmented control, users can tap any one of the buttons contained within it. Doing so deselects the button that was previously selected.

The following Try It Out shows how to use the segmented control to group several views together. It also shows how you can use this control to select a particular group of views.

TRY IT OUT   **Using a Segmented Control**

Codefile [UsingViews2.zip] available for download at Wrox.com

1. Using Xcode, create a new View-based Application project and name it `UsingViews2`.

2. Double-click the `UsingViews2ViewController.xib` file to edit it using Interface Builder.

3. Add the following views to the View window (see Figure 4-12):

   ➤ Segmented Control

   ➤ View

   ➤ Label (make sure it is embedded within View)

4. Add another View (from the Library) onto the View window and then add a Label view to it (see Figure 4-13). Be careful when you position the second view — make sure that the second view is not contained within the first view. This is because when you use the mouse and drag the second View over the first, Interface Builder will think that you are trying to make the second View a child of the first View. To prevent this from happening, use the cursor to move the

FIGURE 4-12

second view over the first. The View window should now look like Figure 4-13.

5. You can verify that the two Views are at the same level by viewing the `UsingViews2ViewController.xib` window in List mode (see Figure 4-14).

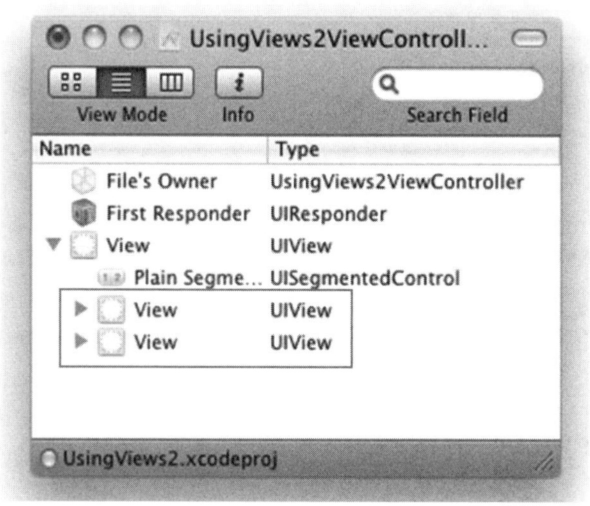

FIGURE 4-13

FIGURE 4-14

6. In the `UsingViews2ViewController.h` file, declare the following outlets:

```
#import <UIKit/UIKit.h>

@interface UsingViews2ViewController : UIViewController {
    IBOutlet UIView *view1;
    IBOutlet UIView *view2;
    IBOutlet UISegmentedControl *segmentedControl;
}

@property (nonatomic, retain) UIView *view1;
@property (nonatomic, retain) UIView *view2;
@property (nonatomic, retain) UISegmentedControl *segmentedControl;

@end
```

7. Back in Interface Builder, connect the outlets to the respective views in the View window. (You may have to move the two Views so that you can connect the two `UIView` outlets to them.)

8. In Xcode, add the following statements that appear in bold to the `UsingViews2ViewController.h` file:

```
#import "UsingViews2ViewController.h"

@implementation UsingViews2ViewController
@synthesize segmentedControl;
@synthesize view1, view2;

- (void)viewDidLoad {
    //---add the event handler for the segmented control---
    [segmentedControl addTarget:self action:@selector(segmentChanged:)
    forControlEvents:UIControlEventValueChanged];

    [super viewDidLoad];
}

//---when the segment has changed---
- (IBAction)segmentChanged:(id)sender {
    NSInteger selectedSegment = segmentedControl.selectedSegmentIndex;
    if (selectedSegment == 0) {
        //---toggle the correct view to be visible---
        [self.view1 setHidden:NO];
        [self.view2 setHidden:YES];
    }
    else{
        //---toggle the correct view to be visible---
        [self.view1 setHidden:YES];
        [self.view2 setHidden:NO];
    }
}

- (void)dealloc {
    [segmentedControl release];
    [view1 release];
    [view2 release];
    [super dealloc];
}
```

9. Press Command-R to test the application on the iPhone Simulator.

10. When you tap the First segment, the First View label appears. When you tap the Second segment, you see the Second View label (see Figure 4-15).

FIGURE 4-15

How It Works

When the View is loaded, you first wire it up so that when the user taps one of its buttons, it triggers a method. In this case, the method is segmentChanged:.

```
[segmentedControl addTarget:self action:@selector(segmentChanged:)
        forControlEvents:UIControlEventValueChanged];
```

In the segmentChanged: method, you determine which button was clicked (via the selectedSegmentIndex property of the segmented control) and show and hide the relevant views:

```
- (IBAction)segmentChanged:(id)sender {
    NSInteger selectedSegment = segmentedControl.selectedSegmentIndex;
    if (selectedSegment == 0) {
        //---toggle the correct view to be visible---
        [self.view1 setHidden:NO];
        [self.view2 setHidden:YES];
    }
    else{
        //---toggle the correct view to be visible---
        [self.view1 setHidden:YES];
        [self.view2 setHidden:NO];
    }
}
```

Using the Web View

If you want to load Web pages from within your application, you can embed a Web browser in your application through the use of the UIWebView. Using the Web view, you can send a request to load Web content, which is a very useful if you want to convert an existing Web application into a native application (such as those written using Dashcode). All you need to do is to embed all the HTML pages into your Resources folder in your Xcode project and load the HTML pages into the Web view during runtime.

 NOTE *Of course, depending on how complex your Web applications are, you may have to do some additional work to port your Web application to a native application if it involves server-side technologies such as CGI, PHP, or others.*

The following Try It Out shows how to use the Web view to load a Web page.

TRY IT OUT Loading a Web Page Using the Web View

Codefile [UsingViews3.zip] available for download at Wrox.com

1. Using Xcode, create a new View-based Application project and name it UsingViews3.

2. Double-click the UsingViews3ViewController.xib file to edit it using Interface Builder.

3. In the View window, add a Web view from the Library (see Figure 4-16). In the Attributes Inspector window for the Web view, check the Scales Page to Fit property.

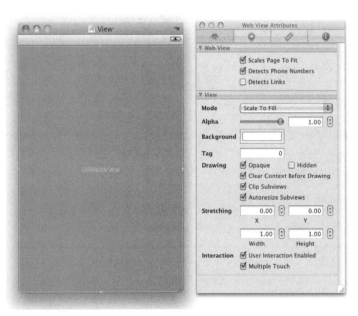

FIGURE 4-16

4. In the `UsingViews3ViewController.h` file, declare an outlet for the Web view:

```
#import <UIKit/UIKit.h>

@interface UsingViews3ViewController : UIViewController {
    IBOutlet UIWebView *webView;
}

@property (nonatomic, retain) UIWebView *webView;

@end
```

5. Back in Interface Builder, connect the `webView` outlet to the Web view.

6. In the `UsingViews3ViewController.m` file, add the following statements that appear in bold:

```
#import "UsingViews3ViewController.h"

@implementation UsingViews3ViewController

@synthesize webView;

- (void)viewDidLoad {

    NSURL *url = [NSURL URLWithString:@"http://www.apple.
com"];
    NSURLRequest *req = [NSURLRequest requestWithURL:url];
    [webView loadRequest:req];

    [super viewDidLoad];
}

- (void)dealloc {
    [webView release];
    [super dealloc];
}
```

7. Press Command-R to test the application on the iPhone Simulator.
You should see the application loading the page from Apple.com (see
Figure 4-17).

FIGURE 4-17

How It Works

To load the Web view with a URL, you first instantiate an NSURL object with a URL via the
URLWithString method:

```
    NSURL *url = [NSURL URLWithString:@"http://www.apple.com"];
```

You then create an NSURLRequest object by passing the NSURL object to its requestWithURL: method:

```
    NSURLRequest *req = [NSURLRequest requestWithURL:url];
```

Finally, you load the Web view with the NSURLRequest object via the loadRequest: method:

```
    [webView loadRequest:req];
```

ADDING VIEWS DYNAMICALLY USING CODE

Up to this point, all the UIs of your application have been created visually using Interface Builder. Although Interface Builder makes it relatively easy to build your UI using drag-and-drop, sometimes you are better off creating the UI using code. One such instance is when you need to create a dynamic UI, such as for games.

 NOTE *I know of developers who swear by creating their UI using code. Interface Builder may be easy to use, but it can be confusing to some people. Because you often have more than one way of doing things in Interface Builder, it can create unnecessary complications.*

In the following Try It Out, you learn how to create views dynamically from code, which will help you understand how views are constructed and manipulated.

TRY IT OUT **Creating Views from Code**

Codefile [UsingViews4.zip] available for download at Wrox.com

1. Using Xcode, create a View-based Application project and name it `UsingViews4`.

2. In the `UsingViews4ViewController.m` file, add the following statements that appear in bold:

```
#import "UsingViews4ViewController.h"

@implementation UsingViews4ViewController

- (void)loadView {

    //---create a UIView object---
    UIView *view =
        [[UIView alloc] initWithFrame:[UIScreen mainScreen].applicationFrame];
    view.backgroundColor = [UIColor lightGrayColor];

    //---create a Label view---
```

```
        CGRect frame = CGRectMake(10, 15, 300, 20);
        UILabel *label = [[UILabel alloc] initWithFrame:frame];
        label.textAlignment = UITextAlignmentCenter;
        label.backgroundColor = [UIColor clearColor];
        label.font = [UIFont fontWithName:@"Verdana" size:20];
        label.text = @"This is a label";
        label.tag = 1000;

        //---create a Button view---
        frame = CGRectMake(10, 70, 300, 50);

        UIButton *button = [UIButton buttonWithType:UIButtonTypeRoundedRect];
        button.frame = frame;

        [button setTitle:@"Click Me, Please!" forState:UIControlStateNormal];
        button.backgroundColor = [UIColor clearColor];
        button.tag = 2000;
        [button addTarget:self action:@selector(buttonClicked:)
            forControlEvents:UIControlEventTouchUpInside];

        [view addSubview:label];
        [view addSubview:button];

        self.view = view;

        [label release];
    }

    -(IBAction) buttonClicked: (id) sender{
        UIAlertView *alert = [[UIAlertView alloc] initWithTitle:@"Action invoked!"
                                    message:@"Button clicked!"
                                    delegate:self
                                    cancelButtonTitle:@"OK"
                                    otherButtonTitles:nil];
        [alert show];
        [alert release];
    }

    @end
```

3. Press Command-R to test the application in the iPhone Simulator.
Figure 4-18 shows that the Label and Round Rect Button view is
displayed on the view. When you click the button, you should see an
alert view displaying a message.

How It Works

To programmatically create your views, you can use the loadView method
defined in your View Controller. You implement this method only if you
are generating your UI during runtime. This method is automatically called
when the view property of your View Controller is called but its current
value is nil.

FIGURE 4-18

The first view you create is the `UIView` object, which allows you to use it as a container for more views:

```
//---create a UIView object---
UIView *view =
    [[UIView alloc] initWithFrame:[UIScreen mainScreen].applicationFrame];

//---set the background color to lightgray---
view.backgroundColor = [UIColor lightGrayColor];
```

Next, you create a Label view and set it to display a string:

```
//---create a Label view---
CGRect frame = CGRectMake(10, 15, 300, 20);
UILabel *label = [[UILabel alloc] initWithFrame:frame];
label.textAlignment = UITextAlignmentCenter;
label.backgroundColor = [UIColor clearColor];
label.font = [UIFont fontWithName:@"Verdana" size:20];
label.text = @"This is a label";
label.tag = 1000;
```

Notice that you have also set the `tag` property, which is very useful for allowing you to search for particular views during runtime.

You also create a Button view by calling the `buttonWithType:` method with the `UIButtonTypeRoundedRect` constant. This method returns a `UIRoundedRectButton` object (which is a subclass of `UIButton`).

```
//---create a Button view---
frame = CGRectMake(10, 70, 300, 50);

UIButton *button = [UIButton buttonWithType:UIButtonTypeRoundedRect];
button.frame = frame;

[button setTitle:@"Click Me, Please!" forState:UIControlStateNormal];
button.backgroundColor = [UIColor clearColor];
button.tag = 2000;
```

You then wire an event handler for its `Touch Up Inside` event so that when the button is tapped, the `buttonClicked:` method is called:

```
[button AddTarget:Self action:@selector(buttonClicked:)
    forControlEvents:UIControlEventTouchUpInside];
```

Finally, you add the `label` and `button` views to the `view` you created earlier:

```
[view addSubview:label];    [view addSubview:button];
```

Finally, you assign the `view` object to the `view` property of the current View Controller:

```
self.view = view;
```

One important point to note here is that within the `loadView` method, you should not get the value of the `view` property (setting it is all right), like this:

```
[self.view addSubView: label];  //---this is not OK---
self.view = view;               //---this is OK---
```

Trying to get the value of the `view` property in this method will result in a circular reference and cause memory overflow.

UNDERSTANDING VIEW HIERARCHY

As views are created and added, they are added to a tree data structure. Views are displayed in the order that they are added. To verify this, modify the location of the `UIButton` object you created earlier by changing its location to `CGRectMake(10, 30, 300, 50)`, as in the following:

```
//---create a Button view---
frame = CGRectMake(10, 30, 300, 50);
UIButton *button = [UIButton buttonWithType:UIButtonTypeRoundedRect];
button.frame = frame;
[button setTitle:@"Click Me, Please!" forState:UIControlStateNormal];
button.backgroundColor = [UIColor clearColor];
button.tag = 2000;
[button addTarget:self action:@selector(buttonClicked:)
    forControlEvents:UIControlEventTouchUpInside];
```

When you now run the application again, you will notice that the button overlaps the label control (see Figure 4-19) since the button was added last:

```
[view addSubview:label];
[view addSubview:button];
```

If you want to switch the order in which the views are displayed after they have been added, you can use the `exchangeSubviewAtIndex:` `withSubviewAtIndex:` method, like this:

```
[self.view addSubview:label];
[self.view addSubview:button];
```

FIGURE 4-19

[self.view exchangeSubviewAtIndex:1 withSubviewAtIndex:0];

```
[button release];
[label release];
```

The preceding statement in bold swaps the order of the Label and Button views. When the application is run again, the Label view will now appear on top of the Button view (See Figure 4-20).

FIGURE 4-20

To know the order of the various views already added, you can use the following code segment to print the value of the `tag` property for each view:

```
[self.view addSubview:label];
[self.view addSubview:button];
[self.view exchangeSubviewAtIndex:1 withSubviewAtIndex:0];

for (int i=0; i<[self.view.subviews count]; ++i) {
    UIView *view = [self.view.subviews objectAtIndex:i];
    NSLog([NSString stringWithFormat:@"%d", view.tag]);
}
```

The following method recursively prints out all the views contained in a `UIView` object:

```
-(void) printViews: (UIView *) view {
    if ([view.subviews count] > 0){
        for (int i=0; i<[view.subviews count]; ++i) {
            UIView *v = [view.subviews objectAtIndex:i];
            NSLog([NSString stringWithFormat:@"View index: %d Tag: %d",i, v.tag]);
            [self printViews:v];
        }
    } else
        return;
}
```

To remove a view from the current view hierarchy, use the removeFromSuperview method of the view you want to remove. For example, the following statement removes the `label` view:

```
[label removeFromSuperview];
```

SWITCHING VIEWS

When you create a View-based Application project in Xcode, you get a project with a single view with a corresponding View Controller. This is what you see when you edit the `.xib` file in Interface Builder. However, sometimes you need more than one view. For example, you may get the user to enter some information in one view and then based on the information that user entered, switch to another view for some actions.

The following Try It Out shows you how to switch between two views and how to wire a new view to a corresponding View Controller.

TRY IT OUT   Switching between Two UIView Views

Codefile [VCExample.zip] available for download at Wrox.com

1.   Using Xcode, create a new View-based Application project and name it VCExample.

2.   Double-click the VCExampleViewController.xib file to edit it in Interface Builder.

3. In the `VCExampleViewController.xib` window, double-click the `View` item and add a Button view to it (see Figure 4-21). Also set the background color of the `View` to green.

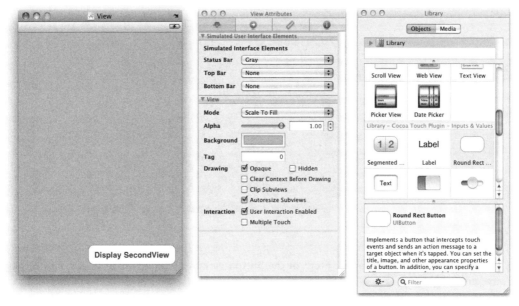

FIGURE 4-21

4. Back in Xcode, edit the `VCExampleViewController.h` file and add the following code that appears in bold:

```
#import <UIKit/UIKit.h>

@interface VCExampleViewController : UIViewController {

}

//---declare an action for the Button view---
-(IBAction) displayView:(id) sender;

@end
```

5. Back in Interface Builder, Control-click and drag the Button view to the File's Owner item and select `displayView:` (see Figure 4-22).

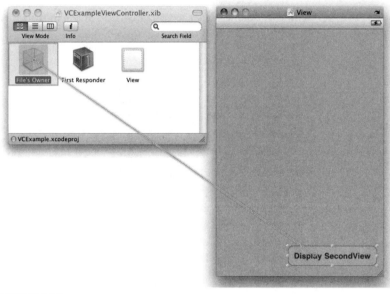

FIGURE 4-22

6.   This connects the `Touch Up Inside` event of the Button view with the `displayView:` action that you have just added.

7.   In Xcode, right-click the Classes group and add a new file. Choose the Cocoa Touch Classes group and then select the `UIViewController` subclass template (see Figure 4-23).

FIGURE 4-23

8. Name the View Controller `SecondViewController.m`.

9. Next, add a new view `.xib` file so that the UI can be created using Interface Builder. Right-click the Resources group in Xcode and add a new file. Choose the User Interfaces group and then select the View XIB template (see Figure 4-24).

FIGURE 4-24

10. Name the `.xib` file `SecondView.xib`. The Xcode should now contain the files that you have just added (see Figure 4-25).

11. Take a look at the `SecondViewController.h` file and observe that the `SecondViewController` class inherits from the `UIViewController` base class:

```
#import <UIKit/UIKit.h>

@interface SecondViewController :
UIViewController {
}

@end
```

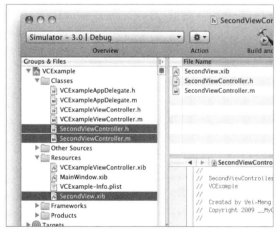

FIGURE 4-25

12. Double-click the `SecondView.xib` file to edit it in Interface Builder. In the `SecondView.xib` window, select the File's Owner item and view its Identity Inspector window (see Figure 4-26). Set its Class to `SecondViewController`.

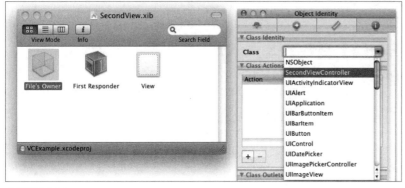

FIGURE 4-26

13. Connect the File's Owner item to the View item by Control-clicking and dragging it over the View item (see Figure 4-27). Select `view`.

14. Double-click the View item and change its background color to orange and then add a Button view (see Figure 4-28).

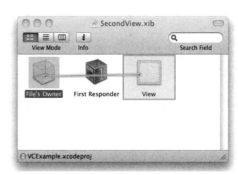

FIGURE 4-27

FIGURE 4-28

15. In Xcode, add the following lines to the `SecondViewController.h` file:

```
#import <UIKit/UIKit.h>

@interface SecondViewController : UIViewController {

}

//---action for the Return button---
-(IBAction) btnReturn:(id) sender;

@end
```

16. Back in Interface Builder, connect the Return button to the File's Owner item and select `btnReturn:`.

17. In the `VCExampleViewController.m` file, add the following lines that appear in bold so that when the Display SecondView button is pressed, the view represented by the second View Controller is added to the current view, thereby making it appear:

```
#import "VCExampleViewController.h"

//---import the header file for the view controller---
#import "SecondViewController.h"

@implementation VCExampleViewController
SecondViewController *secondViewController;

//---add the view of the second view controller to the current view---
-(IBAction) displayView:(id) sender{
    secondViewController = [[SecondViewController alloc]
    initWithNibName:@"SecondView" bundle:nil];
    [self.view addSubview:secondViewController.view];
}
- (void)dealloc {
    //---release the memory used by the view controller---
    [secondViewController release];
    [super dealloc];
}

@end
```

18. In the `SecondViewController.m`, code the `btnReturn:` method so that its view is removed from the current view. This results in having the view disappear and reveal the previous view:

```
#import "SecondViewController.h"

@implementation SecondViewController

-(IBAction) btnReturn:(id) sender {
    [self.view removeFromSuperview];
}

@end
```

19. That's it! Press Command-R to test the application. You see that the second view is displayed when the Display SecondView button is pressed (see Figure 4-29). Likewise, when you press the Return button, the second view disappears.

FIGURE 4-29

How It Works

The first part of this Try It Out shows you how to add a new .xib file to your project. Next, you add a UIViewController subclass that will be used to control the .xib file that you have added. Notice the steps in which you connect the view in the .xib file to the View Controller:

1. In the File's Owner item, set the Class property to the name of the View Controller.

2. Connect the File's Owner item to the view.

The sequence of the preceding steps is important. If you do not specify the class name of the View Controller, you won't be able to connect the File's Owner item to the view.

To display the second view, you create an instance of the second View Controller and then add its view to the current view:

```
secondViewController = [[SecondViewController alloc]
    initWithNibName:@"SecondView" bundle:nil];
    [self.view addSubview:secondViewController.view];
```

To remove the second view, simply call the removeFromSuperview method of the second view:

```
[self.view removeFromSuperview];
```

Animating the Transitions

In the previous section, you saw how to transition from one view to another. The transitioning happens very quickly and is not exciting visually. To live up to the high expectations expected by iPhone users, you need to add some animations to the transition. Fortunately, doing so is very easy using the APIs provided in the SDK, as the following Try It Out demonstrates.

TRY IT OUT Displaying Animations During the Transitioning

1. In the `VCExampleViewController.m`, add the following lines of code that appear in bold:

```
-(IBAction) displayView:(id) sender{
secondViewController = [[SecondViewController alloc]
    initWithNibName:@"SecondView" bundle:nil];

    [UIView beginAnimations:@"flipping view" context:nil];
    [UIView setAnimationDuration:1];
    [UIView setAnimationCurve:UIViewAnimationCurveEaseInOut];
    [UIView setAnimationTransition: UIViewAnimationTransitionCurlDown
        forView:self.view cache:YES];

    [self.view addSubview:secondViewController.view];

    [UIView commitAnimations];
}
```

2. Press Command-R to test the application. Observe what happens when the Display SecondView button is clicked (see Figure 4-30).

3. Back in Xcode, add the following lines that appear in bold to the `SecondViewController.m` file:

```
-(IBAction) btnReturn:(id) sender {

    [UIView beginAnimations:@"flipping view" context:nil];
    [UIView setAnimationDuration:1];
    [UIView setAnimationCurve:UIViewAnimationCurveEaseIn];
    [UIView setAnimationTransition:
       UIViewAnimationTransitionCurlUp
       forView:self.view.superview cache:YES];

    [self.view removeFromSuperview];

    [UIView commitAnimations];

}
```

FIGURE 4-30

4. Press Command-R to test the application. Notice that when you now press the Return button in the second view, the second view flips up (see Figure 4-31).

How It Works

Basically, you added some animation during the transitioning process via the various animations methods in the `UIView` class:

```
[UIView beginAnimations:@"flipping view" context:nil];
[UIView setAnimationDuration:1];
[UIView setAnimationCurve:UIViewAnimationCurveEaseInOut];
[UIView setAnimationTransition:
    UIViewAnimationTransitionCurlDown
    forView:self.view cache:YES];

[self.view addSubview:secondViewController.view];

[UIView commitAnimations];
```

FIGURE 4-31

Here's what you did with the various statements:

➤ You set the animation duration to be one second.

➤ The animation curve is `UIViewAnimationCurveEaseInOut`. You can choose other animation types: `UIViewAnimationCurveEaseIn`, `UIViewAnimationCurveEaseOut`, and `UIViewAnimationCurveLinear`.

➤ The animation transitioning type is `UIViewAnimationTransitionCurlDown`. You can choose other animation transitioning types: `UIViewAnimationTransitionFlipFromLeft`, `UIViewAnimationTransitionFlipFromRight`, and `UIViewAnimationTransitionCurlUp`.

Passing Data Between Views

Sometimes you need to pass data from one view to another. So how do you do that? The easiest way is to create a property on the target view and set the property on the calling view. The following Try It Out shows you how to do this.

Passing Data from One View to Another

1. Double-click the `VCExampleViewController.xib` file and add a `DatePicker` view to the View window (see Figure 4-32).

2. In the `VCExampleViewController.h` file, create an outlet for this `DatePicker` view and then expose it as a property:

```
#import <UIKit/UIKit.h>

@interface VCExampleViewController :
UIViewController {
    //---outlet for the DatePicker view---
    IBOutlet UIDatePicker *datePicker;
}

//---expose this outlet as a property---
@property (nonatomic, retain) UIDatePicker
*datePicker;

-(IBAction) displayView:(id) sender;

@end
```

3. In the `VCExampleViewController.xib` window, Control-click and drag the File's Owner Item to the `DatePicker` view and then select `datePicker`.

FIGURE 4-32

4. In the `SecondViewController.h`, create an object of type `UIDatePicker` and then expose it as a property:

```
#import <UIKit/UIKit.h>

@interface SecondViewController : UIViewController {
    //---object of type UIDatePicker---
    UIDatePicker *selectedDatePicker;
}

//---expose the object as a property---
@property (nonatomic, retain) UIDatePicker *selectedDatePicker;

-(IBAction) btnReturn:(id) sender;

@end
```

5. In the `SecondViewController.m` file, add the following lines that appear in bold to the `viewDidLoad` method:

```
#import "SecondViewController.h"

@implementation SecondViewController
@synthesize selectedDatePicker;

- (void)viewDidLoad {
```

```
    //---display the date and time selected in the previous view---
    NSDateFormatter *formatter = [[[NSDateFormatter alloc] init] autorelease];
    [formatter setDateFormat:@"MMM dd, yyyy HH:mm"];

    UIAlertView *alert = [[UIAlertView alloc]
                             initWithTitle:@"Date and time selected"
                             message:[formatter
                                 stringFromDate:selectedDatePicker.date]
                             delegate:self
                             cancelButtonTitle:@"OK"
                             otherButtonTitles:nil];
    [alert show];
    [alert release];
    [super viewDidLoad];
}

- (void)dealloc {
    //---release the memory used by the property---
    [selectedDatePicker release];
    [super dealloc];
}
```

6. Finally, in the `VCExampleViewController.m` file, add the following lines that appear in bold:

```
#import "VCExampleViewController.h"
#import "SecondViewController.h"

@implementation VCExampleViewController
@synthesize datePicker;
SecondViewController *secondViewController;

-(IBAction) displayView:(id) sender{
    secondViewController = [[SecondViewController alloc]
        initWithNibName:@"SecondView" bundle:nil];

    //---set the property of the second view with the DatePicker view in
    // the current view---
    secondViewController.selectedDatePicker = datePicker;

    [UIView beginAnimations:@"flipping view" context:nil];
    [UIView setAnimationDuration:1];
    [UIView setAnimationCurve:UIViewAnimationCurveEaseInOut];
    [UIView setAnimationTransition: UIViewAnimationTransitionCurlDown
     forView:self.view cache:YES];

    [self.view addSubview:secondViewController.view];

    [UIView commitAnimations];

}
```

7. Press Command-R to test the application on the iPhone Simulator. Select a date and time in the `DatePicker` view and press the Display SecondView button. The selected date and time are displayed when the second view is displayed (see Figure 4-33).

FIGURE 4-33

How It Works

To pass data from one view to another, the easiest way is expose a property on the receiving view and set the property value on the calling end.

The second view exposes the property named `selectedDatePicker`:

```
@interface SecondViewController : UIViewController {
    //---object of type UIDatePicker---
    UIDatePicker *selectedDatePicker;
}

//---expose the object as a property---
@property (nonatomic, retain) UIDatePicker *selectedDatePicker;
```

To pass a value from the first view to the second view, you simply set the property that you have defined:

```
//---set the property of the second view with the DatePicker view in
// the current view---
    secondViewController.selectedDatePicker = datePicker;
```

SUMMARY

In this chapter, you have seen many views in action. You have also seen how views can be dynamically created during runtime. More important, you saw how to wire a view to a View Controller and how to switch between two views during runtime.

EXERCISES

1. Describe the steps to connect a view to a View Controller.

2. When do you use an Alert view and when do you use an action sheet?

3. Create a `UIButton` from code and wire its `Touch Up Inside` event to an event handler.

▶ WHAT YOU HAVE LEARNED IN THIS CHAPTER

TOPIC	KEY CONCEPTS

Using the `UIAlertView`	`UIAlertView *alert = [[UIAlertView alloc]`
	`    initWithTitle:@"Hello"`
	`    message:@"This is an alert view"`
	`    delegate:self`
	`cancelButtonTitle:@"OK"`
	`otherButtonTitles:nil];`

Handling events fired by `UIAlertView`	Ensure that your View Controller conforms to the `UIAlertViewDelegate` protocol.

Using the `UIActionSheet`	`UIActionSheet *action =`
	`    [[UIActionSheet alloc]`
	`    initWithTitle:@"Title of Action Sheet"`
	`    delegate:self`
	`    cancelButtonTitle:@"OK"`
	`    destructiveButtonTitle:`
	`    @"Delete Message"`
	`    otherButtonTitles:@"Option 1",`
	`    @"Option 2", nil];`

Handling events fired by `UIActionSheet`	Ensure that your View Controller conforms to the `UIActionSheetDelegate` protocol.

Wiring up the events for the `UIPageControl`	`[pageControl addTarget:self`
	`    action:@selector(pageTurning:)`
	`    forControlEvents:UIControlEventValueChanged];`

Using the `UIImageView`	`[imageView1 setImage:` `    [UIImage imageNamed:@"iMac_old.jpeg"]];`

Wiring the events for the `UISegmentedControl`	`[segmentedControl addTarget:self`
	`    action:@selector(segmentChanged:)`
	`    forControlEvents:UIControlEventValueChanged];`

Using the `UIWebView`	`NSURL *url =`
	`    [NSURL URLWithString:@"http://www.apple.com"];`
	`NSURLRequest *req =`
	`    [NSURLRequest requestWithURL:url];`
	`[webView loadRequest:req];`

Animating during transitions	`[UIView beginAnimations:@"flipping view"`
	`    context:nil];`
	`[UIView setAnimationDuration:1];`
	`[UIView setAnimationCurve:`
	`    UIViewAnimationCurveEaseInOut];`
	`[UIView setAnimationTransition:`
	`    UIViewAnimationTransitionCurlDown`
	`    forView:self.view cache:YES];`
	
	`[self.view addSubview:`
	`    secondViewController.view];`
	
	`[UIView commitAnimations];`

Passing data between views	Define a property in the receiving view and set its value in the calling view.

5

Keyboard Inputs

WHAT YOU WILL LEARN IN THIS CHAPTER

➤ How to customize the keyboard for different types of inputs

➤ How to make the alphanumeric keyboard go away when you are done typing

➤ How to hide a numeric keyboard

➤ How to detect when a keyboard is visible or not

➤ How to shift views to make way for the keyboard

One of the controversial aspects of the iPhone is the multitouch keyboard that allows users to input data into their iPhone. Critics of the iPhone have long lamented its lack of a physical keyboard for data entry, whereas ardent iPhone supporters swear by its ease of use. Although many mobile platforms have long experimented with virtual keyboards, none is as successful as the iPhone in its implementation.

What made the iPhone keyboard so powerful is its intelligence in tracking what you type, followed by suggestions for the word you are typing, and automatically correcting the spelling and inserting punctuation for you. What's more, the keyboard knows when to appear at the right time — it appears when you tap a TextField view, and it goes away automatically when you tap a non-input view. Also, it lets you input data in different languages.

For iPhone application programmers, the key concern is how to integrate the keyboard into your application. How do you make the keyboard go away when it is no longer needed? And how do you ensure that the view the user is currently interacting with is not blocked by the keyboard? In this chapter, you learn about various ways to deal with the keyboard programmatically.

USING THE KEYBOARD

In iPhone programming, the view that is most commonly associated with the keyboard is the TextField view. When a TextField view is tapped (or clicked, if you are using the Simulator), the keyboard is automatically displayed. The data that the user clicks on the keyboard is then inserted into the TextField view.

TRY IT OUT   Using a TextField for Inputs

Codefile [KeyboardInputs.zip] available for download at Wrox.com

1. Using Xcode, create a new View-based Application project and name it `KeyboardInputs`.

2. Double-click the `KeyboardInputsViewController.xib` file to edit it using Interface Builder.

3. Populate the View with Label and TextField views (see Figure 5-1).

4. Save the `KeyboardInputsViewController.xib` file and press Command-R in Xcode to run the application on the iPhone Simulator. Figure 5-2 (left) shows that when the application is loaded, the keyboard is initially hidden, and when the user clicks the TextField view, the keyboard automatically appears (right).

FIGURE 5-1

FIGURE 5-2

How It Works

The beauty of the iPhone user interface is that when the system detects that the current active view is a TextField view, the keyboard automatically appears; you don't need to do anything to bring up the keyboard. Using the keyboard, you can enter alphanumeric data as well as numbers and special characters (such as symbols). The keyboard in iPhone also supports characters of languages other than English, such as Chinese, Hebrew, and others.

Unfortunately, making the keyboard go away is not as straightforward as making it appear. When you are done with the input, the keyboard does not go away automatically. This is because it does not know when you are done with the input; to do so you need to write some code. You will learn how to do this in the section "Making the Keyboard Go Away."

CUSTOMIZING THE TYPE OF INPUTS

In the previous section, you saw how the TextField view was used for capturing user inputs. To understand more about the input behaviors, go to Interface Builder, select the TextField view, and view its Attributes Inspector window (choose Tools ⇨ Attributes Inspector). Figure 5-3 shows the Attributes Inspector window for the TextField view. In particular, pay attention to the section labeled Text Input Traits.

The Text Input Traits section contains several items for you to use to configure how the keyboard handles the text entered.

➤ The Capitalize item allows you to capitalize the words, sentences, or all characters of the data entered via the keyboard.

➤ The Correction item lets you indicate whether you want the keyboard to provide suggestions for words that are not spelled correctly. You can also choose the Default option so that it defaults to the user's global text correction settings.

➤ The Keyboard item allows you to choose the different types of keyboard for entering different types of data.

FIGURE 5-3

Figure 5-4 shows (from left to right) the keyboard configured with the following Keyboard types: Email Address, Phone Pad, and Number Pad.

FIGURE 5-4

➤   The Appearance item lets you choose how the keyboard should appear.

Figure 5-5 shows the keyboard in Default (top) and Alert (bottom) view.

➤   The Return Key item (see Figure 5-6) allows you to show different types of Return key in your keyboard.

Figure 5-7 shows the keyboard set with the Google key serving as the Return key.

FIGURE 5-5   **FIGURE 5-6**   **FIGURE 5-7**

➤ Finally, the Auto-Enable Return Key check box indicates that if no input is entered for a field, the Return key will be disabled (grayed out). It will be enabled again if at least one character is entered. The Secure check box indicates if the input will be masked (see Figure 5-8). This is usually used for password input.

Making the Keyboard Go Away

In the earlier part of this chapter, you saw that the keyboard in the iPhone automatically appears when you select a TextField view. However, making the keyboard go away requires additional effort on the part of the programmer. In this section, you will see how you can programmatically dismiss the keyboard when you are done with the typing. The first technique is demonstrated in the following Try It Out.

FIGURE 5-8

TRY IT OUT   Dismissing the Keyboard (Technique 1)

1. Using the project you created earlier, double-click the `KeyboardInputsViewController.xib` file to edit it using Interface Builder.

2. With the File's Owner item selected in the `KeyboardInputsViewController.xib` window, view its Identity Inspector window and create a new action called `doneEditing:` (see Figure 5-9).

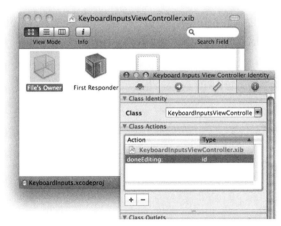

FIGURE 5-9

This creates an `IBAction` that will allow you to connect to an event in the TextField view.

3. Right-click the TextField view in the View window and then click the circle next to the Did End on Exit event and drag it to the File's Owner item (see Figure 5-10). The doneEditing: outlet you have just created should appear. Select it.

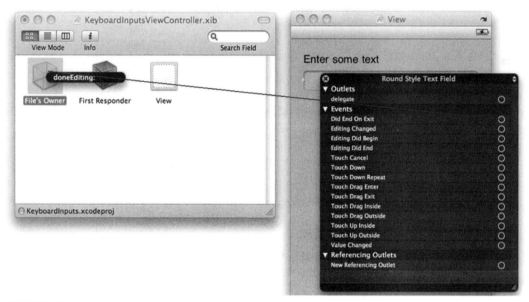

FIGURE 5-10

4. Save the KeyboardInputsViewController.xib file.

5. Back in Xcode, add the following code in the KeyboardInputsViewController.h file:

```
#import <UIKit/UIKit.h>

@interface KeyboardInputsViewController : UIViewController {
}

-(IBAction) doneEditing:(id) sender;

@end
```

6. In the KeyboardInputsViewController.m file, provide the implementation for the doneEditing: action:

```
#import "KeyboardInputsViewController.h"

@implementation KeyboardInputsViewController

-(IBAction) doneEditing:(id) sender{
    [sender resignFirstResponder];
}
```

7. Save the project and press Command-R to run the application on the iPhone Simulator.

8. When the application appears on the iPhone Simulator, click the TextField view. The keyboard should appear. Using the keyboard, type some text into it and press the Return key when you are done. The keyboard now goes away.

How It Works

What you have just done is connect the `Did End on Exit` event of the TextField view with the `doneEditing:` action you have created. When you are editing the content of a TextField view using the keyboard, pressing the Return key on the keyboard fires the `Did End on Edit` event of the TextField view. In this case, it invokes the `doneEditing:` action, which contains the following statement:

```
[sender resignFirstResponder];
```

Basically, the `sender` in this case refers to the TextField view, and `resignFirstResponder` asks the TextField view to resign its First-Responder status. Essentially, it means that you do not want to interact with the TextField view anymore and that the keyboard is no longer needed. Hence, the keyboard should hide itself.

 NOTE *The First Responder in a view always refers to the current view that the user is interacting with. In the example here, when you click the TextField view, it becomes the First Responder and activates the keyboard automatically.*

Set the Keyboard to Number Pad

So far, things have been pretty straightforward. You now know that you can dismiss a keyboard by simply making a TextField resign its First-Responder status. Doing so requires that you handle the `Did End on Exit` event, which is fired whenever the user clicks the Return key on the keyboard. However, the Return key is shown only when you display it using a non-numeric keyboard type. If you display a numeric keyboard, for example, the Return key is no longer available. In this case, you would have trouble getting the `Did End On Exit` event to fire.

Therefore, the following Try It Out teaches another technique for dismissing the keyboard, regardless of the type of keyboard displayed.

Dismissing the Keyboard (Technique 2)

1. Using the same project, double-click the `KeyboardInputsViewCont`
`roller.xib` file to edit it using Interface Builder.

2. Select the TextField view in the View window and view its
Attributes Inspector window (choose Tools ➪ Attributes
Inspector). Change its keyboard type to Number Pad (see
Figure 5-11).

3. Select the File's Owner item in the `KeyboardInputsView`
`Controller.xib` window and view its Identity Inspector window
(see Figure 5-12). Add an action called `bgTouched:` and an outlet
called `textField`.

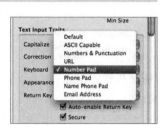

FIGURE 5-11

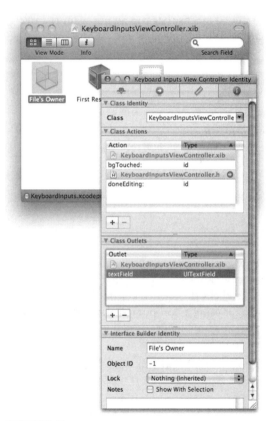

FIGURE 5-12

4. Control-drag the File's Owner item onto the TextField view (see Figure 5-13). The `textField`
outlet should appear. Select it.

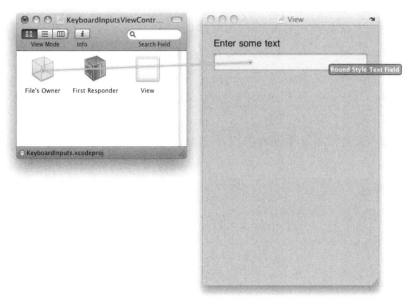

FIGURE 5-13

5. Add a Round Rect Button view to the View window (see Figure 5-14).

FIGURE 5-14

6. With the Round Rect Button view selected, choose Layout ➪ Send to back. This makes the button appear behind the other controls.

7. Resize the Round Rect Button view so that it now covers the entire screen (see Figure 5-15).

FIGURE 5-15

8. In the Attributes Inspector window, set the Type of the Round Rect Button view to Custom (see Figure 5-16).

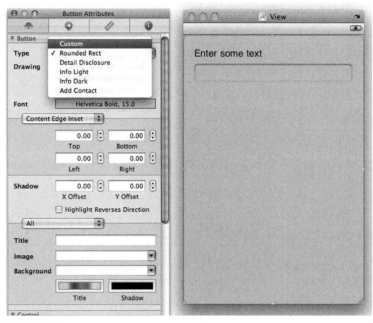

FIGURE 5-16

9. Control-drag the Round Rect Button view onto the File's Owner item in the
KeyboardInputsViewController.xib window (see Figure 5-17). Select the bgTouched:
action.

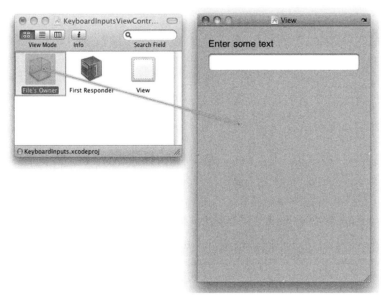

FIGURE 5-17

NOTE *The* Touch Up Inside *event of the Round Rect Button view is wired to
the* bgTouched: *action.*

10. Save the XIB file in Interface Builder.

11. Back in Xcode, edit the KeyboardInputsViewController.h file and add the following statements
highlighted in bold:

```
#import <UIKit/UIKit.h>

@interface KeyboardInputsViewController : UIViewController {
 IBOutlet UITextField *textField;
}

@property (nonatomic, retain) UITextField *textField;

-(IBAction) bgTouched:(id) sender;
-(IBAction) doneEditing:(id) sender;

@end
```

12. In the `KeyboardInputsViewController.m` file, add the following statements highlighted in bold:

```
#import "KeyboardInputsViewController.h"

@implementation KeyboardInputsViewController

@synthesize textField;

-(IBAction) bgTouched:(id) sender{
    [textField resignFirstResponder];
}

-(IBAction) doneEditing:(id) sender{
    [sender resignFirstResponder];
}
```

13. That's it. Press Command-R in Xcode to deploy the application onto the iPhone Simulator. Then, try the following:

➤ Click the TextField view to bring up the keyboard.

➤ When you are done, you can click the Return key on the keyboard to dismiss it. Alternatively, you can click any of the empty spaces outside the TextField view to dismiss the keyboard.

How It Works

In this example, you added a Round Rect Button view to cover up all the empty spaces in the View window of your application. Essentially, the button acts as a net to trap all touches outside of the TextField view on the View window. So when the user clicks (or taps, on a real device) the screen outside the keyboard and the TextField view, the Round Rect Button fires the `Touch Up Inside` event, which is handled by the `bgTouched:` action. In the `bgTouched:` action, you explicitly asked `textField` to resign its First-Responder status, which causes the keyboard to disappear.

The technique used in this example applies even if you have multiple TextField views on your view. Suppose you have three TextField views, named `textField`, `textField2`, and `textField3`. In this case, the `bgTouched:` action looks like this:

```
-(IBAction) bgTouched:(id) sender{
    [textField resignFirstResponder];
    [textField2 resignFirstResponder];
    [textField3 resignFirstResponder];
}
```

So when the `bgTouched:` action is invoked, all three `TextField` views are asked to relinquish their First-Responder status. Calling the `resignFirstResponder` method on a view that is currently not the First Responder is harmless; hence, the preceding statements are safe and will not cause an exception during runtime.

UNDERSTANDING THE RESPONDER CHAIN

The prior Try It Out is a good example of the responder chain in action. In the iPhone, events passed through a series of event handlers known as the responder chain. As you touch on the screen of your iPhone, the iPhone generates events that get passed up the responder chain. Each object in the responder chain checks to see if it can handle the event. In the example above, if the user taps on the Label view, the Label view will check to see if it can handle the event. Since the Label event does not handle the Touch event, it is passed up the responder chain. The large background button that you have added is now next in line to examine the event. Because it handles the `Touch Up Inside` event, the event is consumed by the button.

In summary, objects higher up in the responder chain examine the event first and handle the event if it is applicable. Any object can then stop the propagation of the event up the responder chain, or pass the event up the responder chain if it only partially handles the event.

Automatically Displaying The Keyboard When The View Is Loaded

Sometimes you might want to straightaway set a TextField view as the active view and display the keyboard without waiting for the user to do so. In such cases, you can use the `becomeFirstResponder` method of a view. The following code shows that the TextField view will be the First Responder as soon as the View is loaded:

```
- (void)viewDidLoad {

    [textField becomeFirstResponder];

    [super viewDidLoad];
}
```

DETECTING THE PRESENCE OF THE KEYBOARD

Up to this point, you have seen the various ways to hide the keyboard after you are done using it. However, there is one problem that you need to note. When the keyboard appears, it takes up a signification portion of the screen. If your TextField view is located at the bottom of the screen, it would be covered by the keyboard. As a programmer, it is your duty to ensure that the view is relocated to a visible portion of the screen. Surprisingly, this is not taken care of by the SDK; you have to do the hard work yourself.

NOTE *The current keyboard in the iPhone takes up 216 pixels in height.*

Before you learn how to relocate the views on a screen when the keyboard appears, it is important for you to understand a few key concepts related to the keyboard:

➤ You need to be able to programmatically know when a keyboard is visible or hidden. To do so, your application needs to register for the following notifications — `UIKeyboardWillShowNotification` and `UIKeyboardWillHideNotification`.

➤ You also need to know when and which TextField view is currently being edited so that you can relocate it to a visible portion of the screen. You can know these two pieces of information through the two delegate protocols — `textFieldDidBeginEditing:` and `textFieldDidEndEditing:` — available in the `UITextFieldDelegate` delegate.

Confused? Worry not; the following Try It Out makes it all clear.

TRY IT OUT   **Shifting Views**

Codefile [ScrollingViews.zip] available for download at Wrox.com

1. Using Xcode, create a new View-based Application project and name it `ScrollingViews`.

2. Populate the View with a ScrollView view (see Figure 5-18). Resize the ScrollView view so it covers the entire screen.

3. Add a Text..eld field and a Round Rect Button view onto the ScrollView view (see Figure 5-19).

FIGURE 5-18

FIGURE 5-19

4. Select the `File's Owner` item in the `ScrollingViewsController.xib` window and view its `Identity Inspector` window (see Figure 5-20). Create two outlets: `scrollView` and `textField`.

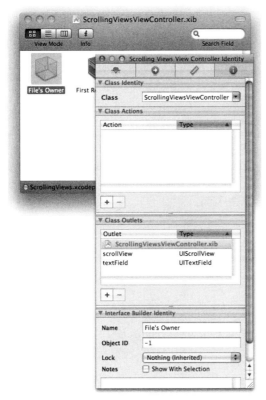

FIGURE 5-20

5. Control-drag the File's Owner item onto the TextField view (see Figure 5-21). Select `textField`.

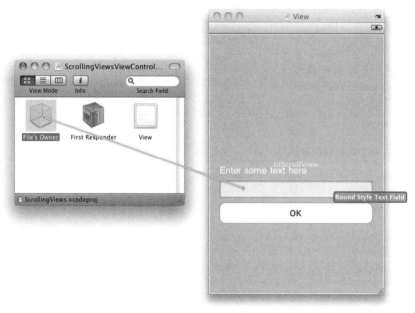

FIGURE 5-21

6. Control-drag the File's Owner item onto the ScrollView view (see Figure 5-22). Select `scrollView`.

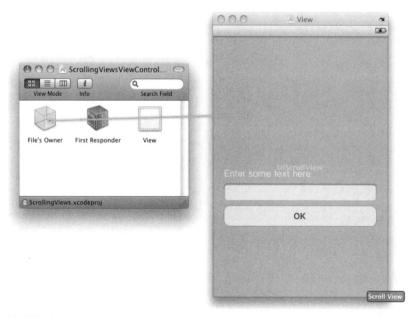

FIGURE 5-22

7. Control-drag the TextField view onto the File's Owner item (see Figure 5-23). Select `delegate`.

 NOTE *This step is important because it enables the delegate protocols* (`textFieldDidBeginEditing:` *and* `textFieldDidEndEditing:`) *to be handled by your View Controller.*

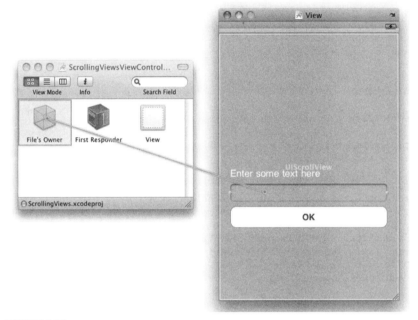

FIGURE 5-23

8. Save the `ScrollViewsViewController.xib` in Interface Builder.

9. Back in Xcode, type the following statements highlighted in bold into the `ScrollingViewsViewController.h` file:

```
#import <UIKit/UIKit.h>

@interface ScrollingViewsViewController :
    UIViewController <UITextFieldDelegate> {

    IBOutlet UITextField *textField;
    IBOutlet UIScrollView *scrollView;

}

@property (nonatomic, retain) UITextField *textField;
@property (nonatomic, retain) UIScrollView *scrollView;

@end
```

10. Type the following statements highlighted in bold in the `ScrollingViewsViewController.m` file:

```
#import "ScrollingViewsViewController.h"

@implementation ScrollingViewsViewController

@synthesize textField;
@synthesize scrollView;

//---size of keyboard---
CGRect keyboardBounds;

//---size of application screen---
CGRect applicationFrame;

//---original size of ScrollView---
CGSize scrollViewOriginalSize;

-(void) moveScrollView:(UIView *) theView {

    //---get the y-coordinate of the view---
    CGFloat viewCenterY = theView.center.y;

    //---calculate how much visible space is left---
    CGFloat freeSpaceHeight = applicationFrame.size.height -
                        keyboardBounds.size.height;

    //---calculate how much the scrollview must scroll---
    CGFloat scrollAmount = viewCenterY - freeSpaceHeight / 2.0;

    if (scrollAmount < 0)  scrollAmount = 0;

    //---set the new scrollView contentSize---
    scrollView.contentSize = CGSizeMake(
                        applicationFrame.size.width,
                        applicationFrame.size.height +
                            keyboardBounds.size.height);

    //---scroll the ScrollView---
    [scrollView setContentOffset:CGPointMake(0, scrollAmount) animated:YES];
}

//---when a TextField view begins editing---
-(void) textFieldDidBeginEditing:(UITextField *)textFieldView {
    [self moveScrollView:textFieldView];
}

//---when a TextField view is done editing---
-(void) textFieldDidEndEditing:(UITextField *) textFieldView {
    [UIView beginAnimations:@"back to original size" context:nil];
    scrollView.contentSize = scrollViewOriginalSize;
```

```
    [UIView commitAnimations];
}


//---when the keyboard appears---
-(void) keyboardWillShow:(NSNotification *) notification
{
    //---gets the size of the keyboard---
    NSDictionary *userInfo = [notification userInfo];
    NSValue *keyboardValue = [userInfo objectForKey:UIKeyboardBoundsUserInfoKey];
    [keyboardValue getValue:&keyboardBounds];
}


//---when the keyboard disappears---
-(void) keyboardWillHide:(NSNotification *) notification
{
}


-(void) viewWillAppear:(BOOL)animated
{
    //---registers the notifications for keyboard---
    [[NSNotificationCenter defaultCenter]
        addObserver:self
        selector:@selector(keyboardWillShow:)
        name:UIKeyboardWillShowNotification
        object:self.view.window];

    [[NSNotificationCenter defaultCenter]
        addObserver:self
        selector:@selector(keyboardWillHide:)
        name:UIKeyboardWillHideNotification
        object:nil];
}

-(void) viewWillDisappear:(BOOL)animated
{
    [[NSNotificationCenter defaultCenter]
        removeObserver:self
        name:UIKeyboardWillShowNotification
        object:nil];

    [[NSNotificationCenter defaultCenter]
        removeObserver:self
        name:UIKeyboardWillHideNotification
        object:nil];
}

-(void) viewDidLoad {
    scrollViewOriginalSize = scrollView.contentSize;
    applicationFrame = [[UIScreen mainScreen] applicationFrame];
```

```
    [super viewDidLoad];
}

-(BOOL) textFieldShouldReturn:(UITextField *) textFieldView {
    if (textFieldView == textField){
        [textField resignFirstResponder];
    }
    return NO;
}

-(void) dealloc {
    [textField release];
    [scrollView release];
    [super dealloc];
}
```

11. Save the project in Xcode and press Command-R to deploy the application onto the iPhone Simulator. Figure 5-24 shows that when you click the TextField view, the keyboard appears and the TextField view (along with other views) is scrolled to the center of the screen. To hide the keyboard, simply press the Return key, and the views are restored to their original positions.

FIGURE 5-24

How It Works

This example demonstrates the various ways in which you can detect the presence of a keyboard and how the view involved can be relocated so that it is not covered by the keyboard.

First, you declare three private variables:

```
//---size of keyboard---
CGRect keyboardBounds;

//---size of application screen---
CGRect applicationFrame;

//---original size of ScrollView---
CGSize scrollViewOriginalSize;
```

The `keyboardBounds` is used to store the size of the keyboard (in particular, to obtain the height of the keyboard). Although you can always hard-code the height of the keyboard to be 216, I don't recommend doing so because the size of the keyboard may change at a later time. A better practice is to dynamically obtain the size of the keyboard during runtime.

The `applicationFrame` is used to store the size of the screen. As with obtaining the size of the keyboard, it is always better to obtain this figure dynamically during runtime.

The `scrollViewOriginalSize` is used to save the original size of the ScrollView view. Doing so allows you to restore the ScrollView to its original size after the user is done with the editing (at which time all the views need to be moved back to their original positions).

When the View is loaded, you first save the size of the ScrollView view as well as obtain the size of the screen:

```
-(void) viewDidLoad {
    scrollViewOriginalSize = scrollView.contentSize;
    applicationFrame = [[UIScreen mainScreen] applicationFrame];
    [super viewDidLoad];
}
```

In the `viewWillAppear:` event (this method is invoked before the View appears on-screen), you register for the two notifications — `UIKeyboardWillShowNotification` and `UIKeyboardWillHide Notification`. When the keyboard appears (`UIKeyboardWillShowNotification`), the `keyboardWillShow:` method is invoked. When the keyboard disappears, the `keyboardWillHide:` method is invoked:

```
-(void) viewWillAppear:(BOOL)animated
{
    //---registers the notifications for keyboard---
    [[NSNotificationCenter defaultCenter]
        addObserver:self
        selector:@selector(keyboardWillShow:)
        name:UIKeyboardWillShowNotification
        object:self.view.window];

    [[NSNotificationCenter defaultCenter]
        addObserver:self
```

```
            selector:@selector(keyboardWillHide:)
            name:UIKeyboardWillHideNotification
            object:nil];
    }
```

Before the view disappears, you remove the notifications you had previously set:

```
-(void) viewWillDisappear:(BOOL)animated
{
    //---removes the notifications for keyboard---
    [[NSNotificationCenter defaultCenter]
        removeObserver:self
        name:UIKeyboardWillShowNotification
        object:nil];

    [[NSNotificationCenter defaultCenter]
        removeObserver:self
        name:UIKeyboardWillHideNotification
        object:nil];
}
```

When you click a TextField view, the `keyboardWillShow:` method is invoked. With this method, you try to obtain the size of the keyboard by passing a reference to the `keyboardBounds` variable:

```
//---when the keyboard appears---
-(void) keyboardWillShow:(NSNotification *) notification
{
    //---gets the size of the keyboard---
    NSDictionary *userInfo = [notification userInfo];
    NSValue *keyboardValue = [userInfo objectForKey:UIKeyboardBoundsUserInfoKey];
    [keyboardValue getValue:&keyboardBounds];
}
```

After the keyboard is displayed, the `textFieldDidBeginEditing:` method is invoked. With this method, you know which TextField view is being edited and you are now ready to move the ScrollView view so that the TextField view can be centered in the remaining visible space not covered by the keyboard. You perform the scrolling by calling the `moveScrollView:` method, which you define next:

```
//---when a TextField view begins editing---
-(void) textFieldDidBeginEditing:(UITextField *)textFieldView {
    [self moveScrollView:textFieldView];
}
```

In the `moveScrollView:` method, you calculate the number of pixels to scroll and then get the ScrollView view to scroll the views contained within it until the TextField view currently being edited is at the center of the visible area of the screen:

```
-(void) moveScrollView:(UIView *) theView {

    //---get the y-coordinate of the view---
    CGFloat viewCenterY = theView.center.y;

    //---calculate how much visible space is left---
```

```
        CGFloat freeSpaceHeight = applicationFrame.size.height -
                        keyboardBounds.size.height;

        //---calculate how much the scrollview must scroll---
        CGFloat scrollAmount = viewCenterY - freeSpaceHeight / 2.0;

        if (scrollAmount < 0)  scrollAmount = 0;

        //---set the new scrollView contentSize---
        scrollView.contentSize = CGSizeMake(
                        applicationFrame.size.width,
                        applicationFrame.size.height +
                            keyboardBounds.size.height);

        //---scroll the ScrollView---
        [scrollView setContentOffset:CGPointMake(0, scrollAmount) animated:YES];
    }
```

When the TextField view resigns its First Responder status, the `textFieldDidEndEditing:` method will be invoked. At this point, you restore the ScrollView view to its original content size:

```
    //---when a TextField view is done editing---
    -(void) textFieldDidEndEditing:(UITextField *) textFieldView {
        [UIView beginAnimations:@"back to original size" context:nil];
        scrollView.contentSize = scrollViewOriginalSize;
        [UIView commitAnimations];
    }
```

A noteworthy point to highlight here is that you use the `beginAnimations` method of the `UIView` class to animate the ScrollView view in the process of restoring to its original size. If you do not use this method, the ScrollView will very abruptly restore to its original size, causing a flicker.

Just before the keyboard disappears, the `keyboardWillHide:` method is invoked. In this case, you don't have much to do:

```
    //---when the keyboard disappears---
    -(void)keyboardWillHide:(NSNotification *) notification
    {
    }
```

Finally, in the `dealloc` method, you release all the outlets you have created:

```
    -(void) dealloc {
        [textField release];
        [scrollView release];
        [super dealloc];
    }
```

HANDLING THE RETURN KEY OF THE KEYBOARD

Earlier, you saw how you can connect an IBAction with the Did End On Exit
event of a TextField view to hide the keyboard when the user presses the Return
key. Alternatively, you can also implement the textFieldShouldReturn:
method. This method is invoked whenever the user presses the Return key on the
keyboard:

```
-(BOOL) textFieldShouldReturn:(UITextField *) textFieldView {
    if (textFieldView == textField){
        [textField resignFirstResponder];
    }
    return NO;
}
```

SUMMARY

In this chapter, you learned the various techniques to deal with the keyboard in your iPhone
application. In particular, you have seen:

➤   How to make the keyboard go away when you are done with the data entry

➤   How to detect the presence or absence of the keyboard

➤   How to ensure that views are not blocked by the keyboard

EXERCISES

1.   How do you hide the keyboard for a UITextField object?

2.   How do you detect whether the keyboard is visible or not?

3.   How do you get the size of the keyboard?

▶ **WHAT YOU HAVE LEARNED IN THIS CHAPTER**

TOPIC	KEY CONCEPTS
Making the keyboard go away	Use the `resignFirstResponder` method on a `UITextField` object to resign its First-Responder status
Display the different types of keyboard displayed	Modify the keyboard type by changing the Text Input Traits of a `UITextField` object in the Attributes Inspector window.
Handling the return key of the keyboard	You either handle the `Did End on Exit` event of a `UITextField` object, or implement the `textFieldShouldReturn:` method in your view controller (remember to ensure that your view controller class is the delegate for the `UITextField` object).
Detecting when the keyboard appears or hides	Register for the two notifications — UIKeyboardWillShowNotification and UIKeyboardWillHideNotification.
Detecting which `UITextField` object has started editing	Implement the `textFieldDidBeginEditing:` method in your view controller.
Detecting which `UITextField` object has ended editing	Implement the `textFieldDidEndEditing:` method in your view controller.

Screen Rotations

With the Hello World! application in Chapter 2, you saw how your iPhone application can
be written so that it supports viewing in either the portrait or landscape mode. This chapter
dives deeper into the topic of screen orientation. In particular, you will learn how to manage
the orientation of your application when the device is rotated. You will also learn how to
reposition your views when the device is rotated so that your application can take advantage
of the change in screen dimensions.

RESPONDING TO DEVICE ROTATIONS

One of the features that modern mobile devices support is the ability to detect the current
orientation — portrait or landscape — of the device. An application can take advantage of
this ability to readjust the device's screen to maximize the use of the new orientation. A good
example is Safari on the iPhone. When you rotate the device to landscape orientation, Safari
automatically rotates its view so that you have a wider screen to view the content of the page
(see Figure 6-1).

FIGURE 6-1

In the iPhone SDK, there are several events that you can handle to ensure that your application is aware of changes in orientation. You can check it out in the following Try it Out.

TRY IT OUT Supporting Different Screen Orientations

Codefile [ScreenRotations.zip] available for download at Wrox.com

1. Using Xcode, create a new View-Based Application project and name it `ScreenRotations`.

2. Press Command-R to test the application on the iPhone Simulator.

3. Change the iPhone Simulator orientation by pressing either the Command-→ (rotate it to the right) or Command-← (rotate it to the left) key combination. Notice that the screen orientation of your application does not change with the change in device orientation (see Figure 6-2); the status bar is now vertical.

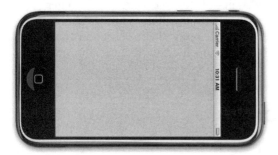

FIGURE 6-2

How It Works

By default, the iPhone application project you created using Xcode supports a single orientation — portrait mode. If you want to support screen orientations other than the default portrait mode, you can do so by overriding the shouldAutorotateToInterfaceOrientation: method in a view controller. This event is commented out by default in the ScreenRotationsViewController.m file:

```
/*
// Override to allow orientations other than the default portrait orientation.
- (BOOL)shouldAutorotateToInterfaceOrientation:
    (UIInterfaceOrientation)interfaceOrientation {
    // Return YES for supported orientations
    return (interfaceOrientation == UIInterfaceOrientationPortrait);
}
*/
```

 NOTE *On the iPhone, screen rotation is automatically handled by the OS. When the OS detects a change in screen orientation, it fires the* shouldAutorotateToInterfaceOrientation: *event; it is up to the developer to decide how the application should display in the target orientation.*

The shouldAutorotateToInterfaceOrientation: method is called when the View is loaded and when orientation of the device changes. This event passes in a single parameter — the orientation that the device has been changed to. The returning value of this event determines whether the current orientation is supported.

If you want to support all screen orientations, simply return a YES:

```
- (BOOL)shouldAutorotateToInterfaceOrientation:
(UIInterfaceOrientation)interfaceOrientation {

    return YES;

}
```

This means that your application will rotate to all orientations (the status bar will always appear at the top) when the device is rotated.

To support specific orientations, simply perform an equality check to specify the orientation supported. For example, the following code snippet shows that only the left landscape orientation is supported.

```
- (BOOL)shouldAutorotateToInterfaceOrientation:
(UIInterfaceOrientation)interfaceOrientation {

    return (interfaceOrientation == UIInterfaceOrientationLandscapeLeft);

}
```

This means that your application will display only in landscape mode (see Figure 6-3) with the Home button on its left (hence the constant name UIInterfaceOrientationLandscapeLeft).

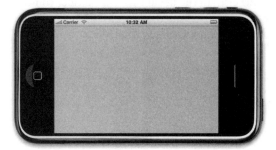

FIGURE 6-3

If the user rotates the device to portrait mode or landscape mode with the Home button on the right (UIInterfaceOrientationLandscapeRight), the application will not change its orientation (see Figure 6-4).

FIGURE 6-4

NOTE *Here is one easy way to differentiate between* UIInterfaceOrientationLandscapeLeft *and* UIInterfaceOrientationLandscapeRight. *Just remember that* UIInterfaceOrientationLandscapeLeft *refers to the Home button positioned on the left and* UIInterfaceOrientationLandscapeRight *refers to the Home button positioned on the right.*

Different Types of Screen Orientations

So far, you have seen a few constants related to screen orientations: UIInterfaceOrientationPortrait, UIInterfaceOrientationLandscapeLeft, and UIInterfaceOrientationLandscapeRight. You have a total of four constants to use for specifying screen orientations:

➤ UIInterfaceOrientationPortrait — displays the screen in portrait mode

➤ UIInterfaceOrientationPortraitUpsideDown — displays the screen in portrait mode but with the Home button at the top of the screen

➤ UIInterfaceOrientationLandscapeLeft — displays the screen in landscape mode with the Home button on the left

➤ UIInterfaceOrientationLandscapeRight — displays the screen in landscape mode with the Home button on the right

Of the four modes, it is usually not recommended to use the UIInterfaceOrientationPortraitUpsideDown mode because it could easily disorient your users (see Figure 6-5).

FIGURE 6-5

If your application supports multiple screen orientations, you should override the shouldAutorotateToInterfaceOrientation: method and then use the || (logical OR) operator to specify all the orientations it supports, like this:

```
- (BOOL)shouldAutorotateToInterfaceOrientation:
    (UIInterfaceOrientation)interfaceOrientation {

    return (interfaceOrientation == UIInterfaceOrientationPortrait ||
           interfaceOrientation == UIInterfaceOrientationLandscapeRight);

}
```

The preceding code snippet enables your application to support both the portrait and landscape-right modes.

Handling Rotations

The iPhone SDK view controller exposes several events that you can handle during the rotation of the screen. The ability to handle events fired during rotation is important because it allows you to reposition the views on the View, or you can stop media playback while the screen is rotating. The events that you can handle are:

➤   willAnimateFirstHalfOfRotationToInterfaceOrientation:

➤   willAnimateSecondHalfOfRotationFromInterfaceOrientation:

➤   willRotateToInterfaceOrientation:

➤   willAnimateRotationToInterfaceOrientation:

The following sections take a more detailed look at each of these events.

willAnimateFirstHalfOfRotationToInterfaceOrientation:

First, the willAnimateFirstHalfOfRotationToInterfaceOrientation: event is fired just before the rotation of the View starts. The method looks like this:

```
- (void)willAnimateFirstHalfOfRotationToInterfaceOrientation:
    (UIInterfaceOrientation) toInterfaceOrientation
    duration: (NSTimeInterval) duration {

}
```

The toInterfaceOrientation parameter indicates the orientation that the View is changing to, and the duration parameter indicates the duration of the first half of the rotation, in seconds.

In this event, you can insert your code to perform tasks that you want to perform before the rotation starts, such as pausing media playback, pausing animations, and so on.

willAnimateSecondHalfOfRotationFromInterfaceOrientation:

The willAnimateSecondHalfOfRotationFromInterfaceOrientation: event is fired when the rotation is halfway through (see Figure 6-6). The method looks like this:

```
- (void)willAnimateSecondHalfOfRotationFromInterfaceOrientation:
    (UIInterfaceOrientation) fromInterfaceOrientation
    duration: (NSTimeInterval) duration {

}
```

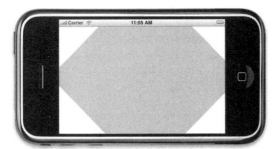

FIGURE 6-6

The `fromInterfaceOrientation` parameter indicates the orientation that it is changing from, whereas the `duration` parameter indicates the duration of the second half of the rotation, in seconds.

In this event, you typically perform tasks when the rotation is halfway done, such as repositioning the views on the View, resuming media playback, and so on.

willRotateToInterfaceOrientation:

The previous two events are fired consecutively — first the `willAnimateFirstHalfOfRotationToInterfaceOrientation:` is fired, followed by the `willAnimateSecondHalfOfRotationFromInterfaceOrientation` event. If you do not need two separate events for handling rotation, you can use the simpler `willRotateToInterfaceOrientation:` event.

The `willRotateToInterfaceOrientation:` event is fired before the orientation starts. In contrast to the previous two events, this is a one-step process. Note that if you handle this event, the `willAnimateFirstHalfOfRotationToInterfaceOrientation:` and `willAnimateSecondHalfOfRotationFromInterfaceOrientation:` events will not be fired anymore.

The method looks like this:

```
- (void)willRotateToInterfaceOrientation:
    (UIInterfaceOrientation) toInterfaceOrientation
    duration: (NSTimeInterval) duration {

}
```

The `toInterfaceOrientation` parameter indicates the orientation that it is changing to, and the `duration` parameter indicates the duration of the rotation, in seconds.

willAnimateRotationToInterfaceOrientation:

Besides the `willRotateToInterfaceOrientation:` event, there is yet another event that you can handle before the rotation starts — the `willAnimateRotationToInterfaceOrientation:` event. The `willAnimateRotationToInterfaceOrientation:` event is fired before the animation of the rotation starts.

 NOTE *If you handle both the* `willRotateToInterfaceOrientation:` *and* `willAnimateRotationToInterfaceOrientation:` *events, the former will fire first, followed by the latter.*

The method looks like this:

```
- (void)willAnimateRotationToInterfaceOrientation:
    (UIInterfaceOrientation) interfaceOrientation
    duration: (NSTimeInterval) duration {

}
```

The `interfaceOrientation` parameter specifies the target orientation to which it is rotating.

 NOTE *If you handle this event, the* `willAnimateFirstHalfOfRotationToInterfaceOrientation:` *and* `willAnimateSecondHalfOfRotationFromInterfaceOrientation:` *events will not fire anymore.*

In the following Try It Out, you will see how you can reposition the views on your UI when the device changes orientation.

TRY IT OUT   **Repositioning Views during Orientation Change**

1. Using the same project created earlier, double-click the `ScreenRotationsViewController.xib` file and add a Round Rect Button view to the View (see Figure 6-7).

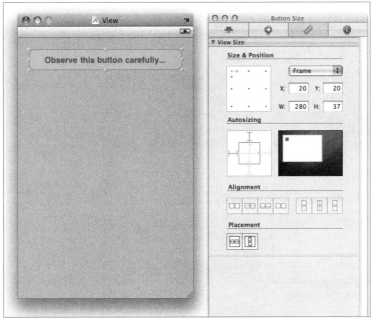

FIGURE 6-7

2. Observe its size and positioning by viewing the Size Inspector window. Here, its position is (20,20) and its size is 280 by 37 pixels.

3. Rotate the orientation of the View by clicking the arrow icon on the upper-right corner of the window (see Figure 6-8).

4. Reposition the Round Rect Button view by relocating it to the bottom-right corner of the View window (see Figure 6-9). Also observe and record its position.

FIGURE 6-8

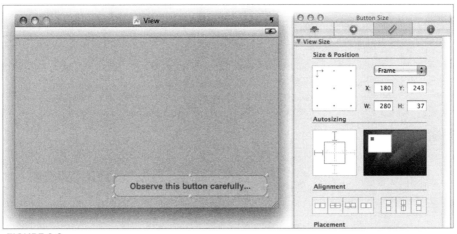

FIGURE 6-9

5. In the `ScreenRotationsViewController.xib` window, select the File's Owner item and create an outlet named `btn` (of type `UIButton`) in the Identity Inspector window (see Figure 6-10).

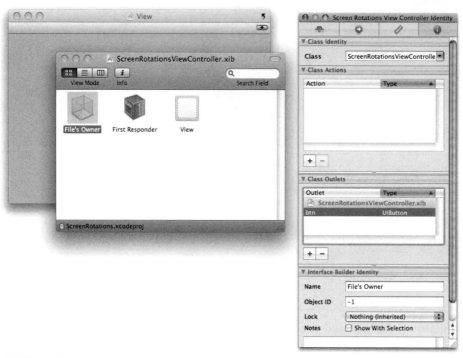

FIGURE 6-10

6. Connect the outlet you have created by control-clicking the File's Owner item and dragging over to the Round Rect Button view (see Figure 6-11). Select `btn`.

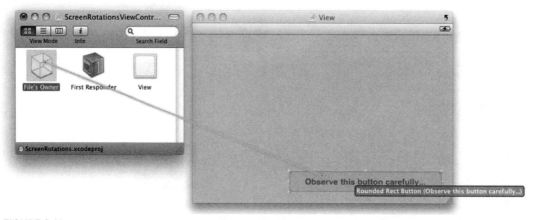

FIGURE 6-11

7.   Save the project in Interface Builder.

8.   Back in Xcode, insert the following code into the ScreenRotationsViewController.h file:

```
#import <UIKit/UIKit.h>

@interface ScreenRotationsViewController : UIViewController {
    IBOutlet UIButton *btn;
}

@property (nonatomic, retain) UIButton *btn;

@end
```

9.   In the ScreenRotationsViewController.m file, add the following code:

```
@implementation ScreenRotationsViewController

@synthesize btn;

...
...

- (void)willAnimateSecondHalfOfRotationFromInterfaceOrientation:
    (UIInterfaceOrientation) fromInterfaceOrientation
    duration: (NSTimeInterval) duration {

    UIInterfaceOrientation destOrientation = self.interfaceOrientation;

    if (destOrientation == UIInterfaceOrientationPortrait)
    {
        //---if rotating to portrait mode---
        btn.frame = CGRectMake(20,20,280,37);
    }
    else
    {
        //---if rotating to landscape mode---
        btn.frame = CGRectMake(180,243,280,37);
    }
}

- (void)dealloc {
    [btn release];
    [super dealloc];
}
```

10.   Save the project and press Command-R in Xcode to deploy the application onto the iPhone Simulator.

11.   Observe that when the iPhone Simulator is in portrait mode, the Round Rect Button view is displayed in the top-left corner. But when you change the orientation to landscape mode, it is repositioned to the bottom-right corner (see Figure 6-12).

FIGURE 6-12

How It Works

This project illustrates how you can reposition the views on your application when the device changes orientation. You first create an outlet and connect it to the Round Rect Button view on the View window.

When the device is being rotated, you handle the `willAnimateSecondHalfOfRotationFrom InterfaceOrientation:` event because doing so allows you to know the destination orientations that the device is changing to. In this method, you can either obtain the destination orientation using the `fromInterfaceOrientation` parameter, or you can obtain it via the `interfaceOrientation` property of the current View (`self`), like this:

```
UIInterfaceOrientation destOrientation = self.interfaceOrientation;
```

Using this information, you position the view according to the destination orientation by altering its `frame` property:

```
if (destOrientation == UIInterfaceOrientationPortrait)
{
    btn.frame = CGRectMake(20,20,280,37);
}
else
{
    btn.frame = CGRectMake(180,243,280,37);
}
```

PROPERTIES FOR DEALING WITH POSITIONING OF VIEWS

In the previous example, you used the `frame` property to change the position of a view during runtime. The `frame` property defines the rectangle occupied by the view, with respect to its *superview* (the view that contains it). Using the `frame` property allows you to set the positioning and size of a view. Besides using the `frame` property, you can also use the `center` property, which sets the center of the view, also with respect to its superview. You usually use the `center` property when you are performing some animation and just want to change the position of a view.

PROGRAMMATICALLY ROTATING THE SCREEN

In the previous section, you saw how your application can handle the changes in device orientation when the user rotates the device. There are times (such as when you are developing a game), however, when you want to force the application to display in certain rotations independently of how the orientation the device is held.

There are two scenarios to consider:

➤ rotating the screen orientation during runtime when your application is running; or

➤ displaying the screen in a particular orientation when the View is loaded.

Rotating During Runtime

During runtime, you can programmatically rotate the screen by using the `setOrientation:` method on an instance of the `UIDevice` class. Using the project created earlier, suppose you want the user to change the screen orientation when the user presses the Round Rect Button view. You can code it as follows:

```
-(IBAction) btnClicked: (id) sender{
    [[UIDevice currentDevice] setOrientation:UIInterfaceOrientationLandscapeLeft];
}
```

The `setOrientation:` method takes in a single parameter specifying the orientation you want to change to.

> **NOTE** *After you have programmatically switched the orientation of your application, your application's rotation can still be changed when you physically rotate the device. The orientation that it can be changed to is dependent of what you set in the* `shouldAutorotateToInterfaceOrientation:` *method.*

Displaying the View in a Specific Orientation When Loading

When a View is loaded, by default it is always displayed in portrait mode. If your application requires that you display the View in a particular orientation when it is loaded, you can do so by setting the orientation of the status bar, like this:

```
- (void)viewDidLoad {
    [UIApplication sharedApplication].statusBarOrientation
=UIInterfaceOrientationLandscapeRight;
    [super viewDidLoad];
}
```

It's interesting to note that the `setOrientation:` method described in the previous section cannot be used to change the orientation of the View during loading time:

```
//---does not work during View loading time---
[[UIDevice currentDevice] setOrientation:UIInterfaceOrientationLandscapeLeft];
```

Likewise, setting the orientation of the status bar does not work during runtime (after the View has loaded):

```
//---does not work during run time---
[UIApplication sharedApplication].statusBarOrientation =
    UIInterfaceOrientationLandscapeLeft;
```

 NOTE *The orientation to which you are changing must first of all be specified in the* `shouldAutorotateToInterfaceOrientation:` *event. This can also be specified in the* `info.plist` *file for the application by setting the* `InitialInterfaceOrientation` *key to the desired orientation.*

SUMMARY

In this chapter, you have seen how changes in screen orientations are handled by the various events in the view controller class. Proper handling of screen orientations will make your application more useable and improve the user experience.

EXERCISES

1. Suppose you want your application to only support the landscape right and landscape left orientation. How should you modify your code?

2. What is the difference between the `frame` and `center` property of a view?

▶ **WHAT YOU HAVE LEARNED IN THIS CHAPTER**

TOPIC	KEY CONCEPTS
Handling device rotations	Implement the `shouldAutorotateToInterfaceOrientation:` method
Four orientations supported	`UIInterfaceOrientationPortrait`
	`UIInterfaceOrientationLandscapeLeft`
	`UIInterfaceOrientationLandscapeRight`
	`UIInterfaceOrientationPortraitUpsideDown`
Events fired when device is rotated	`willAnimateFirstHalfOfRotationToInterfaceOrientation:`
	`willAnimateSecondHalfOfRotationFromInterfaceOrientation:`
	`willRotateToInterfaceOrientation:`
	`willAnimateRotationToInterfaceOrientation:`
Properties for changing the position of a view	Use the `frame` property for changing the positioning and size of a view
	Use the `center` property for changing the positioning of a view

PART II
Building Different Types of iPhone Applications

7

View Controllers

WHAT YOU WILL LEARN IN THIS CHAPTER

➤ How to create a Window-based Application and manually add a View Controller and a View window to it

➤ How to create views dynamically during runtime

➤ How to wire up events of views with event handlers via code

➤ How to switch to another view during runtime

➤ How to animate the switching of views

Until this point, you have been dealing with single view applications; that is, applications with a single View Controller. The previous chapters have all been using the View-based Application template available in the iPhone SDK because it is the simplest way to get started in iPhone programming. When you create a View-based application, there is by default one View Controller (named *<project_name>*ViewController by the iPhone SDK). In real-life applications, you often need more than one View Controller, with each controlling a different view displaying different information. A good example of a multiview application is the Weather application shipped with the iPhone. The main view shows the weather of a region you have selected, and you can swipe the screen to view the weather of other locations. You can also press the *i* icon to flip to another view and add locations.

This chapter teaches you how to create multiple views in your application and then programmatically switch among them during runtime. In addition, you learn how to animate the switching of views using the built-in animation methods available in the iPhone SDK.

CREATING A WINDOW-BASED APPLICATION

In this section, you discover another type of application template you can create using the iPhone SDK: the Window-based Application template. Unlike the View-based Application template, the Window-based Application template does not include a View Controller by default. Instead, it provides only the skeleton of an iPhone application and leaves the rest to the developer — you need to add your own views and View Controllers. Because of this, a Window-based Application presents a very good way for you to understand how View Controllers work and appreciate all the work needed to connect the View Controllers and XIB files. When you understand how View Controllers work, you will be on your way to creating multiview applications.

To put first things first, execute the following Try it Out to write a Window-based Application and then progressively add a View Controller to it. You will need to download the project files as indicated here for this and other Try It Out features in this chapter.

TRY IT OUT Adding a View Controller Using Interface Builder

Codefile [WinBasedApp.zip] available for download on Wrox.com

1. Using Xcode, create a Window-based Application project and name it WinBasedApp. Observe the files created for this project type (see Figure 7-1). Apart from the other, usual supporting file, note that there is only one XIB file (MainWindow.xib) and two delegate files (WinBasedAppAppDelegate.h and WinBasedAppAppDelegate.m).

2. Press Command-R to test the application, and you will realize that an empty screen is displayed on the iPhone Simulator. This is because the Window-based Application template provides only the skeleton structure for a simple iPhone application containing just a window and the application delegate.

3. Back in Xcode, double-click MainWindow.xib to edit it in Interface Builder. Observe that there are four items in the MainWindow.xib window (see Figure 7-2):

➤ File's Owner

➤ First Responder

➤ Win Based App App Delegate

➤ Window

FIGURE 7-1

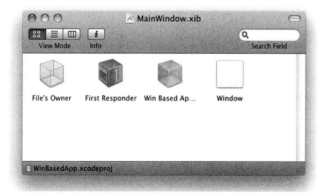

FIGURE 7-2

4. From the Library window, drag and drop a `View Controller` item onto the `MainWindow.xib` window (see Figure 7-3). You will connect this `View Controller` item to a view that you will add to the project.

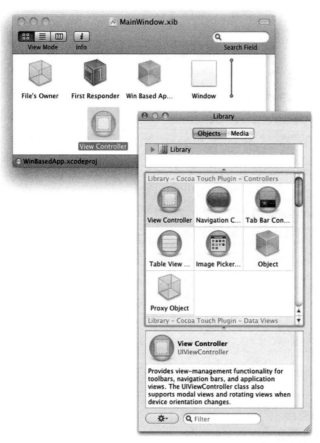

FIGURE 7-3

5. Back in Xcode, right-click the Classes group in Xcode and add a new file. Select the `UIViewController` subclass item and name it `MyViewController`. As you will be adding the XIB file manually in the later steps, uncheck the "With XIB for user interface" checkbox. Xcode should now look like Figure 7-4. The two files will serve as the `View Controller` class for the `View Controller` item you have added previously in Interface Builder.

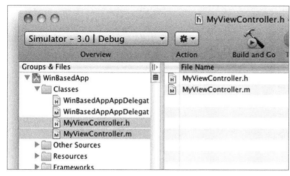

FIGURE 7-4

6. Right-click the Resources group in Xcode and add a new file. Select the View XIB item and name it `MyView.xib`. Xcode should now look like Figure 7-5.

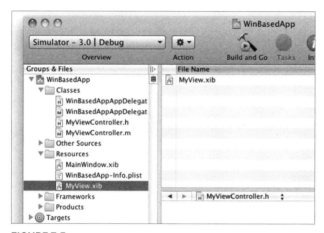

FIGURE 7-5

7. Back in Interface Builder, select the `View Controller` item in the `MainWindow.xib` window and view its Identity Inspector window. In the Class drop-down list, select `MyViewController` (see Figure 7-6). The name of the View Controller will now change to `My View Controller`.

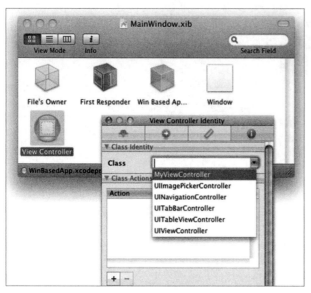

FIGURE 7-6

8. View the Attributes Inspector window for the My View Controller, and for the NIB Name drop-down list, select MyView (see Figure 7-7).

FIGURE 7-7

9. Double-click `MyView.xib` in Xcode to edit it in Interface Builder. In the `MyView.xib` window, select the File's Owner item and in its Identity Inspector window, select the `MyViewController` as its Class name (see Figure 7-8). This means that the XIB file will be controlled by the `MyViewController` class.

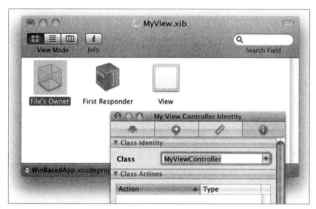

FIGURE 7-8

10. Control-click and drag the File's Owner item to the `View` item. Select `view`.

 NOTE *The step is important as it indicates that MyViewController will be actually be controlling the View window. Failure to perform this step will result in a runtime error.*

11. Double-click the `View` item in the `MyView.xib` window and add a Button view to the View window (see Figure 7-9).

12. Back in Xcode, insert the bold lines in the following code into the `WinBasedAppAppDelegate.h` file:

FIGURE 7-9

```
#import <UIKit/UIKit.h>

@class MyViewController;

@interface WinBasedAppAppDelegate : NSObject <UIApplicationDelegate> {
    UIWindow *window;

    //---create an instance of the view controller---
    MyViewController *myViewController;
}

@property (nonatomic, retain) IBOutlet UIWindow *window;

//---expose the view controller as a property---
@property (nonatomic, retain) IBOutlet MyViewController *myViewController;

@end
```

In the WinBasedAppAppDelegate.m file, insert the following code lines that appear in bold:

```
#import "WinBasedAppAppDelegate.h"

#import "MyViewController.h"

@implementation WinBasedAppAppDelegate

@synthesize window;

//---synthesize the property---
@synthesize myViewController;

- (void)applicationDidFinishLaunching:(UIApplication *)application {

    // Override point for customization after application launch
    //---add the new view to the current window---
    [window addSubview:myViewController.view];

    [window makeKeyAndVisible];
}

- (void)dealloc {
    [myViewController release];
    [window release];
    [super dealloc];
}

@end
```

13. In the MainWindow.xib window, Control-click and drag the Win Based App App Delegate item to the My View Controller item (see Figure 7-10). Select myViewController. This will associate the window with the View Controller.

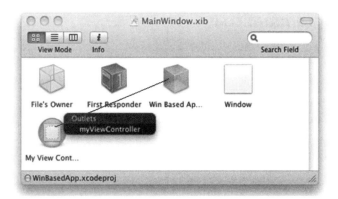

FIGURE 7-10

14. That's it! Press Command-R to test the application on the iPhone Simulator. You should now see the button appearing on the main screen of the application (see Figure 7-11).

FIGURE 7-11

 NOTE *As an exercise, you might want to create an action to display an alert view when the button is pressed.*

How It Works

When you create an iPhone project using the Window-based Application template, Xcode provides you with only the bare minimum number of items in your project — a MainWindow.xib file and the application delegate. You are supposed to add your own View Controller and view.

In the preceding exercise, you first added a View Controller item to the MainWindow.xib window. You then added an instance of the UIViewController class (which you named MyViewController) so that it could be connected to the View Controller you just added. This controller class contains the code that you will write to handle the interactions between the view and the user.

You also added a XIB file to the project (MyView.xib) representing a View in Interface Builder. Take note of the various steps that you need to perform to connect the relevant classes to the correct XIB and View Controller items.

When the application has finished launching, you add the View represented by the myViewController object to the window so that it is visible using the addSubview: method of the UIWindow instance:

```
[window addSubview:myViewController.view];
```

Adding a View Controller Programmatically

Besides adding a View Controller and views using Interface Builder, a commonly used technique is to programmatically create the views during runtime. This provides a lot of flexibility, especially when you are writing games for which the UI of the application is constantly changing.

In the following Try It Out, you learn how you can create a View using an instance of the UIViewController class and then programmatically add views to it.

Adding a View Controller Programmatically

1. Using the same project, right-click the Classes group in Xcode and add a new file. Select the UIViewController subclass item and name it MySecondViewController. Xcode should now look like Figure 7-12.

2. In the WinBasedAppAppDelegate.h file, add the following code that appears in bold:

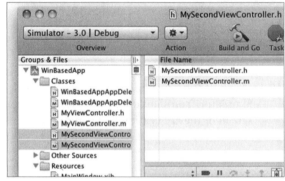

FIGURE 7-12

```
#import "WinBasedAppAppDelegate.h"
#import "MyViewController.h"

#import "MySecondViewController.h"

@implementation WinBasedAppAppDelegate

@synthesize window;
@synthesize myViewController;

//---create an instance of the second view controller---
MySecondViewController *mySecondViewController;

- (void)applicationDidFinishLaunching:(UIApplication *)application {

    //---instantiate the second view controller---
    mySecondViewController = [[MySecondViewController alloc]
                              initWithNibName:nil
                              bundle:nil];

    //---add the view from the second view controller---
    [window addSubview:mySecondViewController.view];

    //---comment this out so that it doesn't load the myViewController---
    //[window addSubview:myViewController.view];
    [window makeKeyAndVisible];
}

- (void)dealloc {
    [mySecondViewController release];
```

```
        [myViewController release];
        [window release];
        [super dealloc];
    }
```

3. In the `MySecondViewController.h` file, insert the following lines of code that appear in bold:

```
#import <UIKit/UIKit.h>

@interface MySecondViewController : UIViewController {
    //---create two outlets - label and button---
    UILabel *label;
    UIButton *button;
}

//---expose the outlets as properties---
@property (nonatomic, retain) UILabel *label;
@property (nonatomic, retain) UIButton *button;

@end
```

4. In the `MySecondViewController.m` file, add the `viewDidLoad()` method:

```
//---synthesize the properties---
@synthesize label, button;

- (void)viewDidLoad {

    //---create a CGRect for the positioning---
    CGRect frame = CGRectMake(10, 10, 300, 50);

    //---create a Label view---
    label = [[UILabel alloc] initWithFrame:frame];
    label.textAlignment = UITextAlignmentCenter;
    label.font = [UIFont fontWithName:@"Verdana" size:20];
    label.text = @"This is a label";

    //---create a Button view---
    frame = CGRectMake(10, 250, 300, 50);
    button = [UIButton buttonWithType:UIButtonTypeRoundedRect];
            button.frame = frame;
    [button setTitle:@"OK" forState:UIControlStateNormal];
    button.backgroundColor = [UIColor clearColor];

    [self.view addSubview:label];
    [self.view addSubview:button];

    [super viewDidLoad];

}
```

5. Press Command-R to test the application on the iPhone Simulator. You will now see the Label and Button views on the main screen of the application (see Figure 7-13).

How It Works

In contrast to the previous example, in which you added a `View Controller` item, an instance of the `UIViewController` class, and a XIB file to your project, this example simply creates an instance of the `UIViewController` class and adds the views programmatically to the main View window.

In the application delegate, after the application has finished launching, you create an instance of the `UIViewController` class that you have created:

```
//---instantiate the view controller---
mySecondViewController = [[MySecondViewController alloc]
                               initWithNibName:nil
                               bundle:nil];
```

FIGURE 7-13

You do not need an XIB file because the various views that you will be using will be added programmatically. Hence the `initWithNibName:` parameter can be set to `nil`.

To load the View window represented by the instance of the `UIViewController` class, you use the `addSubview:` method of the `UIWindow` instance:

```
//---add the view from the view controller---
[window addSubview:mySecondViewController.view];
```

To programmatically create your views during runtime, you need to override the `viewDidLoad()` method of the `UIViewController` class. Here, you create instances of the Label and Button views manually, specifying their positions as well as their text captions. Finally, you add them to the main View window:

```
- (void)viewDidLoad {
    //---create a CGRect for the positioning---
    CGRect frame = CGRectMake(10, 10, 300, 50);

    //---create a Label view---
    label = [[UILabel alloc] initWithFrame:frame];
    label.textAlignment = UITextAlignmentCenter;
    label.font = [UIFont fontWithName:@"Verdana" size:20];
    label.text = @"This is a label";

    //---create a Button view---
    frame = CGRectMake(10, 250, 300, 50);
```

```
button = [UIButton buttonWithType:UIButtonTypeRoundedRect];
        button.frame = frame;
[button setTitle:@"OK" forState:UIControlStateNormal];
button.backgroundColor = [UIColor clearColor];

//---add the views to the current View---
[self.view addSubview:label];
[self.view addSubview:button];

[super viewDidLoad];
}
```

Creating and Connecting Actions

In the previous section, you saw that you can programmatically add views during runtime. Also, in the example, you saw how you can add a Label and Button view to the main View. However, you would need to handle the events raised by the Button view so that when the user presses it, you can perform some work. In Chapter 3, you learned about using outlets and actions and how you connect your code to them using Interface Builder. In the following Try it Out, the views are created using code, and hence you cannot use Interface Builder to connect the actions and outlets — you have to do it by code, too.

TRY IT OUT   Linking Actions to Views

1.   Using the same project created in the previous section, declare the `buttonClicked:` action (shown in bold) in the `MySecondViewController.h` file as follows:

```
#import <UIKit/UIKit.h>

@interface MySecondViewController : UIViewController {
    UILabel *label;
    UIButton *button;
}

@property (nonatomic, retain) UILabel *label;
@property (nonatomic, retain) UIButton *button;

//---declaring the IBAction---
-(IBAction) buttonClicked: (id) sender;

@end
```

2.   In the `MySecondViewController.m` file, you provide the implementation for the `buttonClicked:` action:

```
-(IBAction) buttonClicked: (id) sender{
    UIAlertView *alert = [[UIAlertView alloc] initWithTitle:@"Action invoked!"
                          message:@"Button clicked!"
```

```
                                delegate:self
                                cancelButtonTitle:@"OK"
                                otherButtonTitles:nil];
        [alert show];
        [alert release];
    }
```

3. To connect the relevant event (Touch Up Inside) of the Button view with the buttonClicked: action, add the following code that appears in bold to the loadView() method:

```
- (void)viewDidLoad {

    CGRect frame = CGRectMake(10, 10, 300, 50);

    //---create a Label view---
    label = [[UILabel alloc] initWithFrame:frame];
    label.textAlignment = UITextAlignmentCenter;
    label.font = [UIFont fontWithName:@"Verdana" size:20];
    label.text = @"This is a label";

    //---create a Button view---
    frame = CGRectMake(10, 50, 300, 50);
    button = [[UIButton buttonWithType:UIButtonTypeRoundedRect]
            initWithFrame:frame];
    [button setTitle:@"OK" forState:UIControlStateNormal];
    button.backgroundColor = [UIColor clearColor];

    //---add the action handler and set current class as
target---
    [button addTarget:self
        action:@selector(buttonClicked:)
        forControlEvents:UIControlEventTouchUpInside];

    //---add the views to the current View---
    [self.view addSubview:label];
    [self.view addSubview:button];

    [super viewDidLoad];

}
```

4. That's it! Press Command-R to test the application on the iPhone Simulator. Pressing the OK button displays an alert view (see Figure 7-14).

FIGURE 7-14

CONTROL EVENTS

The list of events you can use for control objects are:

➤ `UIControlEventTouchDown`

➤ `UIControlEventTouchDownRepeat`

➤ `UIControlEventTouchDragInside`

➤ `UIControlEventTouchDragOutside`

➤ `UIControlEventTouchDragEnter`

➤ `UIControlEventTouchDragExit`

➤ `UIControlEventTouchUpInside`

➤ `UIControlEventTouchUpOutside`

➤ `UIControlEventTouchCancel`

➤ `UIControlEventValueChanged`

➤ `UIControlEventEditingDidBegin`

➤ `UIControlEventEditingChanged`

➤ `UIControlEventEditingDidEnd`

➤ `UIControlEventEditingDidEndOnExit`

➤ `UIControlEventAllTouchEvents`

➤ `UIControlEventAllEditingEvents`

➤ `UIControlEventApplicationReserved`

➤ `UIControlEventSystemReserved`

➤ `UIControlEventAllEvents`

The use of each event is detailed at: `http://developer.apple.com/iphone/library/documentation/UIKit/Reference/UIControl_Class/Reference/Reference.html#//apple_ref/doc/constant_group/Control_Events`.

SWITCHING TO ANOTHER VIEW

So far, you have been learning about single-view applications. However, in real life, you often have a number of views, each representing different pieces of information. Depending on the selections made by the user, you then switch to different views to perform different tasks.

Hence, in this section you learn how you can switch to another view depending on the selection made by the user.

TRY IT OUT   Switching Views

1.   Using the same project created in the previous section, add the following code that appears in bold to the MySecondViewController.m file:

```
#import "MySecondViewController.h"

#import "MyViewController.h"

@implementation MySecondViewController
@synthesize label, button;

//---create an instance of the view controller---
MyViewController *myViewController;

-(IBAction) buttonClicked: (id) sender{

    //---add the view of the view controller to the current View---
    myViewController = [[MyViewController alloc]
                            initWithNibName:@"MyView" bundle:nil];
    [self.view addSubview:myViewController.view];

    //---comment out this section---
    /*
    UIAlertView *alert = [[UIAlertView alloc] initWithTitle:@"Action invoked!"
                            message:@"Button clicked!"
                            delegate:self
                            cancelButtonTitle:@"OK"
                            otherButtonTitles:nil];
    [alert show];
    [alert release];
    */

}

- (void)dealloc {
    [myViewController release];
    [label release];
    [super dealloc];
}
```

2.   Declare a btnClicked: action in the MyViewController.h file:

```
#import <UIKit/UIKit.h>

@interface MyViewController : UIViewController {

}

-(IBAction) btnClicked:(id) sender;

@end
```

3. In the `MyViewController.m` file, define the `btnClicked:` action as follows:

```
-(IBAction) btnClicked:(id) sender{
    //---remove the current view; essentially hiding the view---
    [self.view removeFromSuperview];
}
```

4. Double-click the `MyView.xib` file to edit it in Interface Builder.

Control-click and drag the OK button in the View window to the File's Owner item in the `MyView.xib` window and select `btnClicked:`.

5. Back in Xcode, press Command-R to test the application. When you now click the OK button in the main View, you are brought to the second View (see Figure 7-15). To close the second View, press the OK button.

FIGURE 7-15

How It Works

For this example, you simply add the View of the view controller (that you are switching to) to the current view using the `addSubview:` method:

```
        //---add the view of the view controller to the current View---
        myViewController = [[MyViewController alloc]
                            initWithNibName:@"MyView" bundle:nil];
        [self.view addSubview:myViewController.view];
```

To dismiss a view, you use the `removeFromSuperview:` method:

```
        //---remove the current view; essentially hiding the view---
        [self.view removeFromSuperview];
```

ANIMATING THE SWITCHING OF VIEWS

The switching of Views that you have just seen in the previous section happens instantaneously — the two Views change immediately without any visual cues. One of the key selling points of the iPhone is its animation capabilities. Therefore for the switching of views, you can make the display a little more interesting by performing some simple animations, such as flipping one View to reveal another. Here is how to do that.

TRY IT OUT Animating the Transitions

1. Using the same project, add the following code that appears in bold to the `MySecondViewController.m` file:

```
-(IBAction) buttonClicked: (id) sender{

    myViewController = [[MyViewController alloc]
                                  initWithNibName:@"MyView" bundle:nil];

    [UIView beginAnimations:@"flipping view" context:nil];
    [UIView setAnimationDuration:1];
    [UIView setAnimationCurve:UIViewAnimationCurveEaseInOut];
    [UIView setAnimationTransition: UIViewAnimationTransitionFlipFromLeft
            forView:self.view cache:YES];

    [self.view addSubview:myViewController.view];

    [UIView commitAnimations];
}
```

2. In the `MyViewController.m` file, add the following code that appears in bold:

```
-(IBAction) btnClicked:(id) sender{

    [UIView beginAnimations:@"flipping view" context:nil];
    [UIView setAnimationDuration:1];
    [UIView setAnimationCurve:UIViewAnimationCurveEaseIn];
    [UIView setAnimationTransition: UIViewAnimationTransitionFlipFromRight
        forView:self.view.superview cache:YES];

    [self.view removeFromSuperview];

    [UIView commitAnimations];
}
```

3. Press Command-R to test the application on the iPhone Simulator. Click the OK buttons on both Views and notice the direction in which the two Views flipped to one another (see Figure 7-16).

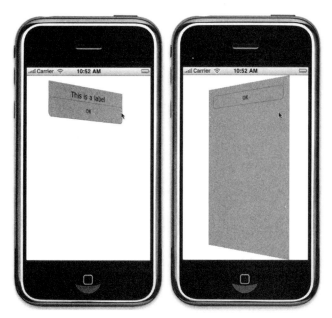

FIGURE 7-16

How It Works

First, examine the animation that is applied to the `MySecondViewController`. You perform the animation by first calling the `beginAnimations:` method of the `UIView` class to start the animation block:

```
[UIView beginAnimations:@"flipping view" context:nil];
```

The `setAnimationDuration:` method specifies the duration of the animation in seconds. Here, you set it to one second:

```
[UIView setAnimationDuration:1];
```

The `setAnimationCurve:` method sets the curve of the animating property changes within an animation:

```
[UIView setAnimationCurve:UIViewAnimationCurveEaseInOut];
```

You can use the following constants for the curve of the animation:

➤ `UIViewAnimationCurveEaseInOut` — causes the animation to begin slowly, accelerate through the middle of its duration, and then slow again before completing

➤ `UIViewAnimationCurveEaseIn` — causes the animation to begin slowly and then speed up as it progresses

➤ `UIViewAnimationCurveEaseOut` — causes the animation to begin quickly and then slow as it completes

➤ `UIViewAnimationCurveLinear` — causes an animation to occur evenly over its duration

The `setAnimationTransition:` method applies a transition type to be applied to a view during the animation duration.

```
[UIView setAnimationTransition: UIViewAnimationTransitionFlipFromLeft
        forView:self.view cache:YES];
```

The cache: parameter specifies whether the iPhone should cache the image of the view and use it during the transition. Caching the image speeds up the animation process. The following constants can be used for the animation transition:

➤ `UIViewAnimationTransitionNone` — no transition

➤ `UIViewAnimationTransitionFlipFromLeft` — flips a view around a vertical axis from left to right

➤ `UIViewAnimationTransitionFlipFromRight` — flips a view around a vertical axis from right to left

➤ `UIViewAnimationTransitionCurlUp` — curls a view up from the bottom

➤ `UIViewAnimationTransitionCurlDown` — curls a view down from the top

To end the animation, call the `commitAnimations:` method:

```
[UIView commitAnimations];
```

The animation performed on the `MyViewController` is similar to that of the `MySecondViewController,` except that the view to animate must be set to `self.view.superview:`

```
[UIView setAnimationTransition: UIViewAnimationTransitionFlipFromRight
        forView:self.view.superview cache:YES];
```

SUMMARY

In this chapter, you had your first experience with Window-based Application projects. The Window-based Application template is a good starting point for you to really understand the nuts and bolts of the UI of an iPhone application. You also learned how to switch between two views and apply animations to the transition process. In the next chapter, you learn the next type of application template supported by the iPhone SDK: Tab Bar applications. A Tab Bar application is another type of multiview application that you can build, except that all the groundwork has already been done for you to make your life easy.

EXERCISES

1. Write the code snippet that allows you to create a View Controller programmatically.

2. Write the code snippet that creates a view dynamically during runtime.

3. Write the code snippet that wires up an event of a view with an event handler.

▶ WHAT YOU HAVE LEARNED IN THIS CHAPTER

TOPIC	KEY CONCEPTS
Adding a View Controller manually	Add an instance of the `UIViewController` subclass item to your project.

Creating a `Label` view by code	`label = [[UILabel alloc] initWithFrame:frame];`
	`label.textAlignment = UITextAlignmentCenter;`
	`label.font = [UIFont fontWithName:@"Verdana" size:20];`
	`label.text = @"This is a label";`

Creating a `Button` view by code	`frame = CGRectMake(10, 250, 300, 50);`
	`button = [[UIButton buttonWithType:`
	`UIButtonTypeRoundedRect]`
	`initWithFrame:frame];`
	`[button setTitle:@"OK" forState:UIControlStateNormal];`
	`button.backgroundColor = [UIColor clearColor];`

Wiring up an event with an event handler	`button addTarget:self`
	`action:@selector(buttonClicked:)`
	`forControlEvents:`
	`UIControlEventTouchUpInside];`

Switching to another view	`myViewController = [[MyViewController alloc]`
	`initWithNibName:@"MyView"`
	`bundle:nil];`
	`[self.view addSubview:myViewController.view];`

Animating the view transition	`UIView beginAnimations:@"flipping view"`
	`context:nil];`
	`[UIView setAnimationDuration:1];`
	`[UIView`
	`setAnimationCurve:`
	`UIViewAnimationCurveEaseInOut];`
	`[UIView setAnimationTransition:`
	`UIViewAnimationTransitionFlipFromLeft`
	`forView:self.view cache:YES];`
	`[self.view addSubview:myViewController.view];`
	`[UIView commitAnimations];`

8

Tab Bar and Navigation Applications

WHAT YOU WILL LEARN IN THIS CHAPTER

➤ How to create Tab Bar applications

➤ How to display Tab Bar applications in different orientations

➤ How to create navigation-based applications

➤ How to navigate from one View window to another in a navigation-based application

The previous chapter demonstrated how to create a multiview application by using multiple view controllers. In fact, multiview applications are so common that the iPhone has a special category of application named after it: Tab Bar applications. A Tab Bar application consists of a Tab Bar commonly located at the bottom of the screen. Within the Tab Bar are Tab Bar items, which when touched display a particular view. One good example of a Tab Bar application is the Phone application in iPhone (see Figure 8-1). The Phone application contains five Tab Bar items: Favorites, Recents, Contacts, Keypad, and Voicemail. For example, when you touch the Favorites item, you see a list of editable favorite contacts. Touching the Contacts item displays the entire list of contacts stored on your iPhone.

FIGURE 8-1

In addition to Tab Bar applications, a type of application commonly found on the iPhone is the navigation-based application. A navigation-based application contains a UI that allows users to drill into a hierarchy of items. It has a navigation bar at the top of the screen showing the item that is currently pushed into a stack. Figure 8-2 shows a good example of a navigation-based application — Settings.

FIGURE 8-2

In the Settings application, you can drill down into the settings of an application by selecting the item and navigating to another screen. When you want to go back to the previous screen, you simply touch the little button at the top-left corner of the screen to navigate back.

Hence, this chapter teaches you how to create these two types of applications using the templates provided by the iPhone SDK.

TAB BAR APPLICATIONS

Up until this point, you have seen the use of two types of application templates provided by the iPhone SDK: View-based Application and Window-based Application. The View-based Application template is the easiest to get started while the Window-based Application template provides the skeleton of an iPhone application and lets you create everything by yourself.

For building Tab Bar applications, you can either use the Window-based Application template, or more conveniently, use the Tab Bar Application template provided.

The following Try it Out uses the Tab Bar Application template to create a project and understand the underlying architecture. Download the necessary project files as indicated here.

TRY IT OUT   Creating a Tab Bar Application

Codefile [TabBarApplication.zip] available for download at Wrox.com

1.   Using Xcode, create a new Tab Bar application project and name it `TabBarApplication`.

2.   Examine the content of the project (see Figure 8-3). Besides the usual application delegate files, it also contains a View Controller (`FirstViewController`) and two XIB files: `MainWindow.xib` and `SecondView.xib`.

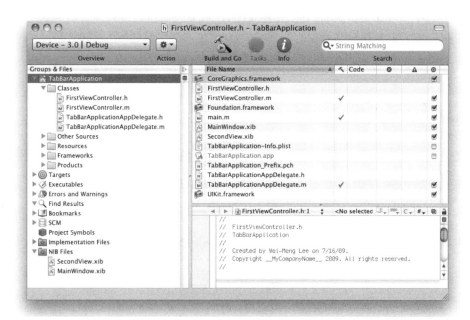

FIGURE 8-3

3. Examine the content of the `TabBarApplicationAppDelegate.h` file, which is as follows:

```
#import <UIKit/UIKit.h>
@interface TabBarApplicationAppDelegate : NSObject
    <UIApplicationDelegate, UITabBarControllerDelegate> {
    UIWindow *window;
    UITabBarController *tabBarController;
}

@property (nonatomic, retain) IBOutlet UIWindow *window;
@property (nonatomic, retain) IBOutlet UITabBarController *tabBarController;

@end
```

Note that instead of the usual `UIViewController` class, you are now using the `UITabBarController` class, which inherits from the `UIViewController` class. A `TabBarController` is a specialized `UIViewController` class that contains a collection of view controllers.

4. When the application has finished loading, the current view of the `UITabBarController` instance is loaded, an occurrence that is evident in the `TabBarApplicationAppDelegate.m` file:

```
import "TabBarApplicationAppDelegate.h"

@implementation TabBarApplicationAppDelegate

@synthesize window;
@synthesize tabBarController;

- (void)applicationDidFinishLaunching:(UIApplication *)application {

    // Add the tab bar controller's current view as a subview of the window
    [window addSubview:tabBarController.view];
}
```

5. Double-click the `MainWindow.xib` file to edit it in Interface Builder. Observe the two Tab Bar Item views contained within the Tab Bar view shown at the bottom of the View.

 NOTE *A Tab Bar Item actually is comprised of a View Controller and a Tab Bar Item object.*

6. Click the first Tab Bar item labeled First (see Figure 8-4). In the Identify Inspector window, observe that this is a View Controller and that the implementing class is `FirstViewController`.

FIGURE 8-4

7. Click the second Tab Bar item and view its Identity Inspector window. Notice that it is pointing to the base `UIViewController` class. Now, view its Attributes Inspector window (see Figure 8-5). Notice that in this case, it is loading its View window from another NIB file — `SecondView`.

 NOTE *If you want users to interact with the UI in the second view, you should add a View Controller class to it so that you can connect outlets and actions to it. You will see how to do this shortly.*

FIGURE 8-5

8. Back in Xcode, press Command-R to run the application on the
    iPhone Simulator (see Figure 8-6). You can now touch the Tab Bar
    items at the bottom of the screen to switch between the two views.

How It Works

Basically, the magic of a Tab Bar application is in the use of the
`UITabBarController` class. If you double-click the `MainWindow.xib` file,
you see that it has a Tab Bar Controller item (see Figure 8-7).

FIGURE 8-6

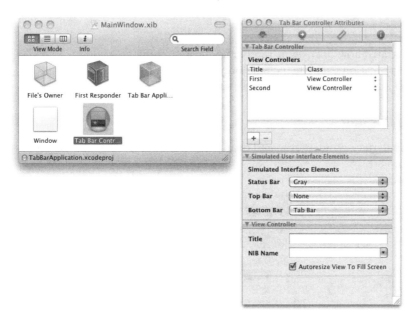

FIGURE 8-7

The Tab Bar Controller contains a collection of View Controllers. In this case, there are two view controllers contained within it. The first view controller inside the `UITabBarController` instance is always displayed when it is added to the current view:

```
- (void)applicationDidFinishLaunching:(UIApplication *)application {

    // Add the tab bar controller's current view as a subview of the window
    [window addSubview:tabBarController.view];
}
```

When the user touches the Tab Bar items, each corresponding view controller is loaded to display its view.

 NOTE *Another way to view the* `MainWindow.xib` *window is to switch it to display in List View (the second button at the top left corner of the window). Doing so allows you to quickly inspect the collection of View Controllers contained in the Tab Bar Controller.*

Adding Tab Bar Items

The previous section demonstrated how to create a Tab Bar application using the template provided by the SDK. By default, the application template includes only two Tab Bar items, so in this section, you see how to add more Tab Bar items to the existing Tab Bar.

TRY IT OUT   Adding Tab Bar Items

1.   Using the same project, in Interface Builder, drag and drop a Tab Bar item from the Library onto the Tab Bar view (see Figure 8-8).

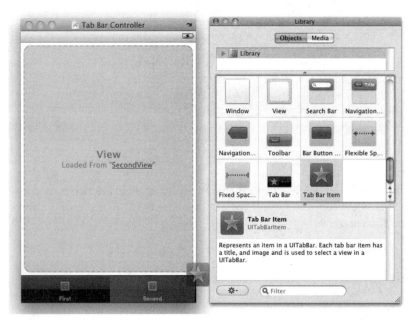

FIGURE 8-8

2.   Select the newly added Tab Bar item and view its Attributes Inspector window. Set the Badge property to 5 and the Identifier property to Search. (see Figure 8-9). Observe the change in appearance of the Tab Bar item.

 NOTE *Click the center of the Tab Bar item so that the Tab Bar item can be selected; if you click the outside, the View Controller is selected.*

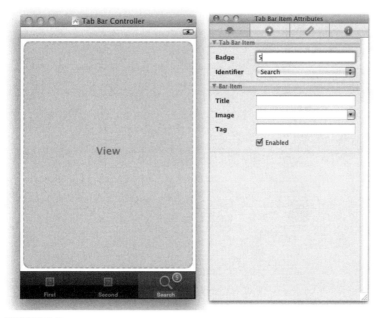

FIGURE 8-9

 NOTE *The Badge property is a nifty way for you to set some numbers or other text on the Tab Bar item so that it can serve as a quick visual cue to users to remind them of something.*

3. Back in Xcode, right-click the Resources folder and choose Add ➪ New File. Click the User Interfaces category and select View XIB. Name the file as `SearchView.xib`.

4. Right-click the Classes folder in Xcode and choose Add ➪ New File. Click the Cocoa Touch Classes category and select the `UIViewController` subclass. Name the file `SearchViewController.m` (uncheck the "With XIB for user interface" option because you have already created your XIB file in the previous step).

5. Double-click the newly created `SearchView.xib` file to open it in Interface Builder. Add a Search Bar view to it (see Figure 8-10).

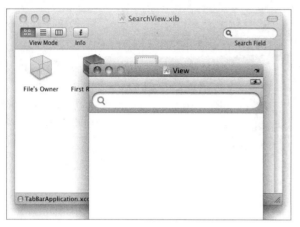

FIGURE 8-10

6. Select the File's Owner item in the `SearchView.xib` window and view its Identity Inspector window. Select `SearchViewController` as its Class.

7. Control-click and drag the File's Owner item to the View item and select `view`.

8. Control-click and drag the Search Bar view to the File's Owner item (see Figure 8-11) and select `delegate`.

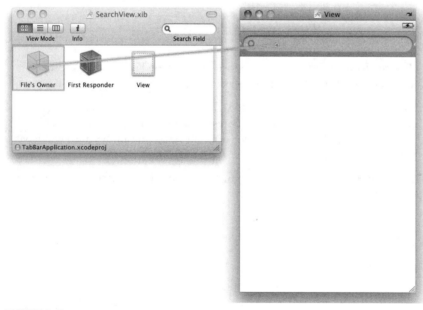

FIGURE 8-11

9. Back in `MainWindow.xib`, select the Tab Bar item and view its Attributes Inspector window (see Figure 8-12). Set its NIB name to `SearchView`.

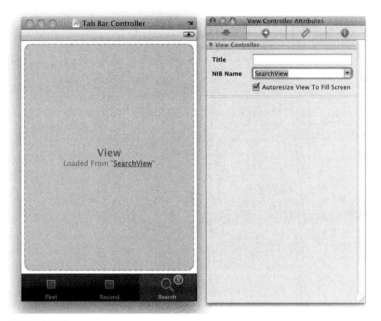

FIGURE 8-12

10. In the Identity Inspector window for the Search Tab Bar item, set the Class name to `SearchViewController` (see Figure 8-13).

 NOTE *This step is important; without it, you will get a runtime error later on when you create outlets and actions on the View Controller class.*

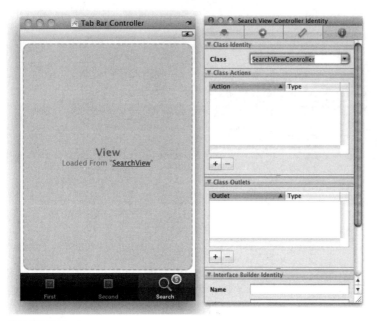

FIGURE 8-13

11. Save the project in Interface Builder.

12. Back in Xcode, insert the following code line that appears in bold into the
SearchViewController.h file:

```
#import <UIKit/UIKit.h>

@interface SearchViewController : UIViewController <UISearchBarDelegate> {

}

@end
```

13. Insert the following code line that appears in bold into the SearchViewController.m file:

```
#import "SearchViewController.h"

@implementation SearchViewController

- (void)searchBarSearchButtonClicked:(UISearchBar *)searchBar
  {
      //---hide the keyboard---
      [searchBar resignFirstResponder];
  }
```

14. That's it! Press Command-R to test the application on the iPhone Simulator. You can now touch the third Tab Bar item (Search) to view the Search Bar (see Figure 8-14). Touching the Search Bar reveals the keyboard automatically. When you are done typing, touch the Search button on the keyboard to hide the keyboard.

FIGURE 8-14

How It Works

In this example, you added a Tab Bar Item view to the Tab Bar view and connected it to an XIB file and its corresponding View Controller class.

Adding new Tab Bar Item views is straightforward: Simply drag the Tab Bar item from the Library and drop it into the Tab Bar view. Alternatively, you can add it through the Attributes Inspector window for the Tab Bar Controller item in the `MainWindow.xib` window (see Figure 8-15). Click the + (plus) button to add new View Controllers, and the Tab Bar view automatically inserts a new Tab Bar Item view for you.

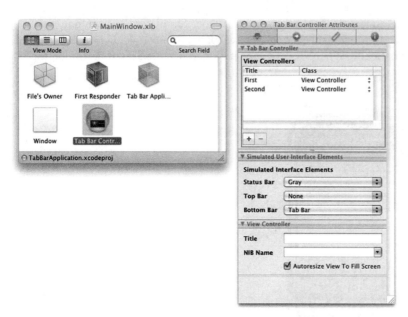

FIGURE 8-15

Displaying Tab Bar Applications in Landscape Mode

In Chapter 6, you learn that screen rotations in iPhone applications can be easily supported by overriding the shouldAutorotateToInterfaceOrientation: method. To support all screen orientations, you simply need to return a YES for this method, like this:

```
- (BOOL)shouldAutorotateToInterfaceOrientation:(UIInterfaceOrientation)
    interfaceOrientation {
    return YES;
}
```

Doing so causes the view to automatically rotate to support the new orientation. For Tab Bar applications, things are a little special. To see how different it is, go ahead and make the following modifications to the FirstViewController.m file:

```
//---FirstViewController.m---
- (BOOL)shouldAutorotateToInterfaceOrientation:(UIInterfaceOrientation)
    interfaceOrientation {
    return YES;
}
```

Press Command-R to test the application and change the screen rotation. What do you notice? Well, the orientation of the application does not change — it is still displayed in portrait mode. In order to support different orientations, all the View Controllers contained within the UITabBarController object must support the same orientations. That is to say, if one View Controller supports landscape left mode, then all the View Controllers must also support landscape left mode.

Hence, in the following Try It Out, you modify the application to support all orientations.

TRY IT OUT Supporting Screen Rotations

1. Using the same project created earlier, observe in the Identity Inspector window that the Second Tab Bar item is set to the base class UIViewController.

2. Right-click the Classes group in Xcode and choose Add ➪ New Files. Select the UIViewController subclass file template and name it SecondViewController.m (uncheck the "With XIB for user interface" option because you already have an XIB file — SecondView.xib).

3. Change the Class name for the Second Tab Bar item to SecondViewController.

4. Double-click on the SecondView.xib file in Xcode to edit it in Interface Builder. Select the File's Owner item and in the Identity Inspector window, change its Class to SecondViewController.

5. In the FirstViewController.m, SecondViewController.m, and SearchViewController.m files, ensure that you return YES for the shouldAutorotateToInterfaceOrientation: method:

```
- (BOOL)shouldAutorotateToInterfaceOrientation:(UIInterfaceOrientation)
    interfaceOrientation {
    return YES;
}
```

6. That's it! Press Command-R and you should now be able to rotate the application to any orientation (see Figure 8-16).

FIGURE 8-16

How It Works

You may recall that the original project files created by the Tab Bar Application template contain only one view controller — `FirstViewController` — which corresponds to the first view in the Tab Bar View Controller. The second view is represented by the `SecondView.xib`, but it does not have a corresponding View Controller class. To ensure that this view supports all orientations, you need to add a new View Controller class to the project so that it can override the implementation provided by the base `UIViewController` class. You then override the `shouldAutorotateToInterfaceOrientation:` method so that each View Controller returns `YES` to support all orientations.

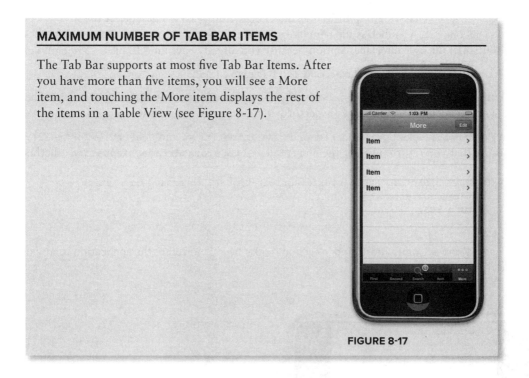

MAXIMUM NUMBER OF TAB BAR ITEMS

The Tab Bar supports at most five Tab Bar Items. After you have more than five items, you will see a More item, and touching the More item displays the rest of the items in a Table View (see Figure 8-17).

FIGURE 8-17

NAVIGATION-BASED APPLICATIONS

Tab Bar applications are suitable for situations in which you have several views, each view displaying different information so the user can quickly switch among them. However, sometimes you have hierarchical data that requires users to move from one screen to another based on what they have selected. In this situation, it is better to use a Navigation-based application.

To see how a Navigation-based application works, you can create one now, in the following Try It Out.

TRY IT OUT   Creating a Navigation-Based Application

Codefile [NavApplication.zip] available for download at Wrox.com

1.   Using Xcode, create a Navigation-based Application project and name it NavApplication.

2.   Observe the files created by the template (see Figure 8-18). As usual, there are the application delegate files, as well as a View Controller named RootViewController. There are two XIB files: RootViewController.xib and MainWindow.xib.

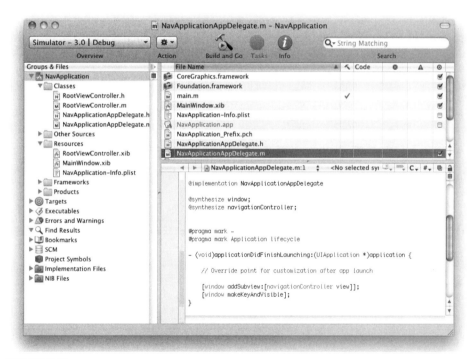

FIGURE 8-18

3.   Examine the content of the `NavAplicationAppDelegate.h` file:

```
@interface NavApplicationAppDelegate : NSObject <UIApplicationDelegate> {

    UIWindow *window;
    UINavigationController *navigationController;
}

@property (nonatomic, retain) IBOutlet UIWindow *window;
@property (nonatomic, retain) IBOutlet UINavigationController
    *navigationController;

@end
```

4.   Instead of using a generic View Controller, it is now using a `UINavigationController` class. The `UINavigationController` class is a specialized View Controller that manages the navigation of hierarchical content.

5.   Examine the content of the `NavAplicationAppDelegate.m` file, in particular the `application-DidFinishLaunching:` method:

```
#import "NavApplicationAppDelegate.h"
#import "RootViewController.h"

@implementation NavApplicationAppDelegate

@synthesize window;
@synthesize navigationController;

#pragma mark -
#pragma mark Application lifecycle

- (void)applicationDidFinishLaunching:(UIApplication *)application {

    // Override point for customization after app launch

    [window addSubview:[navigationController view]];
    [window makeKeyAndVisible];
}
```

6.   Here, you are adding the view of the navigation controller to the current view to make it visible when the application is loaded.

7.   Double-click the `MainWindow.xib` file to edit it in Interface Builder. Figure 8-19 shows that the `MainWindow.xib` window (shown in List View) contains a Navigation Controller item. The Navigation Controller item itself contains a Navigation Bar item as well as a View that is loaded from the `RootViewController` class.

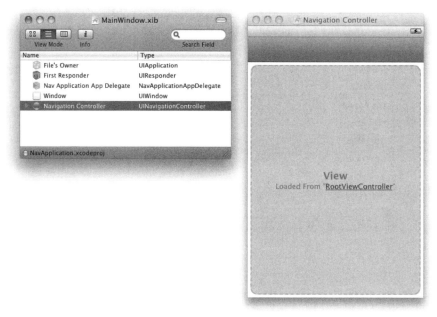

FIGURE 8-19

8. Double-click the `RootViewController.xib` file to open it in Interface Builder. Observe that by default, the Navigation-Application template uses a Table view for the root View Controller (See Figure 8-20).

 NOTE *Navigation-based applications do not necessarily have to use the Table view. However, because the Table view is such a popular view and is often used in a Navigation-based application, Apple has included it by default into the Navigation-based Application template. The Table view is discussed in more detail in Chapter 10.*

FIGURE 8-20

9. Press Command-R to test the application. By itself, the application doesn't show much; all you see are rows of lines (see Figure 8-21). You learn how to populate the Table view next.

10. In the `RootViewController.m` file, add the following statements highlighted in bold to declare and initialize an array containing a list of movies:

```
#import "RootViewController.h"

@implementation RootViewController

NSMutableArray *listOfMovies;

- (void)viewDidLoad {

    //---initialize the array---
    listOfMovies = [[NSMutableArray alloc] init];

    //---add items---
    [listOfMovies addObject:@"Training Day"];
    [listOfMovies addObject:@"Remember the Titans"];
```

FIGURE 8-21

```
        [listOfMovies addObject:@"John Q."];
        [listOfMovies addObject:@"The Bone Collector"];
        [listOfMovies addObject:@"Ricochet"];
        [listOfMovies addObject:@"The Siege"];
        [listOfMovies addObject:@"Malcom X"];
        [listOfMovies addObject:@"Antwone Fisher"];
        [listOfMovies addObject:@"Courage Under Fire"];
        [listOfMovies addObject:@"He Got Game"];
        [listOfMovies addObject:@"The Pelican Brief"];
        [listOfMovies addObject:@"Glory"];
        [listOfMovies addObject:@"The Preacher's Wife"];

        //---set the title of the navigation bar---
        self.navigationItem.title = @"Movies";

    [super viewDidLoad];
}

- (void)dealloc {
    [listOfMovies release];
    [super dealloc];
}
```

11. Insert the following statement in bold in the `tableview:numberOfRowsInSection:` method to specify the number of rows to display for the Table view:

```
//---specify the number of rows in the table view---
- (NSInteger)tableView:(UITableView *)tableView
            numberOfRowsInSection:(NSInteger)section {

    //---set it to the number of items in the array---
    return [listOfMovies count];

}
```

12. Insert the following statements in bold in the `tableview:cellForRowAtIndexPath:` method to specify the appearance of each cell:

```
// Customize the appearance of table view cells.
- (UITableViewCell *)tableView:(UITableView *)tableView
                    cellForRowAtIndexPath:(NSIndexPath *)indexPath {

    static NSString *CellIdentifier = @"Cell";

    UITableViewCell *cell = [tableView
        dequeueReusableCellWithIdentifier:CellIdentifier];
    if (cell == nil) {
        cell = [[[UITableViewCell alloc] initWithStyle:UITableViewCellStyleDefault
                                        reuseIdentifier:CellIdentifier]
                                        autorelease];
```

```
        }

            NSString *cellValue = [listOfMovies objectAtIndex:
        indexPath.row];
                cell.textLabel.text = cellValue;

            return cell;
        }
```

13. Save the project and press Command-R to test the application on the iPhone Simulator. Observe the list of movies shown in the table view (see Figure 8-22).

How It Works

Up until this point, you have not really seen the use of the `UINavigationController` object. Basically, all you did was prepare the Table view to load the list of movies and then display it in the view. In the next section, you modify the project so that when you touch an item in the Table View, the application navigates to another view displaying the name of the movie that you have just touched.

FIGURE 8-22

Navigating to Another View

The true use of a Navigation-based application is to navigate from one view to another. Therefore, this section shows you how to modify the application so that when the user touches a movie, the application navigates to another view.

TRY IT OUT **Displaying the movie title selected in another view**

1. Using the same project, right-click the Classes group in Xcode and choose File ➪ Add Files. Select the `UIViewController` subclass item and click Next. Name the file `DetailsViewController.m` (uncheck the "With XIB for user interface" option as you will add it manually in the next step).

2. Right-click the Resources folder and choose Add ➪ New File. Select the View XIB item and click Next. Name the XIB file `DetailsView.xib`.

3. Double-click the `DetailsView.xib` file to edit it in Interface Builder. Add a Label view to the View window (see Figure 8-23).

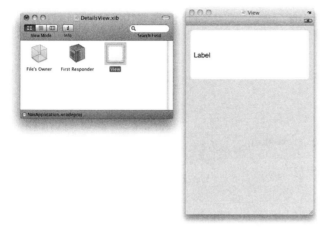

FIGURE 8-23

4. Back in Xcode, add the following lines that appear in bold to DetailsViewController.h:

```
#import <UIKit/UIKit.h>

@interface DetailsViewController : UIViewController {
      IBOutlet UILabel *label;
      NSString *textSelected;
}

@property (nonatomic, retain) UILabel *label;
@property (nonatomic, retain) NSString *textSelected;

-(id) initWithTextSelected:(NSString *) text;

@end
```

5. Back in Interface Builder, set the Class property of the File's Owner item for the DetailsView.xib window to be DetailsViewController.

6. Control-click and drag the File's Owner item to the Label view and select label. Doing so connects the Label view to the label outlet.

7. Control-click the File's Owner Item to the View item and select view. This action connects the View Controller to the view.

8. Add the following implementation code in bold in `DetailsViewController.m`:

```
#import "DetailsViewController.h"

@implementation DetailsViewController

@synthesize label;
@synthesize textSelected;

- (id) initWithTextSelected:(NSString *) text {
    self.textSelected = text;
    [label setText:[self textSelected]];
    return self;
}

- (void)viewDidLoad {
    [label setText:[self textSelected]];
    self.title = @"Movie Details";
    [super viewDidLoad];
}

- (void)dealloc {
    [label release];
    [textSelected release];
    [super dealloc];
}
```

9. Add the following code in bold in `RootViewController.h`:

```
#import "DetailsViewController.h"

@interface RootViewController : UITableViewController {
    DetailsViewController *detailsViewController;
}

@property (nonatomic, retain) DetailsViewController *detailsViewController;

@end
```

10. Add the following code in bold in `RootViewController.m`:

```
#import "RootViewController.h"

@implementation RootViewController
NSMutableArray *listOfMovies;

@synthesize detailsViewController;
```

11. Modify the `tableView:didSelectRowAtIndexPath:` method as shown in the following code highlighted in bold:

```
// Override to support row selection in the table view.
- (void)tableView:(UITableView *)tableView
```

```
            didSelectRowAtIndexPath:(NSIndexPath *)indexPath {

    NSUInteger row = [indexPath row];
    NSString *rowValue = [listOfMovies objectAtIndex:row];
    NSString *message = [[NSString alloc]
                            initWithFormat:@"You have selected \"%@\"", rowValue];

    //---create an instance of the DetailsViewController---
    if (self.detailsViewController == nil)
    {
        DetailsViewController *d = [[DetailsViewController alloc]
                                    initWithNibName:@"DetailsView"
                                    bundle:[NSBundle mainBundle]];
        self.detailsViewController = d;
        [d release];
    }

    //---set the movies selected in the method of the
    // DetailsViewController---//
    [self.detailsViewController initWithTextSelected:message];

    //---Navigate to the details view---
    [self.navigationController pushViewController:self.detailsViewController
        animated:YES];
}
```

12. Press Command-R to test the application on the iPhone Simulator. Observe the result when you touch an item (see Figure 8-24).

FIGURE 8-24

How It Works

The preceding example is a bit more interesting than the examples earlier in the chapter. Basically, you added a new XIB file and a corresponding View Controller class to the project. This new View window will be used to display the movie that you have touched in the View containing the Table view.

Now, in order for the View window containing the Table view to be able to pass the name of the movie selected to the details View window, you would need to create a property on the details View window. This is done through the `textSelected` property:

```
@property (nonatomic, retain) NSString *textSelected;
```

At the same time, you create method called `initWithTextSelected:` so that the calling view can set the value of the `textSelected` property:

```
- (id) initWithTextSelected:(NSString *) text {
    self.textSelected = text;
    [label setText:[self textSelected]];
    return self;
}
```

To navigate from the View containing the Table view to the details view, you use the `pushViewController:` method of the `UINavigationController` object within the `tableView:didSelectRowAtIndexPath:` method:

```
            //---create an instance of the DetailsViewController---
            if (self.detailsViewController == nil)
            {
                DetailsViewController *d = [[DetailsViewController alloc]
                                        initWithNibName:@"DetailsView"
                                        bundle:[NSBundle mainBundle]];
                self.detailsViewController = d;
                [d release];
            }

            //---set the movies selected in the method of the
            // DetailsViewController---//
            [self.detailsViewController initWithTextSelected:message];

            //---Navigate to the details view---
            [self.navigationController pushViewController:self.detailsViewController
                animated:YES];
```

Missing Back Button

Recall that earlier on, you set the title of the navigation item in the `RootViewController.m` file like this:

```
- (void)viewDidLoad {

    //---initialize the array---
    listOfMovies = [[NSMutableArray alloc] init];

    //---add items---
```

```
    [listOfMovies addObject:@"Training Day"];
    //...

    //---set the title of the navigation bar---
    self.navigationItem.title = @"Movies";

    [super viewDidLoad];
}
```

One very common mistake that developers make is forgetting to set this title. So what happens if you forget to set the title of the navigation item? Figure 8-25 shows the effect. Notice that the root view does not have any title, and that the details view does not have the button to bring you back to the previous view. Interestingly, if you touch the area that is supposed to display the back button, it still brings you back to the previous view.

FIGURE 8-25

SUMMARY

In this chapter, you have seen the two major types of iPhone applications supported by the SDK — Tab Bar applications and Navigation-based applications. Understanding how these two types of applications work will allow you to build multi-view applications that look just like those available on your iPhone.

EXERCISE

1. Create a Tab Bar application with two Tab Bar items. When the user taps on the second Tab Bar item, display a list of movie titles.

▶ **WHAT YOU HAVE LEARNED IN THIS CHAPTER**

TOPIC	KEY CONCEPTS
Creating a Tab Bar application	Use a `UITabBarController` instead of the usual `UIViewController`.
Determining which view is loaded first in a Tab Bar application	Change the sequence of View Controllers listed in the `UITabBarController` instance.
Adding Tab Bar Items to a Tab Bar application	After the Tab Bar item has been added to the Tab Bar, be sure to set its NIB Name property to a XIB file in your project. You also need to set its Class property to a View Controller class.
Supporting orientation change in a Tab Bar application	Ensure that all View Controllers implement the `shouldAutorotateToInterfaceOrientation:` method.

Navigating to another View Controller in a Navigation-based application	`[self.navigationController`
	`    pushViewController:self.detailsViewController`
	`        animated:YES];`

Utility Applications

➤ How to develop a Utility Application using the template provided by the SDK

➤ Understand how to flip views in a Utility Application

➤ How to apply different transition styles when flipping views

➤ How to add additional views to a Utility application

The previous two chapters have demonstrated quite a few types of applications you can build using the iPhone SDK: View-Based applications, Navigation-Based applications, and Tab Bar applications. Another type of application that is prevalent in the iPhone is *Utility Applications*. A Utility Application is an application that performs simple tasks requiring minimum user inputs. The Weather and Stocks applications that come with your iPhone are two great examples of utility applications. Figure 9-1 shows the Weather application showing the weather of a particular city. When you touch the small i icon located at the bottom-right corner of the screen, the screen flips to another screen. The flipping of views is one of the characteristics of a Utility Application.

FIGURE 9-1

According to Apple's UI guidelines for iPhone applications, a Utility Application "performs a simple task that requires a minimum of user input." Hence, if you are developing an application that shows a summary of information that the user can digest quickly, the Utility Application would be the ideal application framework to focus on. Some good examples of Utility Applications include:

➤ Currency exchanges

➤ Units conversion calculators

➤ RSS readers

Hence, in this chapter, you will learn how to build Utility Applications using the template included in the iPhone SDK.

CREATING UTILITY APPLICATIONS

The iPhone SDK includes a template for building Utility Applications. Using the template, all the necessary coding needed to flip the views is created for you. If you are building a simple Utility Application, you just need to focus on your application logic. If you are building a more sophisticated Utility Application, the generated code provides a very good base for you to use to extend the application.

To get started, create a Utility Application using the template in the SDK and learn about how it works in the following Try It Out.

TRY IT OUT   Creating a Utility Application

Codefile [UtilityApplication.zip] available for download at Wrox.com

1.   Using Xcode, create a new Utility Application project and name it `UtilityApplication`.

2.   Examine the content of the project (see Figure 9-2). Basically, two views are involved here: `MainView.xib` and `FlipsideView.xib`. The `MainView.xib` is the main view that users see when the application is loaded. It contains a small i icon that when clicked will flip to another view:`FlipsideView.xib`. Each .xib file is represented by two files — one for its view and one for its view controller. Hence, the `MainView.xib` is accompanied by the `MainView.h` and `MainView.m` files, as well as the `MainViewController.h` and `MainViewController.m` files.

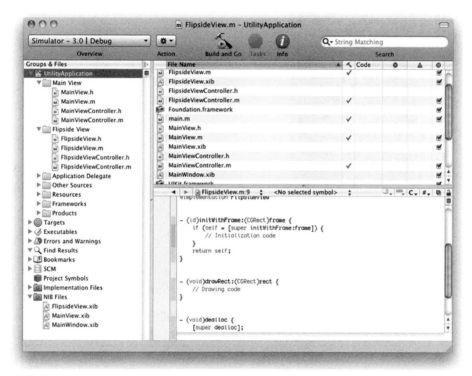

FIGURE 9-2

3. Without writing any additional code, you can test the Utility Application by pressing Command-R. Figure 9-3 shows the application in action. Pressing the i icon flips the display to another view. Pressing the Done button returns you to the main view.

FIGURE 9-3

How It Works

Much of the work needed in a Utility Application is already done for you. But it is always good to understand how things work under the hood so that you can extend it for your own use.

As you have seen, the project contains two main views controlled by two view controllers: MainViewController and FlipsideViewController.

First, examine the content of the FlipsideViewController.h file:

```
@protocol FlipsideViewControllerDelegate;

@interface FlipsideViewController : UIViewController {
    id <FlipsideViewControllerDelegate> delegate;
}
@property (nonatomic, assign) id <FlipsideViewControllerDelegate> delegate;

- (IBAction)done;

@end

@protocol FlipsideViewControllerDelegate
- (void)flipsideViewControllerDidFinish:(FlipsideViewController *)controller;
@end
```

Notice that in this controller, the code defines a protocol called the FlipsideViewControllerDelegate, which contains a single method called flipsideViewControllerDidFinish:. Using this protocol, the FlipsideViewController then exposes a property called delegate of type FlipsideView ControllerDelegate. The actual implementation of the flipsideViewControllerDidFinish:

method is not defined in this controller; instead, it must be defined by whatever calls it (in this case, it is the `MainViewController`). Its use is to signal to the calling view controller that it is done and control should return to the calling view controller.

> **NOTE** *Appendix C discusses protocols in more detail.*

In the `FlipsideViewController.m` file, the implementation for the `done:` method is defined in the header file:

```
- (IBAction)done {
    [self.delegate flipsideViewControllerDidFinish:self];
}
```

Basically this method calls the `flipsideViewControllerDidFinish:` method that you have defined (but implemented elsewhere) in the `FlipsideViewControllerDelegate` protocol.

Now, double-click the `FlipsideView.xib` file to open it in Interface Builder. Observe the following:

➤   The Flipside view contains a Navigation Bar view and a Bar Button view (see Figure 9-4).

➤   The `done:` action is connected to the Done button. (Right-click the File's Owner item to view its connected actions and outlets.)

FIGURE 9-4

Now you can examine the `MainViewController.h` file:

```
#import "FlipsideViewController.h"

@interface MainViewController : UIViewController <FlipsideViewController
Delegate> {
}

- (IBAction)showInfo;

@end
```

Observe that the `MainViewController` implements the `FlipsideViewControllerDelegate` protocol. In other words, it must implement the method that is defined in the protocol (which in this case is the `flipsideViewControllerDidFinish:` method).

In the `MainViewController.m` file, a method named `flipsideViewControllerDidFinish:` is defined. Its use is to close the `FlipsideView` when it is done:

```
- (void)flipsideViewControllerDidFinish:(FlipsideViewController *)
controller {
    [self dismissModalViewControllerAnimated:YES];
}
```

The `MainViewController.m` file also contains an action called `showInfo()`. This action is invoked when the user presses the Info button. The `showInfo()` action loads the `FlipsideView` modally:

```
- (IBAction)showInfo {

    FlipsideViewController *controller = [[FlipsideViewController alloc]
                                initWithNibName:@"FlipsideView"
                                bundle:nil];
    controller.delegate = self;

    controller.modalTransitionStyle = UIModalTransitionStyleFlipHorizontal;
    [self presentModalViewController:controller animated:YES];

    [controller release];
}
```

If you double-click the `MainView.xib` to edit it in Interface Builder, you can right-click the Info button to confirm that its `Touch Up Inside` event is connected to the `showInfo()` action (see Figure 9-5).

FIGURE 9-5

So there you have it — a Utility Application that works magically without the need for you to write any code!

TRANSITIONING STYLES

In the previous section, you saw that when you press the i info button, the view flips to reveal another View. This is controlled by the modalTransitionStyle property of the ViewController class:

```
- (IBAction)showInfo {

    FlipsideViewController *controller = [[FlipsideViewController alloc]
                                          initWithNibName:@"FlipsideView"
                                          bundle:nil];
    controller.delegate = self;

    controller.modalTransitionStyle = UIModalTransitionStyleFlipHorizontal;
    [self presentModalViewController:controller animated:YES];

    [controller release];
}
```

NOTE The `modalTransitionStyle` *property is available only in the iPhone SDK 3.0. If you try to run your application using an older version of the SDK, it will not work.*

The default transitioning is the horizontal flip, in which the main view flips horizontally (see Figure 9-6) to reveal the `FlipsideView`.

Besides flipping horizontally, you can also flip the view vertically or make it dissolve slowly. These features are controlled by the following constants (shown in bold):

```
    //---flip vertically---
    controller.modalTransitionStyle =
UIModalTransitionStyleCoverVertical;

    //---dissolves slowly to reveal another view---
    controller.modalTransitionStyle =
UIModalTransitionStyleCrossDissolve;
```

As an exercise, you should try modifying the transition styles to see for yourself how they differ.

FIGURE 9-6

ADDING ANOTHER VIEW TO THE UTILITY APPLICATION

Now that you have seen how to create a Utility Application using the template provided by the SDK, you might want to add more views to the application so that it has more functionality. Back at the Weather application on the iPhone, observe that the flip side view has an additional plus (+) button that allows you to add more weather information (see Figure 9-7).

FIGURE 9-7

In the following Try It Out, you can see how to add another View to the project created earlier so that it behaves like the Weather application.

Adding a New View to the Utility Application

1. Using the same project created earlier, double-click the `FlipsideView.xib` file to edit it in Interface Builder.

2. Add a Bar Button view onto the Navigation Bar view (see Figure 9-8). Note that the Navigation Bar view can accommodate only at two Bar Button Item views.

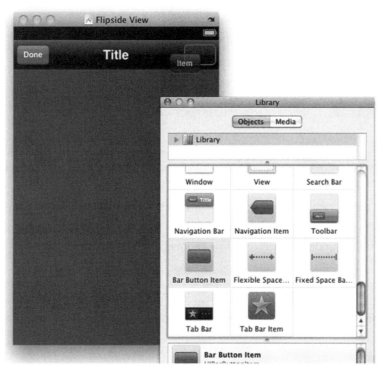

FIGURE 9-8

3. Select the newly added Bar Button item view and view its Attributes Inspector window. Change its Identifier attribute to Add (see Figure 9-9). Notice how it changes the button caption to a plus sign (+).

FIGURE 9-9

4. In the `FlipsideView.xib` window, select the File's Owner item and add a new action called `add` in the Identity Inspector window.

5. After the action is defined, connect it to the + button by control-clicking and then dragging the + button to the File's Owner item in the `FlipsideView.xib` window.

6. Back in Xcode, add a new Group under the project name and name it AddCountryView.

7. Under the newly added AddCountry View group, add a new `UIViewController` subclass item and name it `AddCountryViewController.m`. The .m and .h files are now added to the group (see Figure 9-10). Note that when adding a new `UIViewController` subclass item, Xcode will offer you an option to create an XIB file. Uncheck this option because you add it manually later.

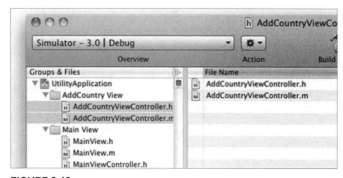

FIGURE 9-10

8. Under the `Resources` group, add a new View XIB item and name it as `AddCountryView.xib`.

9. Double-click on the `AddCountryView.xib` file to edit it in Interface Builder. Populate it with a Search Bar view and a Round Rect Button view (see Figure 9-11).

10. In the `AddCountryView.xib` window, select the File's Owner item and view the Identity Inspector window. Set the Class to `AddCountryView Controller`. Also, add a `done` action to the File's Owner item (see Figure 9-12).

11. Control-click and drag the File's Owner item to the View item and select `view`.

12. Control-click and drag the Done button to the File's Owner item. Select the `done` action.

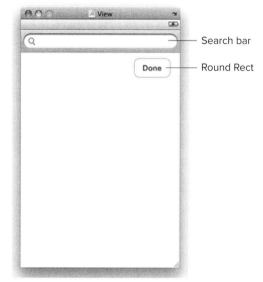

FIGURE 9-11

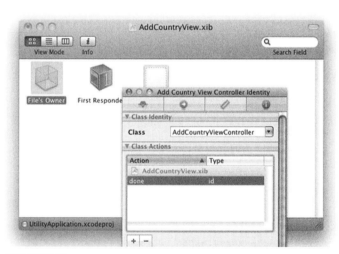

FIGURE 9-12

13. Back in Xcode, insert the following code that appears in bold in the `AddCountryViewController.h` file:

```
#import <UIKit/UIKit.h>

//---defines the protocol---
@protocol AddCountryViewControllerDelegate;

@interface AddCountryViewController : UIViewController {
    //---delegate---
    id <AddCountryViewControllerDelegate> delegate;
}
```

```
//---exposes the delegate as a property---
@property (nonatomic, assign) id <AddCountryViewControllerDelegate> delegate;

  //---the done action; called when the Done button is clicked---- (IBAction)done;

@end

//---defines the protocol---
@protocol AddCountryViewControllerDelegate
- (void)addCountryViewControllerDidFinish:(AddCountryViewController *)controller;
@end
```

14. In the `AddCountryViewController.m` file, add the following code that appears in bold:

```
#import "AddCountryViewController.h"

@implementation AddCountryViewController

  //---synthesize the delegate---
  @synthesize delegate;


  //---invokes the method defined in the protocol---
  - (IBAction)done {
      [self.delegate addCountryViewControllerDidFinish:self];
  }
```

15. In the `FlipsideViewController.h` file, insert the following code that appears in bold:

```
//---import the header file of the AddCountryViewController class---
#import "AddCountryViewController.h";

@protocol FlipsideViewControllerDelegate;

    //---implements the AddCountryViewControllerDelegate protocol---
    @interface FlipsideViewController : UIViewController
                                 <AddCountryViewControllerDelegate>
  {
     id <FlipsideViewControllerDelegate> delegate;
  }

@property (nonatomic, assign) id <FlipsideViewControllerDelegate> delegate;

- (IBAction)done;

//---the add: action; called when the "+" button is clicked---
- (IBAction)add;

@end

@protocol FlipsideViewControllerDelegate
- (void)flipsideViewControllerDidFinish:(FlipsideViewController *)controller;
@end
```

16. In the `FlipsideViewController.m` file, insert the following code that appears in bold:

```
//---defines the addCountryViewControllerDidFinish: method---
- (void)addCountryViewControllerDidFinish:(AddCountryViewController *)controller {
    [self dismissModalViewControllerAnimated:YES];


}


//---defines the add: action---
- (IBAction)add {
AddCountryViewController *controller = [[AddCountryViewController alloc]
                                    initWithNibName:@"AddCountryView"
                                    bundle:nil];
    controller.delegate = self;

    //---use the vertical transition---
    controller.modalTransitionStyle =
    UIModalTransitionStyleCoverVertical;
    [self presentModalViewController:controller
    animated:YES];
    [controller release];
}
```

17. That's it! Press Command-R to deploy the application onto the iPhone Simulator. Figure 9-13 shows the `AddCountryView` moving vertically upward when you press the + button.

18. Pressing the Done button hides the `AddCountryView`.

How It Works

This example illustrates the steps you need to take to add more views to a Utility Application. You first create the XIB file of the additional view as well as its corresponding `UIViewController` class. Within this controller, you define a protocol:

FIGURE 9-13

```
//---defines the protocol---
@protocol AddCountryViewControllerDelegate
- (void)addCountryViewControllerDidFinish:(AddCountryViewController *)controller;
@end
```

You then expose a property of this protocol type:

```
@interface AddCountryViewController : UIViewController {
    //---delegate---
    id <AddCountryViewControllerDelegate> delegate;
}

//---exposes the delegate as a property---
@property (nonatomic, assign) id <AddCountryViewControllerDelegate> delegate;
```

The view that will call this new view needs to implement the method defined in this protocol, which is as follows:

```
- (void)addCountryViewControllerDidFinish:
(AddCountryViewController *)controller;
```

When the user presses the Done button in this view, you invoke the `done:` method:

```
//---invokes the method defined in the protocol---
- (IBAction)done {
    [self.delegate addCountryViewControllerDidFinish:self];
}
```

In the `FlipsideViewController.m` file, you need to implement the protocol defined in the additional view, which is `AddCountryViewControllerDelegate`:

```
//---implements the AddCountryViewControllerDelegate protocol---
@interface FlipsideViewController : UIViewController
                            <AddCountryViewControllerDelegate> {
```

Specifically, you need to implement the `addCountryViewControllerDidFinish:` method, which dismisses the view controller:

```
//---defines the addCountryViewControllerDidFinish: method---
- (void)addCountryViewControllerDidFinish:
(AddCountryViewController *)controller {
    [self dismissModalViewControllerAnimated:YES];
}
```

Finally, you define the `add:` method, which shows the additional view using the vertical transition:

```
//---defines the add: action---
- (IBAction)add {
    AddCountryViewController *controller = [[AddCountryViewController alloc]
                                initWithNibName:@"AddCountryView"
                                bundle:nil];
    controller.delegate = self;

    //---use the vertical transition---
    controller.modalTransitionStyle = UIModalTransitionStyleCoverVertical;
    [self presentModalViewController:controller animated:YES];

    [controller release];
}
```

SUMMARY

In this chapter, you saw the Utility Application template provided by the iPhone SDK to help developers create Utility Applications. Understanding how the transitioning between the Views works is important because it allows you to extend the template for your custom use. In Chapter 10, you will see how Utility Applications are often used together with application settings to persist users' preferences and data.

EXERCISES

1. Observe that as you click on the Info button of a Utility Application, the Info button is highlighted. How do you turn off the effect?

2. How you pass data from one view to another in a Utility Application? Assume that you need to pass a string from the `FlipsideViewController` to the `MainViewController`.

▶ **WHAT YOU HAVE LEARNED IN THIS CHAPTER**

TOPIC	KEY CONCEPTS
Create a Utility Application	Use the Utility Application template provided by the iPhone SDK.
Transition between views in a Utility Application	Use the `modalTransitionStyle` property and set it to one of the following values: `UIModalTransitionStyleFlipHorizontal`, `UIModalTransitionStyleCoverVertical`, and `UIModalTransitionStyleCrossDissolve`.
Add a new view to a Utility Application	First, create a new XIB file and its accompanying `UIViewController` subclass (`.h` and `.m` files). Next, define a protocol in the view controller and expose an instance of the protocol delegate as a property.

PART III
Displaying and Persisting Data

10

Using the Table View

WHAT YOU WILL LEARN IN THIS CHAPTER

➤   How to manually add a Table view to a View, and wire the data source and delegate to your View Controller

➤   How to handle the various events in the table view to populate it with items

➤   How to handle the various events in the Table view so that users can select the items contained within it

➤   How to display text and images in the rows of the table view

➤   How to display the items from a property list in a table view

➤   How to group the items in a table view into sections

➤   How to add indexing to the table view

➤   How to add search capabilities to the table view

➤   How to add disclosures and checkmarks to rows in the table view

One of the most commonly used views in iPhone applications is the Table view. The Table view is used to display lists of items from which users can select, or they can tap it to display more information. Figure 10-1 shows a Table view in action in the Settings Application.

In Chapter 8, you had your first taste of the Table view when you developed a Navigation-based Application project. That chapter didn't fully dive into how the Table view works, and a lot of details were purposely left out. The Table view is such an important topic that it deserves a chapter on its own.

Hence, in this chapter, you examine the Table view in more details and understand the various building blocks that make it such a versatile view.

A SIMPLE TABLE VIEW

The best way to understand how to use a table view in your application is to create a new View-based Application project and then manually add a Table view to the view and wire it to a View Controller. That way, you understand the various building blocks of the Table view.

Without further ado, use the following Try It Out to create a new project and see how to put a Table view together!

FIGURE 10-1

TRY IT OUT   **Using a Table View**

Codefile [TableViewExample.zip] available for download at Wrox.com

1.   Create a new View-based Application project and name it `TableViewExample`.

2.   Double-click the `TableViewExampleViewController.xib` file to edit it in Interface Builder.

3.   Drag the `Table View Object` from the Library and drop it onto the View window (see Figure 10-2).

FIGURE 10-2

4. Right-click the Table view and connect the `dataSource` outlet to the File's Owner item (see Figure 10-3). Do the same for the `delegate` outlet.

FIGURE 10-3

5. In the `TableViewExampleViewController.h` file, add the following statement that appears in bold:

```
#import <UIKit/UIKit.h>

@interface TableViewExampleViewController : UIViewController
    <UITableViewDataSource> {
}

@end
```

> **NOTE** *Strictly speaking, if you have connected the `dataSource` outlet to the File's Owner item, you don't need to add the preceding statement. Either you write the preceding statement (`UITableViewDataSource`) or connect the outlet in Interface Builder. However, doing both doesn't hurt anything. There is one advantage to adding the <UITableViewDataSource> protocol, though — the compiler will warn you if you forget to implement any mandatory methods in your code, helping to prevent errors.*

6. In the `TableViewExampleViewController.m` file, add the following statements that appear in bold:

```objc
#import "TableViewExampleViewController.h"

@implementation TableViewExampleViewController

NSMutableArray *listOfMovies;

//---insert individual row into the table view---
- (UITableViewCell *)tableView:(UITableView *)tableView
    cellForRowAtIndexPath:(NSIndexPath *)indexPath {

    static NSString *CellIdentifier = @"Cell";

    //---try to get a reusable cell---
    UITableViewCell *cell = [tableView
        dequeueReusableCellWithIdentifier:CellIdentifier];

    //---create new cell if no reusable cell is available---
    if (cell == nil) {
        cell = [[[UITableViewCell alloc] initWithStyle:UITableViewCellStyleDefault
                    reuseIdentifier:CellIdentifier] autorelease];
    }

    //---set the text to display for the cell---
    NSString *cellValue = [listOfMovies objectAtIndex:indexPath.row];
    cell.textLabel.text = cellValue;

    return cell;
}

//---set the number of rows in the table view---
- (NSInteger)tableView:(UITableView *)tableView
    numberOfRowsInSection:(NSInteger)section {

    return [listOfMovies count];

}

- (void)viewDidLoad {
    //---initialize the array---
    listOfMovies = [[NSMutableArray alloc] init];

    //---add items---
    [listOfMovies addObject:@"Training Day"];
    [listOfMovies addObject:@"Remember the Titans"];
    [listOfMovies addObject:@"John Q."];
    [listOfMovies addObject:@"The Bone Collector"];
    [listOfMovies addObject:@"Ricochet"];
    [listOfMovies addObject:@"The Siege"];
    [listOfMovies addObject:@"Malcolm X"];
    [listOfMovies addObject:@"Antwone Fisher"];
    [listOfMovies addObject:@"Courage Under Fire"];
```

```
    [listOfMovies addObject:@"He Got Game"];
    [listOfMovies addObject:@"The Pelican Brief"];
    [listOfMovies addObject:@"Glory"];
    [listOfMovies addObject:@"The Preacher's Wife"];

    [super viewDidLoad];
}

- (void)dealloc {
    [listOfMovies release];
    [super dealloc];
}
```

7. Press Command-R to test the application on the iPhone Simulator. Figure 10-4 shows the Table view displaying the list of movies.

How It Works

You first start the application by creating an NSMutableArray object called listOfMovies containing a list of movies names. The items stored in this array will be displayed by the Table view.

```
- (void)viewDidLoad {
    //---initialize the array---
    listOfMovies = [[NSMutableArray alloc] init];

    //---add items---
    [listOfMovies addObject:@"Training Day"];
    [listOfMovies addObject:@"Remember the Titans"];
    [listOfMovies addObject:@"John Q."];
    [listOfMovies addObject:@"The Bone Collector"];
    [listOfMovies addObject:@"Ricochet"];
    [listOfMovies addObject:@"The Siege"];
    [listOfMovies addObject:@"Malcolm X"];
    [listOfMovies addObject:@"Antwone Fisher"];
    [listOfMovies addObject:@"Courage Under Fire"];
    [listOfMovies addObject:@"He Got Game"];
    [listOfMovies addObject:@"The Pelican Brief"];
    [listOfMovies addObject:@"Glory"];
    [listOfMovies addObject:@"The Preacher's Wife"];

    [super viewDidLoad];
}
```

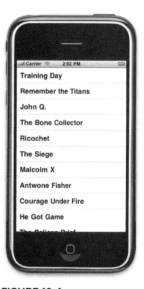

FIGURE 10-4

To populate the Table view with items, you need to handle several events contained in the UITableViewDataSource protocol. Hence, you need to ensure that your view controller conforms to this protocol:

```
@interface TableViewExampleViewController : UIViewController
    <UITableViewDataSource> {
}
```

The `UITableViewDataSource` protocol contains several events that you can implement to supply data to the Table view. Two events that you have handled in this example are:

➤   `tableView:numberOfRowsInSection:`

➤   `tableView:cellForRowAtIndexPath:`

The `tableView:numberOfRowsInSection:` event indicates how many rows you want the Table view to display. In this case, you set it to the number of items in the `listOfMovies` array.

```
//---insert individual row into the table view---
- (NSInteger)tableView:(UITableView *)tableView
    numberOfRowsInSection:(NSInteger)section {

    return [listOfMovies count];

}
```

The `tableView:cellForRowAtIndexPath:` event inserts a cell in a particular location of the Table view. This event is fired once for each row of the Table view.

 NOTE The `tableView:cellForRowAtIndexPath:` *event is not fired continuously from start to finish. For example, if the Table view has 100 rows to be displayed, the event is fired continuously for the first, say, 10 rows that are visible. When the user scrolls down the Table view, the* `tableView:cellForRowAtIndexPath:` *event is fired for the next couple of visible rows.*

Here, you retrieve the individual item from the array and insert it into the Table view:

```
- (UITableViewCell *)tableView:(UITableView *)tableView
    cellForRowAtIndexPath:(NSIndexPath *)indexPath {

    static NSString *CellIdentifier = @"Cell";

    //---try to get a reusable cell---
    UITableViewCell *cell = [tableView
        dequeueReusableCellWithIdentifier:CellIdentifier];

    //---create new cell if no reusable cell is available---
    if (cell == nil) {
        cell = [[[UITableViewCell alloc] initWithStyle:UITableViewCellStyleDefault
                    reuseIdentifier:CellIdentifier] autorelease];
    }

    //---set the text to display for the cell---
    NSString *cellValue = [listOfMovies objectAtIndex:indexPath.row];
    cell.textLabel.text = cellValue;

    return cell;
}
```

Specifically, you use the `dequeueReusableCellWithIdentifier:` method of the `UITableView` class to obtain an instance of the `UITableViewCell` class. The `dequeueReusableCellWithIdentifier:` method returns a reusable Table view cell object. This is important because if you have a large table (say, with 10,000 rows) and you create a single `UITableViewCell` object for each row, you would generate a great performance and memory hit. Also, because a Table view displays only a fixed number of rows at any one time, reusing the cells that have been scrolled out of view would make sense. This is exactly what the `dequeueReusableCellWithIdentifier:` method does. So, for example, if 10 rows are visible in the Table view, only 10 `UITableViewCell` objects are ever created — they always get reused when the user scrolls through the Table view.

Adding a Header and Footer

You can display a header and footer for the Table view by simply implementing the following two methods in your View Controller:

```
- (NSString *)tableView:(UITableView *)tableView
    titleForHeaderInSection:(NSInteger)section{
    //---display "Movie List" as the header---
    return @"Movie List";

}

- (NSString *)tableView:(UITableView *)tableView
    titleForFooterInSection:(NSInteger)section {
    //---display "by Denzel Washington" as the footer---
    return @"by Denzel Washington";

}
```

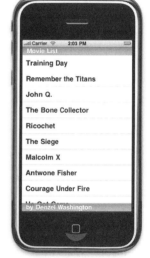

If you insert the preceding statements in the `TableViewExampleViewController.m` file and rerun the application, you see the header and footer of the Table view as shown in Figure 10-5.

FIGURE 10-5

Adding an Image

In addition to text, you can display an image next to the text of a cell in a Table view. Suppose you have an image named `apple.jpeg` in the `Resources` folder of your project (see Figure 10-6).

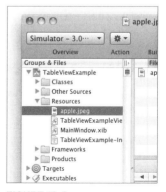

FIGURE 10-6

NOTE *You can simply drag and drop an image to the Resources folder of Xcode. When prompted, ensure that you save a copy of the image in your project.*

To display an image next to the text of a cell, insert the following statements that appear in bold into the `tableView:cellForRowAtIndexPath:` method:

```
- (UITableViewCell *)tableView:(UITableView *)tableView
   cellForRowAtIndexPath:(NSIndexPath *)indexPath {

   static NSString *CellIdentifier = @"Cell";

   //---try to get a reusable cell---
   UITableViewCell *cell = [tableView
       dequeueReusableCellWithIdentifier:CellIdentifier];

   //---create new cell if no reusable cell is available---
   if (cell == nil) {
       cell = [[[UITableViewCell alloc] initWithStyle:UITableViewCellStyleDefault
                   reuseIdentifier:CellIdentifier] autorelease];
   }

   //---set the text to display for the cell---
   NSString *cellValue = [listOfMovies objectAtIndex:indexPath.row];
   cell.text = cellValue;

   UIImage *image = [UIImage imageNamed:@"apple.jpeg"];
   cell.imageView.image = image;

   return cell;
}
```

Press Command-R to test the application and you see that the image is displayed next to each row (see Figure 10-7).

Notice that the `UITableViewCell` object already has the `imageView` property. All you need to do is to create an instance of the `UIImage` class and then load the image from the `Resources` folder of your project.

Displaying the Item Selected

So far, you have seen how to populate the Table view with items by ensuring that your View Controller conforms to the `UITableViewDataSource` protocol. This protocol takes care of populating the Table view, but if you want to select the items in a Table view, you need to conform to another protocol, `UITableViewDelegate`.

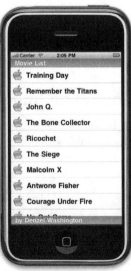

FIGURE 10-7

The `UITableViewDelegate` protocol contains events that allow you to manage selections, edit and delete rows, and display a header and footer.

To use the `UITableViewDelegate` protocol, modify the `TableViewExampleViewController.h` file by adding the statement in bold as follows:

```
#import <UIKit/UIKit.h>

@interface TableViewExampleViewController : UIViewController
    <UITableViewDataSource,
    UITableViewDelegate>{

}

@end
```

Strictly speaking, if you have connected the `delegate` outlet to the File's Owner item previously (see Figure 10-8), you don't need to add the preceding statement (`UITableViewDelegate`). Either you write the preceding statement or connect the outlet in Interface Builder. However, doing both doesn't hurt.

FIGURE 10-8

The following Try It Out shows how you can allow users to make selections in a Table view.

TRY IT OUT Making a Selection in a Table View

1. Using the same project created earlier, add the following statements that appear in bold to the
`TableViewExampleViewController.m` file:

```
#import "TableViewExampleViewController.h"

@implementation TableViewExampleViewController

NSMutableArray *listOfMovies;

- (void)tableView:(UITableView *)tableView
  didSelectRowAtIndexPath:(NSIndexPath *)indexPath {

    NSString *movieSelected = [listOfMovies objectAtIndex:[indexPath row]];
    NSString *msg = [[NSString alloc] initWithFormat:@"You have selected %@",
                    movieSelected];

    UIAlertView *alert = [[UIAlertView alloc] initWithTitle:@"Movie selected"
                            message:msg
                            delegate:self
                            cancelButtonTitle: @"OK"
                            otherButtonTitles:nil];

    [alert show];
    [alert release];
    [movieSelected release];
    [msg release];
}
```

2. Press Command-R to test the application on the iPhone Simulator.

3. Select a row by tapping it. When a row is selected, you see an alert
view displaying the row you have selected (see Figure 10-9).

How It Works

One of the events in the `UITableViewDelegate` protocol is `tableView:`
`didSelectRowAtIndexPath:`, which is fired when the user selects a row in
the Table view. One of the parameters contained in `tableView:didSelec-`
`tRowAtIndexPath:` event is of the type `NSIndexPath`. The `NSIndexPath`
class represents the path of a specific item in a nested array collection.

For this event, to know which row has been selected, you simply call the
row property of the `NSIndexPath` object (`indexPath`) and then use
the row number to reference against the `listOfMovies` array:

FIGURE 10-9

```
NSString *movieSelected = [listOfMovies objectAtIndex:[indexPath row]];
```

NOTE *The* row *property of the* NSIndexPath *class is one of the additions made by the UIKit framework to enable the identification of rows and sections in a Table view. So be aware that the original class definition of the* NSIndexPath *class does not contain the* row *property.*

After the selected movie is retrieved, you simply display it using the UIAlertView class:

```
NSString *msg = [[NSString alloc] initWithFormat:@"You have selected %@",
                 movieSelected];

UIAlertView *alert = [[UIAlertView alloc] initWithTitle:@"Movie selected"
                                       message:msg
                                       delegate:self
                                       cancelButtonTitle: @"OK"
                                       otherButtonTitles:nil];
```

Indenting

Another event in the UITableViewDelegate protocol is tableView: indentationLevelForRowAtIndexPath:. When you handle this event, it is fired for every row that is visible on the screen. To set an indentation for a particular row, simply return an integer indicating the level of indentation:

```
- (NSInteger)tableView:(UITableView *)tableView
   indentationLevelForRowAtIndexPath:(NSIndexPath
*)indexPath {

   return [indexPath row] % 2;

}
```

In the preceding example, the indentation alternates between 0 and 1, depending on the current row number. Figure 10-10 shows how the Table view looks if you insert the preceding code in the TableViewExampleViewController.m file.

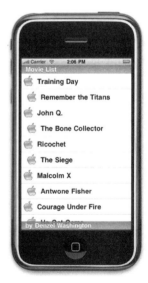

FIGURE 10-10

DISPLAYING SECTIONS

In the previous sections, you create a View-based Application project and then manually add a Table view to the View window and connect the data source and delegate to the File's Owner item. You then handle all the relevant events defined in the two protocols, UITableViewDelegate and UITableViewDataSource, so that you can populate the Table view with items as well as make them selectable.

In real life, the Table view is often used with a Navigation-based Application because it is very common for users to select an item from a Table view and then navigate to another screen showing the details of the item selected. For this reason, the Navigation-based Application template in the iPhone SDK by default uses the `TableView` class instead of the `View` class.

In addition, you can group items in a Table view into sections so that you can group related items with a header for each section. In the following Try It Out, you learn how to use the Table view from within a Navigation-based Application project. At the same time, you learn how to display items stored in a property list, as opposed to an array.

Displaying Sections in a Table View

1. Create a new Navigation-based Application project and name it `TableView`.

2. Double-click the `RootViewController.xib` file to edit it in Interface Builder.

3. Notice that in the `RootViewController.xib` window you now have a `TableView` item instead of the usual `View` item (see Figure 10-11).

4. Double-click the `TableView` item and observe that you have a Table view within it (see Figure 10-12).

FIGURE 10-11

5. Examine `RootViewController.h` file and notice that the `RootViewController` class now extends the `UITableViewController` base class:

```
@interface RootViewController : UITableViewController {
}

@end
```

6. Also examine the `RootViewController.m` file and observe that it includes a number of event stubs that you can use by removing the comment statements.

7. Right-click the Resources folder and choose Add ➪ New File.

FIGURE 10-12

8. Select the Other category on the left of the New File dialog and select the Property List template on the right of the dialog (see Figure 10-13).

 NOTE *The .PLIST template is moved in XCode3.2 to the Mac OS X ⇨ Resources tab.*

FIGURE 10-13

9. Name the property list `Movies.plist`. The property list is now saved in the Resources folder of your project. Select it and create the list of items as shown in Figure 10-14.

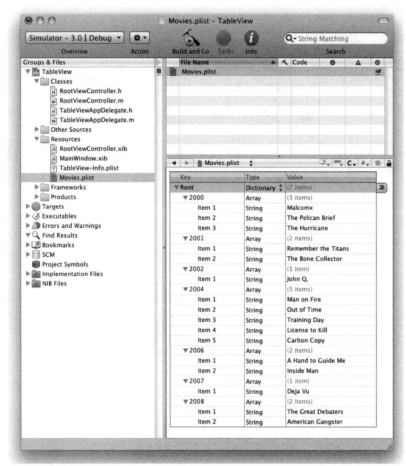

FIGURE 10-14

10. In the `RootViewController.h` file, add the following statements that appear in bold:

```
@interface RootViewController : UITableViewController {
    NSDictionary *movieTitles;
    NSArray *years;
}

@property (nonatomic, retain) NSDictionary *movieTitles;
@property (nonatomic, retain) NSArray *years;

@end
```

11. In the `RootViewController.m` file, add the following statements that appear in bold:

```
#import "RootViewController.h"

@implementation RootViewController

@synthesize movieTitles, years;

- (void)viewDidLoad {

    //---path to the property list file---
    NSString *path = [[NSBundle mainBundle] pathForResource:@"Movies"
                            ofType:@"plist"];

    //---load the list into the dictionary---
    NSDictionary *dic = [[NSDictionary alloc] initWithContentsOfFile:path];

    //---save the dictionary object to the property---
    self.movieTitles = dic;
    [dic release];

    //---get all the keys in the dictionary object and sort them---
    NSArray *array = [[movieTitles allKeys]
                    sortedArrayUsingSelector:@selector(compare:)];

    //---save the keys in the years property---
    self.years = array;

    [super viewDidLoad];

}

- (NSInteger)numberOfSectionsInTableView:(UITableView *)tableView {

    //---returns the number of years as the number of sections you want to see---
    return [years count];
}

// Customize the number of rows in the table view.
- (NSInteger)tableView:(UITableView *)tableView
  numberOfRowsInSection:(NSInteger)section {

    //---check the current year based on the section index---
    NSString *year = [years objectAtIndex:section];

    //---returns the movies in that year as an array---
    NSArray *movieSection = [movieTitles objectForKey:year];

    //---return the number of movies for that year as the number of rows in that
    // section ---
```

```
    return [movieSection count];

}

// Customize the appearance of table view cells.
- (UITableViewCell *)tableView:(UITableView *)tableView
  cellForRowAtIndexPath:(NSIndexPath *)indexPath {

    static NSString *CellIdentifier = @"Cell";

    UITableViewCell *cell = [tableView
        dequeueReusableCellWithIdentifier:CellIdentifier];

    if (cell == nil) {
        cell = [[[UITableViewCell alloc] initWithStyle:UITableViewCellStyleDefault
                    reuseIdentifier:CellIdentifier] autorelease];
    }

    // Configure the cell.
    //---get the year---
    NSString *year = [years objectAtIndex:[indexPath section]];

    //---get the list of movies for that year---
    NSArray *movieSection = [movieTitles objectForKey:year];

    //---get the particular movie based on that row---
    cell.textLabel.text = [movieSection objectAtIndex:[indexPath row]];

    return cell;

}

- (NSString *)tableView:(UITableView *)tableView
  titleForHeaderInSection:(NSInteger)section {

    //---get the year as the section header---
    NSString *year = [years objectAtIndex:section];

    return year;
}

- (void)dealloc {
    [years release];
    [movieTitles release];
    [super dealloc];
}

@end
```

12. Press Command-R to test the application. You can now see the movies grouped into sections organized by year (see Figure 10-15).

FIGURE 10-15

You can also change the style of the Table view by clicking the `TableView` item in Interface Builder and then changing the `Style` property in the Attributes Inspector window to `Grouped` (see Figure 10-16).

FIGURE 10-16

FIGURE 10-17

If you rerun the application, you see that the look of the Table view is now different (see Figure 10-17).

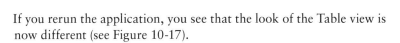

Codefile [TableView.zip] available for download at Wrox.com

How It Works

The exercise covers quite a number of concepts, and you will need some time to understand them all.

First, you created a property list in your project. You populated the property list with several key/value pairs. Essentially, you can visualize the key/value pairs stored in the property list as shown in Figure 10-18.

Key	Value
2000	"Malcolm X", "The Pelican Brief", "The Hurricane"
2001	"Remember the Titans", "The Bone Collector"
2002	"John Q."
2004	"Man on Fire", "Out of Time", " Training Day", "License to Kill", "Carbon Copy"
2006	"A Hand to Guide Me", "Inside Man"
2007	"Deja Vu"
2008	"The Great Debaters", "American Gangster"

FIGURE 10-18

Each key represents a year, and the value for each key represents the movies released in that particular year. You will use the values stored in the property list and display them in the Table view.

Within the `RootViewController` class, you create two properties: `movieTitles` (an `NSDictionary` object) and `years` (an `NSArray` object).

When the view is loaded, you first locate the property list and load the list into the `NSDictionary` object, followed by retrieving all the years into the `NSArray` object:

```
- (void)viewDidLoad {
    //---path to the property list file---
    NSString *path = [[NSBundle mainBundle] pathForResource:@"Movies"
                                ofType:@"plist"];

    //---load the list into the dictionary---
    NSDictionary *dic = [[NSDictionary alloc] initWithContentsOfFile:path];

    //---save the dictionary object to the property---
    self.movieTitles = dic;
    [dic release];

    //---get all the keys in the dictionary object and sort them---
    NSArray *array = [[movieTitles allKeys]
                sortedArrayUsingSelector:@selector(compare:)];

    //---save the keys in the years property---
    self.years = array;

    [super viewDidLoad];
}
```

Because the Table view now displays the list of movies in sections, with each section representing a year, you need to tell the Table view how many sections are there. You do so by implementing the `numberOfSectionsInTableView:` method:

```
- (NSInteger)numberOfSectionsInTableView:(UITableView *)tableView {

    //---returns the number of years as the number of sections you want to see---
    return [years count];
}
```

After the Table view knows how many sections to display, it must also know how many rows to display in each section. You tell it that information by implementing the `tableView:numberOfRowsInSection:` method:

```
// Customize the number of rows in the table view.
- (NSInteger)tableView:(UITableView *)tableView
  numberOfRowsInSection:(NSInteger)section {

    //---check the current year based on the section index---
    NSString *year = [years objectAtIndex:section];

    //---returns the movies in that year as an array---
    NSArray *movieSection = [movieTitles objectForKey:year];

    //---return the number of movies for that year as the number of rows in that
    // section ---
    return [movieSection count];

}
```

To display the movies for each section, you implement the `tableView:cellForRowAtIndexPath:` method and extract the relevant movie titles from the `NSDictionary` object:

```
// Customize the appearance of table view cells.
- (UITableViewCell *)tableView:(UITableView *)tableView
  cellForRowAtIndexPath:(NSIndexPath *)indexPath {

    static NSString *CellIdentifier = @"Cell";

    UITableViewCell *cell = [tableView
        dequeueReusableCellWithIdentifier:CellIdentifier];

    if (cell == nil) {
        cell = [[[UITableViewCell alloc] initWithStyle:UITableViewCellStyleDefault
                    reuseIdentifier:CellIdentifier] autorelease];
    }

    // Configure the cell.
    //---get the year---
    NSString *year = [years objectAtIndex:[indexPath section]];

    //---get the list of movies for that year---
```

```
      NSArray *movieSection = [movieTitles objectForKey:year];

      //---get the particular movie based on that row---
      cell.text = [movieSection objectAtIndex:[indexPath row]];

      return cell;

}
```

Finally, you implement the `tableView:titleForHeaderInSection:` method to retrieve the year as the header for each section:

```
- (NSString *)tableView:(UITableView *)tableView
  titleForHeaderInSection:(NSInteger)section {

    //---get the year as the section header---
    NSString *year = [years objectAtIndex:section];

    return year;
}
```

Adding Indexing

The list of movies is pretty short, so scrolling through the list is not too much of a hassle. However, imagine that the list contains 10,000 titles spanning 100 years. In this case, scrolling from the top of the list to the bottom of the list can take a long time. A very useful feature of the Table view is its ability to display an index on the right side of the view. An example is the A–Z index list available in your Contacts list (see Figure 10-19).

To add an index list to your Table view, you just need to implement the `sectionIndexTitlesForTableView:` method and return the array containing the section headers, which is the `years` array in this case:

```
- (NSArray *)sectionIndexTitlesForTableView:(UITableView
*)tableView {
    return years;
}
```

FIGURE 10-19

 NOTE *Before you run the application, be sure to change the style of the Table view back to Plain. If you set it to Grouped style, the index will overlap with the layout of the Table view.*

Figure 10-20 shows the index displayed on the right side of the Table view.

FIGURE 10-20

Adding Search Capability

One very common function associated with the Table view is the
ability to search the items contained within a Table view. For example,
the Contacts application has the Search Bar at the top
(see Figure 10-21) for easy searching of contacts.

FIGURE 10-21

In the following Try It Out, you will learn how to add search
functionality to the Table view.

TRY IT OUT Adding a Search Bar to the Table View

1. Using the same project created in the previous section, in Interface
Builder drag a Search Bar from the Library and drop it onto the
Table view (see Figure 10-22).

2. Right-click the Search Bar and connect the `delegate` to the File's
Owner item (see Figure 10-23).

FIGURE 10-22

FIGURE 10-23

In the `RootViewController.h` file, add the following statements that appear in bold:

```
@interface RootViewController : UITableViewController
<UISearchBarDelegate>{

    NSDictionary *movieTitles;
    NSArray *years;

    //---search---
    IBOutlet UISearchBar *searchBar;
    BOOL isSearchOn;
    BOOL canSelectRow;
    NSMutableArray *listOfMovies;
    NSMutableArray *searchResult;
}

@property (nonatomic, retain) NSDictionary *movieTitles;
@property (nonatomic, retain) NSArray *years;

//---search---
@property (nonatomic, retain) UISearchBar *searchBar;
- (void) doneSearching: (id)sender;
- (void) searchMoviesTableView;

@end
```

NOTE *As before, the addition of the preceding statement is not absolutely necessary after you have connected the delegate to the File's Owner item in Interface Builder.*

3. In Interface Builder, Control-click and drag the File's Owner item to the Search Bar and select `searchBar`.

4. In the `RootViewController.m` file, add the following statements that appear in bold:

```
#import "RootViewController.h"

@implementation RootViewController

@synthesize movieTitles, years;
@synthesize searchBar;

- (void)viewDidLoad {

    NSString *path = [[NSBundle mainBundle] pathForResource:@"Movies"
                    ofType:@"plist"];
    NSDictionary *dic = [[NSDictionary alloc] initWithContentsOfFile:path];

    self.movieTitles = dic;

    NSArray *array = [[movieTitles allKeys]
                    sortedArrayUsingSelector:@selector(compare:)];
    self.years = array;

    [dic release];
    //---display the searchbar---
    self.tableView.tableHeaderView = searchBar;
    searchBar.autocorrectionType = UITextAutocorrectionTypeYes;

    //---copy all the movie titles in the dictionary into the listOfMovies array---
    listOfMovies = [[NSMutableArray alloc] init];
    for (NSString *year in array)    //---get all the years---
    {
        //---get all the movies for a particular year---
        NSArray *movies = [movieTitles objectForKey:year];
        for (NSString *title in movies)
        {
            [listOfMovies addObject:title];
        }
    }

    //---used for storing the search result---
    searchResult = [[NSMutableArray alloc] init];

    isSearchOn = NO;
```

```
    canSelectRow = YES;

    [super viewDidLoad];

}
//---fired when the user taps on the searchbar---
- (void)searchBarTextDidBeginEditing:(UISearchBar *)searchBar {

    isSearchOn = YES;
    canSelectRow = NO;
    self.tableView.scrollEnabled = NO;

    //---add the Done button at the top---
    self.navigationItem.rightBarButtonItem = [[[UIBarButtonItem alloc]

        initWithBarButtonSystemItem:UIBarButtonSystemItemDone
        target:self action:@selector(doneSearching:)] autorelease];
}

//---done with the searching---
- (void) doneSearching:(id)sender {

    isSearchOn = NO;
    canSelectRow = YES;
    self.tableView.scrollEnabled = YES;
    self.navigationItem.rightBarButtonItem = nil;

    //---hides the keyboard---
    [searchBar resignFirstResponder];

    //---refresh the TableView---
    [self.tableView reloadData];
}

//---fired when the user types something into the searchbar---
- (void)searchBar:(UISearchBar *)searchBar textDidChange:(NSString *)searchText {
    //---if there is something to search for---
    if ([searchText length] > 0) {
        isSearchOn = YES;
        canSelectRow = YES;
        self.tableView.scrollEnabled = YES;
        [self searchMoviesTableView];
    }
    else {
        //---nothing to search---
        isSearchOn = NO;
        canSelectRow = NO;
        self.tableView.scrollEnabled = NO;
    }
    [self.tableView reloadData];
}

//---performs the searching using the array of movies---
```

```objc
- (void) searchMoviesTableView {

    //---clears the search result---
    [searchResult removeAllObjects];

    for (NSString *str in listOfMovies)
    {
        NSRange titleResultsRange = [str rangeOfString:searchBar.text
            options:NSCaseInsensitiveSearch];

        if (titleResultsRange.length > 0)
            [searchResult addObject:str];
    }

}

//---fired when the user taps the Search button on the keyboard---
- (void)searchBarSearchButtonClicked:(UISearchBar *)searchBar {

[self searchMoviesTableView];

}

- (NSInteger)numberOfSectionsInTableView:(UITableView *)tableView {

    if (isSearchOn)
        return 1;
    else
        return [years count];

}

// Customize the number of rows in the table view.
- (NSInteger)tableView:(UITableView *)tableView
   numberOfRowsInSection:(NSInteger)section {

    if (isSearchOn) {
        return [searchResult count];
    } else
    {
        NSString *year = [years objectAtIndex:section];
        NSArray *movieSection = [movieTitles objectForKey:year];
        return [movieSection count];
    }

}

// Customize the appearance of table view cells.
- (UITableViewCell *)tableView:(UITableView *)tableView
   cellForRowAtIndexPath:(NSIndexPath *)indexPath {

    static NSString *CellIdentifier = @"Cell";

    UITableViewCell *cell = [tableView
```

```
              dequeueReusableCellWithIdentifier:CellIdentifier];

    if (cell == nil) {
        cell = [[[UITableViewCell alloc] initWithStyle:UITableViewCellStyleDefault
                reuseIdentifier:CellIdentifier] autorelease];
    }

    // Configure the cell.
    if (isSearchOn) {
        NSString *cellValue = [searchResult objectAtIndex:indexPath.row];
        cell.textLabel.text = cellValue;
    } else {
        NSString *year = [years objectAtIndex:[indexPath section]];
        NSArray *movieSection = [movieTitles objectForKey:year];
        cell.textLabel.text = [movieSection objectAtIndex:[indexPath row]];
    }
    return cell;
}

- (NSString *)tableView:(UITableView *)tableView
  titleForHeaderInSection:(NSInteger)section {

    NSString *year = [years objectAtIndex:section];
    if (isSearchOn)
        return nil;
    else
        return year;

}

- (NSArray *)sectionIndexTitlesForTableView:(UITableView *)tableView {
    if (isSearchOn)
        return nil;
    else
        return years;

}

//---fired before a row is selected---
- (NSIndexPath *)tableView :(UITableView *)theTableView
  willSelectRowAtIndexPath:(NSIndexPath *)indexPath {
    if (canSelectRow)
        return indexPath;
    else
        return nil;

}

- (void)didReceiveMemoryWarning {
    // Releases the view if it doesn't have a superview.
```

```
    [super didReceiveMemoryWarning];

    // Release any cached data, images, etc that aren't in use.
}

- (void)viewDidUnload {
    // Release anything that can be recreated in viewDidLoad or on demand.
    // e.g. self.myOutlet = nil;
}

- (void)dealloc {
    [years release];
    [movieTitles release];
    [searchBar release];
    [super dealloc];
}

@end
```

6. Press Command-R to test the application on the iPhone Simulator.

7. Tap the Search Bar and the keyboard will appear (see Figure 10-24). Observe the following:

➤ As you type, the Table view displays the movies whose title contains the characters that you are typing. You can select the search result by tapping them.

➤ When the keyboard appears and the Search Bar has no text in it, the Table view contains the original list and the rows are not searchable.

➤ When you click the Done button, the keyboard disappears and the original list appears.

FIGURE 10-24

How It Works

That is quite a lot of work, isn't it? But not to worry: It is actually quite easy to follow. Go ahead and dive in into the details.

First, you add an outlet to connect to the Search Bar:

```
IBOutlet UISearchBar *searchBar;
```

You then define two Boolean variables so that you can track whether the search process is ongoing and whether the user can select the rows in the Table view:

```
BOOL isSearchOn;
BOOL canSelectRow;
```

You then define two NSMutableArray objects so that you can use one to store the list of movies and use another to temporarily store the result of the search:

```
NSMutableArray *listOfMovies;
NSMutableArray *searchResult;
```

When the view is first loaded, you first associate the Search Bar with the Table view and then copy the entire list of movie titles from the NSDictionary object into the NSMutableArray:

```
//---display the searchbar---
self.tableView.tableHeaderView = searchBar;
searchBar.autocorrectionType = UITextAutocorrectionTypeYes;

//---copy all the movie titles in the dictionary into the listOfMovies array---
listOfMovies = [[NSMutableArray alloc] init];
for (NSString *year in array)      //---get all the years---
{
    //---get all the movies for a particular year---
    NSArray *movies = [movieTitles objectForKey:year];
    for (NSString *title in movies)
    {
        [listOfMovies addObject:title];
    }
}

//---used for storing the search result---
searchResult = [[NSMutableArray alloc] init];

isSearchOn = NO;
canSelectRow = YES;
```

When the user taps the Search Bar, the searchBarTextDidBeginEditing: event (one of the methods defined in the UISearchBarDelegate protocol) fires. In this method, you add a Done button to the top-right corner of the screen. When the Done button is clicked, the doneSearching: method is called (which you define next).

```
//---fired when the user taps on the searchbar---
- (void)searchBarTextDidBeginEditing:(UISearchBar *)searchBar {
```

```
        isSearchOn = YES;
        canSelectRow = NO;
        self.tableView.scrollEnabled = NO;

        //---add the Done button at the top---
        self.navigationItem.rightBarButtonItem = [[[UIBarButtonItem alloc]
            initWithBarButtonSystemItem:UIBarButtonSystemItemDone
            target:self action:@selector(doneSearching:)] autorelease];
    }
```

The `doneSearching:` method makes the Search Bar resign its First Responder status (thereby hiding the keyboard). At the same time, you reload the Table view by calling the `reloadData` method of the Table view. This causes the various events associated with the Table view to be fired again.

```
    //---done with the searching---
    - (void) doneSearching:(id)sender {

        isSearchOn = NO;
        canSelectRow = YES;
        self.tableView.scrollEnabled = YES;
        self.navigationItem.rightBarButtonItem = nil;

        //---hides the keyboard---
        [searchBar resignFirstResponder];

        //---refresh the TableView---
        [self.tableView reloadData];
    }
```

As the user types into the Search Bar, the `searchBar:textDidChange:` event is fired for each character entered. In this case, if the Search Bar has at least one character, you call the `searchMoviesTableView` method (which you define next):

```
    //---fired when the user types something into the searchbar---
    - (void)searchBar:(UISearchBar *)searchBar textDidChange:(NSString *)searchText {
        //---if there is something to search for---
        if ([searchText length] > 0) {
            isSearchOn = YES;
            canSelectRow = YES;
            self.tableView.scrollEnabled = YES;
            [self searchMoviesTableView];
        }
        else {
            //---nothing to search---
            isSearchOn = NO;
            canSelectRow = NO;
            self.tableView.scrollEnabled = NO;
        }
        [self.tableView reloadData];
    }
```

The `searchMoviesTableView` method performs the searching on the `listOfMovies` array. You use the `rangeOfString:options:` method of the `NSString` class to perform a case-insensitive search of each movie title using the specified string. The returning result is an `NSRange` object, which contains the location and length of the search string in the string being searched. If the length is more than zero, this means that a match has been found, and hence you add it to the searchResult array:

```
//---performs the searching using the array of movies---
- (void) searchMoviesTableView {

    //---clears the search result---
    [searchResult removeAllObjects];

    for (NSString *str in listOfMovies)
    {
        NSRange titleResultsRange = [str rangeOfString:searchBar.text
            options:NSCaseInsensitiveSearch];

        if (titleResultsRange.length > 0)
            [searchResult addObject:str];
    }

}
```

When the user taps the Search button (on the keyboard), you make a call to the searchMoviesTableView method:

```
//---fired when the user taps the Search button on the keyboard---
- (void)searchBarSearchButtonClicked:(UISearchBar *)searchBar {

    [self searchMoviesTableView];

}
```

The rest of the methods are straightforward. If the search is currently active (as determined by the isSearchOn variable), you display the list of titles contained in the searchResult array. If not, you display the entire list of movies.

Disclosures and Check Marks

Because users often select rows in a Table view to view more detailed information, rows in a Table view often spot images containing an arrow or a checkmark. Figure 10-25 shows an example of such arrows.

There are three types of images that you can display:

➤ Disclosure button

➤ Checkmark

➤ Disclosure indicator

FIGURE 10-25

To display a disclosure or checkmark, insert the following statement that appears in bold in the
`tableView:cellForRowAtIndexPath:` event:

```
- (UITableViewCell *)tableView:(UITableView *)tableView
    cellForRowAtIndexPath:(NSIndexPath *)indexPath {

    static NSString *CellIdentifier = @"Cell";

    UITableViewCell *cell = [tableView
        dequeueReusableCellWithIdentifier:CellIdentifier];

    if (cell == nil) {
        cell = [[[UITableViewCell alloc] initWithStyle:UITableViewCellStyleDefault
                    reuseIdentifier:CellIdentifier] autorelease];
    }

    // Configure the cell.
    if (isSearchOn) {
        NSString *cellValue = [searchResult objectAtIndex:indexPath.row];
        cell.text = cellValue;
    } else {
        NSString *year = [years objectAtIndex:[indexPath section]];
        NSArray *movieSection = [movieTitles objectForKey:year];
        cell.text = [movieSection objectAtIndex:[indexPath row]];
    }
    cell.accessoryType = UITableViewCellAccessoryDetailDisclosureButton;

    return cell;
}
```

You can use the following constants for the `accessoryType` property:

➤ `UITableViewCellAccessoryDetailDisclosureButton`

➤ `UITableViewCellAccessoryCheckmark`

➤ `UITableViewCellAccessoryDisclosureIndicator`

Figure 10-26 shows the different types of images corresponding to the three preceding constants.

FIGURE 10-26

Of the three image types, only the `UITableViewCellAccessoryDetailDisclosureButton` can handle a user's tap event. (The other two images are used only for display purposes.) To handle the event when the user taps the Disclosure button, you need to implement the `tableView:accessoryButtonTappedForRowWithIndexPath:` method:

```
- (void)tableView:(UITableView *)tableView
    accessoryButtonTappedForRowWithIndexPath:(NSIndexPath *)indexPath {

    //---insert code here---
    // e.g. navigate to another view to display detailed information, etc
}
```

Figure 10-27 shows the two different events fired when a user taps the content of the cell as well as the Disclosure button.

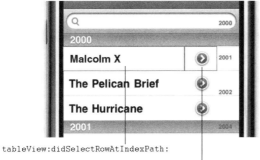

```
tableView:didSelectRowAtIndexPath:

      tableView:accessoryButtonTappedForRowWithIndexPath:
```

FIGURE 10-27

Commonly, you use the Disclosure button to display detailed information about the selected row.

SUMMARY

In this chapter, you had a good look at the Table view and how to customize it to display items in the various forms. You also learned how to implement search functionality in the Table view, which is an essential function in real-world applications.

EXERCISES

1. Name the two protocols that your View Controller must conform to when using the Table view in your view. Briefly describe their uses.

2. Which is the method to implement if you want to add an index in a Table view?

3. Name the three disclosure and checkmark images that you can use. Which one of them handles user taps?

▶ **WHAT YOU HAVE LEARNED IN THIS CHAPTER**

TOPIC	KEY CONCEPTS
Add items to a Table view	Handle the various events in the `UITableViewDataSource` protocol.
Allow users to select rows in a Table view	Handle the various events in the `UITableViewDelegate` protocol.
Add images to rows in a Table view	Use the image property of the `UITableViewCell` class and set it to an instance of the `UIImage` class containing an image.

Use a property list with a Table view	Use the following code snippet to locate the property list:
	
	`NSString *path = [[NSBundle mainBundle]`
	`pathForResource:@"Movies"`
	`ofType:@"plist"];`
	
	Then use a combination of `NSDictionary` and `NSArray` objects to retrieve the key/value pairs stored in the property list.

Group items in a Table view in sections	Implement the following methods: ➤ `numberOfSectionsInTableView:` ➤ `tableView:numberOfRowsInSection:` ➤ `tableView:titleForHeaderInSection:`
Add an index to a Table view	Implement the `sectionIndexTitlesForTableView:` method.
Add disclosure and checkmark images to a row in a Table view	Set the `accessoryType` property of an UITableViewCell object to one of the following: ➤ UITableViewCellAccessoryDetailDisclosureButton ➤ UITableViewCellAccessoryCheckmark ➤ UITableViewCellAccessoryDisclosureIndicator
Implement a search in a Table view	Use the Search Bar view and handle the various events in the `UISearchBarDelegate` protocol.

11

Application Preferences

WHAT YOU WILL LEARN IN THIS CHAPTER

➤ How to add application preferences to your application

➤ How to programmatically access the Settings values

➤ How to reset your application's preference settings

If you are a relatively seasoned Mac OS X user, you're likely familiar with the concept of application preferences. Almost every Mac OS X application has application-specific settings that are used for configuring the application's appearance and behavior. These settings are known as the *application preferences*.

In the iPhone OS, applications also have application preferences. In contrast to Mac OS X applications, however, whose application preferences are an integral part of the application, iPhone preferences are centrally managed by an application called Settings (see Figure 11-1).

FIGURE 11-1

The main page of the Settings application displays the preferences of system applications as well as third-party applications. Tapping any setting brings you to another page, where you can configure the preferences of an application.

In this chapter, you learn how to incorporate application preferences into your application and modify them programmatically during runtime.

CREATING APPLICATION PREFERENCES

Creating application preferences for your iPhone application is a pretty straightforward process. The process involves adding a resource called the Settings Bundle to your project, configuring a property list file, and then deploying your application. When your application is deployed, the application preferences are automatically created for you in the Settings application.

The following Try It Out shows how to add application preferences to your iPhone application project in Xcode.

TRY IT OUT Adding Application Preferences

1. Using Xcode, create a new Utility Application project and name it `ApplicationSettings`.

2. Right-click the project name in Xcode and add a new file. Select the Resources template category and click Settings Bundle (see Figure 11-2). Click Next.

FIGURE 11-2

3. When asked to name the file, use the default name of `Settings.bundle` and click Finish.

4. The `Settings.bundle` item should now be part of your project (see Figure 11-3). Click it and view the content of the `Root.plist` file using the default Property List editor.

FIGURE 11-3

5. Press Command-R to test the application on the iPhone Simulator. When the application is loaded on the Simulator, press the Home key to return to the main screen of the iPhone. Tap the Settings application. You can now see a new Settings entry named ApplicationSettings (see Figure 11-4).

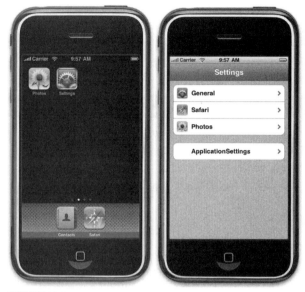

FIGURE 11-4

6. When you touch the `ApplicationSettings` entry, you see the default settings created for you (see Figure 11-5).

How It Works

It seems almost magical that without coding a single line, you have incorporated your application preferences into your application. The magic part is actually the `Settings.bundle` file that you have added to your project. It contains two files: `Root.plist` and `Root.strings`. The `Root.plist` file is an XML file that contains a collection of dictionary objects (key/value pairs). These key/value pairs are translated into the preferences entries you see in the Settings application.

FIGURE 11-5

> **NOTE** *Note that the key/value pair in the* `Root.plist` *file is case sensitive. Hence, you need to be careful when modifying the entries. A typo can result in a nonfunctional application.*

Take a moment to understand the use of the various keys used in the `Root.plist` file. There are two root-level keys in the `Root.plist` file, as follows:

➤ `StringsTable`, which contains the name of the strings file associated with this file. In this case, it is pointing to `Root.strings`.

➤ `PreferenceSpecifiers`, which is of type `Array` and contains an array of dictionaries, with each item containing the information for a single preference.

Each preference is represented by an item (known as `PreferenceSpecifiers`), such as `Item 1`, `Item 2`, `Item 3`, and so on. Each item has a `Type` key, which indicates the type of data stored. It can be one of the following, as shown in Table 11-1.

TABLE 11-1: List of Preference Specifiers and Usage

ELEMENT TYPE	DESCRIPTION
`PSTextFieldSpecifier`	A text field preference. Displays an optional title and an editable text field. Use this type for preferences that require the user to specify a custom string value.
`PSTitleValueSpecifier`	A read-only string preference. Use this type to display preference values as formatted strings.
`PSToggleSwitchSpecifier`	A toggle switch preference. Use this type to configure a preference that can have only one of two values.
`PSSliderSpecifier`	A slider preference. Use this type for a preference that represents a range of values. The value for this type is a real number whose minimum and maximum you specify.
`PSMultiValueSpecifier`	A multivalue preference. Use this type for a preference that supports a set of mutually exclusive values.
`PSGroupSpecifier`	A group item preference. The group type is a way for you to organize groups of preferences on a single page.
`PSChildPaneSpecifier`	A child pane preference. Use this type to link to a new page of preferences.

Each `PreferenceSpecifiers` key contains a list of subkeys that you can use. For example, for the `PSTextFieldSpecifier` key, you can use the following keys: `Type`, `Title`, `Key`, `DefaultValue`, `IsSecure`, `KeyBoardType`, `AutocapitalizationType`, and `AutocorrectionType`. You then set each key with its appropriate values.

> **NOTE** *For more information of the use of each key, refer to Apple's "Settings Application Schema Reference" documentation. The easiest way to locate it is to do a Web search for the title of this document. The URL for this document is:* `http://developer.apple.com/iPhone/library/documentation/PreferenceSettings/Conceptual/SettingsApplicationSchemaReference/Introduction/Introduction.html`.

Examine the `Root.plist` file in more detail. Take, for example, `Item 3`. Observe that it has four keys under it: `Type`, `Title`, `Key`, and `DefaultValue`. The `Type` key specifies the type of information it is going to store. In this case, it is a `PSToggleSwitchSpecifier`, which means it will be represented visually as an ON/OFF switch. The `Title` key specifies the text that will be shown for this item (Item 3). The `Key` key is the identifier that uniquely identifies this key so that you can programmatically retrieve the value of this item in your application. Finally, the `DefaultValue` key specifies the default value of this item. In this case, it is checked, indicating that the value is ON.

In the next Try It Out, you modify the `Root.plist` file so that you can use it to store some user's credentials. This is very useful in cases where you are writing an application that requires users to log in to a server. When the user uses your application for the first time, he will supply his login credentials, such as username and password. Your application can then store the credentials in the application preferences so that the next time the user uses your application, the application can automatically retrieve the credentials without asking the user to supply them.

TRY IT OUT Modifying the Application Preferences

1. Back in Xcode, select the `Root.plist` file and remove all four items under the `PreferenceSpecifiers` key. You do so by selecting individual items under the `PreferenceSpecifiers` key and then pressing the Delete key.

2. To add a new item under the `PreferenceSpecifiers` key, select the `PreferenceSpecifiers` key and press the Add Child button (see Figure 11-6).

 NOTE *The Add Child button looks basically like a square with three horizontal bars inside it.*

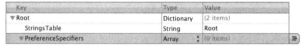

Key	Type	Value
▼ Root	Dictionary	(2 items)
StringsTable	String	Root
▼ PreferenceSpecifiers	Array	(0 items)

FIGURE 11-6

3. A new item is added for you. To add additional items, click the Add Child button (see Figure 11-7). Click the Add Sibling button three more times.

 NOTE *The Add Sibling button is the square with the plus (+) sign inside it.*

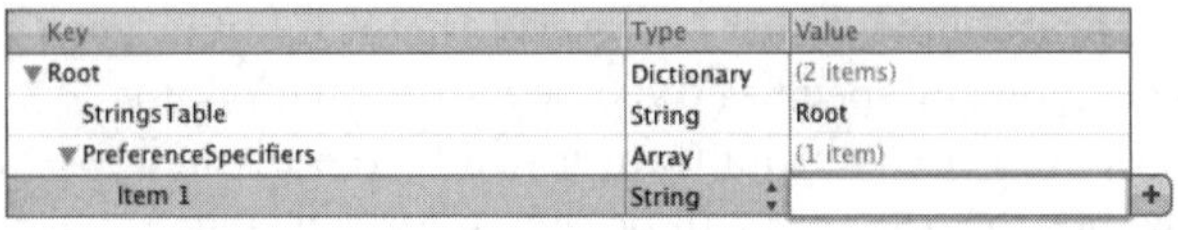

Key	Type	Value
▼ Root	Dictionary	(2 items)
StringsTable	String	Root
▼ PreferenceSpecifiers	Array	(1 item)
Item 1	String	

FIGURE 11-7

4. The `Root.plist` file should now look like Figure 11-8.

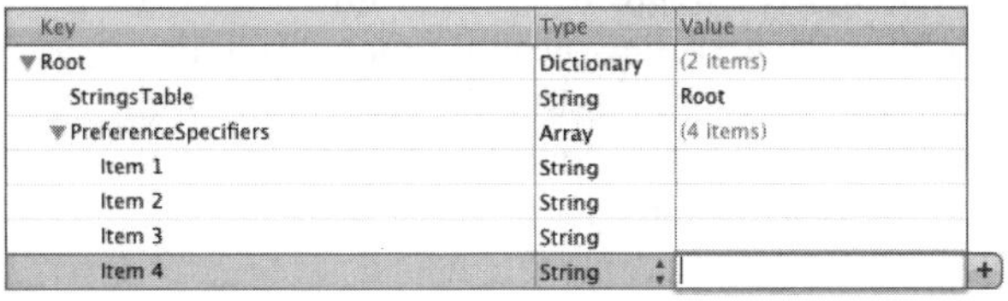

Key	Type	Value
▼ Root	Dictionary	(2 items)
StringsTable	String	Root
▼ PreferenceSpecifiers	Array	(4 items)
Item 1	String	
Item 2	String	
Item 3	String	
Item 4	String	

FIGURE 11-8

5. Change the Type of `Item 1` to Dictionary and expand it by clicking the arrow displayed to the left of it (see Figure 11-9). Press the Add Child button to add a child to `Item 1`.

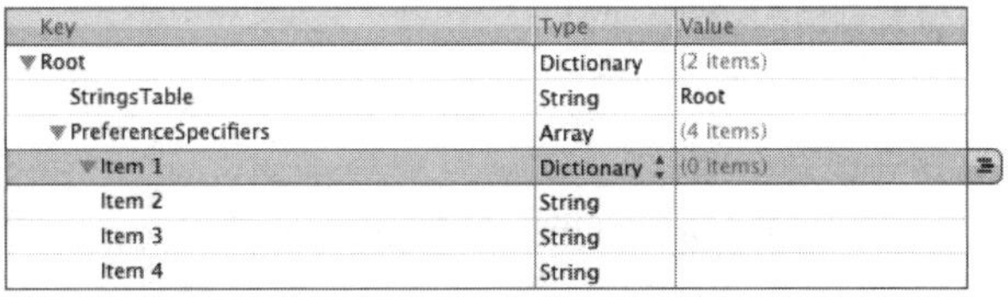

Key	Type	Value
▼ Root	Dictionary	(2 items)
StringsTable	String	Root
▼ PreferenceSpecifiers	Array	(4 items)
▼ Item 1	Dictionary	(0 items)
Item 2	String	
Item 3	String	
Item 4	String	

FIGURE 11-9

6. A new item is added under `Item 1` (see Figure 11-10). Click the Add Sibling button to add another item under `Item 1`.

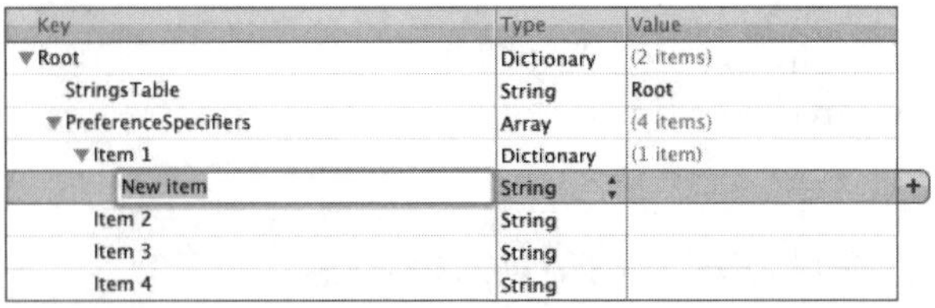

Key	Type	Value
▼ Root	Dictionary	(2 items)
StringsTable	String	Root
▼ PreferenceSpecifiers	Array	(4 items)
▼ Item 1	Dictionary	(1 item)
New item	String	
Item 2	String	
Item 3	String	
Item 4	String	

FIGURE 11-10

Remember, you use the Add Sibling button to add a new item within the same level. Use the Add Child button to add a new child item under the current level.

7. The `Root.plist` file should now look like Figure 11-11.

Key	Type	Value
▼ Root	Dictionary	(2 items)
StringsTable	String	Root
▼ PreferenceSpecifiers	Array	(4 items)
▼ Item 1	Dictionary	(2 items)
New item	String	
New item – 2	String	
Item 2	String	
Item 3	String	
Item 4	String	

FIGURE 11-11

8. Modify the entire `Root.plist` file so that it looks like Figure 11-12. Ensure that the capitalization of each key and value pairs is correct.

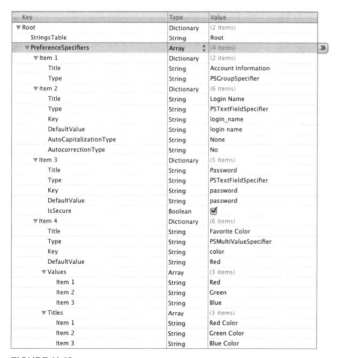

Key	Type	Value
▼ Root	Dictionary	(2 items)
StringsTable	String	Root
▼ PreferenceSpecifiers	Array	(4 items)
▼ Item 1	Dictionary	(2 items)
Title	String	Account Information
Type	String	PSGroupSpecifier
▼ Item 2	Dictionary	(6 items)
Title	String	Login Name
Type	String	PSTextFieldSpecifier
Key	String	login_name
DefaultValue	String	login name
AutoCapitalizationType	String	None
AutocorrectionType	String	No
▼ Item 3	Dictionary	(5 items)
Title	String	Password
Type	String	PSTextFieldSpecifier
Key	String	password
DefaultValue	String	password
IsSecure	Boolean	☑
▼ Item 4	Dictionary	(6 items)
Title	String	Favorite Color
Type	String	PSMultiValueSpecifier
Key	String	color
DefaultValue	String	Red
▼ Values	Array	(3 items)
Item 1	String	Red
Item 2	String	Green
Item 3	String	Blue
▼ Titles	Array	(3 items)
Item 1	String	Red Color
Item 2	String	Green Color
Item 3	String	Blue Color

FIGURE 11-12

NOTE *Pay particular attention to the* `Type` *of each item.*

9. Save the project and press Command-R to test the application on the iPhone Simulator. Press the Home button and launch the Settings application again. Select the `ApplicationSettings` settings and observe the preferences shown (see Figure 11-13).

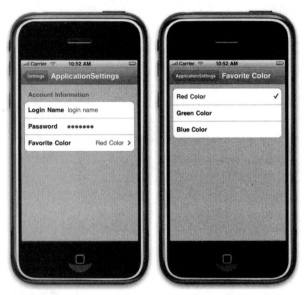

FIGURE 11-13

10. Make some changes to the settings values and then press the Home button to return to the Home screen. The changes in the settings are automatically saved to the phone. When you return to the Settings page again, the new values will be displayed.

How It Works

What you have done is basically modify the `Root.plist` file to store three preferences — Login Name, Password, and Favorite Color. For the password field, you use the `IsSecure` key to indicate that the value must be masked when displaying it to the user. Also of particular interest is the Favorite Color preference, for which you use the `Titles` and `Values` keys to display a list of selectable choices and their corresponding values to store on the phone.

In this example, you have used the following preference specifiers:

➤ PSGroupSpecifier – Used to display a group for the settings. In this case, all the settings are grouped under the Account Information group.

➤ PSTextFieldSpecifier – Specifies a text field.

➤ PSMultiValueSpecifier – Specifies a list of selectable values. The Titles item contains a list of visible text that users can select from. The Values item is the corresponding value for the text selected by the user. For example, if the user selects Blue Color as his favorite color, the value Blue will be stored on the iPhone.

PROGRAMMATICALLY ACCESSING THE SETTINGS VALUES

The preferences settings are of little use if you can't programmatically access them from within your application. In the following sections, you modify the application so that you can load the preferences settings as well as make changes to them programmatically.

First, use the following Try It Out to prepare the UI by connecting the necessary outlets and actions.

TRY IT OUT Preparing the Main and Flipside Views

1. Double-click the MainView.xib file to edit it in Interface Builder.

2. In the MainView.xib window, double-click the Main View item to display the Main View window (see Figure 11-14). Add a Button view to it and label it as Load Settings Values.

FIGURE 11-14

3. Double-click the `FlipsideView.xib` file to edit it in Interface Builder.

4. In the `FlipsideView.xib` window, double-click the Flipside View item and add the following views to the Flipside View window (see Figure 11-15):

➤ `Label`

➤ `TextField`

➤ `PickerView`

FIGURE 11-15

5. Back in Xcode, insert the following code that appears in bold into the `MainViewController.h` file:

```
#import "FlipsideViewController.h"

@interface MainViewController : UIViewController <FlipsideViewControllerDelegate> {
}

- (IBAction)loadSettings: (id) sender;
- (IBAction)showInfo;

@end
```

6. In the `FlipsideViewController.h` file, insert the following code that appears in bold:

```
@protocol FlipsideViewControllerDelegate;

@interface FlipsideViewController : UIViewController
    <UIPickerViewDataSource, UIPickerViewDelegate> {
    id <FlipsideViewControllerDelegate> delegate;

    IBOutlet UITextField *loginName;
    IBOutlet UITextField *password;
    IBOutlet UIPickerView *favoriteColor;

}
@property (nonatomic, retain) UITextField *loginName;
@property (nonatomic, retain) UITextField *password;
@property (nonatomic, retain) UIPickerView *favoriteColor;

@property (nonatomic, assign) id <FlipsideViewControllerDelegate> delegate;
- (IBAction)done;

@end

@protocol FlipsideViewControllerDelegate
- (void)flipsideViewControllerDidFinish:(FlipsideViewController *)controller;
@end
```

7. In the `FlipsideViewController.m` file, add the following statements:

```
#import "FlipsideViewController.h"

@implementation FlipsideViewController

@synthesize delegate;
@synthesize loginName;
@synthesize password;
@synthesize favoriteColor;
```

8. In Interface Builder, connect the outlets and action to the various views. In the `FlipsideView`
`.xib` window, do the following:

➤ Control-click and drag the File's Owner item to the first TextField view and select
`loginName`.

➤ Control-click and drag the File's Owner item to the second TextField view and select
`password`.

➤ Control-click and drag the File's Owner item to the Picker view and select `favoriteColor`.

➤ Control-click and drag the Picker view to the File's Owner item and select `dataSource`.

➤ Control-click and drag the Picker view to the File's Owner item and select `delegate`.

9. Right-click the File's Owner item to verify that all the connections are connected properly
(see Figure 11-16).

FIGURE 11-16

10. In the `MainView.xib` window, Control-click and drag the Button view to the File's Owner item and select `loadSettings:`.

11. Save the project in Interface Builder.

12. In Xcode, add the following code in bold to the `FlipsideViewController.m` file:

```
#import "FlipsideViewController.h"

@implementation FlipsideViewController

@synthesize delegate;
@synthesize loginName;
@synthesize password;
@synthesize favoriteColor;

NSMutableArray *colors;
NSString *favoriteColorSelected;

- (void)viewDidLoad {
    //---create an array containing the colors values---
    colors = [[NSMutableArray alloc] init];
    [colors addObject:@"Red"];
```

```
    [colors addObject:@"Green"];
    [colors addObject:@"Blue"];


    [super viewDidLoad];
    self.view.backgroundColor = [UIColor viewFlipsideBackgroundColor];
}

//---number of components in the Picker view---
- (NSInteger)numberOfComponentsInPickerView:(UIPickerView *)thePickerView {
    return 1;
}

//---number of items(rows) in the Picker view---
- (NSInteger)pickerView:(UIPickerView *)thePickerView
    numberOfRowsInComponent:(NSInteger)component {
    return [colors count];
}

//---populating the Picker view---
- (NSString *)pickerView:(UIPickerView *)thePickerView titleForRow:(NSInteger)row
    forComponent:(NSInteger)component {
    return [colors objectAtIndex:row];
}

//---the item selected by the user---
- (void)pickerView:(UIPickerView *)thePickerView didSelectRow:(NSInteger)row
    inComponent:(NSInteger)component {
    favoriteColorSelected = [colors objectAtIndex:row];
}

- (void)dealloc {
    [colors release];
    [favoriteColorSelected release];
    [loginName release];
    [password release];
    [favoriteColor release];
    [super dealloc];
}
```

13. That's it! Press Command-R to test the application on the iPhone Simulator. Figure 11-17 shows the UI of the application for the Main and Flipside views.

> **NOTE** Note that the compiler may generate a warning because you have not implemented the `loadSettings:` action in the `MainViewController.m` file yet. This is all right, as you just want to check out how the user interface looks.

FIGURE 11-17

How It Works

So far, all the work that has been done prepares the UI for displaying the values retrieved from the pref-erences settings. In particular, you need to prepare the Picker view to display a list of colors from which the user can choose. In the Flipside view, you make use of the Done button to save the values of the preferences settings. That is, your code for saving the preferences settings will be inserted into the done action (this will be done in the "Saving the Settings Values" section).

To load the Picker view with the three colors, you first need to ensure that the FlipsideViewController class conforms to the UIPickerViewDataSource and UIPickerViewDelegate protocols:

```
//---FlipsideViewController.h---
@protocol FlipsideViewControllerDelegate;

@interface FlipsideViewController : UIViewController
    <UIPickerViewDataSource, UIPickerViewDelegate> {
    id <FlipsideViewControllerDelegate> delegate;
```

The UIPickerViewDataSource protocol defines the methods to populate the Picker view with items while the UIPickerViewDelegate protocol defines methods to enable users to select an item from the Picker view.

In the `FlipsideViewController.m` file, you first create an `NSMutableArray` object to store the list of colors available for selection, in the `viewDidLoad` method:

```
- (void)viewDidLoad {
    //---create an array containing the colors values---
    colors = [[NSMutableArray alloc] init];
    [colors addObject:@"Red"];
    [colors addObject:@"Green"];
    [colors addObject:@"Blue"];
    [super viewDidLoad];
    self.view.backgroundColor = [UIColor viewFlipsideBackgroundColor];
}
```

To set the number of components (columns) in the Picker view, implement the `numberOfComponentsInPickerView:` method:

```
//---number of components in the Picker view---
- (NSInteger)numberOfComponentsInPickerView:(UIPickerView *)thePickerView {
    return 1;
}
```

To set the number of items (rows) you want to display in the Picker view, implement the `pickerView:numberOfRowsInComponent:` method:

```
//---number of items(rows) in the Picker view---
- (NSInteger)pickerView:(UIPickerView *)thePickerView
    numberOfRowsInComponent:(NSInteger)component {
    return [colors count];
}
```

To populate the Picker view with the three colors, implement the `pickerView:titleForRow:forComponent:` method:

```
//---populating the Picker view---
- (NSString *)pickerView:(UIPickerView *)thePickerView titleForRow:(NSInteger)row
    forComponent:(NSInteger)component {
    return [colors objectAtIndex:row];
}
```

To save the color selected by the user in the Picker view, implement the `pickerView:didSelectRow:inComponent:` method:

```
//---the item selected by the user---
- (void)pickerView:(UIPickerView *)thePickerView didSelectRow:(NSInteger)row
    inComponent:(NSInteger)component {
    favoriteColorSelected = [colors objectAtIndex:row];
}
```

The color selected will now be saved in the `favoriteColorSelected` object.

Loading the Settings Values

With the user interface of the application ready, it is now time to see how you can programmatically load the values of the preference settings and then display them in your application. This display is useful because it gives your user a chance to view the values of the settings without needing to go to the Settings application.

TRY IT OUT Loading Settings Values

1. Insert the following lines of code that appear in bold to the `MainViewController.m` file (make sure that the code line with password and favorite color markers is entered all on one line, unlike how it appears in the following code):

```
#import "MainViewController.h"
#import "MainView.h"

@implementation MainViewController

- (IBAction) loadSettings: (id) sender{

    NSUserDefaults *defaults = [NSUserDefaults standardUserDefaults];

    NSString *strLoginname = [defaults objectForKey:@"login_name"];
    NSString *strPassword = [defaults objectForKey:@"password"];
    NSString *strColor = [defaults objectForKey:@"color"];

    NSString *str = [[NSString alloc] initWithFormat:@"Login name is \"%@\",
password is \"%@\", and favorite color is \"%@\"",
                    strLoginname, strPassword, strColor];

    UIAlertView *alert = [[UIAlertView alloc]
                         initWithTitle:@"Settings Values"
                         message:str
                         delegate:nil
                         cancelButtonTitle: @"Done"
                         otherButtonTitles:nil];
    [alert show];

    [strLoginname release];
    [strPassword release];
    [strColor release];
    [str release];
    [alert release];
}
```

FIGURE 11-18

2. Press Command-R to test the application on the iPhone Simulator. When the application is loaded, tap on the Load Settings Values button and you should see the settings values displayed in an alert view (see Figure 11-18).

How It Works

To load the values of the preferences settings, you use a class known as the NSUserDefaults:

```
NSUserDefaults *defaults = [NSUserDefaults standardUserDefaults];
```

The preceding statement returns the one-and-only-one instance of the NSUserDefaults class. Think of NSUserDefaults as a common database that you can use to store your application preference settings.

To retrieve the values of the preference settings, you use the objectForKey: method and specify the name of the preference setting you want to retrieve:

```
NSString *strLoginname = [defaults objectForKey:@"login_name"];
NSString *strPassword = [defaults objectForKey:@"password"];
NSString *strColor = [defaults objectForKey:@"color"];
```

Resetting the Preference Settings Values

Sometimes you may want to reset the values of the preference settings of your application. This is especially true if you have made an error in the Root.plist file and want to reset all the settings. The easiest way to do this is to remove the application from the phone or Simulator. To do so, simply tap and hold the application's icon, and when the icons start to wriggle, tap the X button to remove the application. The preference settings associated with the application will also be removed.

Another way to clear the values of the preference settings would be to navigate to the folder containing your application (on the iPhone Simulator). The applications on the iPhone Simulator are stored in the following folder: ~/Library/Application Support/iPhone Simulator/User/ Applications/ (note that the tilde symbol (~) represents your home directory and not your root hard disk). Inside this folder, you need to find the folder containing your application. Within the application folder is a Library/Preferences folder. Delete the file ending with *application_name*.plist (see Figure 11-19) and your preferences settings will now be reset.

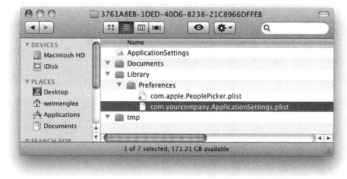

FIGURE 11-19

Saving the Settings Values

Now that you have seen how to load the values of preferences settings, use the following Try It Out to see how to save the values back to the preferences settings. This allows users to directly modify their preferences settings from within your application, instead of using the Settings application to do so.

TRY IT OUT Saving Settings Values

1. In the `FlipsideViewController.m` file, insert the following code that appears in bold:

```
#import "FlipsideViewController.h"

@implementation FlipsideViewController

@synthesize delegate;
@synthesize loginName;
@synthesize password;
@synthesize favoriteColor;

NSMutableArray *colors;
NSString *favoriteColorSelected;

- (void)viewDidLoad {
    colors = [[NSMutableArray alloc] init];
    [colors addObject:@"Red"];
    [colors addObject:@"Green"];
    [colors addObject:@"Blue"];


    NSUserDefaults *defaults = [NSUserDefaults standardUserDefaults];
    loginName.text = [defaults objectForKey:@"login_name"];
    password.text = [defaults objectForKey:@"password"];

    //---find the index of the array for the color saved---
    favoriteColorSelected = [[NSString alloc] initWithString:
                               [defaults objectForKey:@"color"]];
    int selIndex = [colors indexOfObject:favoriteColorSelected];

    //---display the saved color in the Picker view---
    [favoriteColor selectRow:selIndex inComponent:0 animated:YES];

    [super viewDidLoad];
    self.view.backgroundColor = [UIColor viewFlipsideBackgroundColor];
}

- (IBAction)done {

    NSUserDefaults *defaults = [NSUserDefaults standardUserDefaults];
    [defaults setObject:loginName.text forKey:@"login_name"];
```

```
[defaults setObject:password.text forKey:@"password"];
[defaults setObject:favoriteColorSelected forKey:@"color"];

[self.delegate flipsideViewControllerDidFinish:self];
}
```

2. Press Command-R to test the application on the iPhone Simulator. When the application is loaded, tap the i icon to switch to the Flipside view. Make some changes to the login name, password, and favorite color (see Figure 11-20). When you press Done, all the changes are made to the phone. When you return to the Main view, tapping the Load Settings Values button displays the updated settings values.

How It Works

You use the same approach to save the values back to the preferences settings as you do to retrieve those settings; that is, you use the NSUserDefaults class:

```
NSUserDefaults *defaults = [NSUserDefaults
standardUserDefaults];
[defaults setObject:loginName.text forKey:@"login_
name"];
[defaults setObject:password.text forKey:@"password"];
[defaults setObject:favoriteColorSelected forKey:@"color"];
```

FIGURE 11-20

Rather than use the objectForKey: method, you now use the setObject:forKey: method to save the values.

A particular challenge for the Flipside view is that the existing value for the favorite color must be displayed in a Picker view; therefore, during the viewDidLoad: method, you need to load the values of the preferences settings and then determine the index of the Picker view to display the correct color. You do this via the indexOfObject: method of the NSMutableArray class:

```
//---find the index of the array for the color saved---
favoriteColorSelected = [[NSString alloc] initWithString:
                        [defaults objectForKey:@"color"]];
int selIndex = [colors indexOfObject:favoriteColorSelected];

//---display the saved color in the Picker view---
[favoriteColor selectRow:selIndex inComponent:0 animated:YES];
```

SUMMARY

In this chapter, you have seen how you can make use of the Application Preferences feature of the iPhone to save your application's preferences to the Settings application. Doing so allows you to delegate most of the mundane tasks of saving and loading an application's preferences settings to the OS. All you need to do is to use the NSUserDefaults class to programmatically access the preferences settings.

EXERCISES

1. You have learned that you can use the NSUserDefaults class to access the preferences settings values for your application. What are the methods for retrieving and saving the values?

2. What are the two ways in which you can remove the preferences settings for an application?

3. What is the difference between the Add Child button and the Add Sibling button in the Property List editor?

► **WHAT YOU'VE LEARNED IN THIS CHAPTER**

TOPIC	KEY CONCEPTS
Adding application preferences to your application	Add a Settings Bundle file to your project and modify the `Root.plist` file.

Loading the value of a preference setting	`NSUserDefaults *defaults =`
	`    [NSUserDefaults standardUserDefaults];`
	`NSString *strLoginname =`
	`    [defaults objectForKey:@"login_name"];`

Resetting preference settings values	Either remove the entire application from the Home screen, or remove it via the iPhone Simulator folder on your Mac.

Saving the value of a preference setting	`NSUserDefaults *defaults =`
	`    [NSUserDefaults standardUserDefaults];`
	`[defaults setObject:loginName.text`
	`    forKey:@"login_name"];`

12

Database Storage Using SQLite3

WHAT YOU WILL LEARN IN THIS CHAPTER

➤ How to use the SQLite3 database in your Xcode project

➤ How to create and open a SQLite3 database

➤ How to use the various SQLite3 functions to execute SQL strings

➤ How to use bind variables to insert values into a SQL string

In the previous chapter, you learned about data persistence using files. For simple applications, you can write the data you want to persist to a simple text file. For more structured data, you can use a property list. For large and complex data, it is more efficient to store them using a database. The iPhone comes with the SQLite3 database library, which you can use to store your data. With your data stored in a database, your application can populate a Table view or store a large amount of data in a structured manner.

This chapter shows you how to use the embedded SQLite3 database in your applications.

USING SQLITE3

To use a SQLite3 database in your application, you first need to add the `libsqlite3.dylib` library to your Xcode project. Use the following Try It Out to find out how. You will need to download the code files indicated for this and the rest of the Try It Out features in this chapter.

TRY IT OUT **Preparing Your Project to Use SQLite3**

Codefile [Databases.zip] available for download at Wrox.com

1. Using Xcode, create a new View-based Application project and name it `Databases`.

2. Right-click the `Frameworks` folder in your project and choose Project ➪ Add to Project from the menu bar.

3. Navigate to `/Developer/Platforms/iPhoneSimulator.platform/Developer/SDKs/iPhoneSimulator<version>.sdk/usr/lib` and select the file named `libsqlite3.dylib`.

 NOTE *<version> represents the version of the iPhone SDK you are using. For example, if the version you are using is 3.1, the path is* `/Developer/Platforms/iPhoneSimulator.platform/Developer/SDKs/iPhoneSimulator3.1.sdk/usr/lib`.

4. When the Add dialog is displayed, deselect the Copy Items into Destination Group's Folder (If Needed) check box, and for the reference type, select Relative to Current SDK (see Figure 12-1).

5. In the `DatabasesViewController.h` file, declare a variable of type `sqlite3` as well as a method named `filePath` (see the code in bold):

```
#import <UIKit/UIKit.h>
#import "sqlite3.h"

@interface DatabasesViewController :
UIViewController {
    sqlite3 *db;
}

-(NSString *) filePath;

@end
```

FIGURE 12-1

6. In the `DatabasesViewController.m` file, define the `filePath` method as shown in bold:

```
#import "DatabasesViewController.h"

@implementation DatabasesViewController

-(NSString *) filePath {
    NSArray *paths = NSSearchPathForDirectoriesInDomains(
                      NSDocumentDirectory, NSUserDomainMask, YES);
    NSString *documentsDir = [paths objectAtIndex:0];
    return [documentsDir stringByAppendingPathComponent:@"database.sql"];
```

```
    }

    - (void)viewDidLoad {
        [super viewDidLoad];
    }

    @end
```

How It Works

To work with SQLite3, you need to link your application to a dynamic library called `libsqlite3.dylib`. The `libsqlite3.dylib` that you selected is an alias to the latest version of the SQLite3 library. On an actual iPhone device, the `libsqlite3.dylib` is located in the `/usr/lib/` directory.

To use a SQLite database, you need to create an object of type `sqlite3`:

```
        sqlite3 *db;
```

The `filePath` method returns the full path to the SQLite database that will be created in the `Documents` directory on your iPhone (within your application's sandbox):

```
    -(NSString *) filePath {
        NSArray *paths = NSSearchPathForDirectoriesInDomains(
                        NSDocumentDirectory, NSUserDomainMask, YES);
        NSString *documentsDir = [paths objectAtIndex:0];
        return [documentsDir stringByAppendingPathComponent:@"database.sql"];
    }
```

 NOTE *Chapter 13 discusses the various folders that you can access within your application's sandbox.*

CREATING AND OPENING A DATABASE

After the necessary library is added to the project, you can open a database for usage. You will use the various C functions included with SQLite3 to create or open a database, as demonstrated in the following Try It Out.

TRY IT OUT   Opening a Database

1. Using the same project created previously, define the `openDB` method in the `DatabasesViewController.m` file:

```
#import "DatabasesViewController.h"

@implementation DatabasesViewController

-(NSString *) filePath {
    //...
}
```

```
-(void) openDB {
    //---create database---
    if (sqlite3_open([[self filePath] UTF8String], &db) != SQLITE_OK )
    {
        sqlite3_close(db);
        NSAssert(0, @"Database failed to open.");
    }
}

- (void)viewDidLoad {
    [self openDB];
    [super viewDidLoad];
}

@end
```

How It Works

The `sqlite3_open()` C function opens an SQLite database whose filename is specified as the first argument:

```
[[self filePath] UTF8String]
```

In this case, the filename of the database is specified as a C string using the `UTF8String` method of the `NSString` class because the `sqlite3_open()` C function does not understand an `NSString` object.

The second argument contains a handle to the `sqlite3` object, which in this case is `db`.

If the database is available, it opens the database. If the specified database is not found, a new database is created. If the database is successfully opened, the function will return a value of `0` (represented using the `SQLITE_OK` constant).

The following list from `http://www.sqlite.org/c3ref/c_abort.html` shows the result codes returned by the various SQLite functions:

```
#define SQLITE_OK           0    /* Successful result */
#define SQLITE_ERROR        1    /* SQL error or missing database */
#define SQLITE_INTERNAL     2    /* Internal logic error in SQLite */
#define SQLITE_PERM         3    /* Access permission denied */
#define SQLITE_ABORT        4    /* Callback routine requested an abort */
#define SQLITE_BUSY         5    /* The database file is locked */
#define SQLITE_LOCKED       6    /* A table in the database is locked */
#define SQLITE_NOMEM        7    /* A malloc() failed */
#define SQLITE_READONLY     8    /* Attempt to write a readonly database */
#define SQLITE_INTERRUPT    9    /* Operation terminated by sqlite3_interrupt()*/
#define SQLITE_IOERR        10   /* Some kind of disk I/O error occurred */
#define SQLITE_CORRUPT      11   /* The database disk image is malformed */
#define SQLITE_NOTFOUND     12   /* NOT USED. Table or record not found */
#define SQLITE_FULL         13   /* Insertion failed because database is full */
#define SQLITE_CANTOPEN     14   /* Unable to open the database file */
#define SQLITE_PROTOCOL     15   /* NOT USED. Database lock protocol error */
#define SQLITE_EMPTY        16   /* Database is empty */
#define SQLITE_SCHEMA       17   /* The database schema changed */
#define SQLITE_TOOBIG       18   /* String or BLOB exceeds size limit */
#define SQLITE_CONSTRAINT   19   /* Abort due to constraint violation */
#define SQLITE_MISMATCH     20   /* Data type mismatch */
```

```
#define SQLITE_MISUSE      21   /* Library used incorrectly */
#define SQLITE_NOLFS       22   /* Uses OS features not supported on host */
#define SQLITE_AUTH        23   /* Authorization denied */
#define SQLITE_FORMAT      24   /* Auxiliary database format error */
#define SQLITE_RANGE       25   /* 2nd parameter to sqlite3_bind out of range */
#define SQLITE_NOTADB      26   /* File opened that is not a database file */
#define SQLITE_ROW        100   /* sqlite3_step() has another row ready */
#define SQLITE_DONE       101   /* sqlite3_step() has finished executing */
```

Examining the Database Created

If the database is created successfully, it can be found in the `Documents` folder of your application's sandbox. As discussed in Chapter 13, you can locate the `Documents` folder of your application on the iPhone Simulator in the `~/Library/Application Support/iPhone Simulator/User/Applications/<App_ID>/Documents/` folder. Figure 12-2 shows the `database .sql` file.

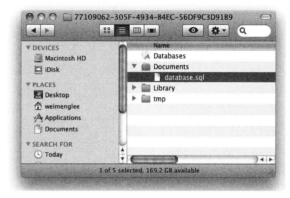

FIGURE 12-2

Creating a Table

After the database is created, you can create a table to store some data. In the following Try It Out, you learn how to create a table with two text fields. For illustration purposes, create a table named `Contacts`, with two fields called `email` and `name`.

TRY IT OUT Creating a Table

This is a one-step process. Using the same project as that used earlier in the chapter, define the `createTableNamed:withField1:withField2:` method as follows:

```
#import "DatabasesViewController.h"

@implementation DatabasesViewController

-(NSString *) filePath {
    //...
}

-(void) openDB {
    //...
}

-(void) createTableNamed:(NSString *) tableName
withField1:(NSString *) field1
```

```
withField2:(NSString *) field2 {

    char *err;
    NSString *sql = [NSString stringWithFormat:
        @"CREATE TABLE IF NOT EXISTS '%@' ('%@' TEXT PRIMARY KEY, '%@' TEXT);",
        tableName, field1, field2];

    if (sqlite3_exec(db, [sql UTF8String], NULL, NULL, &err) != SQLITE_OK) {
        sqlite3_close(db);
        NSAssert(0, @"Tabled failed to create.");
    }

}

- (void)viewDidLoad {
    [self openDB];
    [self createTableNamed:@"Contacts" withField1:@"email" withField2:@"name"];
    [super viewDidLoad];
}

@end
```

How It Works

The `createTableNamed:withField1:withField2:` method takes in three parameters: `tableName`, `field1`, and `field2`.

Using these three parameters, you first formulate a SQL string and then create a table using the `sqlite3_exec()` C function, with the important arguments to this function being the `sqlite3` object, the SQL query string, and a pointer to a variable for error messages. If an error occurs in creating the database, you will use the `NSAssert` method to halt the application and close the database connection.

Figure 12-3 shows the `Contacts` table that is created if the operation is successful.

email	name

FIGURE 12-3

 NOTE *For a jumpstart in the SQL language, check out the SQL tutorial at:* `http://w3schools.com/sql/default.asp.`

Inserting Records

After the table is created, you can insert some records into it. The following Try It Out shows you how to write two rows of records into the table created in the previous section.

TRY IT OUT Inserting Records

1. Still using the same project as before, define the `insertRecordIntoTableNamed:withField1:field1Value:andField2:field2Value:` method as follows and modify the `viewDidLoad` method as shown in bold:

```objc
#import "DatabasesViewController.h"

@implementation DatabasesViewController

-(NSString *) filePath {
    //...
}

-(void) openDB {
    //...
}

-(void) createTableNamed:(NSString *) tableName
withField1:(NSString *) field1
withField2:(NSString *) field2 {

    //...
}

-(void) insertRecordIntoTableNamed: (NSString *) tableName
withField1: (NSString *) field1 field1Value: (NSString *) field1Value
andField2: (NSString *) field2 field2Value: (NSString *) field2Value {

    NSString *sql = [NSString stringWithFormat:
        @"INSERT OR REPLACE INTO '%@' ('%@', '%@') VALUES ('%@','%@')",
        tableName, field1, field2, field1Value, field2Value];

    char *err;
    if (sqlite3_exec(db, [sql UTF8String], NULL, NULL, &err) != SQLITE_OK)
    {
        sqlite3_close(db);
        NSAssert(0, @"Error updating table.");
    }

}

- (void)viewDidLoad {
    [self openDB];
    [self createTableNamed:@"Contacts" withField1:@"email" withField2:@"name"];

    for (int i=0; i<=2; i++)
```

```
        {
            NSString *email = [[NSString alloc] initWithFormat:
                                    @"user%d@learn2develop.net",i];
            NSString *name = [[NSString alloc] initWithFormat: @"user %d",i];
            [self insertRecordIntoTableNamed:@"Contacts"
                withField1:@"email" field1Value:email
                andField2:@"name" field2Value:name];
        }
        [super viewDidLoad];
    }

@end
```

How It Works

The code in this example is similar to that of the previous one; you formulate a SQL string and use the `sqlite3_exec()` C function to insert a record into the database:

```
NSString *sql = [NSString stringWithFormat:
    @"INSERT OR REPLACE INTO '%@' ('%@', '%@') VALUES ('%@','%@')",
    tableName, field1, field2, field1Value, field2Value];

char *err;
if (sqlite3_exec(db, [sql UTF8String], NULL, NULL, &err) != SQLITE_OK)
{
    sqlite3_close(db);
    NSAssert(0, @"Error updating table.");
}
```

In the `viewDidLoad` method, you insert two records into the database by calling the `insertRecordIntoTableNamed:withField1:field1Value:andField2:field2Value:` method:

```
for (int i=0; i<=2; i++)
{
    NSString *email = [[NSString alloc] initWithFormat:
                            @"user%d@learn2develop.net",i];
    NSString *name = [[NSString alloc] initWithFormat: @"user %d",i];

    [self insertRecordIntoTableNamed:@"Contacts"
        withField1:@"email" field1Value:email
        andField2:@"name" field2Value:name];
}
```

Figure 12-4 shows the content of the table after the rows are inserted into the table.

email	name
user0@learn2develop.net	user 0
user1@learn2develop.net	user 1

FIGURE 12-4

Bind Variables

One of the common tasks involved in formulating SQL strings is the need to insert values into the query string and making sure that the string is well formulated and that it does not contain invalid characters. Earlier in the Inserting Records section, you saw that to insert a row into the database, you had to formulate your SQL statement like this:

```
NSString *sql = [NSString stringWithFormat:
    @"INSERT OR REPLACE INTO '%@' ('%@', '%@') VALUES ('%@','%@')",
    tableName, field1, field2, field1Value, field2Value];

char *err;
if (sqlite3_exec(db, [sql UTF8String], NULL, NULL, &err) != SQLITE_OK)
{
    sqlite3_close(db);
    NSAssert(0, @"Error updating table.");
}
```

SQLite supports a feature known as *bind variables* to help you formulate your SQL string. For example, the preceding SQL string can be formulated as follows using bind variables:

```
NSString *sqlStr = [NSString stringWithFormat:
    @"INSERT OR REPLACE INTO '%@' ('%@', '%@') VALUES (?,?)",
    tableName, field1, field2];

const char *sql = [sqlStr UTF8String];
```

Here, the ? is a placeholder for you to replace with the actual value of the query. In the preceding statement, assuming that `tableName` is `Contacts`, `field1` is `email`, and `field2` is `name`, the `sql` is now:

```
INSERT OR REPLACE INTO Contacts ('email', 'name') VALUES (?,?)
```

 NOTE *Note that the* ? *can be inserted only into the* VALUES *and* WHERE *section of the SQL statement; you cannot insert it into a table name, for example. The following statement would be invalid:* INSERT OR REPLACE INTO ? ('email', 'name') VALUES (?,?).

To substitute the values for the `?`, you need to create a `sqlite3_stmt` object and use the `sqlite3_prepare_v2()` function to compile the SQL string into a binary form and then insert the placeholder values using the `sqlite3_bind_text()` function, like this:

```
sqlite3_stmt *statement;

if (sqlite3_prepare_v2(db, sql, -1, &statement, nil) == SQLITE_OK) {
    sqlite3_bind_text(statement, 1, [field1Value UTF8String], -1, NULL);
    sqlite3_bind_text(statement, 2, [field2Value UTF8String], -1, NULL);
}
```

> **NOTE** *To bind integer values, use the* `sqlite3_bind_int()` *function.*

After the preceding call, the SQL string looks like this:

```
INSERT OR REPLACE INTO Contacts ('email', 'name') VALUES
    ('user0@learn2develop.net', 'user0')
```

To execute the SQL statement, you use the `sqlite3_step()` function, followed by the `sqlite3_finalize()` function to delete the prepared SQL statement:

```
if (sqlite3_step(statement) != SQLITE_DONE)
    NSAssert(0, @"Error updating table.");

sqlite3_finalize(statement);
```

> **NOTE** *Note that in the previous section, you used the* `sqlite3_exec()` *function to execute SQL statements. In this example, you actually use a combination of* `sqlite3_prepare()`, `sqlite3_step()`, *and* `sqlite3_finalize()` *functions to do the same thing. In fact, the* `sqlite3_exec()` *function is actually a wrapper for these three functions. For nonquery SQL statements (such as for creating tables, inserting rows, and so on), it is always better to use the* `sqlite3_exec()` *function.*

Retrieving Records

Now that the records have been successfully inserted into the table, it is time to get them out. This is a good way to ensure that they really have been saved. The following Try It Out shows you how to retrieve your records.

TRY IT OUT Retrieving the Records

1. Using the same project as you've been using in this chapter, define the `getAllRowsFromTableNamed:` method as follows and modify the `viewDidLoad` method as shown in bold:

```
#import "DatabasesViewController.h"

@implementation DatabasesViewController

-(NSString *) filePath {
    //...
}

-(void) openDB {
    //...
}

-(void) createTableNamed:(NSString *) tableName
```

```
withField1:(NSString *) field1
withField2:(NSString *) field2 {
    //...
}

-(void) insertRecordIntoTableNamed: (NSString *) tableName
withField1: (NSString *) field1 field1Value: (NSString *) field1Value
andField2:(NSString *) field2  field2Value: (NSString *) field2Value {
    //...
}

-(void) getAllRowsFromTableNamed: (NSString *) tableName {
    //---retrieve rows---
    NSString *qsql = @"SELECT * FROM CONTACTS";
    sqlite3_stmt *statement;

if (sqlite3_prepare_v2( db, [qsql UTF8String], -1, &statement, nil) ==
    SQLITE_OK) {

        while (sqlite3_step(statement) == SQLITE_ROW)
        {
            char *field1 = (char *) sqlite3_column_text(statement, 0);
            NSString *field1Str = [[NSString alloc] initWithUTF8String: field1];

            char *field2 = (char *) sqlite3_column_text(statement, 1);
            NSString *field2Str = [[NSString    alloc] initWithUTF8String: field2];

            NSString *str = [[NSString alloc] initWithFormat:@"%@ - %@",
                                field1Str, field2Str];
            NSLog(str);

            [field1Str release];
            [field2Str release];
            [str release];
        }
        //---deletes the compiled statement from memory---
        sqlite3_finalize(statement);
    }

}

- (void)viewDidLoad {
    [self openDB];
    [self createTableNamed:@"Contacts" withField1:@"email" withField2:@"name"];

    for (int i=0; i<=2; i++)
    {
        NSString *email = [[NSString alloc] initWithFormat:
                            @"user%d@learn2develop.net",i];
        NSString *name = [[NSString alloc] initWithFormat: @"user %d",i];

        [self insertRecordIntoTableNamed:@"Contacts"
            withField1:@"email" field1Value:email
```

```
                    andField2:@"name" field2Value:name];
        }

    [self getAllRowsFromTableNamed:@"Contacts"];
    sqlite3_close(db);
    [super viewDidLoad];
    }

@end
```

2. Press Command-R to test the application. In Xcode, press Command-Shift-R to display the Debugger Console window. When the application has loaded, you should see the records displayed in the Debugger Console (see Figure 12-5), proving to you that the rows are indeed in the table.

FIGURE 12-5

How It Works

To retrieve the records from the table, you first prepare the SQL statement and then use the `sqlite3_step()` function to execute the prepared statement. The `sqlite3_step()` function returns a value of 100 (represented by the `SQLITE_ROW` constant) if another row is ready. In this case, you call the `sqlite3_step()` function using a `while` loop, continuing as long as it returns a `SQLITE_ROW`:

```
if (sqlite3_prepare_v2( db, [qsql UTF8String], -1, &statement, nil) ==
    SQLITE_OK) {

        while (sqlite3_step(statement) == SQLITE_ROW)
        {
            char *field1 = (char *) sqlite3_column_text(statement, 0);
            NSString *field1Str = [[NSString alloc] initWithUTF8String: field1];

            char *field2 = (char *) sqlite3_column_text(statement, 1);
```

```
          NSString *field2Str = [[NSString   alloc] initWithUTF8String: field2];

          NSString *str = [[NSString alloc] initWithFormat:@"%@ - %@",
                          field1Str, field2Str];
          NSLog(str);

          [field1Str release];
          [field2Str release];
          [str release];
      }
      //---deletes the compiled statement from memory---
      sqlite3_finalize(statement);
  }
```

To retrieve the value for the first field in the row, you use the `sqlite3_column_text()` function by passing it the `sqlite3_stmt` object as well as the index of the field you are retrieving. For example, to retrieve the first field of the returned row, you use:

```
          char *field1 = (char *) sqlite3_column_text(statement, 0);
```

To retrieve an integer column (field), use the `sqlite3_column_int()` function.

SUMMARY

This chapter provides a whirlwind introduction to the SQLite3 database used in the iPhone. With SQLite3, you can now store all your structured data in an efficient manner and perform complex aggregations on your data.

EXERCISES

1. Explain the difference between the `sqlite3_exec()` function and the other three functions: `sqlite3_prepare()`, `sqlite3_step()`, and `sqlite3_finalize()`.

2. How do you obtain a C-style string from an `NSString` object?

3. Write the code segment to retrieve a set of rows from a table.

▶ **WHAT YOU HAVE LEARNED IN THIS CHAPTER**

TOPIC	KEY CONCEPTS
Use a SQLite3 database in your application	Need to add a reference to the `libsqlite3.dylib` to your project.
Obtain a C string from a `NSString` object	Use the `UTF8String` method of the `NSString` class.
Create and open a SQLite3 database	Use the `sqlite3_open()` C function.
Execute a SQL query	Use the `sqlite3_exec()` C function.
Close a database connection	Use the `sqlite3_close()` C function.
Use bind variables	Create a `sqlite3_stmt` object. Use the `sqlite3_prepare_v2()` C function to prepare the statement. Use the `sqlite3_bind_text()` (or `sqlite3_bind_int()`, and so on) C function to insert the values into the statement. Use the `sqlite3_step()` C function to execute the statement. Use the `sqlite3_finalize()` C function to delete the statement from memory.
Retrieve records	Use the `sqlite3_step()` C function to retrieve each individual row.
Retrieve columns from a row	Use the `sqlite3_column_text()` (or `sqlite3_column_int()`, and so on) C function.

13

File Handling

WHAT YOU WILL LEARN IN THIS CHAPTER

- ➤ Where your applications are stored on the iPhone
- ➤ The various folders within your `Applications` folder
- ➤ How to read and write to files in the `Documents` and `tmp` folders
- ➤ How to use a property to store structured data
- ➤ How to programmatically retrieve values stored in a property list
- ➤ How to modify the values retrieved from a property list and save the changes to a file

All the applications you have developed up to this point are pretty straightforward — the application starts, performs something interesting, and ends. In Chapter 11, you saw how you can make use of the application settings feature to save the preferences of your application to a central location managed by the Settings application. Sometimes, however, you simply need to save some data to your application's folder for use later. For example, rather than keep files you download from a remote server in memory, a better (and more effective and memory efficient) method might be to save them in a file so that you can use them later (maybe even after the application has shut down and restarted).

In this chapter, you learn more about how you can persist data in your application so that you can use it later, even after the application has restarted. You learn the two available approaches: saving the data as files and as a property list.

UNDERSTANDING THE APPLICATION FOLDERS

So far, you have been busy deploying your applications onto the iPhone Simulator and have not spent much time exploring where the applications get stored in the iPhone file system. This section helps you understand the folder structure of the iPhone.

On the desktop, the content of the iPhone Simulator is stored in the `~/Library/Application Support/iPhone Simulator/User/` folder.

 NOTE *The ~ (tilde) represents the current user's directory. Specifically, the preceding directory is equivalent to:*

`/Users/<username>/Library/Application Support/iPhone Simulator/User/.`

Within this folder are five Subfolders:

➤   `Applications`

➤   `Library`

➤   `Media`

➤   `Root`

➤   `tmp`

The `Applications` folder is the folder that contains all your installed applications (see Figure 13-1). Within the `Applications` folder are several folders with long filenames. These filenames are generated by Xcode to uniquely identify each of your applications. Within each application's folder, you can find your application's executable file (the `.app` file, which includes all embedded resources), together with a few other folders, such as `Documents`, `Library`, and `tmp`. On the iPhone, all applications run within their own sandboxed environment — that is, an application can access only the files stored within its own folder; it cannot access the folders of other applications.

FIGURE 13-1

Using the Documents and Library Folders

The Documents folder is where you can store files used by your application, whereas the Library folder stores the application-specific settings. The tmp folder stores temporary data required by your application.

So how you do write to these folders? See the following Try It Out for an example of doing just that. You need to download the indicated code files to work through the project.

TRY IT OUT **Writing and Reading from Files**

[FilesHandling.zip] available for download at Wrox.com

1. Using Xcode, create a new View-based Application project and name it FilesHandling.

2. In the FilesHandlingViewController.h file, add in the following statements that appear in bold:

```
#import <UIKit/UIKit.h>

@interface FilesHandlingViewController : UIViewController {

}


-(NSString *) documentsPath;
-(NSString *) readFromFile:(NSString *) filePath;
-(void) writeToFile:(NSString *) text withFileName:(NSString *) filePath;

@end
```

3. In the FilesHandlingViewController.m file, add in the following statements that appear in bold:

```
#import "FilesHandlingViewController.h"

@implementation FilesHandlingViewController

//---finds the path to the application's Documents directory---
-(NSString *) documentsPath {

    NSArray *paths = NSSearchPathForDirectoriesInDomains(
                        NSDocumentDirectory, NSUserDomainMask, YES);

    NSString *documentsDir = [paths objectAtIndex:0];
    return documentsDir;
```

```
    }

    //---read content from a specified file path---
    -(NSString *) readFromFile:(NSString *) filePath {

        //---check if file exists---
        if ([[NSFileManager defaultManager] fileExistsAtPath:filePath])
        {
            NSArray *array = [[NSArray alloc] initWithContentsOfFile: filePath];
            NSString *data = [[NSString alloc] initWithFormat:@"%@",
                                    [array objectAtIndex:0]];
            [array release];
            return data;
        }
        else
            return nil;

    }


    //---write content into a specified file path---
    -(void) writeToFile:(NSString *) text withFileName:(NSString *) filePath {

        NSMutableArray *array = [[NSMutableArray alloc] init];
        [array addObject:text];
        [array writeToFile:filePath atomically:YES];
        [array release];
    }

    // Implement viewDidLoad to do additional setup after loading the view,
    // typically from a nib.
    - (void)viewDidLoad {
        //---formulate filename---
        NSString *fileName = [[self documentsPath]
                                stringByAppendingPathComponent:@"data.txt"];

        //---write something to the file---
        [self writeToFile:@"a string of text" withFileName:fileName];

        //---read it back---
        NSString *fileContent = [self readFromFile:fileName];

        //---display the content read in the Debugger Console window---
        NSLog(fileContent);

        [super viewDidLoad];
    }
```

4. Press Command-R to test the application on the iPhone Simulator.

5. If you go to Finder and navigate to the Documents folder of your application, you see that the data.txt file is now visible (see Figure 13-2).

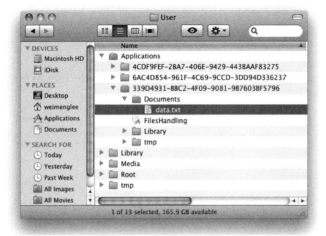

FIGURE 13-2

6. If you deploy the application to a real device, the location of the file is `/private/var/mobile/`
`Applications/<application_id>/Documents/data.txt`.

7. If you double-click the `data.txt` file, you see its content as follows:

```
<?xml version="1.0" encoding="UTF-8"?>
<!DOCTYPE plist PUBLIC "-//Apple//DTD PLIST 1.0//EN"
     "http://www.apple.com/DTDs/PropertyList-1.0.dtd">
<plist version="1.0">
<array>
    <string>a string of text</string>
</array>
</plist>
```

8. If you turn on the Debugger Console window (Shift-Command-R), you see the application print
the string `"a string of text"`.

How It Works

You first define the `documentsPath` method, which returns the path to the `Documents` directory:

```
//---finds the path to the application's Documents directory---
-(NSString *) documentsPath {
    NSArray *paths = NSSearchPathForDirectoriesInDomains(
                   NSDocumentDirectory, NSUserDomainMask, YES);

    NSString *documentsDir = [paths objectAtIndex:0];
    return documentsDir;
}
```

Basically, you use the `NSSearchPathForDirectoriesInDomains()` function to create a list of
directory search paths, indicating that you want to look for the `Documents` directory (using the
`NSDocumentDirectory` constant). The `NSUserDomainMask` constant indicates that you want to search

from the application's home directory, and the YES argument indicates that you want to obtain the full path of all the directories found.

To obtain the path to the Documents folder, simply extract the first item of the paths array (because there is one and only one Documents folder in an iPhone application's folder). In fact, this block of code is derived from the Mac OS X API, where multiple folders might be returned. But in the case of the iPhone, there can only be one Documents folder per application.

You next define the writeToFile:withFileName: method, which creates an NSMutableArray and adds the text to be written to file to it.

```
//---write content into a specified file path---
-(void) writeToFile:(NSString *) text withFileName:(NSString *) filePath {
    NSMutableArray *array = [[NSMutableArray alloc] init];
    [array addObject:text];
    [array writeToFile:filePath atomically:YES];
    [array release];
}
```

To persist the content (a process known as serialization) of the NSMutableArray to a file, you use its writeToFile:atomically: method. The atomically: parameter indicates that the file should first be written to a temporary file before it is renamed to the file name specified. This approach guarantees that the file will never be corrupted, even if the system crashes during the writing process.

To read the content from a file, you define the readFromFile: method:

```
//---read content from a specified file path---
-(NSString *) readFromFile:(NSString *) filePath {
    //---check if file exists---
    if ([[NSFileManager defaultManager] fileExistsAtPath:filePath])
    {
        NSArray *array = [[NSArray alloc] initWithContentsOfFile: filePath];
        NSString *data = [[NSString alloc] initWithFormat:@"%@",
                              [array objectAtIndex:0]];
        [array release];
        return data;
    }
    else
        return nil;
}
```

You first use an instance of the NSFileManager class to check to see whether the specified file exists. If it does, you read the content of the file into an NSArray object. In this case, because you know that the file contains a single line of text, you extract the first element in the array.

With all the methods in place, you are ready to make use of them. When the view is loaded, you first create the pathname for a file that you want to save. You then write a string of text into the file and immediately read it back and print it in the Debugger Console window:

```
- (void)viewDidLoad {
    //---filename---
    NSString *fileName = [[self documentsPath]
                    stringByAppendingPathComponent:@"data.txt"];
```

```
    //---write something to the file---
    [self writeToFile:@"a string of text" withFileName:fileName];

    //---read it back---
    NSString *fileContent = [self readFromFile:fileName];

    //---display the content read in the Debugger Console window---
    NSLog(fileContent);

    [super viewDidLoad];
}
```

Storing Files in the Temporary Folder

In addition to storing files in the `Documents` directory, you can store temporary files in the `tmp` folder. Files stored in the `tmp` folder are not backed up by iTunes, so you need to find a permanent place for the files you want to be sure to keep. To get the path to the `tmp` folder, you can call the `NSTemporaryDirectory()` function, like this:

```
-(NSString *) tempPath{
    return NSTemporaryDirectory();
}
```

On a real device, the path returned for the `tmp` folder would be: `/private/var/mobile/ Applications/<application_id>/tmp/`.

However, on the iPhone Simulator, the path returned is actually `/var/folders/<application_ id>/-Tmp-/data.txt`, not `~/Library/Application Support/iPhone Simulator/User/ Applications/<application_id>/tmp/`.

The following statement returns the path of a file to be stored in the `tmp` folder:

```
NSString *fileName = [[self tempPath]
    stringByAppendingPathComponent:@"data.txt"];
```

USING PROPERTY LISTS

In iPhone programming, you can use property lists to store structured data using key/value pairs. Property lists are stored as XML files and are highly transportable across file systems and networks. For example, you might want to store a list of AppStore applications titles in your application. Because applications in the AppStore are organized into category, it would be natural to store this information using a property list employing the structure shown in Figure 13-3.

Category	Titles
Games	"Animal Park", "Biology Quiz", "Calculus Test"
Entertainment	"Eye Balls — iBlower", "iBell", "iCards Birthday"
Utilities	"Battery Monitor", "iSystemInfo"

FIGURE 13-3

In Xcode, you can create and add a property list in the Resources folder of your application and populate it with items using the built-in Property List Editor. When the application is deployed, the property list is deployed together with the application. Programmatically, you can retrieve the values stored in a property list using the NSDictionary class. More important, if you need to make changes to a property list, you can write the changes to a file so that subsequently you can refer to the file directly instead of the property list.

In the following Try It Out, you will create a property list and populate it with some values. You will then read the values from the property list during runtime, make some changes, and then save the modified values to another property list file.

 NOTE *If you want to store application-specific settings that the user can modify outside your application, you should consider using the* NSUserDefaults *class to store the settings in the Settings application. Application Settings are discussed in Chapter 11.*

TRY IT OUT Creating and Modifying a Property List

1. Using the same project created earlier, right-click the project name in Xcode and choose Add ⇨ New File.

2. Select the Other item on the left of the New File dialog and select the Property List template on the right of the dialog (see Figure 13-4).

FIGURE 13-4

3. Name the property list as `Apps.plist`.

4. Populate the `Apps.plist` as shown in Figure 13-5.

FIGURE 13-5

In the `viewDidLoad` method, add the following statements that appear in bold:

```
- (void)viewDidLoad {
    //---filename---
    NSString *fileName = [[self documentsPath]
                            stringByAppendingPathComponent:@"data.txt"];

    //---write something to the file---
    [self writeToFile:@"a string of text" withFileName:fileName];

    //---read it back---
    NSString *fileContent = [self readFromFile:fileName];

    //---display the content read in the Debugger Console window---
    NSLog(fileContent);

    //---get the path to the property list file---
    NSString *plistFileName = [[self documentsPath]
    stringByAppendingPathComponent:@"Apps.plist"];
```

```objc
        //---if the property list file can be found---
        if ([[NSFileManager defaultManager] fileExistsAtPath:plistFileName])
        {
            //---load the content of the property list file into a NSDictionary
            // object---
            NSDictionary *dict = [[NSDictionary alloc]
                                    initWithContentsOfFile:plistFileName];

            //---for each category---
            for (NSString *category in dict)
            {
                NSLog(category);
                NSLog(@"========");

                //---return all titles in an array---
                NSArray *titles = [dict valueForKey:category];

                //---print out all the titles in that category---
                for (NSString *title in titles)
                {
                    NSLog(title);
                }
            }
            [dict release];
        }
        else {
            //---load the property list from the Resources folder---
            NSString *pListPath = [[NSBundle mainBundle] pathForResource:@"Apps"
                                    ofType:@"plist"];

            NSDictionary *dict = [[NSDictionary alloc]
                                    initWithContentsOfFile:pListPath];

            //---make a mutable copy of the dictionary object---
            NSMutableDictionary *copyOfDict = [dict mutableCopy];

            //---get all the different categories---
            NSArray *categoriesArray = [[copyOfDict allKeys]
                                    sortedArrayUsingSelector:@selector(compare:)];

            //---for each category---
            for (NSString *category in categoriesArray)
            {
                //---get all the app titles in that category---
                NSArray *titles = [dict valueForKey:category];

                //---make a mutable copy of the array---
                NSMutableArray *mutableTitles = [titles mutableCopy];

                //---add a new title to the category---
                [mutableTitles addObject:@"New App title"];

                //---set the array back to the dictionary object---
                [copyOfDict setObject:mutableTitles forKey:category];
```

```
            [mutableTitles release];
        }

        //---write the dictionary to file---
        fileName = [[self documentsPath]
                        stringByAppendingPathComponent:@"Apps.plist"];

        [copyOfDict writeToFile:fileName atomically:YES];

        [dict release];
        [copyOfDict release];
    }

    [super viewDidLoad];
}
```

5. Press Command-R to test the application on the iPhone Simulator.

6. When you first run the application, you see that the application creates a new .plist file in the Documents directory of your application. If you double-click the .plist file to view it using the Property List Editor, you see that for each category of applications, you have a new item named New App title (see Figure 13-6).

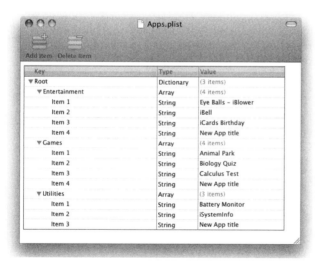

FIGURE 13-6

7. If you now run the application a second time, the application prints the content of the .plist file in the Documents directory to the Debugger Console window (see Figure 13-7).

FIGURE 13-7

How It Works

The first part of this example shows how you can add a property list file to your application. In the property list file, you add three keys representing the category of applications in the AppStore: Entertainment, Games, and Utilities. Each category contains a list of application titles.

When the view is loaded, you first try to locate a file named Apps.plist in the Documents directory of your application:

```
//---get the path to the property list file---
NSString *plistFileName = [[self documentsPath]
                    stringByAppendingPathComponent:@"Apps.plist"];
```

If the file is found, you then load its content into an NSDictionary object:

```
//---if the property list file can be found---
if ([[NSFileManager defaultManager] fileExistsAtPath:plistFileName])
{
    //---load the content of the property list file into a NSDictionary
    // object---
    NSDictionary *dict = [[NSDictionary alloc]
                    initWithContentsOfFile:plistFileName];
    //...
}
```

Next, you enumerate through all the keys in the dictionary object and print the titles of each application in the Debugger Console window:

```
//---for each category---
for (NSString *category in dict)
{
```

```
                    NSLog(category);
                    NSLog(@"=======");
                    //---return all titles in an array---
                    NSArray *titles = [dict valueForKey:category];

                    //---print out all the titles in that category---
                    for (NSString *title in titles)
                    {
                        NSLog(title);
                    }
                }
                [dict release];
```

When the application is run for the first time, the `Apps.plist` file is not available, so you load it from the `Resources` folder:

```
            else {
                //---load the property list from the Resources folder---
                NSString *pListPath = [[NSBundle mainBundle] pathForResource:@"Apps"
                                        ofType:@"plist"];

                NSDictionary *dict = [[NSDictionary alloc]
                                        initWithContentsOfFile:pListPath];
                //...
            }
```

Because you are making changes to the dictionary object, you need to make a mutable copy of the dictionary object and assign it to an `NSMutableDictionary` object:

```
                //---make a mutable copy of the dictionary object---
                NSMutableDictionary *copyOfDict = [dict mutableCopy];
```

This step is important because the `NSDictionary` object is immutable, meaning that after the items are populated from the property list, you cannot add content to the dictionary object. Using the `mutableCopy` method of the `NSDictionary` class allows you to create a mutable instance of the dictionary object, which is `NSMutableDictionary`.

You then retrieve an array containing all the keys in the mutable dictionary object:

```
                //---get all the different categories---
                NSArray *categoriesArray = [[copyOfDict allKeys]
                                        sortedArrayUsingSelector:@selector(compare:)];
```

You use this array to loop through all the keys in the dictionary so that you can add some additional titles to each category:

```
                //---for each category---
                for (NSString *category in categoriesArray)
                {

                }
```

Note that you cannot enumerate using the `NSMutableDictionary` object like this:

```
for (NSString *category in copyOfDict)
{
    //...
}
```

This is because you cannot add items to the `NSMutableDictionary` object while it is being enumerated. Therefore, you need to loop using an `NSArray` object.

When you're inside the loop, you extract all the titles of the applications in each category and make a mutable copy of the array containing the titles of the applications:

```
//---get all the app titles in that category---
NSArray *titles = [dict valueForKey:category];

//---make a mutable copy of the array---
NSMutableArray *mutableTitles = [titles mutableCopy];
```

You can now add a new title to the mutable array containing the application titles:

```
//---add a new title to the category---
[mutableTitles addObject:@"New App title"];
```

After the additional item is added to the mutable array, set it back to the mutable dictionary object:

```
//---set the array back to the dictionary object---
[copyOfDict setObject:mutableTitles forKey:category];
[mutableTitles release];
```

Finally, you write the mutable dictionary object to a file using the `writeToFile:atomically:` method:

```
//---write the dictionary to file---
fileName = [[self documentsPath]
                stringByAppendingPathComponent:@"Apps.plist"];
[copyOfDict writeToFile:fileName atomically:YES];

[dict release];
[copyOfDict release];
```

SUMMARY

This chapter demonstrated how to write a file to the file system of the iPhone and how to read it back. In addition, you saw how structured data can be represented using a property list and how you can programmatically work with a property list using a dictionary object. In the next chapter, you will see how you can make use of databases to store more complex data.

EXERCISES

1. Describe the uses of the various folders within an application's folder.

2. What is the difference between the `NSDictionary` and `NSMutableDictionary` classes?

3. Name the paths of the `Documents` and `tmp` folders on a real device.

▶ **WHAT YOU HAVE LEARNED IN THIS CHAPTER**

TOPIC	KEY CONCEPTS
Subdirectories in each of the applications folder	`Documents`, `Library`, and `tmp`

Getting the path of the `Documents` directory	`NSArray *paths = NSSearchPathForDirectoriesInDomains(`
	 `                    NSDocumentDirectory,`
	 `                    NSUserDomainMask, YES);`
	
	 `NSString *documentsDir = [paths objectAtIndex:0];`

Getting the path of the `tmp` directory	`-(NSString *) tempPath {`
	 `    return NSTemporaryDirectory();`
	 `}`

Check whether file exists	`if ([[NSFileManager defaultManager]`
	 `fileExistsAtPath:filePath]) {`
	 `}`

Location of the `Documents` directory on a real device	`/private/var/mobile/Applications/<application_id>/` `Documents/`
Location of the `tmp` directory on a real device	`/private/var/mobile/Applications/<application_id>/tmp/`

Load a property list from the `Resources` folder	`NSString *pListPath = [[NSBundle mainBundle]`
	 `                    pathForResource:@"Apps"`
	 `                    ofType:@"plist"];`

Create a mutable copy of an `NSDictionary` object	`NSDictionary *dict = [[NSDictionary alloc]`
	 `                    initWithContentsOfFile:pListPath];`
	 `NSMutableDictionary *copyOfDict = [dict mutableCopy];`

PART IV
Advanced iPhone Programming Techniques

14

Programming Multi-touch Applications

WHAT YOU WILL LEARN IN THIS CHAPTER

➤ How to detect touches in your application

➤ How to differentiate between single and double taps

➤ How to implement the pinch gesture

➤ How to implement the drag gesture

One of the most important selling points of the iPhone is its screen, which can detect multiple points of input. Multi-touch inputs allow for very natural interaction between users and your applications. Because of multi-touch, the mobile Safari Web browser is easily one of the most user-friendly Web browsers available on a smart phone.

In this chapter, you learn how to detect touches in your application and then implement some cool features that improve the interaction between the user and the application, such as a Jigsaw Puzzle application. By detecting touches in your application, the user can rearrange the locations of the images on the screen, as well as change the size of the images using the pinching gesture.

DETECTING TOUCHES

Before you learn how to detect touches in your application, you first need to acquaint yourself with a few events that handle the detection of touches. You will then be able to know whether the user has single-tapped or double-tapped on your application and react accordingly.

Time to get the engine rolling! Make sure you download the code indicated here so you can work through the following Try It Out activity.

TRY IT OUT Detecting for Taps

[MultiTouch.zip] is available for download at Wrox.com

1. Using Xcode, create a new View-based Application project and name it MultiTouch.

2. Drag and drop an image into the Resources folder. Figure 14-1 shows an image named apple.jpeg located in the Resources folder.

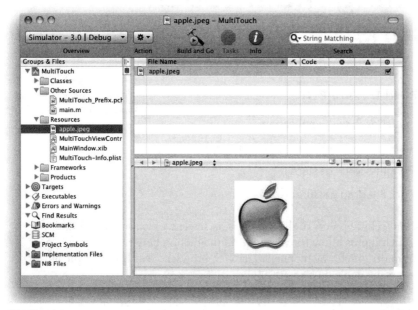

FIGURE 14-1

3. Double-click the MultiTouchViewController.xib file to edit it in Interface Builder.

4. Populate the View window with the ImageView view. Ensure that the ImageView covers the entire View window.

5. Select the ImageView view and view its Attributes window (see Figure 14-2). Set its Image property to `apple.jpeg`.

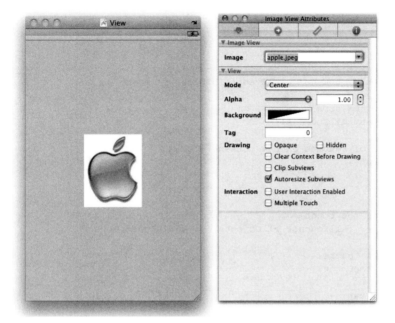

FIGURE 14-2

6. In the `MultiTouchViewController.h` file, add the following statements that appear in bold:

```
#import <UIKit/UIKit.h>

@interface MultiTouchViewController : UIViewController {

IBOutlet UIImageView *imageView;

}

@property (nonatomic, retain) UIImageView *imageView;

@end
```

7. Back in Interface Builder, Control-click and drag the File's Owner item to the ImageView view. Select ImageView.

8. In the `MultiTouchViewController.m` file, add the following statements that appear in bold:

```
#import "MultiTouchViewController.h"

@implementation MultiTouchViewController

@synthesize imageView;

//---fired when the user finger(s) touches the screen---
-(void) touchesBegan: (NSSet *) touches withEvent: (UIEvent *) event {

    //---get all touches on the screen---
    NSSet *allTouches = [event allTouches];

    //---compare the number of touches on the screen---
    switch ([allTouches count])
    {
        //---single touch---
        case 1: {
            //---get info of the touch---
            UITouch *touch = [[allTouches allObjects] objectAtIndex:0];

            //---compare the touches---
            switch ([touch tapCount])
            {
                //---single tap---
                case 1: {
                    imageView.contentMode = UIViewContentModeScaleAspectFit;
                } break;

                //---double tap---
                case 2: {
                    imageView.contentMode = UIViewContentModeCenter;
                } break;
            }
        } break;
    }
}

- (void)dealloc {
    [imageView release];
    [super dealloc];
}
```

9. Press Command-R to test the application on the iPhone Simulator.

10. Single-tap the apple icon to enlarge it. Double-tap it to return it to its original size (see Figure 14-3).

FIGURE 14-3

How It Works

The preceding application works by sensing the user's touch on the screen of the iPhone or iPod Touch. When the user touches the screen, the View or View Controller fires a series of events that you can handle. There are four such events:

➤ `touchesBegan:withEvent:`

➤ `touchesEnded:withEvent:`

➤ `touchesMoved:withEvent:`

➤ `touchesCancelled:withEvent:`

Take a closer look at the first event. First, the `touchesBegan:withEvent:` event is fired when at least one touch is sensed on the screen. In this event, you can know how many fingers are on the screen by calling the `allTouches` method of the `UIEvent` object (event):

```
//---get all touches on the screen---
NSSet *allTouches = [event allTouches];
```

The `allTouches` method returns an `NSSet` object containing a set of `UITouch` objects. To know how many fingers are on the screen, simply count the number of `UITouch` objects in the `NSSet` object using the `count` method. In this case, you are (at this moment) interested only in a single touch, therefore you implement only the case for one touch:

```
//---compare the number of touches on the screen---
switch ([allTouches count])
{
    //---single touch---
    case 1: {
        //---get info of the touch---
        UITouch *touch = [[allTouches allObjects] objectAtIndex:0];

        //---compare the touches---
        switch ([touch tapCount])
        {
            //---single tap---
            case 1: {
                imageView.contentMode = UIViewContentModeScaleAspectFit;
            } break;

            //---double tap---
            case 2: {
                imageView.contentMode = UIViewContentModeCenter;
            } break;
        }
    } break;
}
```

You extract details of the first touch by using the `allObjects` method of the `NSSet` object to return an `NSArray` object. You then use the `objectAtIndex:` method to obtain the first array item.

The `UITouch` object (`touch`) contains the `tapCount` property, which tells you whether the user has single-tapped the screen or performed a double tap (or more). If the use single-tapped the screen, you resize the image to fit the entire `ImageView` view using the `UIViewContentModeScaleAspectFit` constant. If it is a double-tap, you restore it to its original size using the `UIViewContentModeCenter` constant.

The other three events, which are not discussed in this section, are `touchesEnded:withEvent:`, `touchesMoved:withEvent:`, and `touchesCancelled:withEvent:`.

The `touchesEnded:withEvent:` event is fired when the user's finger(s) is lifted from the screen. The `touchesMoved:withEvent:` event is fired continuously when the user's finger or fingers are touching and moving on the screen. Finally, if the application is interrupted while the user's finger is on the screen, the `touchesCancelled:withEvent:` event is fired.

 NOTE *In addition to detecting taps in the* `touchesBegan:withEvent:` *event, you can detect them in the* `touchesEnded:withEvent:` *event.*

UNDERSTANDING MULTI-TAPPING

When a user performs a multi-tap on the screen, your application will fire the `touchesBegan:` and `touchesEnded:` events multiple times. For example, if the user taps on the screen once, the `touchesBegan:` and `touchesEnded:` events will be fired once, with the `tapCount` property of the `UITouch` object returning a value of 1. However, if the user taps the screen twice (in quick succession), then the `touchesBegan:` and `touchesEnded:` events will be fired twice; the first time these events are fired, the `tapCount` property will be 1, the second time the `tapCount` property will be 2.

Understanding the way multi-taps are detected is important because if you are detecting double-taps your application might redundantly execute blocks of code that are designed for single-tap. For example, in the preceding Try It Out, double-tapping on the image will first try to change the mode of the image to `UIViewContentModeScaleAspectFit` (which is what single-tap is supposed to do; in this case because the image is already in the `UIViewContentModeScaleAspectFit` mode the user won't notice any difference), then it changes back to the `UIViewContentModeCenter` mode (which is what double-tap is supposed to do). Ideally, it should not need to execute the block of code for single-tap.

To solve this problem, you have to write some code to check if a second tap is indeed coming:

➤ When a single-tap is detected, use a timer using a `NSTimer` object.

➤ When a double-tap is detected, stop the timer and check to see if the time difference between the second tap and the first tap is small enough (such as a fraction of a second) to constitute a double-tap. If it is, execute the code for double-tap. Else, execute the code for single-tap.

In the next section, you learn how to detect for multi-touches in your application.

DETECTING MULTI-TOUCHES

Detecting for multi-touches is really very simple after you understand the concepts in previous section. The ability to detect for multi-touches is very useful because you can use this ability to zoom in on views in your application.

The following Try It Out shows you how to detect multi-touches.

1. Using the same project created in the previous section, modify the `touchesBegan:withEvent:` method by adding the following statements that appear in bold:

```
-(void) touchesBegan: (NSSet *) touches withEvent: (UIEvent *) event {

    //---get all touches on the screen---
    NSSet *allTouches = [event allTouches];

    //---compare the number of touches on the screen---
    switch ([allTouches count])
    {
        //---single touch---
        case 1: {
            //---get info of the touch---
            UITouch *touch = [[allTouches allObjects] objectAtIndex:0];

            //---compare the touches---
            switch ([touch tapCount])
            {
                //---single tap---
                case 1: {
                    imageView.contentMode = UIViewContentModeScaleAspectFit;
                } break;

                case 2: {
                    imageView.contentMode = UIViewContentModeCenter;
                } break;
            }
        } break;

        //---double-touch---
        case 2: {
            //---get info of first touch---
            UITouch *touch1 = [[allTouches allObjects] objectAtIndex:0];

            //---get info of second touch---
            UITouch *touch2 = [[allTouches allObjects] objectAtIndex:1];

            //---get the points touched---
            CGPoint touch1PT = [touch1 locationInView:[self view]];
            CGPoint touch2PT = [touch2 locationInView:[self view]];

            NSLog(@"Touch1: %.0f, %.0f", touch1PT.x, touch1PT.y);
            NSLog(@"Touch2: %.0f, %.0f", touch2PT.x, touch2PT.y);
        } break;
    }
}
```

2. Press Command-R to test the application on the iPhone Simulator.

3. In the iPhone Simulator, press the Option key, and two circles should appear (see Figure 14-4). Clicking the screen simulates two fingers touching the screen of the device. Click and move the mouse to simulate pinching the screen.

4. Open the Debugger Console window (press Command-Shift-R) and observe the output as you Option-click the screen of the iPhone Simulator:

```
2009-08-25 10:01:15.510 MultiTouch[2230:207] Touch1: 107, 201
2009-08-25 10:01:15.511 MultiTouch[2230:207] Touch2: 213, 239
2009-08-25 10:01:15.758 MultiTouch[2230:207] Touch1: 105, 201
2009-08-25 10:01:15.759 MultiTouch[2230:207] Touch2: 215, 239
2009-08-25 10:01:15.918 MultiTouch[2230:207] Touch1: 215, 239
2009-08-25 10:01:15.919 MultiTouch[2230:207] Touch2: 105, 201
2009-08-25 10:01:16.054 MultiTouch[2230:207] Touch1: 105, 201
2009-08-25 10:01:16.055 MultiTouch[2230:207] Touch2: 215, 239
2009-08-25 10:01:16.238 MultiTouch[2230:207] Touch1: 105, 201
2009-08-25 10:01:16.239 MultiTouch[2230:207] Touch2: 215, 239
```

FIGURE 14-4

NOTE *Using the iPhone Simulator, the coordinates for the two touches are often interchanged as you Option-click the same spot on the screen of the iPhone Simulator.*

How It Works

As you do when detecting for single-touch, you check for multi-touches in the `touchesBegan:withEvent:` event. Rather than receive information about the first touch, you now obtain information for both the first and second touch:

```
//---get info of first touch---
UITouch *touch1 = [[allTouches allObjects] objectAtIndex:0];

//---get info of second touch---
UITouch *touch2 = [[allTouches allObjects] objectAtIndex:1];
```

NOTE *Basically, to detect more than two touches, you simply extend the preceding code by getting information about the third touch, fourth touch, and so on.*

To get the coordinates (represented as a `CGPoint` structure) of each touch, you use the `locationInView:` method of the `UITouch` class and pass it the view that it is currently in:

```
//---get the points touched---
CGPoint touch1PT = [touch1 locationInView:[self view]];
CGPoint touch2PT = [touch2 locationInView:[self view]];
```

The coordinates returned by the `locationInView:` method are relative to the view specified. In the preceding snippet, the coordinates displayed are relative to the main View window.

The x and y coordinates of a `CGPoint` structure are represented using the `CGFloat` type, so you need to use the `%f` format specifier when printing them in the Debugger Console window:

```
NSLog(@"Touch1: %.0f, %.0f", touch1PT.x, touch1PT.y);
NSLog(@"Touch2: %.0f, %.0f", touch2PT.x, touch2PT.y);
```

One important thing to understand is that the coordinates values displayed are relative to a specified view. Figure 14-5 shows that the top-left corner has a coordinate of (0,-20) and the bottom-right corner a coordinate of (320,460) when you reference against the main View window:

```
//---get the points touched---
CGPoint touch1PT = [touch1 locationInView:[self view]];
CGPoint touch2PT = [touch2 locationInView:[self view]];
```

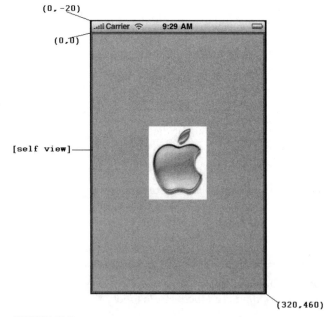

FIGURE 14-5

Suppose the size of the image view was shrunk to the size shown in Figure 14-6 (remember that it is currently filling up the entire screen). If you referenced that against the ImageView view, the (0,0) position would then start at the top-left corner of the image view. All other points to the top left of the (0,0) point would have negative x- and y-coordinates:

```
//---get the points touched---
CGPoint touch1PT = [touch1 locationInView:imageView];
CGPoint touch2PT = [touch2 locationInView:imageView];
```

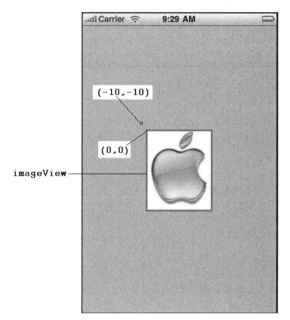

FIGURE 14-6

Implementing the Pinch Gesture

Now that you know the technique for detecting multi-touches in your application, you can write some cool applications that make use of multi-touches. A cool example would be to implement the famous iPhone pinch gesture that differentiates it from the competition.

Using the pinch gesture, you place two fingers on the screen and pinch by moving the two fingers closer to each other. This often translates to a zoom-out action when applying this gesture to, say, a photo that you are viewing, or to a Web page in Mobile Safari. When you move the two fingers apart, you zoom in on a photo or Web page.

To use the pinch gesture on an image, you actually need to enlarge the image first. This is because the image can only be resized if its display mode is set to UIViewContentModeScaleAspectFit. Hence, in this case, you need to single-tap on the image (which actually sets the image mode to UIViewContentModeScaleAspectFit) before you can try the pinching effect.

In the following Try It Out, you learn how to implement the pinch gesture to zoom the image in and out in the image view.

TRY IT OUT Zooming In and Out

1. Using the same project created earlier, add the following statement that appears in bold to the `MultiTouchViewController.h` file:

```
#import <UIKit/UIKit.h>

@interface MultiTouchViewController : UIViewController {
    IBOutlet UIImageView *imageView;
}

@property (nonatomic, retain) UIImageView *imageView;

-(CGFloat) distanceBetweenTwoPoints: (CGPoint)fromPoint toPoint: (CGPoint)toPoint;

@end
```

2. In the `MultiTouchViewController.m` file, implement the `distanceBetweenTwoPoints:toPoint:` and `touchesMoved:withEvent:` methods and add the statements that appear in bold to the `touchesBegan:withEvent:` method:

```
#import "MultiTouchViewController.h"

@implementation MultiTouchViewController

@synthesize imageView;

CGFloat originalDistance;

-(CGFloat) distanceBetweenTwoPoints:(CGPoint)fromPoint toPoint:(CGPoint)toPoint {

    float lengthX = fromPoint.x - toPoint.x;
    float lengthY = fromPoint.y - toPoint.y;
    return sqrt((lengthX * lengthX) + (lengthY * lengthY));

}

-(void) touchesBegan: (NSSet *) touches withEvent: (UIEvent *) event {

    //---get all touches on the screen---
    NSSet *allTouches = [event allTouches];

    //---compare the number of touches on the screen---
    switch ([allTouches count])
    {
        //---single touch---
        case 1: {
            //---get info of the touch---
            UITouch *touch = [[allTouches allObjects] objectAtIndex:0];

            //---compare the touches---
            switch ([touch tapCount])
            {
                //---single tap---
```

```
                    case 1: {
                        imageView.contentMode = UIViewContentModeScaleAspectFit;
                    } break;

                    case 2: {
                        imageView.contentMode = UIViewContentModeCenter;
                    } break;
                }
            } break;

            //---double-touch---
            case 2: {
                //---get info of first touch---
                UITouch *touch1 = [[allTouches allObjects] objectAtIndex:0];
                //---get info of second touch---
                UITouch *touch2 = [[allTouches allObjects] objectAtIndex:1];

                //---get the points touched---
                CGPoint touch1PT = [touch1 locationInView:[self view]];
                CGPoint touch2PT = [touch2 locationInView:[self view]];

                NSLog(@"Touch1: %.0f, %.0f", touch1PT.x, touch1PT.y);
                NSLog(@"Touch2: %.0f, %.0f", touch2PT.x, touch2PT.y);

                //---record the distance made by the two touches---
                originalDistance = [self distanceBetweenTwoPoints:touch1PT
                                    toPoint: touch2PT];

            } break;
        }
}

//---fired when the user moved his finger(s) on the screen---
-(void) touchesMoved: (NSSet *) touches withEvent: (UIEvent *) event {

    //---get all touches on the screen---
    NSSet *allTouches = [event allTouches];

    //---compare the number of touches on the screen---
    switch ([allTouches count])
    {
        //---single touch---
        case 1: {
        } break;

        //---double-touch---
        case 2: {
            //---get info of first touch---
            UITouch *touch1 = [[allTouches allObjects] objectAtIndex:0];

            //---get info of second touch---
            UITouch *touch2 = [[allTouches allObjects] objectAtIndex:1];

            //---get the points touched---
```

```
CGPoint touch1PT = [touch1 locationInView:[self view]];
CGPoint touch2PT = [touch2 locationInView:[self view]];

NSLog(@"Touch1: %.0f, %.0f", touch1PT.x, touch1PT.y);
NSLog(@"Touch2: %.0f, %.0f", touch2PT.x, touch2PT.y);

CGFloat currentDistance = [self distanceBetweenTwoPoints: touch1PT
                                          toPoint: touch2PT];

//---zoom in---
if (currentDistance > originalDistance)
{
    imageView.frame = CGRectMake(imageView.frame.origin.x - 2,
                                 imageView.frame.origin.y - 2,
                                 imageView.frame.size.width + 4,
                                 imageView.frame.size.height + 4);
}
else {
    //---zoom out---
    imageView.frame = CGRectMake(imageView.frame.origin.x + 2,
                                 imageView.frame.origin.y + 2,
                                 imageView.frame.size.width - 4,
                                 imageView.frame.size.height - 4);
}
originalDistance = currentDistance;
} break;
}
}
```

3. Press Command-R to test the application on the iPhone Simulator.

4. Single-tap the image view to enlarge. To zoom the image in and out, Option-click the image (see Figure 14-7).

How It Works

To detect for the pinch gesture, you need to find out the distance between the two fingers and constantly compare their distances so that you know whether the two fingers are moving toward or away from each other.

To find the distance between two fingers, you define the `distanceBetweenTwoPoints:toPoint:` method:

```
-(CGFloat) distanceBetweenTwoPoints:(CGPoint)fromPoint
toPoint:(CGPoint)toPoint {

    float lengthX = fromPoint.x - toPoint.x;
    float lengthY = fromPoint.y - toPoint.y;
    return sqrt((lengthX * lengthX) + (lengthY * lengthY));

}
```

FIGURE 14-7

This method takes in two `CGPoint` structures and then calculates the distance between them. No rocket science here — just the Pythagorean theorem in action.

When the two fingers first touch the screen, you record their distance in the
`touchesBegan:withEvent:` method (see the code in bold):

```
-(void) touchesBegan: (NSSet *) touches withEvent: (UIEvent *) event {

        //...
        //---double-touch---
        case 2: {
            //---get info of first touch---
            UITouch *touch1 = [[allTouches allObjects] objectAtIndex:0];
            //---get info of second touch---
            UITouch *touch2 = [[allTouches allObjects] objectAtIndex:1];

            //---get the points touched---
            CGPoint touch1PT = [touch1 locationInView:[self view]];
            CGPoint touch2PT = [touch2 locationInView:[self view]];

            NSLog(@"Touch1: %.0f, %.0f", touch1PT.x, touch1PT.y);
            NSLog(@"Touch2: %.0f, %.0f", touch2PT.x, touch2PT.y);

            //---record the distance made by the two touches---
            originalDistance = [self distanceBetweenTwoPoints:touch1PT
                                    toPoint: touch2PT];

        } break;
    }
}
```

As the two fingers move on the screen, you constantly compare their current distance with the original
distance (see Figure 14-8).

FIGURE 14-8

If the current distance is greater than the original distance, this is a zoom-in gesture. If not, it is a zoom-out gesture:

```
//---fired when the user moved his finger(s) on the screen---
-(void) touchesMoved: (NSSet *) touches withEvent: (UIEvent *) event {

    //...
    //---double-touch---
    case 2: {
    //---get info of first touch---
    UITouch *touch1 = [[allTouches allObjects] objectAtIndex:0];

    //---get info of second touch---
    UITouch *touch2 = [[allTouches allObjects] objectAtIndex:1];

    //---get the points touched---
    CGPoint touch1PT = [touch1 locationInView:[self view]];
    CGPoint touch2PT = [touch2 locationInView:[self view]];

    NSLog(@"Touch1: %.0f, %.0f", touch1PT.x, touch1PT.y);
    NSLog(@"Touch2: %.0f, %.0f", touch2PT.x, touch2PT.y);

    CGFloat currentDistance = [self distanceBetweenTwoPoints: touch1PT
                                       toPoint: touch2PT];

    //---zoom in---
    if (currentDistance > originalDistance)
    {
        imageView.frame = CGRectMake(imageView.frame.origin.x - 2,
                                     imageView.frame.origin.y - 2,
                                     imageView.frame.size.width + 4,
                                     imageView.frame.size.height + 4);
    }
    else {
        //---zoom out---
        imageView.frame = CGRectMake(imageView.frame.origin.x + 2,
                                     imageView.frame.origin.y + 2,
                                     imageView.frame.size.width - 4,
                                     imageView.frame.size.height - 4);
        }
        originalDistance = currentDistance;
    } break;
    }
}
```

Implementing the Drag Gesture

Another gesture that you can implement is the drag gesture, in which you tap an item on the screen and drag the item by moving the finger. In the following Try It Out, you learn how to drag an image view on the screen by implementing the drag gesture.

TRY IT OUT Dragging the ImageView

1. Using the same project created earlier, resize the ImageView view so that it fits the size of the image (see Figure 14-9).

2. Add the following statements that appear in bold to the touchesMoved:withEvent: method:

```
//---fired when the user moved his finger(s) on
the screen---
-(void) touchesMoved: (NSSet *) touches withEvent:
(UIEvent *) event {

    //---get all touches on the screen---
    NSSet *allTouches = [event allTouches];

    //---compare the number of touches on the
    screen---
    switch ([allTouches count])
    {
        //---single touch---
        case 1: {
            //---get info of the touch---
            UITouch *touch = [[allTouches
            allObjects] objectAtIndex:0];

            //---check to see if the image is being touched---
            CGPoint touchPoint = [touch locationInView:[self view]];

            if (touchPoint.x > imageView.frame.origin.x &&
                touchPoint.x < imageView.frame.origin.x +
                            imageView.frame.size.width &&
                touchPoint.y > imageView.frame.origin.y &&
                touchPoint.y <imageView.frame.origin.y +
                            imageView.frame.size.height) {
                [imageView setCenter:touchPoint];
            }
        } break;

        //---double-touch---
        case 2: {
            //---get info of first touch---
            UITouch *touch1 = [[allTouches allObjects] objectAtIndex:0];
            //---get info of second touch---
            UITouch *touch2 = [[allTouches allObjects] objectAtIndex:1];

            //...
            //...

        } break;
    }
}
```

FIGURE 14-9

3. Press Command-R to test the application on the iPhone Simulator.

4. You can now tap the image view and then move the image anywhere on the screen simply by moving your finger (see Figure 14-10).

How It Works

The concept for this example is very simple. When a finger taps the screen, you check to see whether the position of the finger falls within the range of the image view:

```
CGPoint touchPoint = [touch locationInView:[self
view]];

if (touchPoint.x > imageView.frame.origin.x &&
    touchPoint.x < imageView.frame.origin.x +
                   imageView.frame.size.width &&
    touchPoint.y > imageView.frame.origin.y &&
    touchPoint.y <imageView.frame.origin.y +
                  imageView.frame.size.height)
                  {
    [imageView setCenter:touchPoint];
}
```

FIGURE 14-10

If it does, you simply reposition the image view by calling its `setCenter` property.

Using this technique, you can easily write a jigsaw puzzle application in which users can rearrange the different pieces of the jigsaw puzzle simply by dragging them on the screen.

SUMMARY

In this chapter, you have seen the various events that you need to handle in order to know whether the user is single- or double-tapping your application. You also saw how to detect multiple touches on your application and use this knowledge to create some really interesting applications.

EXERCISES

1. Name the four events for detecting touches in your application.

2. What is the difference between multi-taps and multi-touches?

3. How do you simulate multi-touch on the iPhone Simulator?

▶ **WHAT YOU HAVE LEARNED IN THIS CHAPTER**

TOPIC	KEY CONCEPTS
Detect touches on the view	Handle the following event in the view or View Controller: * `touchesBegan:withEvent:` * `touchesEnded:withEvent:` * `touchesMoved:withEvent:` * `touchesCancelled:withEvent:`
Detect for taps (single, double, and so on)	You can detect for taps either in the `touchesBegan:withEvent:` or `touchesEnded:withEvent:` methods.
Implement "pinch" gesture	Compare the distance made by the two touch points and deduce whether the gesture is zoom in or out.
Implement "drag" gesture	Ensure that the touch point falls within the area occupied by the view in question.

15

Simple Animations

WHAT YOU WILL LEARN IN THIS CHAPTER

➤ How to use the NSTimer class to create timers that will call methods at regular time intervals

➤ How to perform some simple animations using the NSTimer class

➤ How to perform affine transformation on the ImageView

➤ How to animate a series of images using the ImageView

Up to this point, the applications you have written have all made use of the standard views provided by the iPhone SDK. As Apple has reiterated, the iPhone and iPod Touch are more than just phones. The iPhone is also a music player and, more important for this chapter, the iPhone is also a gaming platform.

In this chapter, you can have some fun and create something visual. You learn how to perform some simple animations using a timer object and then perform some transformations on a view. Although it is beyond the scope of this book to show you how to create animations using OpenGL, this chapter does show you some interesting techniques that you can use to make your applications come alive!

USING THE NSTIMER CLASS

One of the easiest ways to get started with animation is to use the NSTimer class. The NSTimer class creates timer objects, which allow you to call a method at a regular time intervals. Using an NSTimer object, you can update an image at regular time intervals, thereby creating an impression that it is being animated.

In the following Try It Out, you learn how to display a bouncing ball on the screen using the NSTimer class. When the ball touches the sides of the screen, it bounces off in the opposite direction. You also learn how to control the frequency with which the ball animates. You need to download the code files indicated here for this and other Try It Out features within this chapter.

TRY IT OUT   **Animating the Ball**

Codefile [Animation.zip] is available for download at Wrox.com

1.   Using Xcode, create a new View-based Application project and name it Animation.

2.   Drag and drop an image named tennisball.jpg to the Resources folder in Xcode. When the Add dialog appears, select the Copy Item into Destination Group's Folder (If Needed) check box so that a copy of the image is copied into the project.

3.   Double-click the AnimationViewController.xib file to edit it in Interface Builder.

4.   In the View window, drag and drop an ImageView onto it and set its Image property to tennisball.jpg (see Figure 15-1).

 NOTE *Ensure that the size of the ImageView fits the tennis ball image. Later, you move the ImageView on the screen, so it is important not to fill the entire screen with the ImageView.*

FIGURE 15-1

5.   Select the View (outside the ImageView) and change the background color to black (see Figure 15-2).

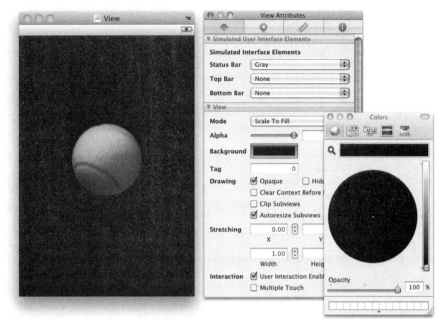

FIGURE 15-2

6.   Add a Label and a Slider view from the Library onto the View window (see Figure 15-3). Set the `Initial` property of the Slider view to `0.01`.

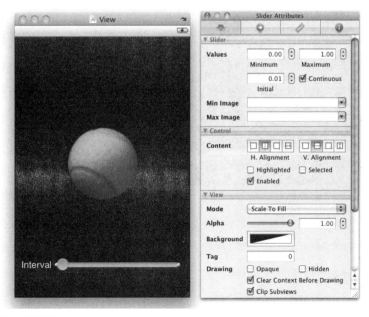

FIGURE 15-3

7. In the `AnimationViewController.h` file, declare the following outlets, actions, and fields:

```
#import <UIKit/UIKit.h>

@interface AnimationViewController : UIViewController {
    IBOutlet UIImageView *imageView;
    IBOutlet UISlider *slider;

    CGPoint position;
    NSTimer *timer;

    float ballRadius;
}

@property (nonatomic, retain) UIImageView *imageView;
@property (nonatomic, retain) UISlider *slider;

-(IBAction) sliderMoved:(id) sender;

@end
```

8. Back in Interface Builder, connect the outlets and actions as shown in Figure 15-4.

FIGURE 15-4

9. In the `AnimationViewController.m` file, add the following statements that appear in bold:

```
#import "AnimationViewController.h"

@implementation AnimationViewController

@synthesize imageView;
@synthesize slider;

-(void) onTimer {
    imageView.center = CGPointMake(
                        imageView.center.x + position.x,
                        imageView.center.y + position.y);

    if (imageView.center.x > 320 - ballRadius || imageView.center.x < ballRadius)
        position.x = -position.x;
    if (imageView.center.y > 460 - ballRadius || imageView.center.y < ballRadius)
        position.y = -position.y;
}

- (void)viewDidLoad {
    ballRadius = imageView.frame.size.width/2;
    [slider setShowValue:YES];

    position = CGPointMake(12.0,4.0);
    timer = [NSTimer scheduledTimerWithTimeInterval:slider.value
            target:self
            selector:@selector(onTimer)
            userInfo:nil
            repeats:YES];

    [super viewDidLoad];
}

-(IBAction) sliderMoved:(id) sender {
    [timer invalidate];
    timer = [NSTimer scheduledTimerWithTimeInterval:slider.value
            target:self
            selector:@selector(onTimer)
            userInfo:nil
            repeats:YES];
}

- (void)didReceiveMemoryWarning {
[super didReceiveMemoryWarning];
}

- (void)dealloc {
    [timer invalidate];
```

```
    [imageView release];
    [slider release];
    [super dealloc];
}

@end
```

10. Press Command-R to test the application on the iPhone Simulator. You should now see the tennis ball animating on the screen (see Figure 15-5). To vary the speed of the animation, move the slider. Moving the slider to the right slows down the animation; moving it to the left speeds it up.

How It Works

When the view is loaded, the first thing you do is get the radius of the tennis ball, which in this case is half the width of the image:

```
ballRadius = imageView.frame.size.width/2;
```

This value will be used during the animation to check whether the tennis ball has touched the edges of the screen.

To set the slider to show its value, you use the `setShowValue:` method:

FIGURE 15-5

```
    [slider setShowValue:YES];
```

> **NOTE** Note that the `setShowValue:` method is undocumented and hence the compiler will sound a warning.

You also initialize the `position` variable:

```
    position = CGPointMake(12.0,4.0);
```

The `position` variable is used to specify how much the image must move every time the timer fires. The preceding code tells it to move 12 pixels horizontally and 4 pixels vertically.

You next call the `scheduledTimerWithTimeInterval:target:selector:userInfo:repeats:` class method of the `NSTimer` class to create a new instance of the `NSTimer` object:

```
timer = [NSTimer scheduledTimerWithTimeInterval:slider.value
            target:self
            selector:@selector(onTimer)
            userInfo:nil
            repeats:YES];
```

The `scheduledTimerWithTimeInterval:` specifies the number of seconds between firings of the timer. Here, you set it to the value of the Slider view, which takes on a value from 0.0 to 1.0. If the slider's value is 0.5, the timer object will fire every half-second.

The `selector:` parameter specifies the method to call when the timer fires, and the `repeats:` parameter indicates whether the timer object will repeatedly reschedule itself. In this case, when the timer fires, it will call the `onTimer` method, which you define next.

In the `onTimer` method, you change the position of the ImageView by setting its `center` property to a new value. After repositioning, you check whether the image has touched the edges of the screen; if it has, the value of the `position` variable is negated:

```
-(void) onTimer {
    imageView.center = CGPointMake(
                        imageView.center.x + position.x,
                        imageView.center.y + position.y);

    if (imageView.center.x > 320 - ballRadius || imageView.center.x < ballRadius)
        position.x = -position.x;
    if (imageView.center.y > 460 - ballRadius || imageView.center.y < ballRadius)
        position.y = -position.y;
}
```

When you move the slider, the `sliderMoved:` method is called. In this method, first invalidate the timer object and then create another instance of the `NSTimer` class:

```
-(IBAction) sliderMoved:(id) sender {
    [timer invalidate];
    timer = [NSTimer scheduledTimerWithTimeInterval:slider.value
            target:self
            selector:@selector(onTimer)
            userInfo:nil
            repeats:YES];
}
```

Moving the slider allows you to change the frequency at which the image is animated.

 NOTE *After an* `NSTimer` *object is started, you cannot change its firing interval. Therefore, the only way to change the interval is to invalidate the current one and create a new* `NSTimer` *object.*

Animating the Visual Change

You may have noticed that as you move the slider towards the right, the animation slows and the animation of the tennis ball becomes abrupt.

To make the animation smoother, you can animate the visual changes caused by setting the `center` property of the view within an animation block. The start of the animation block is defined by the `beginAnimations:context:` class method of the `UIView` class:

```
[UIView beginAnimations:@"my_own_animation" context:nil];
    imageView.center = CGPointMake(
                        imageView.center.x + position.x,
                        imageView.center.y + position.y);
[UIView commitAnimations];
```

To end an animation block, you call the `commitAnimations` class method of the `UIView` class. The preceding code tries to animate the ImageView when it moves from one position to another (see Figure 15-6). This results in a much smoother animation than before.

TRANSFORMING VIEWS

FIGURE 15-6

The previous section shows how you can use the `NSTimer` class to simulate some simple animation by constantly changing the position of the ImageView. Besides repositioning the view, you can use the transformation techniques supported by the iPhone SDK to achieve the same effect.

Transforms are defined in Core Graphics, and the iPhone SDK supports standard affine 2D transforms. You can use the iPhone SDK to perform the following affine 2D transforms:

 NOTE An affine transformation *is a linear transformation that preserves co-linearity and ratio of distances. This means that all the points lying on a line initially will remain in a line after the transformation, with their respective ratio of distance between each other maintained.*

➤ Translation — moves the origin of the view by the amount specified using the *x* and *y* axes

➤ Rotation — moves the view by the angle specified

➤ Scaling — changes the scale of the view by the *x* and *y* factors specified

Figure 15-7 shows the effects of the various transformations just described.

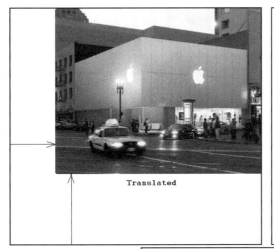

Translated

Rotated

Scaled

FIGURE 15-7

Translation

To perform an affine transform on a view, simply use its `transform` property. Recall that in the previous example, you set the new position of the view through its `center` property:

```
imageView.center = CGPointMake(
                    imageView.center.x + position.x,
                    imageView.center.y + position.y);
```

Using 2D transformation, you can use its `transform` property and set it to a `CGAffineTransform` data structure returned by the `CGAffineTransformMakeTranslation()` function, like this:

```
//---in the AnimationviewController.h file---
CGPoint position;
CGPoint translation;


//---in the viewDidLoad method---
position = CGPointMake(12.0,4.0);
```

```
    translation = CGPointMake(0.0,0.0);


-(void) onTimer {
    imageView.transform = CGAffineTransformMakeTranslation(
        translation.x, translation.y);

    translation.x = translation.x + position.x;
    translation.y = translation.y + position.y;

    if (imageView.center.x + translation.x > 320 - ballRadius ||
        imageView.center.x + translation.x < ballRadius)
        position.x = -position.x;

    if (imageView.center.y + translation.y > 460 - ballRadius ||
        imageView.center.y + translation.y < ballRadius)
        position.y = -position.y;
}
```

The `CGAffineTransformMakeTranslation()` function takes in two arguments — the value to move for the x-axis and the value to move for the y-axis.

The preceding code achieves the same effect as setting the `center` property of ImageView.

Rotation

The rotation transformation allows you to rotate a view using the angle you specified. In the following Try It Out, you modify the code from the previous example so that the tennis ball can be rotated as it bounces across the screen.

TRY IT OUT   Rotating the Tennis Ball

1.   In the `AnimationViewController.h` file, add the declaration for the `angle` variable:

```
#import <UIKit/UIKit.h>

@interface AnimationViewController : UIViewController {
    IBOutlet UIImageView *imageView;
    IBOutlet UISlider *slider;

    CGPoint position;
    NSTimer *timer;

    float ballRadius;
    float angle;
}

@property (nonatomic, retain) UIImageView *imageView;
```

```
@property (nonatomic, retain) UISlider *slider;

-(IBAction) sliderMoved:(id) sender;

@end
```

2. In the `AnimationViewController.m` file, add the following statement that appears in bold:

```
-(void) onTimer {

    //---rotation---
    imageView.transform = CGAffineTransformMakeRotation(angle);
    angle += 0.02;
    if (angle>6.2857) angle = 0;

    imageView.center = CGPointMake(
                        imageView.center.x + position.x,
                        imageView.center.y + position.y);

    if (imageView.center.x > 320 - ballRadius || imageView.center.x < ballRadius)
        position.x = -position.x;
    if (imageView.center.y > 460 - ballRadius || imageView.center.y < ballRadius)
        position.y = -position.y;

}

- (void)viewDidLoad {

    //---set the angle to 0---
    angle = 0;

    ballRadius = imageView.frame.size.width/2;
    [slider setShowValue:YES];
    position = CGPointMake(12.0,4.0);
    timer = [NSTimer scheduledTimerWithTimeInterval:slider.value
            target:self
            selector:@selector(onTimer)
            userInfo:nil
            repeats:YES];
    [super viewDidLoad];
}
```

 NOTE *If you have added the code to perform translation in the Translation section, be sure to remove it before adding the code outlined in this step.*

3. Press Command-R to test the application. The tennis ball now rotates as it bounces across the screen.

How It Works

To rotate a view, set its `transform` property using a `CGAffineTransform` data structure returned by the `CGAffineTransformMakeRotation()` function. The `CGAffineTransformMakeRotation()` function takes a single argument, which contains the angle to rotate (in radians). After each rotation, you increment the angle by 0.02:

```
//---rotation---
imageView.transform = CGAffineTransformMakeRotation(angle);
angle += 0.02;
```

A full rotation takes 360 degrees, which works out to be 2π radian. Hence, if the angle exceeds 6.2857 (=2*3.142857), you reset `angle` to 0:

```
if (angle>6.2857) angle = 0;
```

Scaling

For scaling of views, you use the `CGAffineTransformMakeScale()` function to return a `CGAffineTransform` data structure and set it to the `transform` property of the view:

```
imageView.transform = CGAffineTransformMakeScale(angle,
    angle);
```

The `CGAffineTransformMakeScale()` function takes in two arguments: the factor to scale for the x-axis and the factor to scale for the y-axis.

If you modify the previous example with the preceding statement, the tennis ball gets bigger as it bounces on the screen (see Figure 15-8). It then resets back to its original size and grows again.

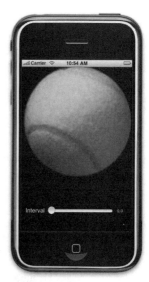

FIGURE 15-8

ANIMATING A SERIES OF IMAGES

So far, you have seen that you can use the ImageView view to display a static image. In addition, you can use it to display a series of images and then alternate between them.

The following Try It Out shows how this is done using the ImageView.

TRY IT OUT   Displaying a Series of Images

Codefile [Animations2.zip] is available for download at Wrox.com

1. Using Xcode, create a new View-based Application project and name it `Animations2`.

2. Add a series of images to the `Resources` folder by dragging and dropping them into the `Resources` folder in Xcode. When the Add dialog appears, select the Copy Item into Destination Group's Folder (If Needed) check box so that a copy of each of the images will be copied into the project. Figure 15-9 shows the images added.

3. In the `Animations2ViewController.m` file, add the following statements that appear in bold:

FIGURE 15-9

```
- (void)viewDidLoad {
    NSArray *images = [NSArray
arrayWithObjects:
                    [UIImage imageNamed:@"MacSE.jpeg"],
                    [UIImage imageNamed:@"imac.jpeg"],
                    [UIImage imageNamed:@"MacPlus.jpg"],
                    [UIImage imageNamed:@"imac_old.jpeg"],
                    [UIImage imageNamed:@"Mac8100.jpeg"],
                    nil];

    CGRect frame = CGRectMake(0,0,320,460);
    UIImageView *imageView = [[UIImageView alloc] initWithFrame:frame];
    imageView.animationImages = images;
    imageView.contentMode = UIViewContentModeScaleAspectFit;
    imageView.animationDuration = 3;    //---seconds to complete one set
                                        // of animation---
    imageView.animationRepeatCount = 0; //---continuous---

    [imageView startAnimating];

    [self.view addSubview:imageView];
    [imageView release];
    [super viewDidLoad];
}
```

4. Press Command-R to test the series of images on the iPhone Simulator. The images are displayed in the ImageView view (see Figure 15-10), one at a time.

How It Works

You first create an NSArray object and initialize it with a few UIImage objects:

```
NSArray *images = [NSArray arrayWithObjects:
                    [UIImage imageNamed:@"MacSE.jpeg"],
                    [UIImage imageNamed:@"imac.jpeg"],
                    [UIImage imageNamed:@"MacPlus.jpg"],
                    [UIImage imageNamed:@"imac_old.jpeg"],
                    [UIImage imageNamed:@"Mac8100.jpeg"],
                    nil];
```

You then instantiate a UIImageView object:

```
CGRect frame = CGRectMake(0,0,320,460);
UIImageView *imageView = [[UIImageView alloc]
    initWithFrame:frame];
```

FIGURE 15-10

To get the ImageView to display the series of images, set its animationImages property to the images object. You also set the display mode of the ImageView:

```
imageView.animationImages = images;
imageView.contentMode = UIViewContentModeScaleAspectFit;
```

To control how fast the images are displayed, you set the animationDuration property to a value. This value indicates the number of seconds that the ImageView will take to display one complete set of images. The animationRepeatCount property allows you to specify how many times you want the animation to occur. Set it to 0 if you want it to display indefinitely:

```
imageView.animationDuration = 3;      //---seconds to complete one set
                                      // of animation---
imageView.animationRepeatCount = 0; //---continuous---
```

Finally, start the animation by calling the startAnimating method. You also need to add the ImageView to the view by calling the addSubView: method:

```
[imageView startAnimating];
[self.view addSubview:imageView];
```

SUMMARY

In this chapter, you have seen the usefulness of the NSTimer class and how it can help you perform some simple animations. You have also learned about the various affine transformations supported by the iPhone SDK. Last, you learned about the ability of the ImageView to animate a series of images at a regular time interval.

EXERCISES

1. Name the three affine transformations supported by the iPhone SDK.

2. How do you pause an NSTimer object and then make it continue?

3. What is the use of enclosing your block of code with the beginAnimations and commitAnimations methods of the UIView class?

```
[UIView beginAnimations:@"some_text" context:nil];
    //---code to effect visual change---
[UIView commitAnimations];
```

▶ **WHAT YOU HAVE LEARNED IN THIS CHAPTER**

TOPIC	KEY CONCEPTS

Using the `NSTimer` object to create timers	Create a timer object that will call the `onTimer` method every half-second:
	 `Timer = [NSTimer scheduledTimerWithTimeInterval:0.5`
	           `target:self`
	           `selector:@selector(onTimer)`
	           `userInfo:nil`
	           `repeats:YES];`

Stopping the `NSTimer` object	`[timer invalidate];`

Animating visual changes	`[UIView beginAnimations:@"some_text" context:nil];`
	 `//---code to effect visual change---`
	 `[UIView commitAnimations];`

Performing affine transformations	Use the `transform` property of the view.
Translation	Use the `CGAffineTransformMakeTranslation()` function to return a `CGAffineTransform` data structure and set it to the `transform` property.
Rotation	Use the `CGAffineTransformMakeRotation()` function to return a `CGAffineTransform` data structure and set it to the `transform` property.
Scaling	Use the `CGAffineTransformMakeScale()` function to return a `CGAffineTransform` data structure and set it to the `transform` property.
Animating a series of images using ImageView	Set the `animationImages` property to an array containing `UIImage` objects. Set the `animationDuration` property. Set the `animationRepeatCount` property. Call the `startAnimating` method.

16

Accessing Built-in Applications

WHAT YOU WILL LEARN IN THIS CHAPTER

➤ How to send emails from within your application

➤ How to invoke Safari from within your application

➤ How to invoke the Phone from within your application

➤ How to send SMS messages from within your application

➤ How to access the camera and Photo Library

➤ How to access the Contacts application

➤ How to add and remove contact information from the Contacts application

The iPhone comes with a number of built-in applications that make it one of the most popular mobile devices of all time. Some of these applications are Contacts, Mail, Phone, Safari, SMS, and Calendar. These applications perform most of the tasks you would expect of a mobile phone. As an iPhone developer, you can also programmatically invoke these applications from within your application using the various APIs provided by the iPhone SDK.

In this chapter, you learn how to invoke some of the built-in applications that come bundled with iPhone as well as how to interact with them from within your iPhone application.

SENDING EMAILS

Sending emails is one of the many tasks performed by iPhone users. Sending emails on the iPhone is accomplished using the built-in Mail application, which is a rich HTML mail client that supports POP3, IMAP, Exchange email systems, and most web-based emails such as Yahoo! and Gmail.

There are times where you need to send an email in your iPhone application. A good example is embedding a feedback button in your application that users can click to send feedback to you directly. You have two ways to send emails programmatically:

➤ Build your own email client and implement all the necessary protocols necessary to communicate with an email server

➤ Invoke the built-in Mail application and ask it to send the email for you

Unless you are well versed in network communications and familiar with all the email protocols, your most logical choice is to go for option two — invoke the Mail application to do the job. The following Try It Out shows you how (you need to download the code files indicated here to work through this example).

TRY IT OUT   Sending Emails Using the Mail Application

Codefile [Emails.zip] is available for download at Wrox.com

1. Using Xcode, create a View-based Application project and name it `Emails`.

2. Double-click the `EmailViewController.xib` file to edit it in Interface Builder.

3. Populate the View window with the following views (see Figure 16-1):

➤ `Label`

➤ `TextField`

➤ `Button`

4. Insert the following statements in bold into the `EmailsViewController.h` file:

FIGURE 16-1

```
#import <UIKit/UIKit.h>

@interface EmailsViewController : UIViewController {
    IBOutlet UITextField *to;
    IBOutlet UITextField *subject;
    IBOutlet UITextField *body;
}

@property (nonatomic, retain) UITextField *to;
@property (nonatomic, retain) UITextField *subject;
```

```
@property (nonatomic, retain) UITextField *body;

-(IBAction) btnSend: (id) sender;

@end
```

5. Back in Interface Builder, Control-click and drag the File's Owner item to each of the three TextField views and select `to`, `subject`, and `body`, respectively.

6. Control-click and drag the Button view to the File's Owner item and select `btnSend:`.

7. Insert the following code in bold into the `EmailsViewController.m` file:

```
#import "EmailsViewController.h"

@implementation EmailsViewController
@synthesize to, subject, body;

- (void) sendEmailTo:(NSString *) toStr
    withSubject: (NSString *) subjectStr
    withBody:   (NSString *) bodyStr {

    NSString *emailString = [[NSString alloc]
        initWithFormat:@"mailto:?to=%@&subject=%@&body=%@",
        [toStr stringByAddingPercentEscapesUsingEncoding:NSASCIIStringEncoding],
        [subjectStr
            stringByAddingPercentEscapesUsingEncoding:NSASCIIStringEncoding],
        [bodyStr stringByAddingPercentEscapesUsingEncoding:NSASCIIStringEncoding]];

    [[UIApplication sharedApplication] openURL:[NSURL URLWithString:emailString]];
    [emailString release];
}

-(IBAction) btnSend: (id) sender{
    [self sendEmailTo:to.text withSubject:subject.text withBody:body.text];
}

- (void)dealloc {
    [to release];
    [subject release];
    [body release];
    [super dealloc];
}
```

8. Press Command-R to test the application on a real iPhone. Figure 16-2 shows the application in action. After you have filled in the TextField views with the necessary information, click the Send button to invoke the Mail application and fill it with all the information you have typed in your application. Clicking the Send button in Mail sends the email.

NOTE *Remember, this example only works on a real device. Testing it on the iPhone Simulator will not work. Appendix D discusses how to prepare your iPhone for testing.*

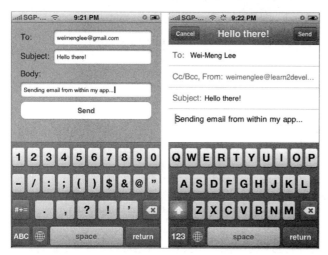

FIGURE 16-2

How It Works

The magic of invoking the Mail application lies in the string that you create in the sendEmailTo:withSubject:withBody: method that you have defined:

```
NSString *emailString = [[NSString alloc]
    initWithFormat:@"mailto:?to=%@&subject=%@&body=%@",
    [toStr stringByAddingPercentEscapesUsingEncoding:NSASCIIStringEncoding],
    [subjectStr
        stringByAddingPercentEscapesUsingEncoding:NSASCIIStringEncoding],
    [bodyStr stringByAddingPercentEscapesUsingEncoding:NSASCIIStringEncoding]];
```

Basically, this is a URL string with the mailto: protocol indicated. The various parameters, such as to, subject, and body, are inserted into the string. Note that you use the stringByAddingPercentEscapesUsingEncoding: method of the NSString class to encode with various parameters with the correct percent escapes so that the end result is a valid URL string.

To invoke the Mail application, simply call the sharedApplication method to return the singleton application instance and then use the openURL: method to invoke the Mail application:

```
[[UIApplication sharedApplication] openURL:[NSURL URLWithString:emailString]];
[emailString release];
```

Invoking Safari

If you want to invoke the Safari Web browser on your iPhone, you can also make use of a URL string and then use the `openURL:` method of the application instance, like this:

```
[[UIApplication sharedApplication]
        openURL:[NSURL URLWithString: @"http://www.apple
        .com"]];
```

The preceding code snippet invokes Safari to open the `www.apple.com` page (see Figure 16-3).

Invoking the Phone

To make a phone call using the iPhone's dialer, use the following URL string:

```
[[UIApplication sharedApplication]
    openURL:[NSURL URLWithString:@"tel:1234567890"]];
```

FIGURE 16-3

The preceding statement invokes the dialer of the iPhone using the phone number specified.

> **NOTE** *Note that the preceding statement works only for iPhone and not iPod Touch because the iPod Touch does not have phone capabilities. Also, you would need to a real device to test this out; the code does not have an effect on the iPhone Simulator. Appendix E discusses how to prepare your iPhone for testing.*

Invoking SMS

You can also use a URL string to send SMS messages using the SMS application:

```
[[UIApplication sharedApplication]
    openURL:[NSURL URLWithString:
    @"sms:96924065"]];
```

The preceding statement invokes the SMS application (see Figure 16-4).

FIGURE 16-4

NOTE *Note that the preceding statement works only for iPhone and not iPod Touch, because the iPod Touch does not have phone capabilities. Also, you would need to a real device to test this out; the code does not have an effect on the iPhone Simulator. Appendix E discusses how to prepare your iPhone for testing.*

INTERCEPTING SMS MESSAGES

One of the most requested features of the iPhone SDK is the ability to intercept incoming SMS messages from within an iPhone application. Unfortunately, the current version of the SDK does not provide a means to do this.

Likewise, you cannot send SMS messages directly from within your application; the messages must be sent from the built-in SMS application itself. This requirement prevents rogue applications from sending SMS messages without the user's knowledge.

ACCESSING THE CAMERA AND THE PHOTO LIBRARY

The iPhone and iPod Touch both have cameras that allow you to take pictures as well as record videos. All the pictures taken and videos recorded are saved in the Photos application. As a developer, you have a number of options to manipulate the cameras as well as access the pictures and videos stored in the Photos application:

➤ You can invoke the Camera to take pictures or record a video.

➤ You can invoke the Photos application to allow users to select a picture or video from the photo albums. You can then use the picture or video selected in your application.

Accessing the Photo Library

Every iPhone and iPod Touch device includes the Photos application, in which all the pictures taken and videos recorded are stored. Using the iPhone SDK, you can use the `UIImagePickerController` class to programmatically display a UI to let the user select your pictures and videos from the Photos application. The following Try It Out demonstrates how you can do that in your application.

TRY IT OUT Accessing the Photo Library

Codefile [PhotoLibrary.zip] is available for download at Wrox.com

1. Using Xcode, create a View-based Application project and name it PhotoLibrary.

2. Double-click the PhotoLibraryViewController.xib file to edit it in Interface Builder.

3. Populate the View window with the following views (see Figure 16-5):

➤ Button

➤ ImageView

4. In the Attributes Inspector window for the ImageView view, set the Mode to Aspect Fit.

5. In the PhotoLibraryViewController.h file, insert the following statements that appear in bold:

```
##import <UIKit/UIKit.h>

@interface PhotoLibraryViewController :
UIViewController
    <UINavigationControllerDelegate,
    UIImagePickerControllerDelegate> {

    IBOutlet UIImageView *imageView;
    UIImagePickerController *imagePicker;
}

@property (nonatomic, retain) UIImageView *imageView;

-(IBAction) btnClicked: (id) sender;

@end
```

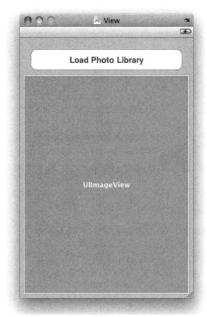

FIGURE 16-5

6. Back in Interface Builder, Control-click and drag the File's Owner item to the ImageView view and select imageView.

7. Control-click and drag the Button view to the File's Owner item select btnClicked:.

8. In the PhotoLibraryViewController.m file, insert the following statements that appear in bold:

```
#import "PhotoLibraryViewController.h"

@implementation PhotoLibraryViewController

@synthesize imageView;

- (void)viewDidLoad {
    imagePicker = [[UIImagePickerController alloc] init];
```

```objc
    [super viewDidLoad];
}

- (IBAction) btnClicked: (id) sender{
    imagePicker.delegate = self;
    imagePicker.sourceType = UIImagePickerControllerSourceTypePhotoLibrary;

    //---show the Image Picker---
    [self presentModalViewController:imagePicker animated:YES];
}

- (void)imagePickerController:(UIImagePickerController *)picker
    didFinishPickingMediaWithInfo:(NSDictionary *)info {

    UIImage *image;
    NSURL *mediaUrl;

    mediaUrl = (NSURL *)[info valueForKey:UIImagePickerControllerMediaURL];

    if (mediaUrl == nil)
    {
        image = (UIImage *) [info valueForKey:UIImagePickerControllerEditedImage];
        if (image == nil)
        {
            //---original image selected---
            image = (UIImage *)
                [info valueForKey:UIImagePickerControllerOriginalImage];

            //---display the image---
            imageView.image = image;
        }
        else //---edited image picked---
        {
            //---get the cropping rectangle applied to the image---
            CGRect rect =
                [[info valueForKey:UIImagePickerControllerCropRect] CGRectValue ];

            //---display the image---
            imageView.image = image;
        }
    }
    else
    {
        //---video picked---
        //...
    }

    //---hide the Image Picker---
    [picker dismissModalViewControllerAnimated:YES];
}

- (void)imagePickerControllerDidCancel:(UIImagePickerController *)picker
```

```
    {
        //---user did not select image/video; hide the Image Picker---
        [picker dismissModalViewControllerAnimated:YES];
    }

    - (void)dealloc {
        [imageView release];
        [imagePicker release];
        [super dealloc];
    }
```

9. Press Command-R to test the application on the iPhone Simulator.

10. When the application is loaded, tap the Load Photo Library button, and the Photo Albums on the iPhone Simulator appears (see Figure 16-6). Select a picture; the selected picture is then displayed on the ImageView view.

FIGURE 16-6

How It Works

Access to the Photo Library is provided by the UIImagePickerController class, which provides the UI for choosing and taking pictures and videos on your iPhone. All you need to do is create an instance of this class and provide a delegate that conforms to the UIImagePickerControllerDelegate protocol. In addition, your delegate must conform to the UINavigationControllerDelegate protocol because the

`UIImagePickerController` class uses the navigation controller to allow users to select the photos in the photo library. Therefore, you first need to specify the protocols in `PhotoLibraryViewController.h`:

```
@interface PhotoLibraryViewController : UIViewController
    <UINavigationControllerDelegate, UIImagePickerControllerDelegate> {
    . . .
```

When the Load Library button is clicked, you set the type of picker interface displayed by the `UIImagePickerController` class and then display it modally:

```
- (IBAction) btnClicked: (id) sender{

    //---the delegate that implements the methods defined in the protocols---
    imagePicker.delegate = self;

    //---type of source---
    imagePicker.sourceType = UIImagePickerControllerSourceTypePhotoLibrary;

    //---show the Image Picker---
    [self presentModalViewController:imagePicker animated:YES];
}
```

Note that if you want the picture to be editable when the user chooses the picture, you can add the following statement:

```
imagePicker.allowsImageEditing = YES;
```

By default, the source type is always `UIImagePickerControllerSourceTypePhotoLibrary`. However, you can also change it to one of the following:

➤ `UIImagePickerControllerSourceTypeCamera`

➤ `UIImagePickerControllerSourceTypeSavedPhotosAlbum`

When a picture/video has been selected by the user, the `imagePickerController:didFinishPickingMediaWithInfo:` event fires, and you handle it by checking the type of media selected by the user:

```
- (void)imagePickerController:(UIImagePickerController *)picker
    didFinishPickingMediaWithInfo:(NSDictionary *)info {

    UIImage *image;
    NSURL *mediaUrl;

    mediaUrl = (NSURL *)[info valueForKey:UIImagePickerControllerMediaURL];

    if (mediaUrl == nil)
    {
        image = (UIImage *) [info valueForKey:UIImagePickerControllerEditedImage];
        if (image == nil)
        {
            //---original image selected---
            image = (UIImage *)
```

```
                [info valueForKey:UIImagePickerControllerOriginalImage];

            //---display the image---
            imageView.image = image;
        }
        else //---edited image picked---
        {
            //---get the cropping rectangle applied to the image---
            CGRect rect =
                [[info valueForKey:UIImagePickerControllerCropRect] CGRectValue ];

            //---display the image---
            imageView.image = image;
        }
    }
    else
    {
        //---video picked---
        //...
    }

    //---hide the Image Picker---
    [picker dismissModalViewControllerAnimated:YES];
}
```

The type of media selected by the user is encapsulated in the didFinishPickingMediaWithInfo: parameter. You use the valueForKey: method to extract the different types of media type and then typecast it to the respective type:

```
        mediaUrl = (NSURL *)[info valueForKey:UIImagePickerControllerMediaURL];
```

If the user cancels the selection, the imagePickerControllerDidCancel: event fires. In this case, you simply dismiss the Image Picker:

```
    - (void)imagePickerControllerDidCancel:(UIImagePickerController *)picker
    {
        //---user did not select image/video; hide the Image Picker---
        [picker dismissModalViewControllerAnimated:YES];
    }
```

Accessing the Camera

Besides accessing the Photo Library, you can also access the camera on your iPhone. Although accessing the hardware is the focus of the next chapter, you take a look here at how to access the camera in this chapter because it is also accomplished using the UIImagePickerController class.

To access the camera, you modify the existing project created in the previous section. There isn't much to modify because most of the code you have written still applies.

TRY IT OUT Activating the Camera

1. Using the same project created in the previous section, edit the `PhotoLibraryViewController.m` file and change the source type of the Image Picker to camera (see code highlighted in bold):

```
-(IBAction) btnClicked: (id) sender{
    imagePicker.delegate = self;

    //---comment this out---
    //imagePicker.sourceType = UIImagePickerControllerSourceTypePhotoLibrary;

    //---invoke the camera---
    imagePicker.sourceType = UIImagePickerControllerSourceTypeCamera;

    imagePicker.allowsImageEditing = YES;
    [self presentModalViewController:imagePicker animated:YES];
}
```

2. In `PhotoLibraryViewController.h` file, declare the following two methods highlighted in bold so that you can save the image captured by the camera to the application's `Documents` folder (on the device):

```
#import <UIKit/UIKit.h>

@interface PhotoLibraryViewController : UIViewController
    <UINavigationControllerDelegate, UIImagePickerControllerDelegate> {

    IBOutlet UIImageView *imageView;
    UIImagePickerController *imagePicker;
}

@property (nonatomic, retain) UIImageView *imageView;

-(IBAction) btnClicked: (id) sender;

- (NSString *) filePath: (NSString *) fileName;
- (void) saveImage;

@end
```

3. In the `PhotoLibraryViewController.m` file, define the two methods that you have declared in the previous step:

```
- (NSString *) filePath: (NSString *) fileName {
    NSArray *paths = NSSearchPathForDirectoriesInDomains(
                        NSDocumentDirectory, NSUserDomainMask, YES);
    NSString *documentsDir = [paths objectAtIndex:0];
    return [documentsDir stringByAppendingPathComponent:fileName];
}

- (void) saveImage{
    //---get the date from the ImageView---
    NSData *imageData =
        [NSData dataWithData:UIImagePNGRepresentation(imageView.image)];
```

```
        //---write the date to file---
        [imageData writeToFile:[self filePath:@"MyPicture.png"] atomically:YES];
}
```

4. Right-click the Frameworks group in Xcode and choose Add ⇨ Existing Frameworks. Select
`Frameworks/MediaPlayer.framework`.

5. In the `PhotoLibraryViewController.h` file, import the following header file:

```
#import <UIKit/UIKit.h>
#import <MediaPlayer/MediaPlayer.h>
```

6. Insert the following statements that appear in bold:

```
- (void)imagePickerController:(UIImagePickerController *)picker
    didFinishPickingMediaWithInfo:(NSDictionary *)info {

    UIImage *image;
    NSURL *mediaUrl;

    mediaUrl = (NSURL *)[info valueForKey:UIImagePickerControllerMediaURL];
    if (mediaUrl == nil)
    {
        image = (UIImage *) [info valueForKey:UIImagePickerControllerEditedImage];
        if (image == nil)
        {
            //---original image selected---
            image = (UIImage *)
                [info valueForKey:UIImagePickerControllerOriginalImage];

            //---display the image---
            imageView.image = image;

            //---save the image captured---
            [self saveImage];
        }
        else
        {
            //---edited image picked---
            //---get the cropping rectangle applied to the image---
            CGRect rect =
                [[info valueForKey:UIImagePickerControllerCropRect] CGRectValue ];

            //---display the image---
            imageView.image = image;

            //---save the image captured---
            [self saveImage];
        }
    }
    else
```

```
        {
            //---video picked---
            MPMoviePlayerController *player = [[MPMoviePlayerController alloc]
                                                initWithContentURL:mediaUrl];
            [player play];
        }

        //---hide the Image Picker---
        [picker dismissModalViewControllerAnimated:YES];
    }
```

7. Press Command-R to test the application on a real iPhone.

 NOTE *Appendix E discusses how to prepare your iPhone for testing.*

8. Tap the Load Photo Library button, and you are now able to use your iPhone's camera to take photos and videos. If you use it to take a picture, the picture you take is saved onto the `Document` folder of your application. If you take a video, the video can be played back using the media player on your device.

How It Works

What you did in this exercise was modify the source type of the Image Picker to camera:

```
        imagePicker.sourceType = UIImagePickerControllerSourceTypeCamera;
```

When the camera takes a picture, the picture is passed back in the `imagePickerController:` `didFinishPickingMediaWithInfo:` method and displayed in the ImageView view. However, it is your responsibility to manually save the image to a location on the phone. In this case, you defined the `filePath:` method to save the picture to the `Document` folder of your application:

```
    - (NSString *) filePath: (NSString *) fileName {
        NSArray *paths = NSSearchPathForDirectoriesInDomains(
                            NSDocumentDirectory, NSUserDomainMask, YES);
        NSString *documentsDir = [paths objectAtIndex:0];
        return [documentsDir stringByAppendingPathComponent:fileName];
    }
```

The `saveImage:` method extracts the image data on the ImageView view and then calls the `filePath:` method to save the data into a file named `MyPicture.png`:

```
    - (void) saveImage{
        //---get the date from the ImageView---
        NSData *imageData =
        [NSData dataWithData:UIImagePNGRepresentation(imageView.image)];

        //---write the date to file---
        [imageData writeToFile:[self filePath:@"MyPicture.png"] atomically:YES];
    }
```

For video recording, the video captured by the iPhone's camera is saved on the device and returned as a URL. You can make use of the MPMoviePlayerController class (available in the MediaPlayer framework) to play back the video:

```
//---video picked---
MPMoviePlayerController *player = [[MPMoviePlayerController alloc]
                                   initWithContentURL:mediaUrl];

[player play];
[player release];
```

ACCESSING THE CONTACTS APPLICATION

Another commonly used built-in application in your iPhone and iPod Touch is the Contacts application (see Figure 16-7). The Contacts application contains the list of contacts you have saved on your device.

FIGURE 16-7

As with the Photo Library, you can programmatically access the contacts stored in the Contacts application. This access is useful because your application can rely on the Contacts application as a backend storage area for contact information, rather than need to create your own database to do so.

In the next Try It Out, you see how to access the Contacts application using the
`ABPeoplePickerNavigationController` class from the `AddressBookUI` framework. Don't forget
to download the code files indicated here.

1. Using Xcode, create a View-based Application project and name it `AddressBook`.

2. Right-click the Frameworks group in Xcode and choose Add ⇨ Existing Frameworks.

3. Select `Frameworks/AddressBook.framework` and
`Frameworks/AddressBookUI.framework`. When asked
whether you want to add them to the project, click Add.

4. Double-click the `AddressBookViewController.xib` file
to edit it in Interface Builder.

5. Populate the View window with a Button view (see
Figure 16-8).

6. Insert the following statements that appear in bold into
the `AddressBookViewController.h` file:

```
#import <UIKit/UIKit.h>
#import <AddressBook/AddressBook.h>
#import <AddressBookUI/AddressBookUI.h>

@interface AddressBookViewController :
UIViewController
    <ABPeoplePickerNavigationControllerDelegate> {
}

-(IBAction) btnClicked: (id) sender;

@end
```

FIGURE 16-8

7. In Interface Builder, Control-click and drag the Button
view to the File's Owner item and select `btnClicked:`.

8. Insert the following statements that appear in bold into the `AddressBookViewController.m` file:

```
#import "AddressBookViewController.h"

@implementation AddressBookViewController

-(IBAction) btnClicked: (id) sender{
    ABPeoplePickerNavigationController *picker =
        [[ABPeoplePickerNavigationController alloc] init];
```

```objc
    picker.peoplePickerDelegate = self;

    //---display the People Picker---
    [self presentModalViewController:picker animated:YES];

    [picker release];
}

- (void)peoplePickerNavigationControllerDidCancel:
(ABPeoplePickerNavigationController *)peoplePicker {

    //---hide the People Picker---
    [self dismissModalViewControllerAnimated:YES];
}

- (BOOL)peoplePickerNavigationController:
    (ABPeoplePickerNavigationController *)peoplePicker

    shouldContinueAfterSelectingPerson:(ABRecordRef)person {


    //---get the First Name---
    NSString *str = (NSString *)ABRecordCopyValue(person,
        kABPersonFirstNameProperty);
    str = [str stringByAppendingString:@"\n"];

    //---get the Last Name---
    str = [str stringByAppendingString:(NSString *)ABRecordCopyValue(
    person, kABPersonLastNameProperty)];
    str = [str stringByAppendingString:@"\n"];

    //---get the Emails---
    ABMultiValueRef emailInfo = ABRecordCopyValue(person, kABPersonEmailProperty);

    //---iterate through the emails---
    for (NSUInteger i=0; i< ABMultiValueGetCount(emailInfo); i++) {
        str = [str stringByAppendingString:
            (NSString *)ABMultiValueCopyValueAtIndex(emailInfo, i)];
        str = [str stringByAppendingString:@"\n"];
    }

    //---display the details---
    UIAlertView *alert = [[UIAlertView alloc] initWithTitle:@"Selected Contact"
                            message:str delegate:self
                            cancelButtonTitle:@"OK"
                            otherButtonTitles:nil];
    [alert show];
    [alert release];

    //---hide the People Picker---
    [self dismissModalViewControllerAnimated:YES];
```

```
        return NO;
    }

    - (BOOL)peoplePickerNavigationController:
        (ABPeoplePickerNavigationController *)peoplePicker
        shouldContinueAfterSelectingPerson:(ABRecordRef)person
        property:(ABPropertyID)property
        identifier:(ABMultiValueIdentifier)identifier {

        [self dismissModalViewControllerAnimated:YES];
        return NO;
    }
```

9. If you want to test the application on the iPhone Simulator, ensure
    that you have at least one contact in your Contacts application with
    the following details filled in (see Figure 16-9 for an example):

    ➤ First Name

    ➤ Last Name

    ➤ Email

FIGURE 16-9

10. Press Command-R to test the application on the iPhone Simulator. Tap the Load Contacts button
    to open the Contacts application. Select a contact, and its contact details are displayed in an alert
    view (see Figure 16-10).

FIGURE 16-10

How It Works

Like the previous section where you use the `UIImagePickerController` class to choose a photo from the Photo Library, you can also access the contacts stored in the Contacts application on your iPhone using the `ABPeoplePickerNavigationController` class. Before you use the `ABPeoplePickerNavigationController` class, you need to add the `AddressBook` and `AddressBookUI` frameworks to your project. Like the `UIImagePickerController` class, you need to conform to a specific protocol, specifically, the `ABPeoplePickerNavigationControllerDelegate` protocol. In essence, after you have selected a contact from the Contacts application, the following methods may be invoked:

➤   `peoplePickerNavigationController:shouldContinueAfterSelectingPerson:`

➤   `peoplePickerNavigationController:shouldContinueAfterSelectingPerson:property:`
    `identifier:`

➤   `peoplePickerNavigationControllerDidCancel:`

The `peoplePickerNavigationControllerDidCancel:` method is fired when the you tap on the Cancel button when selecting a contact from the Contacts application.

When you tap on a contact, the `peoplePickerNavigationController:` `shouldContinueAfterSelectingPerson:` method is fired. The details of the selected contact are encapsulated in the `shouldContinueAfterSelectingPerson:` parameter, of type `ABRecordRef`.

In this example, you extracted the various properties of the contact and display it using the `AlertView` class:

```
        //---get the First Name---
NSString *str = (NSString *)ABRecordCopyValue(person,
    kABPersonFirstNameProperty);
str = [str stringByAppendingString:@"\n"];

//---get the Last Name---
str = [str stringByAppendingString:(NSString *)ABRecordCopyValue(
person, kABPersonLastNameProperty)];
str = [str stringByAppendingString:@"\n"];

//---get the Emails---
ABMultiValueRef emailInfo = ABRecordCopyValue(person, kABPersonEmailProperty);

//---iterate through the emails---
for (NSUInteger i=0; i< ABMultiValueGetCount(emailInfo); i++) {
    str = [str stringByAppendingString:
        (NSString *)ABMultiValueCopyValueAtIndex(emailInfo, i)];
    str = [str stringByAppendingString:@"\n"];
}

//---display the details---
UIAlertView *alert = [[UIAlertView alloc] initWithTitle:@"Selected Contact"
                        message:str delegate:self
                        cancelButtonTitle:@"OK"
                        otherButtonTitles:nil];
[alert show];
[alert release];
```

When you are done, you dismiss the People Picker and return NO (which does nothing):

```
//---hide the People Picker---
[self dismissModalViewControllerAnimated:YES];
return NO;
```

What about the peoplePickerNavigationController:shouldContinueAfterSelectingPerson: property:identifier: event? This event is fired when you tap on a contact to view the contacts properties. This event is only fired when the peoplePickerNavigationController: shouldContinueAfterSelectingPerson: method returns a YES. If it returns a YES, the Contacts application will proceed to display the properties of the selected contact. When a property is selected, the peoplePickerNavigationController:shouldContinueAfterSelectingPerson:property: identifier: event will then be fired. In this event, you return a YES to perform the action for the property selected and dismiss the picker. You return NO to show the person in the picker.

Adding a Contact

Besides retrieving the information of contacts stored in the Contacts application, you might also want to add a new contact directly into it. You can do so via the code snippets below:

```
-(void) addContact{

    ABAddressBookRef addressBook = ABAddressBookCreate();
    ABRecordRef person = ABPersonCreate();

    //---add the first name and last name---
    ABRecordSetValue(person, kABPersonFirstNameProperty, @"Wei-Meng" , nil);
    ABRecordSetValue(person, kABPersonLastNameProperty, @"Lee", nil);

    //---add the address---
    ABMutableMultiValueRef address =
        ABMultiValueCreateMutable(kABMultiDictionaryPropertyType);
    NSMutableDictionary *addressDictionary = [[NSMutableDictionary alloc] init];

    [addressDictionary setObject:@"Some Street Name" forKey:(NSString *)
        kABPersonAddressStreetKey];
    [addressDictionary setObject:@"New York" forKey:(NSString *)
        kABPersonAddressCityKey];
    [addressDictionary setObject:@"NY" forKey:(NSString *)
        kABPersonAddressStateKey];
    [addressDictionary setObject:@"12345" forKey:(NSString *)
        kABPersonAddressZIPKey];
    [addressDictionary setObject:@"United States" forKey:(NSString *)
        kABPersonAddressCountryKey];
    [addressDictionary setObject:@"US" forKey:(NSString *)
        kABPersonAddressCountryCodeKey];

    ABMultiValueAddValueAndLabel(address, addressDictionary, kABHomeLabel, NULL);
```

```
        ABRecordSetValue(person, kABPersonAddressProperty, address, nil);

        //---add the address book for the contact and save the addressbook---
        ABAddressBookAddRecord(addressBook, person, nil);
        ABAddressBookSave(addressBook, nil);
        CFRelease(person);
    }
```

The above method - addContact, adds a contact to the Contacts application. It populates the contact with the following information:

➤ First Name

➤ Last Name

➤ Home address

   ➤ Street

   ➤ City

   ➤ State

   ➤ Zip

   ➤ Country

   ➤ Country code

FIGURE 16-11

Figure 16-11 shows the details of the contact added.

 NOTE *For more information about the various methods used to add a contact, refer to the ABAddressBook reference in the Apple's iPhone Reference Library. You can download the reference at:* http://developer.apple.com/ iphone/library/documentation/AddressBook/Reference/ ABAddressBookRef_iPhoneOS/ABAddressBookRef_iPhoneOS.pdf.

Removing a Contact

To remove a contact from the Contacts application, use the following code snippet:

```
    -(void) removeContact: (NSString *) firstName andLastName:(NSString *) lastName {

        ABAddressBookRef addressBook = ABAddressBookCreate();
        CFArrayRef allContacts = ABAddressBookCopyArrayOfAllPeople(addressBook);

        CFIndex contactsCount = ABAddressBookGetPersonCount(addressBook);

        for (int i = 0; i < contactsCount; i++)
```

```
        {
            ABRecordRef ref = CFArrayGetValueAtIndex(allContacts, i);
            NSString *contactFirstName = (NSString *) ABRecordCopyValue(
                ref, kABPersonFirstNameProperty);
            NSString *contactLastName = (NSString *) ABRecordCopyValue(
                ref, kABPersonLastNameProperty);

            if ( [firstName isEqualToString:contactFirstName] &&
                [lastName isEqualToString:contactLastName])
            {
                ABAddressBookRemoveRecord(addressBook, ref, nil);
                ABAddressBookSave(addressBook, nil);
            }
        }
    }
}
```

The preceding method, `removeContact`, takes in two parameters, `firstName` and `lastName`, and searches the Contacts application for a contact with a matching first and last name. If a contact is found, it is removed from the Contacts application.

 NOTE *For more information about the various methods used to remove a contact, refer to the ABAddressBook reference in the Apple's iPhone Reference Library. You can download the reference at* `http://developer.apple.com/ iphone/library/documentation/AddressBook/Reference/ ABAddressBookRef_iPhoneOS/ABAddressBookRef_iPhoneOS.pdf`.

SUMMARY

In this chapter, you saw how you could easily integrate the various built-in applications into your own iPhone applications. In particular, you saw how you can invoke the built-in SMS, Mail, Safari, and phone dialer simply by using a URL string. You also learned about accessing the Contacts and Photo Library using the classes provided by the iPhone SDK.

EXERCISES

1. Name the various URL strings for invoking the Safari, Mail, SMS, and phone dialer applications.

2. What is the class name for invoking the Image Picker UI in the iPhone?

3. What is the class name for invoking the People Picker UI in the iPhone?

▶ **WHAT YOU LEARNED IN THIS CHAPTER**

TOPIC	KEY CONCEPTS

Sending email from within your application	`NSString *emailString =`
	
	`@"mailto:?to=USER@EMAIL.COM&subject=SUBJECT&body=BODY OF EMAIL";`
	
	`[[UIApplication sharedApplication]`
	
	`openURL:[NSURL`
	
	`URLWithString:emailString]];`

Invoking Safari	`[[UIApplication sharedApplication]`
	
	`openURL:[NSURL`
	
	`URLWithString:`
	`@"http://www.apple.com"]];`

Invoking the Phone	`[[UIApplication sharedApplication]`
	`openURL:[NSURL`
	`URLWithString:@"tel:1234567890"]];`

Invoking SMS	`[[UIApplication sharedApplication]`
	`openURL:[NSURL`
	`URLWithString: @"sms:96924065"]];`

Accessing the Photo Library	Use the `UIImagePickerController` class and ensure your View Controller conforms to the `UINavigationControllerDelegate` protocol.
Accessing the Contacts application	Use the `ABPeoplePickerNavigationController` class from the `AddressBookUI` framework.

17

Accessing the Hardware

WHAT YOU WILL LEARN IN THIS CHAPTER

➤ How to obtain accelerometer data from your iPhone or iPod Touch

➤ How to detect shakes to your device

➤ How to obtain geographical data using the Core Location service in the iPhone and iPod Touch

➤ How to display a map in your application

In the previous chapter, you saw how you could access the built-in applications on an iPhone and iPod Touch through various means — URL strings as well as using the specialized classes provided by the iPhone SDK. In this chapter, you learn how to access the hardware of your device, such as the accelerometer, and obtain location information through GPS, cell towers, and wireless hotspots.

USING THE ACCELEROMETER

One of the most innovative features of the iPhone and iPod Touch is the built-in accelerometer. The accelerometer allows the device to detect the orientation of the device and adapts the content to suit the new orientation. For example, when you rotate your device sideways, the Safari Web browser automatically switches the screen to landscape mode so that you now have a wider viewing space. Similarly, the camera relies on the accelerometer to tell it whether you are taking a picture in portrait or landscape mode.

The accelerometer in iPhone and iPod Touch measures the acceleration of the device relative to freefall. A value of 1 indicates that the device is experiencing 1 g of force exerting on it (1 g of force being the gravitational pull of the earth, which your device experiences when it is stationary). The accelerometer measures the acceleration of the device in three different axes: X, Y, and Z. Figure 17-1 shows the different axes measured by the accelerometer.

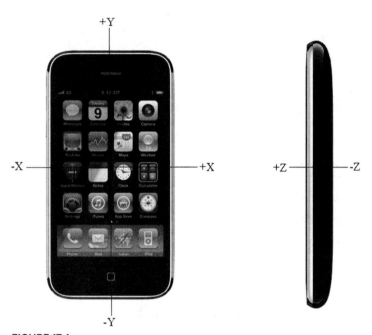

FIGURE 17-1

Table 17-1 shows the various readings of the three axes when the device is in the various positions.

TABLE 17-1: The Various Readings of the X, Y, and Z Axes

POSITION	X	Y	Z
Vertical upright position	0.0	-1.0	0.0
Landscape Left	1.0	0.0	0.0
Landscape Right	-1.0	0.0	0.0
Upside Down	0.0	1	0.0
Flat Up	0.0	0.0	-1.0
Flat Down	0.0	0.0	1.0

If the device is held upright and moved to the right quickly, the value of the X-axis will increase from 0 to a positive value. If it is moved to the left quickly, the value of the X-axis will decrease from 0 to a negative value. If the device is moved upward quickly, the value of the Y-axis will increase from -1.0 to a larger value. If the device is moved download quickly, the value of the Y-axis will decrease from -1.0 to a smaller value.

If the device is lying flat on a table and then dropped, the value of the Z-axis will decrease from -1.0 to a smaller number. If it is moved upward, the value of the Z-axis will increase from -1.0 to a bigger number.

 NOTE *The accelerometer used on the iPhone and iPod Touch gives a maximum reading of about +/- 2.3G with a resolution of about 0.018 g.*

In the following Try it Out, you learn how to programmatically access the data returned by the accelerometer. Obtaining the accelerometer data allows you to build very interesting applications, such as a spirit level, as well as games that depend on motion detection.

TRY IT OUT   Accessing the Accelerometer Data

Codefile [Accelerometer.zip] available for download at Wrox.com

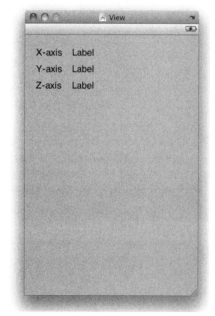

FIGURE 17-2

1. Using Xcode, create a new View-based Application project and name it `Accelerometer`.

2. Double-click the `AccelerometerViewController.xib` file to edit it in Interface Builder.

3. Populate the View window with the six Label views, as shown in Figure 17-2.

4. In the `AccelerometerViewController.h` file, add the following statements that appear in bold:

```
#import <UIKit/UIKit.h>

@interface AccelerometerViewController :
UIViewController
    <UIAccelerometerDelegate> {

    IBOutlet UILabel *labelX;
    IBOutlet UILabel *labelY;
    IBOutlet UILabel *labelZ;
}

@property (nonatomic, retain) UILabel *labelX;
@property (nonatomic, retain) UILabel *labelY;
@property (nonatomic, retain) UILabel *labelZ;

@end
```

5. Back in Interface Builder, Control-click and drag the File's Owner item to each of the three Label views and select `labelX`, `labelY`, and `labelZ`, respectively.

6. In the `AccelerometerViewController.m` file, add the following statements that appear in bold:

```
#import "AccelerometerViewController.h"

@implementation AccelerometerViewController

@synthesize labelX, labelY, labelZ;

- (void)viewDidLoad {
    UIAccelerometer *acc = [UIAccelerometer sharedAccelerometer];
    acc.delegate = self;
    acc.updateInterval = 1.0f/60.0f;
    [super viewDidLoad];
}

- (void)accelerometer:(UIAccelerometer *) acc
    didAccelerate:(UIAcceleration *)acceleration {

    NSString *str = [[NSString alloc] initWithFormat:@"%g", acceleration.x];
    labelX.text = str;
    str = [[NSString alloc] initWithFormat:@"%g", acceleration.y];
    labelY.text = str;
    str = [[NSString alloc] initWithFormat:@"%g", acceleration.z];
    labelZ.text = str;
    [str release];
}

- (void)dealloc {
    [labelX release];
    [labelY release];
    [labelZ release];
    [super dealloc];
}
```

7. Press Command-R to test the application on an iPhone device. Figure 17-3 shows the data displayed on the application when my iPhone is resting on the iPhone docking cradle.

 NOTE *For accelerometer data, you need a real device — either an iPhone or an iPod Touch.*

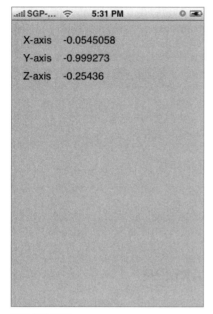

X-axis   -0.0545058
Y-axis   -0.999273
Z-axis   -0.25436

FIGURE 17-3

How It Works

To use the accelerometer in your iPhone or iPod Touch, you need to the implement the
`UIAccelerometerDelegate` protocol in your delegate (such as the View Controller):

```
@interface AccelerometerViewController : UIViewController
    <UIAccelerometerDelegate> {
```

When the view is loaded, you first obtain a single instance of the `UIAccelerometer` class using the
`sharedAccelerometer` method. You then specify the delegate of the instance and the update interval in
which you want to obtain accelerometer data:

```
- (void)viewDidLoad {
    UIAccelerometer *acc = [UIAccelerometer sharedAccelerometer];
    acc.delegate = self;
    acc.updateInterval = 1.0f/60.0f;
    [super viewDidLoad];
}
```

The `updateInterval` property specifies the interval in seconds — that is, the number of seconds
between updates. In the preceding case, you indicate that you want the accelerometer data to be
updated 60 times a second.

The `UIAccelerometerDelegate` protocol defines a single method that you need to implement in order to obtain accelerometer data: `accelerometer:didAccelerate:`. In your case, you extract the values of the three axes and display them on the three Label views:

```
- (void)accelerometer:(UIAccelerometer *) acc
    didAccelerate:(UIAcceleration *)acceleration {

    NSString *str = [[NSString alloc] initWithFormat:@"%g", acceleration.x];
    labelX.text = str;
    str = [[NSString alloc] initWithFormat:@"%g", acceleration.y];
    labelY.text = str;
    str = [[NSString alloc] initWithFormat:@"%g", acceleration.z];
    labelZ.text = str;
    [str release];
}
```

DETECTING SHAKES IN IPHONE OS2 AND EARLIER

In iPhone OS 3.0, Apple provides the Shake API (discussed in the next section), which is a set of methods that allows you to detect shakes to the device. However, how do you detect shakes in iPhone OS 2.0 and earlier?

The answer is actually very simple. You can add some code in the `accelerometer:didAccelerate:` event, like this:

```
#import "AccelerometerViewController.h"

#define kAccelerationThreshold 2.2

//...

//...


- (void)accelerometer:(UIAccelerometer *) acc
    didAccelerate:(UIAcceleration *)acceleration {

    if (fabsf(acceleration.x) > kAccelerationThreshold)
    {
        NSLog(@"Shake detected");
    }
}
```

The `fabsf()` function returns the absolute value of a floating-point number. In this case, if the X-axis value registers an absolute value of more than 2.2, it is deemed that the user is shaking the device.

USING SHAKE API TO DETECT SHAKES IN OS 3.0

In iPhone OS 3.0, Apple announced the availability of a new Shake API that helps you to detect shakes to the device. In reality, this new Shake API comes in the form of three events that you can handle in your code:

➤   `motionBegan:`

➤   `motionEnded:`

➤   `motionCancelled:`

These three events are defined in the `UIResponder` class, which is the super class of `UIApplication`, `UIView`, and its subclasses (including `UIWindow`). The following Try It Out shows you how to detect shakes to your device using these three events.

TRY IT OUT   Using the Shake API

Codefile [Shake.zip] available for download at Wrox.com

1.   Using Xcode, create a new View-based Application project and name it `Shake`.

2.   Double-click the `ShakeViewController.xib` file to edit it in Interface Builder.

3.   Populate the View window with the following views (see Figure 17-4):

➤   TextField

➤   DatePicker

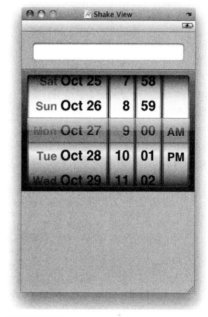

4.   Insert the following statements that appear in bold into the `ShakeViewController.h` file:

```
#import <UIKit/UIKit.h>

@interface ShakeViewController : UIViewController {
    IBOutlet UITextField *textField;
    IBOutlet UIDatePicker *datePicker;
}

@property (nonatomic, retain) UITextField
*textField;
@property (nonatomic, retain) UIDatePicker
*datePicker;

-(IBAction) doneEditing: (id) sender;

@end
```

FIGURE 17-4

5.   In Interface Builder, control-click and drag the File's Owner item to the TextField view and select `textField`.

6. Control-click and drag the File's Owner item to the DatePicker view and select `datePicker`.

7. Right-click the TextField view and connect its `Did End on Exit` event to the File's Owner item (see Figure 17-5). Select `doneEditing:`.

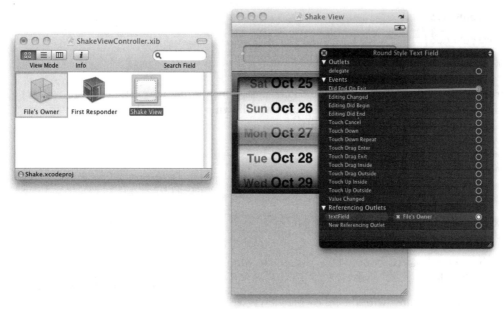

FIGURE 17-5

8. Insert the following statements that appear in bold to the `ShakeViewController.m` file:

```objc
#import "ShakeViewController.h"

@implementation ShakeViewController

@synthesize textField, datePicker;

- (void) viewDidAppear:(BOOL)animated
{
    [self.view becomeFirstResponder];
    [super viewDidAppear:animated];
}

- (IBAction) doneEditing: (id) sender {
    //---when keyboard is hidden, make the view the first responder
    // or else the Shake API will not work---
    [self.view becomeFirstResponder];
}

- (void)motionBegan:(UIEventSubtype)motion withEvent:(UIEvent *)event {
```

```
        if (event.subtype == UIEventSubtypeMotionShake )
        {
            NSLog(@"motionBegan:");
        }
    }

    - (void)motionCancelled:(UIEventSubtype)motion withEvent:(UIEvent *)event {
        if (event.subtype == UIEventSubtypeMotionShake )
        {
            NSLog(@"motionCancelled:");
        }
    }

    - (void)motionEnded:(UIEventSubtype)motion withEvent:(UIEvent *)event {
        if (event.subtype == UIEventSubtypeMotionShake )
        {
            NSLog(@"motionEnded:");
        }
    }

    - (void)dealloc {
        [textField release];
        [datePicker release];
        [super dealloc];
    }
```

9. Right-click the Classes group in Xcode and choose Add ➪ New File. Select the UIView subclass template (see Figure 17-6).

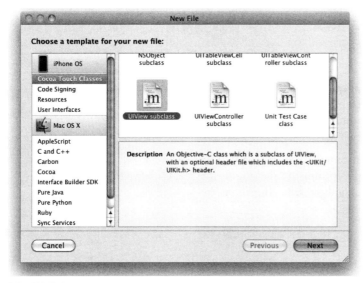

FIGURE 17-6

10. Click Next and name the file `ShakeView.m`.

11. Insert the following statements in bold in `ShakeView.m`:

```
#import "ShakeView.h"

@implementation ShakeView

- (id)initWithFrame:(CGRect)frame {
    if (self = [super initWithFrame:frame]) {
        // Initialization code
    }
    return self;
}

- (void)drawRect:(CGRect)rect {
    // Drawing code
}

- (void)dealloc {
    [super dealloc];
}

- (BOOL)canBecomeFirstResponder {
    return YES;
}

@end
```

12. In Interface Builder, select the View window and view its Identity Inspector window. Select its class name as `ShakeView` (see Figure 17-7).

13. Save the file in Interface Builder.

14. Press Command-R to test the application on the iPhone Simulator. Open the Debugger Console window by pressing Command-Shift-R in Xcode.

FIGURE 17-7

15. With the application in the iPhone Simulator, choose Hardware ➪ Shake Gesture to simulate shaking the device. Observe the information printed in the Debugger Console window (see Figure 17-8).

FIGURE 17-8

16. Tap the TextField view to make the keyboard appear. Choose Hardware ➪ Shake Gesture to simulate shaking the device again. Observe the values printed in the Debugger Console window.

17. Close the keyboard by tapping the return key on the keyboard. Simulate shaking the simulator again and observe the output on the Debugger Console.

How It Works

You need to be aware that the three events used for monitoring shakes are fired only when there is a first responder in your View. Hence, the first thing you do when your View appears is to set it to become the first responder (in the ShakeViewController.m file):

```
- (void) viewDidAppear:(BOOL)animated
{
    [self.view becomeFirstResponder];
    [super viewDidAppear:animated];
}
```

However, by default, the View cannot be a first responder, so you need to create a `UIView` subclass (`ShakeView.m`) so that you can override the default `canBecomeFirstResponder` method to return a `YES`:

```
- (BOOL)canBecomeFirstResponder {
    return YES;
}
```

Doing so allows your View to become a first responder. By default, Interface Builder wires your View with the `UIView` base class (with which you need not do anything most of the time). You now need to tell Interface Builder to use the newly created `ShakeView` subclass.

Next, you handle the three events in the `ShakeViewController.m` file:

```
- (void)motionBegan:(UIEventSubtype)motion withEvent:(UIEvent *)event {
    if (event.subtype == UIEventSubtypeMotionShake )
    {
        NSLog(@"motionBegan:");
    }
}

- (void)motionCancelled:(UIEventSubtype)motion withEvent:(UIEvent *)event {
    if (event.subtype == UIEventSubtypeMotionShake )
    {
        NSLog(@"motionCancelled:");
    }
}

- (void)motionEnded:(UIEventSubtype)motion withEvent:(UIEvent *)event {
    if (event.subtype == UIEventSubtypeMotionShake )
    {
        NSLog(@"motionEnded:");
    }
}
```

For each event, you first check that the motion is indeed a shake; then print a debugging statement in the Debugger Console.

In the `doneEditing:` method (which is fired when the user dismisses the keyboard by tapping the Return key), you make the View the first responder:

```
-(IBAction) doneEditing: (id) sender {
    //---when keyboard is hidden, make the view the first responder
    // or else the Shake API will not work---
    [self.view becomeFirstResponder];
}
```

If you don't do this, the three motion-sensing events are not fired. The key point to remember is that something has to be the first responder.

The `motionBegan:` event is fired when the OS suspects that the device is being shaken. If eventually the OS determines that the action is not a shake, the `motionCancelled:` event is fired. When the OS finally determines that the action is a shake action, the `motionEnded:` event is fired.

PERFORMING AN ACTION WHEN THE DEVICE IS SHAKEN

Now that you know how to detect shaking on your devices, you can put it to good use. Using the same project, modify it so that when the device is shaken, you reset the DatePicker view to today's date.

TRY IT OUT   Resetting the DatePicker when Shaken

1. In the `ShakeViewController.m` file, add the following statements that appear in bold:

```
- (void)ResetDatePicker {
    [datePicker setDate:[NSDate date]];
}

- (void)motionEnded:(UIEventSubtype)motion withEvent:(UIEvent
*)event {
    if (event.subtype == UIEventSubtypeMotionShake )
    {
        NSLog(@"motionEnded:");
        [self ResetDatePicker];
    }
}
```

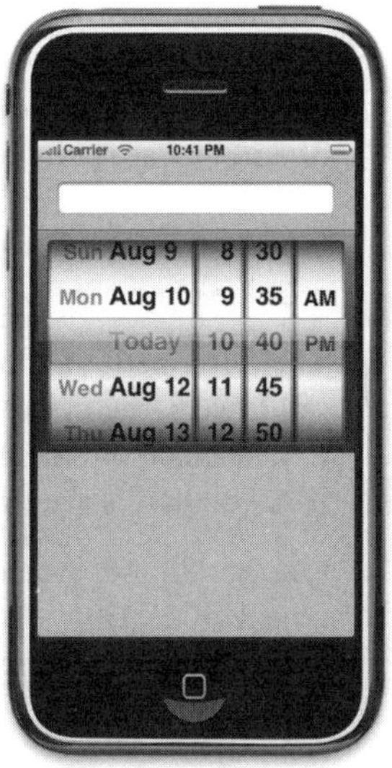

2. Press Command-R to test the application on the iPhone Simulator. Set the DatePicker view to some date. Choose Hardware ➪ Shake Gesture to simulate shaking the device. Notice that the DatePicker view now resets to today's date (see Figure 17-9).

How It Works

In this example, you first added a `ResetDatePicker` method to reset the DatePicker view to today's date:

```
- (void)ResetDatePicker {
    [datePicker setDate:[NSDate date]];
}
```

FIGURE 17-9

When the device is shaken, you then call the `ResetDatePicker` method to reset the DatePicker view to the current date:

```
- (void)motionEnded:(UIEventSubtype)motion withEvent:(UIEvent *)event {
    if (event.subtype == UIEventSubtypeMotionShake )
    {
        NSLog(@"motionEnded:");
        [self ResetDatePicker];
    }
}
```

LOCATION-BASED SERVICES

Nowadays, mobile devices are commonly equipped with GPS receivers. Using a GPS receiver, you find your location easily because of the many satellites orbiting the earth, courtesy of the U.S. government. However, GPS requires a clear sky to work and hence does not work indoors. Also, the first-generation iPhone is not equipped with a GPS receiver.

Besides GPS, another effective way to locate one's position is through cell tower triangulation. When a mobile phone is switched on, it is constantly in contact with base stations surrounding it. By knowing the identity of cell towers, it is possible to correlate this information into a physical location through the use of various databases containing the cell towers' identity and their exact geographical location. Cell tower triangulation has its advantages over GPS because it works indoors, without the need to obtain information from satellites. However, it is not as accurate as GPS because its accuracy depends on the area you are in. Cell tower triangulation works best in densely populated areas where the cell towers are closely located. However, cell tower triangulation is not applicable to iPod Touch because it does not have a cellular phone in it.

The third method of locating one's position is to rely on Wi-Fi triangulation. Rather than connect to cell towers, the device connects to a Wi-Fi network and checks the service provider against databases to determine the location serviced by the provider. Of the three methods described here, Wi-Fi triangulation is the least accurate.

On the iPhone, Apple provides the Core Location framework to help you determine your physical location. The beauty of this framework is that it makes use of all three approaches mentioned, and whichever method it uses is totally transparent to the developer. You simply specify the accuracy you need, and Core Location determines the best way to obtain the results for you.

Sound amazing? It is. The following Try It Out shows you how this is done in code.

TRY IT OUT   **Obtaining Location Coordinates**

Codefile [GPS.zip] available for download at Wrox.com

1.   Using Xcode, create a new View-based Application project and name it `GPS`.

2.   Double-click the `GPSViewController.xib` file to edit it in Interface Builder.

3.   Populate the View window with the following views (see Figure 17-10):

➤   `Label`

➤   `TextField`

4. Right-click the Frameworks group in Xcode and choose Add ⇨ Existing Frameworks. Select `Framework/CoreLocation.framework`.

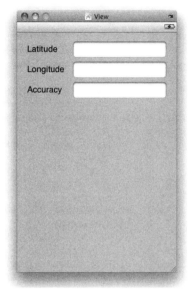

5. Insert the following statements that appear in bold into the `GPSViewController.h` file:

```
#import <UIKit/UIKit.h>
#import <CoreLocation/CoreLocation.h>

@interface GPSViewController : UIViewController
    <CLLocationManagerDelegate> {

    IBOutlet UITextField *latitudeTextField;
    IBOutlet UITextField *longitudeTextField;
    IBOutlet UITextField *accuracyTextField;
    CLLocationManager *lm;
}

@property (retain, nonatomic) UITextField
*latitudeTextField;
@property (retain, nonatomic) UITextField
*longitudeTextField;
@property (retain, nonatomic) UITextField
*accuracyTextField;
```

FIGURE 17-10

```
@end
```

6. Back in Interface Builder, Control-click and drag the File's Owner item to each of the three TextField views and select `latitudeTextField`, `longitudeTextField`, and `accuracyTextField`, respectively.

7. Insert the following statements that appear in bold into the `GPSViewController.m` file:

```
#import "GPSViewController.h"

@implementation GPSViewController

@synthesize latitudeTextField, longitudeTextField, accuracyTextField;

- (void) viewDidLoad {
    lm = [[CLLocationManager alloc] init];
    if ([lm locationServicesEnabled]) {
        lm.delegate = self;
        lm.desiredAccuracy = kCLLocationAccuracyBest;
        lm.distanceFilter = 1000.0f;
        [lm startUpdatingLocation];
    }
}

- (void) locationManager: (CLLocationManager *) manager
    didUpdateToLocation: (CLLocation *) newLocation
```

```
        fromLocation: (CLLocation *) oldLocation{

        NSString *lat = [[NSString alloc] initWithFormat:@"%g",
            newLocation.coordinate.latitude];
        latitudeTextField.text = lat;

        NSString *lng = [[NSString alloc] initWithFormat:@"%g",
            newLocation.coordinate.longitude];
        longitudeTextField.text = lng;

        NSString *acc = [[NSString alloc] initWithFormat:@"%g",
            newLocation.horizontalAccuracy];
        accuracyTextField.text = acc;

        [acc release];
        [lat release];
        [lng release];
    }

- (void) locationManager: (CLLocationManager *) manager
    didFailWithError: (NSError *) error {

        NSString *msg = [[NSString alloc] initWithString:@"Error obtaining location"];
        UIAlertView *alert = [[UIAlertView alloc]
                            initWithTitle:@"Error"
                            message:msg
                            delegate:nil
                            cancelButtonTitle: @"Done"
                            otherButtonTitles:nil];
        [alert show];
        [msg release];
        [alert release];
    }

- (void) dealloc{
        [lm release];
        [latitudeTextField release];
        [longitudeTextField release];
        [accuracyTextField release];
        [super dealloc];
    }
```

8.   Press Command-R to test the application on the iPhone Simulator. Figure 17-11 shows the simulator displaying the latitude and longitude of the location returned. It also shows the accuracy of the result.

 NOTE *You can test the application on the iPhone Simulator. However, note that for the simulator, the device always reports a fixed position. There is no prize for guessing correctly where this position is referring to.*

How It Works

First, to use the `CLLocationManager` class, you need to implement the `CLLocationManagerDelegate` protocol in your View Controller class:

```
@interface GPSViewController : UIViewController
    <CLLocationManagerDelegate> {
```

When the View is loaded, you first create an instance of the `CLLocationManager` class:

```
- (void) viewDidLoad {
    lm = [[CLLocationManager alloc] init];
    if ([lm locationServicesEnabled]) {
        lm.delegate = self;
        lm.desiredAccuracy = kCLLocationAccuracyBest;
        lm.distanceFilter = 1000.0f;
        [lm startUpdatingLocation];
    }
}
```

FIGURE 17-11

Before you proceed to use the object, you check to see whether the user has enabled Location Services on the device. If it is enabled, you then proceed to specify the desired accuracy using the `desiredAccuracy` property. You can use the following constants to specify the accuracy that you want:

➤   kCLLocationAccuracyBest

➤   kCLLocationAccuracyNearestTenMeters

➤   kCLLocationAccuracyHundredMeters

➤   kCLLocationAccuracyKilometer

➤   kCLLocationAccuracyThreeKilometers

While you can specify the best accuracy that you want, the actual accuracy is not guaranteed. Also, specifying a location with greater accuracy takes a significant amount of time and your device's battery power.

The `distanceFilter` property allows you to specify the distance a device must move laterally before an update is generated. The unit for this property is in meters, relative to its last position. If you want to be notified of all movements, use the `kCLDistanceFilterNone` constant. Finally, you start the Location Manager using the `startUpdatingLocation` method.

To obtain location information, you need to handle two events:

➤   locationManager:didUpdateToLocation:fromLocation:

➤   locationManager:didFailWithError:

When a new location value is available, the `locationManager:didUpdateToLocation:fromLocation:` event is fired. If the location manager cannot locate the location value, it fires the `locationManager: didFailWithError:` event. When a location value is obtained, you display its latitude and longitude along with its accuracy using the `CLLocation` object:

```
- (void) locationManager: (CLLocationManager *) manager
    didUpdateToLocation: (CLLocation *) newLocation
    fromLocation: (CLLocation *) oldLocation{

    NSString *lat = [[NSString alloc] initWithFormat:@"%g",
        newLocation.coordinate.latitude];
    latitudeTextField.text = lat;

    NSString *lng = [[NSString alloc] initWithFormat:@"%g",
        newLocation.coordinate.longitude];
    longitudeTextField.text = lng;

    NSString *acc = [[NSString alloc] initWithFormat:@"%g",
        newLocation.horizontalAccuracy];
    accuracyTextField.text = acc;

    [acc release];
    [lat release];
    [lng release];
}
```

The `horizontalAccuracy` property of the `CLLocation` object specifies the radius of accuracy in meters.

Displaying Maps

While obtaining the location value of a position is interesting, it is not of much use if you cannot visually locate it on a map. Hence, the most ideal situation would be to use the location information and display it on a map. Fortunately, iPhone SDK 3.0 comes with the Map Kit API to make displaying Google Maps in your application a snap. You see how this can be done in the following Try it Out.

TRY IT OUT   Displaying a Location Using the Map Kit

1.   Using the same project created in the previous section, add a Button view to the View window in the `GPSViewController.xib` file (see Figure 17-12).

2. Right-click the Frameworks group in Xcode and add the existing framework called `MapKit.framework`.

3. Insert the following statements that appear in bold into the `GPSViewController.h` file:

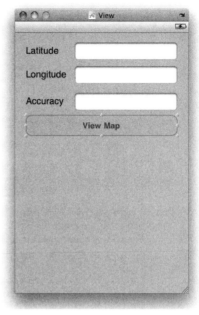

FIGURE 17-12

```
#import <UIKit/UIKit.h>
#import <CoreLocation/CoreLocation.h>
#import <MapKit/MapKit.h>

@interface GPSViewController : UIViewController
    <CLLocationManagerDelegate> {
    IBOutlet UITextField *accuracyTextField;
    IBOutlet UITextField *latitudeTextField;
    IBOutlet UITextField *longitudeTextField;
    CLLocationManager *lm;

    MKMapView *mapView;
}

@property (retain, nonatomic) UITextField
*accuracyTextField;
@property (retain, nonatomic) UITextField
*latitudeTextField;
@property (retain, nonatomic) UITextField
*longitudeTextField;

-(IBAction) btnViewMap: (id) sender;

@end
```

4. Back in Interface Builder, Control-click and drag the Button view to the File's Owner item and select `btnViewMap:`.

5. In the `GPSViewController.m` file, add the following statements that appear in bold:

```
-(IBAction) btnViewMap: (id) sender {
    [self.view addSubview:mapView];
}

- (void) viewDidLoad {
    lm = [[CLLocationManager alloc] init];
    lm.delegate = self;
    lm.desiredAccuracy = kCLLocationAccuracyBest;
    lm.distanceFilter = 1000.0f;
    [lm startUpdatingLocation];

    mapView = [[MKMapView alloc] initWithFrame:self.view.bounds];
    mapView.mapType = MKMapTypeHybrid;
}

- (void) locationManager: (CLLocationManager *) manager
    didUpdateToLocation: (CLLocation *) newLocation
    fromLocation: (CLLocation *) oldLocation{
```

```
       NSString *lat = [[NSString alloc] initWithFormat:@"%g",
          newLocation.coordinate.latitude];
       latitudeTextField.text = lat;

       NSString *lng = [[NSString alloc] initWithFormat:@"%g",
          newLocation.coordinate.longitude];
       longitudeTextField.text = lng;

       NSString *acc = [[NSString alloc] initWithFormat:@"%g",
          newLocation.horizontalAccuracy];
       accuracyTextField.text = acc;

       [acc release];
       [lat release];
       [lng release];

       MKCoordinateSpan span;
       span.latitudeDelta=.005;
       span.longitudeDelta=.005;

       MKCoordinateRegion region;
       region.center = newLocation.coordinate;
       region.span=span;

       [mapView setRegion:region animated:TRUE];
     }

     - (void) dealloc{
       [mapView release];
       [lm release];
       [latitudeTextField release];
       [longitudeTextField release];
       [accuracyTextField release];
       [super dealloc];
     }
```

FIGURE 17-13

6. Press Command-R to test the application on the iPhone Simulator. Tapping the View Map button shows the map displaying the location reported by the location manager (see Figure 17-13).

> **NOTE** *If you test the application on a real device, you will be able to see that the map updates itself dynamically when you move about. Be sure to alter the* distanceFilter *property to a smaller number so that you can track small changes in distance.*

How It Works

To use the Map Kit in your application, you first need to add the `MapKit.framework` to your project.

When the view has loaded, you create an instance of the `MKMapView` class and set the map type (hybrid — map and satellite) to display:

```
- (void) viewDidLoad {
    lm = [[CLLocationManager alloc] init];
    lm.delegate = self;
    lm.desiredAccuracy = kCLLocationAccuracyBest;
    lm.distanceFilter = 1000.0f;
    [lm startUpdatingLocation];

    mapView = [[MKMapView alloc] initWithFrame:self.view.bounds];
    mapView.mapType = MKMapTypeHybrid;
}
```

When the View Map button is tapped, you add the `mapView` object to the current view:

```
-(IBAction) btnViewMap: (id) sender {
    [self.view addSubview:mapView];
}
```

When the location information is updated, you zoom into the location using the `setRegion:` method of the `mapView` object:

```
- (void) locationManager: (CLLocationManager *) manager
    didUpdateToLocation: (CLLocation *) newLocation
    fromLocation: (CLLocation *) oldLocation{

    //...
    //...

    MKCoordinateSpan span;
    span.latitudeDelta=.005;
    span.longitudeDelta=.005;

    MKCoordinateRegion region;
    region.center = newLocation.coordinate;
    region.span=span;

    [mapView setRegion:region animated:TRUE];
}
```

NOTE *For more information on the* `MKMapView` *class, refer to Apple's documentation at* `http://developer.apple.com/iphone/library/navigation/Frameworks/CocoaTouch/MapKit/index.html`.

SUMMARY

In this chapter, you have seen how to manipulate the various types of hardware of your device: the accelerometer, Shake API, and location-based services using Core Location. Combining all this knowledge allows you to create very compelling applications.

EXERCISES

1. Name the protocol that your delegate needs to conform to in order to use the accelerometer on your iPhone and iPod Touch.

2. Name the three events in the Shake API in iPhone SDK 3.0.

3. Core Location uses three different methods to obtain a device's location. Discuss the various methods used by the iPhone and iPod Touch.

▶ **WHAT YOU LEARNED IN THIS CHAPTER**

TOPIC	KEY CONCEPTS
Accessing the accelerometer	Ensure that your view controller conforms to the `UIAccelerometerDelegate` protocol and create an instance of the `UIAccelerometer` class.
	To listen to changes in acceleration, implement the `accelerometer:didAccelerate:` method.
Detecting Shakes	You can either use the accelerometer data or use the new Shake API in iPhone OS 3.0. For the Shake API, handle the following events: `motionBegan:`, `motionEnded:`, and `motionCancelled:`.
Obtaining location data	Add the `CoreLocation` framework to your project.
	Ensure that your view controller conforms to the `CLLocationManagerDelegate` protocol and create an instance of the `CLLocationManager` class.
	To listen to changes in location, implement the `locationManager:didUpdateToLocation: fromLocation:` method.
Specifying accuracy for location data	Use one of the following constants:
	➤ `kCLLocationAccuracyBest`
	➤ `kCLLocationAccuracyNearestTenMeters`
	➤ `kCLLocationAccuracyHundredMeters`
	➤ `kCLLocationAccuracyKilometer`
	➤ `kCLLocationAccuracyThreeKilometers`
Displaying Maps	Add the `MapKit` framework to your project.
	Create an instance of the `MKMapView` class and use the various properties to specify the location.

PART V
Appendices

Answers to Exercises

This appendix provides the solutions for the end-of-chapter exercises located at the end of each chapter, except Chapter 1.

CHAPTER 2 EXERCISE SOLUTIONS

Answer to Question 1

The minimum image size you should design is 57 × 57 pixels. It is all right to design a larger image because the iPhone automatically resizes it for you. In general, try to design a larger image because doing so prepares your application for the newer devices that Apple may roll out.

Answer to Question 2

You should implement the `shouldAutorotateToInterfaceOrientation:` method and code the appropriate statements to support the orientation you want. To support all orientations, simply return a YES in this method, like this:

```
- (BOOL)shouldAutorotateToInterfaceOrientation:(UIInterfaceOrientation)
interfaceOrientation {
    // Return YES for supported orientations
    return YES;
}
```

CHAPTER 3 EXERCISE SOLUTIONS

Answer to Question 1

In the `.h` file:

```
//---declare an outlet---
IBOutlet UITextField *nameTextField;
//...
//...
//---expose the outlet as a property---
@property (nonatomic, retain) UITextField *nameTextField;
```

In the `.m` file:

```
@implementation BasicUIViewController
//---generate the getters and setters for the property---
@synthesize nameTextField;
```

Answer to Question 2

In the `.h` file:

```
- (IBAction)btnClicked:(id)sender;
```

In the `.m` file:

```
@implementation BasicUIViewController
//...
//...
- (IBAction)btnClicked:(id)sender {
    //---your code for the action here---
}
```

CHAPTER 4 EXERCISE SOLUTIONS

Answer to Question 1

To connect a view to its View Controller, do the following within its `.xib` file:

➤   In the File's Owner item, specify the class to the name of the View Controller.

➤   Connect the File's Owner item to the view.

Answer to Question 2

You use an alert view when displaying a message to the user. If you have several options to let the user choose from, you should use the action sheet.

Answer to Question 3

```
- (void)loadView {

    //---create a UIView object---
    UIView *view =
        [[UIView alloc] initWithFrame:[UIScreen mainScreen].applicationFrame];
    view.backgroundColor = [UIColor lightGrayColor];

    //---create a Button view---
    frame = CGRectMake(10, 70, 300, 50);

    UIButton *button = [UIButton buttonWithType:UIButtonTypeRoundedRect];
    button.frame = frame;

    [button setTitle:@"Click Me, Please!" forState:UIControlStateNormal];
    button.backgroundColor = [UIColor clearColor];
    button.tag = 2000;
    [button addTarget:self action:@selector(buttonClicked:)
        forControlEvents:UIControlEventTouchUpInside];

    [view addSubview:button];

    self.view = view;

}
```

CHAPTER 5 EXERCISE SOLUTIONS

Answer to Question 1

First, handle the `Did End on Exit` event (or implement the `textFieldShouldReturn:` method in the View Controller). Then call the `resignFirstResponder` method of the `UITextField` object to release its first-responder status.

Answer to Question 2

Register for the two notificationsL `UIKeyboardWillShowNotification` and `UIKeyboardWillHideNotification`.

Answer to Question 3

```
//---gets the size of the keyboard---
NSDictionary *userInfo = [notification userInfo];
NSValue *keyboardValue = [userInfo objectForKey:UIKeyboardBoundsUserInfoKey];
[keyboardValue getValue:&keyboardBounds];
```

CHAPTER 6 EXERCISE SOLUTIONS

Answer to Question 1

```
-(BOOL)shouldAutorotateToInterfaceOrientation:
(UIInterfaceOrientation)interfaceOrientation {

    return (interfaceOrientation == UIInterfaceOrientationLandscapeLeft ||
            interfaceOrientation == UIInterfaceOrientationLandscapeRight);

}
```

Answer to Question 2

The frame property defines the rectangle occupied by the view, with respect to its superview (the view that contains it). Using the frame property allows you to set the positioning and size of a view. Besides using the frame property, you can also use the center property, which sets the center of the view, also with respect to its superview. You usually use the center property when you are performing some animation and just want to change the position of a view.

CHAPTER 7 EXERCISE SOLUTIONS

Answer to Question 1

```
mySecondViewController = [[MySecondViewController alloc]
                             initWithNibName:nil
                             bundle:nil];
```

Answer to Question 2

```
- (void)viewDidLoad {

    //---create a CGRect for the positioning---
    CGRect frame = CGRectMake(10, 10, 300, 50);

    //---create a Label view---
    label = [[UILabel alloc] initWithFrame:frame];
    label.textAlignment = UITextAlignmentCenter;
    label.font = [UIFont fontWithName:@"Verdana" size:20];
    label.text = @"This is a label";

    //---create a Button view---
    frame = CGRectMake(10, 250, 300, 50);
    button = [[UIButton buttonWithType:UIButtonTypeRoundedRect]
            initWithFrame:frame];
```

```
        [button setTitle:@"OK" forState:UIControlStateNormal];
        button.backgroundColor = [UIColor clearColor];

        [self.view addSubview:label];
        [self.view addSubview:button];

        [super viewDidLoad];
    }
```

Answer to Question 3

```
        //---add the action handler and set current class as target---
        [button addTarget:self
            action:@selector(buttonClicked:)
            forControlEvents:UIControlEventTouchUpInside];

    //...
    //...
    //...

    -(IBAction) buttonClicked: (id) sender{
        //---do something here---
    }
```

CHAPTER 8 EXERCISE SOLUTIONS

Answer to Question 1

Available for
download on
Wrox.com

Codefile [TabBarAndNav.zip]

1. Using Xcode, create a new Tab Bar Application project and name it TabBarAndNav.

2. Double-click MainWindow.xib to edit it in Interface Builder.

3. Select the Tab Bar Controller item and view its Attributes Inspector window (see Figure A-1). Set the Second view controller to Navigation Controller.

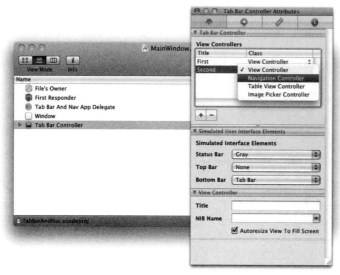

FIGURE A-1

4. Double-click the Tab Bar Controller item (see Figure A-2) and click the second Tab Bar Item view located at the bottom of the view. You should now see a Navigation Bar at the top of the view.

FIGURE A-2

5. Back in Xcode, right-click Classes and add a new `UITableViewController` subclass item. Name it `MoviesListViewController.m`.

6. Right-click the Resources group, add a new View `.xib` file, and name it `MoviesListView .xib`.

7. Double-click the `MoviesListView.xib` file and set its Class name to `MoviesListViewController` (see Figure A-3).

FIGURE A-3

8. Drag and drop the Table View view from the Library onto the `MoviesListView.xib` window (see Figure A-4). Remove the View item from the same window.

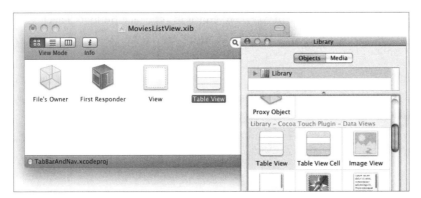

FIGURE A-4

9. Control-click and drag the File's Owner item to Table View and select `view`.

10. Control-click and drag the Table View to the File's Owner item and select `datasource`.

11. Control-click and drag the Table View to the File's Owner item and select `delegate`.

12. Verify the connections of the Table View by right-clicking it. Figure A-5 shows the required connection.

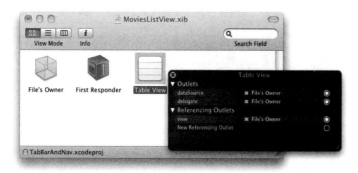

FIGURE A-5

13. Back in the `MainWindow.xib` window, expand the Tab Bar Controller item and select its second View Controller. Set its Class name to `MoviesListViewController` (see Figure A-6).

14. Double-click the `SecondView.xib` file in Xcode to edit it in Interface Builder. Select the File's Owner item, and in the Identity Inspector window, change its Class to `MovieListViewController`.

FIGURE A-6

15. Save the project in Interface Builder.

16. Back in Xcode, insert the following code that appears in bold into the
MoviesListViewController.m file:

```
#import "MoviesListViewController.h"

@implementation MoviesListViewController
NSMutableArray *listOfMovies;

- (void)viewDidLoad {
    //---initialize the array---
    listOfMovies = [[NSMutableArray alloc] init];

    //---add items---
```

```objc
    [listOfMovies addObject:@"Training Day"];
    [listOfMovies addObject:@"Remember the Titans"];
    [listOfMovies addObject:@"John Q."];
    [listOfMovies addObject:@"The Bone Collector"];
    [listOfMovies addObject:@"Ricochet"];
    [listOfMovies addObject:@"The Siege"];
    [listOfMovies addObject:@"Malcolm X"];
    [listOfMovies addObject:@"Antwone Fisher"];
    [listOfMovies addObject:@"Courage Under Fire"];
    [listOfMovies addObject:@"He Got Game"];
    [listOfMovies addObject:@"The Pelican Brief"];
    [listOfMovies addObject:@"Glory"];
    [listOfMovies addObject:@"The Preacher's Wife"];

    //---set the title---
    self.navigationItem.title = @"Movies";

    [super viewDidLoad];
}

- (void)dealloc {
    [listOfMovies release];
    [super dealloc];
}

// Customize the number of rows in the table view.
- (NSInteger)tableView:(UITableView *)tableView
            numberOfRowsInSection:(NSInteger)section {
    return [listOfMovies count];
}

// Customize the appearance of table view cells.
- (UITableViewCell *)tableView:(UITableView *)tableView
                    cellForRowAtIndexPath:(NSIndexPath *)indexPath {

    static NSString *CellIdentifier = @"Cell";

    UITableViewCell *cell = [tableView
        dequeueReusableCellWithIdentifier:CellIdentifier];
    if (cell == nil) {
        cell = [[[UITableViewCell alloc] initWithStyle:
        UITableViewCellStyleDefault
                                        reuseIdentifier:CellIdentifier]
                                        autorelease];
    }

    NSString *cellValue = [listOfMovies objectAtIndex:indexPath.row];
    cell.labelText. text = cellValue;

    return cell;
}
```

17. Press Command-R to test the application on the iPhone Simulator. Clicking the Second Tab Bar item should display a list of movies (see Figure A-7).

FIGURE A-7

18. If you want to display the movie selected on a separate view, just add another .xib file and View Controller to it. This step is outlined in Chapter 8, in the section "Navigating to Another View."

CHAPTER 9 EXERCISE SOLUTIONS

Answer to Question 1

You can turn off the highlighting effect by selecting the Info button in Interface Builder and viewing its attributes in the Attributes Inspector window. Deselect the option named "Show Touch On Highlight."

Answer to Question 2

Assuming that you want to pass a string from the `FlipsideViewController` to the `MainViewController`, the following statements that appear in bold show how you can pass data from one view to another using a property:

FLIPSIDEVIEWCONTROLLER.H

```
#import "AddCountryViewController.h";

@protocol FlipsideViewControllerDelegate;

@interface FlipsideViewController : UIViewController
<AddCountryViewControllerDelegate> {
id <FlipsideViewControllerDelegate> delegate;

//---internal member---
    NSString *str;


}

@property (nonatomic, assign) id <FlipsideViewControllerDelegate> delegate;

//---expose the member as a property---
@property (nonatomic, retain) NSString *str;

- (IBAction)done;
- (IBAction)add;
@end

@protocol FlipsideViewControllerDelegate
- (void)flipsideViewControllerDidFinish:(FlipsideViewController *)controller;
@end
```

FLIPSIDEVIEWCONTROLLER.M

```
#import "FlipsideViewController.h"

@implementation FlipsideViewController

@synthesize delegate;

//---generates the getter and setter for the property---
@synthesize str;

- (IBAction)done {

    //---set a value to the property---
    self.str = @"Some text";

    [self.delegate flipsideViewControllerDidFinish:self];
}
```

MAINVIEWCONTROLLER.M

```
- (void)flipsideViewControllerDidFinish:(FlipsideViewController *)controller {

    //---prints out the string obtained in the Debugger Console window---
    NSLog(controller.str);

    [self dismissModalViewControllerAnimated:YES];
}
```

CHAPTER 10 EXERCISE SOLUTIONS

Answer to Question 1

The two protocols are `UITableViewDataSource` and `UITableViewDelegate`.

The `UITableViewDataSource` protocol contains events in which you can populate the Table view with various items.

The `UITableViewDelegate` protocol contains events in which you can handle the selection of rows in a Table view.

Answer to Question 2

To add an index list to your Table view, you need to implement the `sectionIndexTitlesForTableView:` method.

Answer to Question 3

The three disclosure and checkmark images are as follows:

➤ `UITableViewCellAccessoryDetailDisclosureButton`

➤ `UITableViewCellAccessoryCheckmark`

➤ `UITableViewCellAccessoryDisclosureIndicator`

The `UITableViewCellAccessoryDetailDisclosureButton` image handles a user's tap event. The event name is `tableView:accessoryButtonTappedForRowWithIndexPath:`.

CHAPTER 11 EXERCISE SOLUTIONS

Answer to Question 1

For retrieving preferences settings values, you use the `objectForKey:` method. For saving preferences settings values, you use the `setObject:forKey:` method.

Answer to Question 2

You can either remove the application from the device or Simulator, or you can remove the file ending with *application_name*.plist in the application folder within the Simulator.

Answer to Question 3

The Add Child button is represented by three horizontal lines. It adds a child item to the currently selected item. The Add Sibling button, on the other hand, is represented by a plus sign (+). It adds an item on the same level as the currently selected item.

CHAPTER 12 EXERCISE SOLUTIONS

Answer to Question 1

The sqlite3_exec() function is actually a wrapper for the three functions: sqlite3_prepare(); sqlite3_step(); and sqlite3_finalize(). For nonquery SQL statements (such as for creating tables, inserting rows, and so on), it is always better to use the sqlite3_exec() function.

Answer to Question 2

To obtain a C-style string from an NSString object, use the UTF8String method from the NSString class.

Answer to Question 3

```
NSString *qsql = @"SELECT * FROM CONTACTS";
sqlite3_stmt *statement;

if (sqlite3_prepare_v2( db, [qsql UTF8String], -1, &statement, nil) ==
    SQLITE_OK) {

        while (sqlite3_step(statement) == SQLITE_ROW)
        {
            char *field1 = (char *) sqlite3_column_text(statement, 0);
            NSString *field1Str = [[NSString alloc] initWithUTF8String: field1];

            char *field2 = (char *) sqlite3_column_text(statement, 1);
            NSString *field2Str = [[NSString    alloc] initWithUTF8String: field2];

            NSString *str = [[NSString alloc] initWithFormat:@"%@ - %@",
                                    field1Str, field2Str];
            NSLog(str);

            [field1Str release];
```

```
                [field2Str release];
                [str release];
        }
        //---deletes the compiled statement from memory---
        sqlite3_finalize(statement);
}
```

CHAPTER 13 EXERCISE SOLUTIONS

Answer to Question 1

The three folders are Documents, Library, and tmp. The Documents folder can be used by the developer to store application-related data. The Library stores application-specific settings, such as those used by the NSUserDefaults class. The tmp folder can be used to store temporary data that will not be backed up by iTunes.

Answer to Question 2

The NSDictionary class creates a dictionary object whose items are immutable; that is, after it is populated, you can no longer add items to it. The NSMutableDictionary class, on the other hand, creates a mutable dictionary object that allows items to be added to it after it is loaded.

Answer to Question 3

Location of the Documents directory on a real device:

```
/private/var/mobile/Applications/<application_id>/Documents/
```

Location of the tmp directory on a real device:

```
/private/var/mobile/Applications/<application_id>/tmp/
```

CHAPTER 14 EXERCISE SOLUTIONS

Answer to Question 1

The four events are as follows:

➤   touchesBegan:withEvent:

➤   touchesEnded:withEvent:

➤   touchesMoved:withEvent:

➤   touchesCancelled:withEvent:

Answer to Question 2

When you multi-tap, you tap a single point in quick succession. This is similar to double-clicking in Mac OS X. When you multi-touch, on the other hand, you touch multiple contact points on the screen.

Answer to Question 3

Pressing the Option key allows you to simulate multi-touch on the iPhone Simulator.

CHAPTER 15 EXERCISE SOLUTIONS

Answer to Question 1

The three affine transformations are translation, rotation, and scaling.

Answer to Question 2

The only way to pause the NSTimer object is to call its invalidate method. To make it continue, you have to create a new NSTimer object.

Answer to Question 3

The beginAnimations and commitAnimations methods of the UIView class allow you to enclose blocks of code that cause visual changes so that the changes in visual appearance will be animated and not appear to change abruptly.

CHAPTER 16 EXERCISE SOLUTIONS

Answer to Question 1

For invoking Safari:

```
@"http://www.apple.com"
```

For invoking Mail:

```
@"mailto:?to=weimenglee@gmail.com&subject=Hello&body=Content of email"
```

For invoking SMS:

```
@"sms:96924065"
```

For invoking Phone:

```
@"tel:1234567890"
```

Answer to Question 2

The class name is UIImagePickerController.

Answer to Question 3

The class name is `ABPeoplePickerNavigationController`.

CHAPTER 17 EXERCISE SOLUTIONS

Answer to Question 1

The protocol is `UIAccelerometerDelegate`.

Answer to Question 2

The three events are

➤ `motionBegan:`

➤ `motionEnded:`

➤ `motionCancelled:`

Answer to Question 3

For the first-generation iPhone, Core Location uses cell tower triangulation and Wi-Fi triangulation to determine its position. This is because first-generation iPhone does not have a built-in GPS receiver. For second- and third-generation devices, Core Location uses the three different methods. For iPod Touch, it uses only Wi-Fi triangulation because it has neither a GPS receiver nor cellular connectivity.

B

Getting Around in Xcode

Xcode is the Integrated Development Environment (IDE) that Apple uses for developing Mac OS X and iPhone applications. It is a suite of applications that includes a set of compilers, documentation, and Interface Builder (discussed in Appendix C).

Using Xcode, you can build your iPhone applications from the comfort of an intelligent text editor, coupled with many different tools to help debug your iPhone applications. If you are new to Xcode, this appendix can serve as a useful guide to get you started quickly. Appendix C covers the Interface Builder in more detail.

LAUNCHING XCODE

The easiest way to launch Xcode is to type **Xcode** in the textbox of Spotlight. Alternatively, you can launch Xcode by navigating to the `\Developer\iPhone OS <version_no>\ Applications\` folder and double-clicking the Xcode icon.

> **NOTE** *For convenience, you can also drag the Xcode icon to the Dock so that in future you can launch it directly from the Dock.*

At the time of writing, the version of Xcode available is version 3.1.

Project Types Supported

Xcode supports the building of iPhone and Mac OS X applications. When you create a new project in Xcode (which you do by choosing File ➪ New Project), you see the New Project dialog, as shown in Figure B-1.

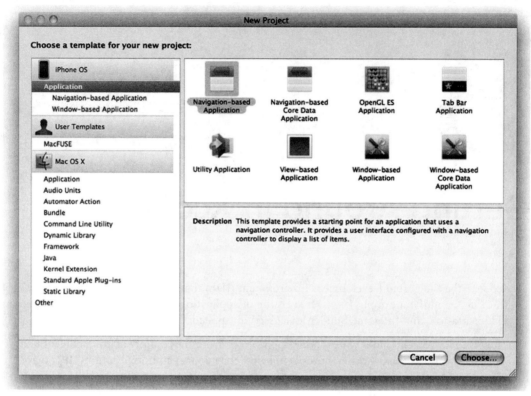

FIGURE B-1

As you can see, you have two main project types to create (iPhone OS and Mac OS X). Under the iPhone OS category, you have the Application item, which is further divided into two categories: Navigation-based Application and Window-based Application. Clicking the Application item displays all the project types you can create, as follows:

➤ Navigation-based Application

➤ Navigation-based Core Data Application

➤ OpenGL ES Application

➤ Tab Bar Application

➤ Utility Application

➤ View-based Application

➤ Window-based Application

➤ Window-based Core Data Application

Select the project type you want to create and click the Choose button. You are then asked to name the project.

When the project is created, Xcode displays all the files that make up your project (see Figure B-2).

FIGURE B-2

The Xcode window is divided into five sections:

> **Toolbar:** displays the buttons for commonly-performed actions.

> **Groups and Files List:** displays the files in a project. Files are grouped into folders and categories for better management.

> **Status bar:** displays the status information about the current action.

> **Detail View:** displays the files contained in the folders and groups selected in the Groups and Files List section.

> **Editor:** displays the appropriate editor showing the file currently selected.

To edit a code file, click the filename of a file to open the editor. Depending on what you click, the appropriate editor is launched. For example, if you click an .h or .m file, the code editor in which you can edit your source code is displayed (see Figure B-3).

FIGURE B-3

If you click a .plist file, the XML Property List editor is launched (see Figure B-4).

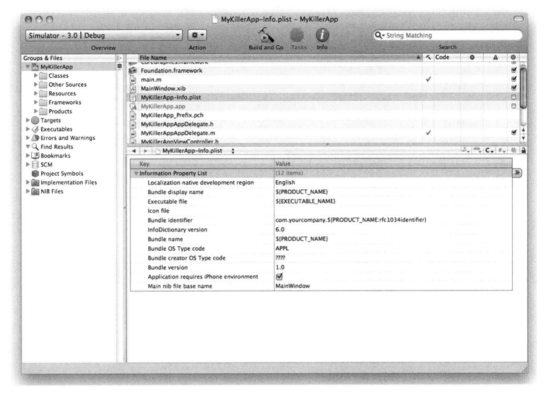

FIGURE B-4

Customizing the Toolbar

The Xcode window contains the toolbar section, in which you can place your favorite items for quick access. By default, the following items are placed in the toolbar:

➤ **Overview:** allows you to select target settings such as the active SDK (iPhone OS version and device versus Simulator) as well as active configurations (Debug or Release).

➤ **Action:** specifies the action you can perform with a selected item.

➤ **Build and Go:** lets you build and deploy the application.

➤ **Tasks:** stops any operation in progress.

➤ **Info:** views the detailed information of a selected item.

➤ **Search:** filters the items currently displayed in the Detail View section.

You can add items to the toolbar by right-clicking the toolbar and selecting Customize Toolbar. You then see a drop-down pane showing all the items that you can add to the toolbar (see Figure B-5). To add an item to the toolbar, drag the item directly onto the toolbar.

FIGURE B-5

Code Sense

One of the most common features of modern IDE is *code completion*, which makes the IDE automatically try to complete the statement you are typing based on the current context. In Xcode, this code-completion feature is known as Code Sense. As an example, when you type the letters **UIA** in a method, such as the viewDidLoad() method, Xcode automatically suggests the UIAlertView class (see Figure B-6; notice that the suggested characters are displayed in gray). If you want to accept the suggested word, simply press the Tab or Enter key.

```
// Implement viewDidLoad to
- (void)viewDidLoad {
    UIAlertView
    [super viewDidLoad];
}
```

FIGURE B-6

Besides getting Xcode to complete the word for you, you can also invoke the Code Sense feature by pressing the Esc key (or press F5). Code Sense displays a list of words matching whatever you have typed (see Figure B-7).

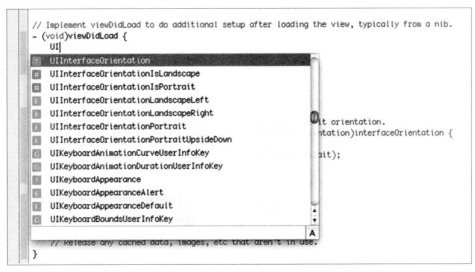

FIGURE B-7

As you type in Xcode, Xcode automatically recognizes the code and inserts the relevant parameters' placeholders. For example, if you invoke the methods of an object, Xcode inserts the placeholders of the various parameters. Figure B-8 shows an example of the placeholders inserted for the UIAlertView object after you type **ini**. To accept the placeholders for the various parameters, press the Tab key.

```
// Implement viewDidLoad to do additional setup after loading the view, typically from a nib.
- (void)viewDidLoad {
    UIAlertView *alert = [[UIAlertView alloc] initWithTitle:(NSString *)title message:(NSString *)message delegate:(id)delegate
    [super viewDidLoad];
}
```

FIGURE B-8

To enter the value for each parameter, press to move to each parameter. Alternatively, click each placeholder and type over it.

Running the Application

To execute an application, you first select the active SDK to use. You also choose whether you want to test it on a real device or use the included iPhone Simulator. You do so by selecting from the Overview list (see Figure B-9).

FIGURE B-9

To run the application, press Command-R, and Xcode will build and deploy the application onto the selected device or Simulator.

DEBUGGING YOUR APPLICATIONS

Debugging your iPhone applications is an essential part of your development journey. Xcode includes debugger utilities that help you trace and examine your code as you execute your application. The following sections show some of the tips and tricks that you can employ when developing your iPhone applications.

Error

When you try to run your application, Xcode first tries to build the project before it can deploy the application onto the real device or Simulator. Any syntax errors that Xcode detects are immediately highlighted in red. Figure B-10 shows Xcode highlighting a syntax error. The error with the code block is the missing brace symbol ([) for the [[UIAlertView alloc] statement:

```
UIAlertView *alert = [UIAlertView alloc]
                        initWithTitle:@"Hello World!"
                        message:@"Hello, my World"
                        delegate:self
                        cancelButtonTitle:@"OK"
                        otherButtonTitles:nil];
```

FIGURE B-10

If you have more than one error, you can also click the error icon to view the list of errors (see Figure B-11).

FIGURE B-11

Warnings

Objective-C is a case-sensitive language, and therefore one of the most common mistakes that beginners make is mixing up the capitalization for some of the method names. Consider the following:

```
- (void)viewDidLoad {
    UIAlertView *alert = [[UIAlertView alloc]
                          initwithTitle:@"Hello World!"
                          message:@"Hello, my World"
                          delegate:self
```

```
                          cancelButtonTitle:@"OK"
                          otherButtonTitles:nil];

    [alert show];
    [alert release];
    [super viewDidLoad];
}
```

Can you spot the error? Syntactically, the preceding statements have no problem. However, one of the parameters appears with the wrong capitalization. It turns out that `initwithTitle:` must be spelled as `initWithTitle:`. When you compile the program, Xcode will not flag the preceding code as an error; instead, it will issue you with a warning message displayed in yellow (see Figure B-12).

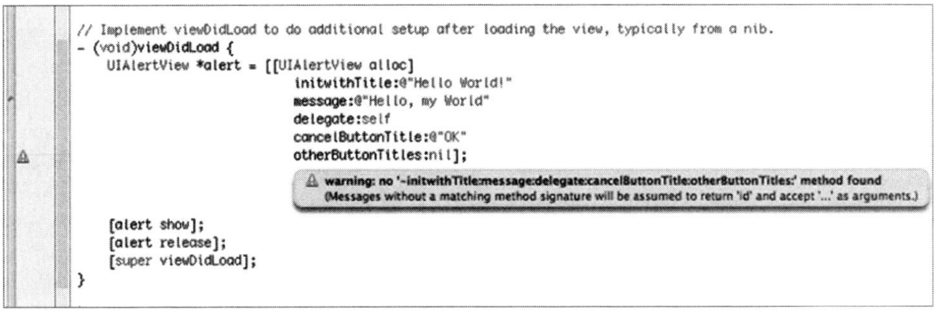

FIGURE B-12

When you see a warning message in Xcode, pay special attention to it and check that the method name is spelled correctly, including the capitalization. Failing to do so may result in a runtime exception. Figure B-13 shows the runtime exception message that Xcode displays when a runtime exception occurs.

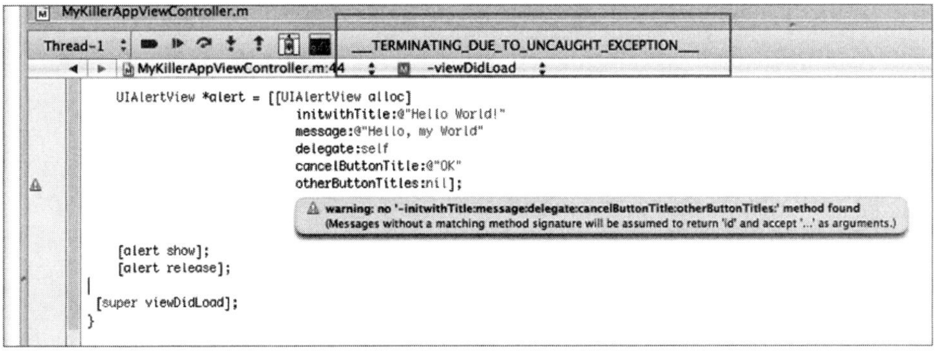

FIGURE B-13

When a runtime exception occurs, the best way to troubleshoot the error is to open the Debugger Console window by pressing Shift-Command-R. The Debugger Console window displays all the debugging information that is printed when Xcode debugs your application. This window usually contains the clue that helps you determine exactly what went wrong behind the scenes. Figure B-14 shows the content of the Debugger Console window when the exception occurs. To find out the cause of the crash, scroll to the bottom of the window and look for the section displayed in bold. In this case, note the reason stated. It is quite obvious that the problem is with the `UIAlertView` object.

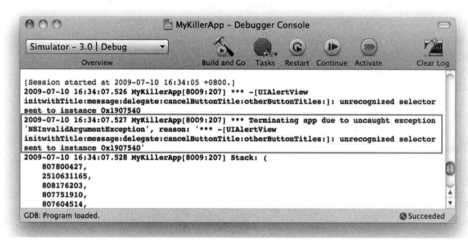

FIGURE B-14

Setting Breakpoints

Setting breakpoints in your code is a very handy tool to use to debug your application. Breakpoints allow you to execute your code line by line and examine the values of variables so that they perform as expected.

In Xcode, you set a breakpoint by clicking the left column of the code editor (see Figure B-15).

```
- (void)willRotateToInterfaceOrientation:
    (UIInterfaceOrientation) toInterfaceOrientation
    duration: (NSTimeInterval) duration {

    UIInterfaceOrientation destOrientation = toInterfaceOrientation;
    if (destOrientation == UIInterfaceOrientationPortrait)
    {
        btn.frame = CGRectMake(20,20,280,37);
    }
    else
    {
        btn.frame = CGRectMake(180,243,280,37);
    }
}
```

FIGURE B-15

NOTE *You can toggle the state of a breakpoint by clicking it to disable or disable it. Breakpoints displayed in dark blue are enabled; those displayed in light blue are disabled.*

After you have set breakpoints in your application, you need to press Command-Y to debug your application so that your breakpoints will be stopped when they are reached.

 NOTE *Pressing Command-R to run the application will not cause the break-points to be stopped.*

When the application reaches the breakpoint you have set, Xcode displays the current line of execution with a red arrow (see Figure B-16).

```
- (void)willRotateToInterfaceOrientation:
    (UIInterfaceOrientation) toInterfaceOrientation
    duration: (NSTimeInterval) duration {

    UIInterfaceOrientation destOrientation = toInterfaceOrientation;
    if (destOrientation == UIInterfaceOrientationPortrait)
    {
        btn.frame = CGRectMake(20,20,280,37);
    }
    else
    {
        btn.frame = CGRectMake(180,243,280,37);
    }
}
```

FIGURE B-16

At this juncture, you can do several things:

➤ Step Into (Shift-Command-I) — Step into the statements in a function/method.

➤ Step Over (Shift-Command-O) — Execute all the statements in a function /method and continue to the next statement.

➤ Step Out (Shift-Command-T) — Finish executing all the statements in a function or method and continue to the next statement after the function call.

➤ If you want to resume the execution of your application, press Option-Command-P.

➤ You can also examine the values of variables and objects by clicking the Show Debugger button (see Figure B-17). You can also move your mouse over the objects and variables you are interested in to view their values.

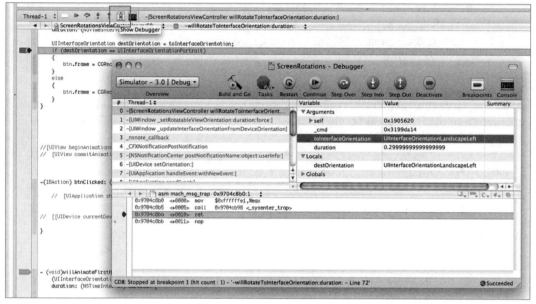

FIGURE B-17

Using NSLog

In addition to setting breakpoints to trace the flow of your application, you can use the NSLog()
method to print debugging messages to the Debugger Console window. The following
NSLog() statement prints a message to the Debugger Console window when the application
changes orientation:

```
- (void)willRotateToInterfaceOrientation:
    (UIInterfaceOrientation) toInterfaceOrientation
    duration: (NSTimeInterval) duration {

    NSLog(@"In the willRotateToInterfaceOrientation: event handler");

    UIInterfaceOrientation destOrientation = toInterfaceOrientation;
    if (destOrientation == UIInterfaceOrientationPortrait)
    {
        btn.frame = CGRectMake(20,20,280,37);
    }
    else
    {
        btn.frame = CGRectMake(180,243,280,37);
    }
}
```

Figure B-18 shows the output in the Debugger Console window (press Shift-Command-R to display it).

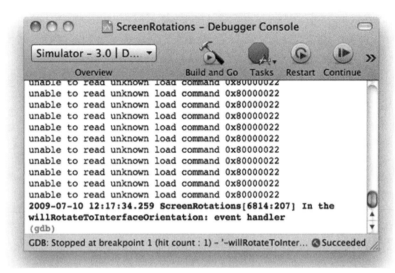

FIGURE B-18

Documentations

During the course of your development, you often need to check on the various methods, classes, and objects used in the iPhone SDK. The best way to check them out is to refer to the documentation. Xcode allows you to quickly and easily browse the definitions of classes, properties, and methods through the use of the Option key. To view the help documentation of an item, simply press the Option key. The cursor changes to a cross-hair. Double-click the item you want to check out, and the Developer Documentation window appears (see Figure B-19).

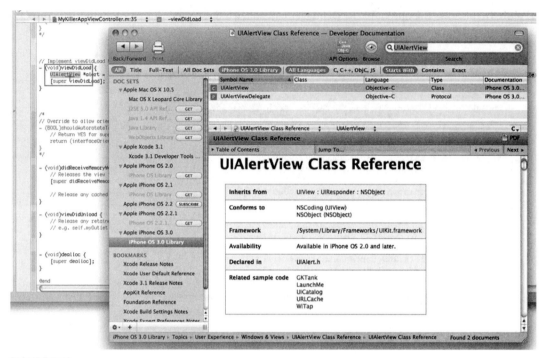

FIGURE B-19

Research Assistant

One very useful tool in the Documentation is the Research Assistant (Help ⇨ Show Research Assistant). The Research Assistant is a window that displays context-sensitive help as you work on your code in Xcode. When you position your cursor on a particular keyword/statement, the Research Assistant will display the following information about the current keyword/statement (see also Figure B-20):

➤ Declaration

➤ Abstract

➤ Availability

➤ Related API

➤ Related Documents

➤ Sample Code

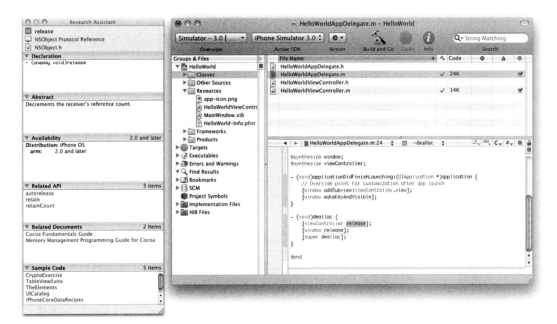

FIGURE B-20

SUMMARY

In this appendix, you had a quick overview of how to use Xcode to develop your iPhone applications. You saw how to use the Debugger Console window to view outputs generated by Xcode while your application is running, as well as how to set breakpoints in your application so that you can step through your code.

Getting Around
in Interface Builder

Interface Builder is one of the tools shipped with the iPhone SDK. It is a visual design tool that you can use to build the user interface of your iPhone applications. Although not strictly required for the development of your iPhone applications, Interface Builder plays an integral role in your journey of learning about iPhone application development. This appendix covers some of the important features of Interface Builder.

.XIB WINDOW

The most direct way to launch Interface Builder is to double-click any of the .xib files in your Xcode project. For example, if you have created a View-based Application project, there would be two .xib files in the Resources folder of Xcode. Double-clicking any one of them launches Interface Builder.

When Interface Builder is launched, the first window that you see has the same name as your .xib file (see Figure C-1).

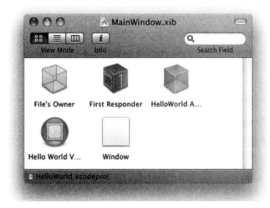

FIGURE C-1

Within this window are several items, and depending on what you double-clicked, you should see some of the following items, such as:

➤   File's Owner

➤   First Responder

➤   View, Table View, Window, and so on

➤   Some View Controllers and delegates

By default, the `.xib` window is displayed in icon mode. But you can also switch to list mode, where you can view some of the items in more detail. For example, Figure C-2 shows that when viewed in list mode, the View item displays a hierarchy of views contained within it.

FIGURE C-2

DESIGNING THE VIEW

To design the user interface of your application, you typically double-click the View (or Table View or other) item on the `.xib` window to visually display the window so that you can drag and drop views onto your View window.

To populate your View window with views, you drag and drop objects listed in the Library window (see the Library section for more information on the Library window). Figure C-3 shows a Label view being dropped onto the View window.

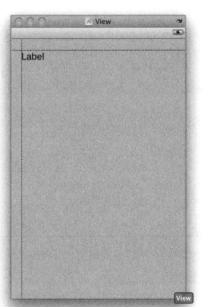 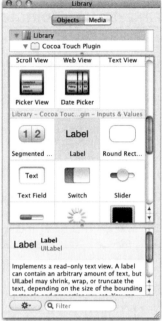

FIGURE C-3

As you position the view on the window, gridlines appear to guide you.

The View window also allows you to rotate the orientation of your view so that you can see how your view looks when it is rotated to the landscape orientation (see Figure C-4).

FIGURE C-4

INTERFACE BUILDER KEYBOARD SHORTCUTS

As you add more views to the View window, you realize that you are spending a lot of time figuring out their actual sizes and locations with respect to other views. So here are some tips to make your life easier:

➤ To make a copy of a view on the View window, simply Option-click and drag a view.

➤ If no view is currently selected, pressing the Option key and then moving the mouse over a view displays its layout and size information (see left side of Figure C-5).

➤ If a view is currently selected, pressing the Option key and then moving the mouse over the view displays that view's size information. If you move the mouse over another view, it displays the distance between that view and the selected view (see right of Figure C-5).

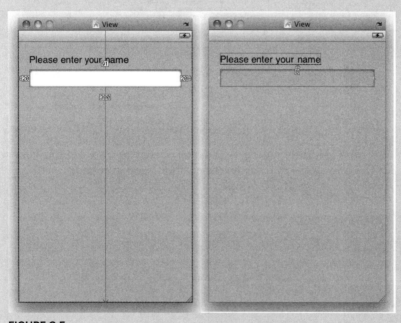

FIGURE C-5

INSPECTOR WINDOW

To customize the various attributes and properties of views, Interface Builder provides what it calls the Inspector window. The Inspector window is divided into four panes:

➤ Attributes Inspector

➤ Connection Inspector

➤ Size Inspector

➤ Identity Inspector

You can invoke the Inspector window by choosing Tools ⇨ Library.

The following sections discuss each of the Inspector panes in more details.

Attributes Inspector pane

The Attributes Inspector window (see Figure C-6) is where you configure the attributes of views in Interface Builder. The content of the Attributes Inspector window is dynamic and will change depending on what is selected in the View window.

You invoke the Attributes Inspector window by choosing Tools ⇨ Attributes Inspector.

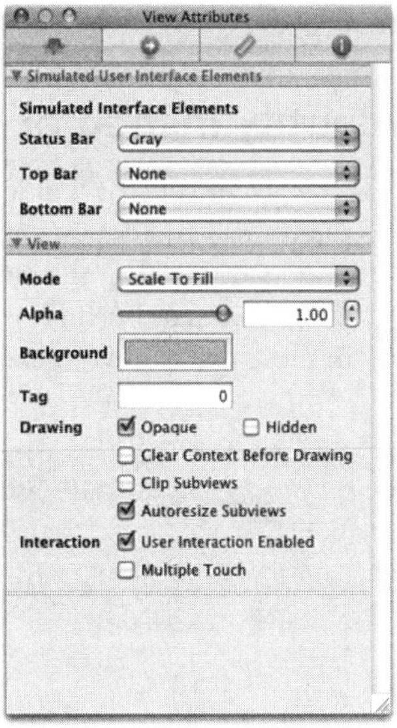

FIGURE C-6

Connections Inspector window

The Connections Inspector window (see Figure C-7) is where you connect the outlets and actions to your View Controller in Interface Builder. The content of the Connections Inspector window is dynamic and will change depending on what is selected in the View window.

You invoke the Connections Inspector window by choosing Tools ⇨ Connections Inspector.

FIGURE C-7

Size Inspector window

The Size Inspector window (see Figure C-8) is where you configure the size and positioning of views in Interface Builder.

The Size Inspector window can be invoked by choosing Tools ⇨ Size Inspector.

Identity Inspector window

The Size Inspector window (see Figure C-9) is where you configure the outlets and actions of your view controller. You add actions and outlets by clicking the plus sign (+) button and remove them using the minus sign button(–). The last section in this appendix discusses in more detail how to create outlets and actions in Interface Builder.

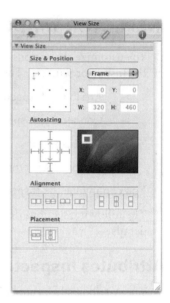

FIGURE C-8

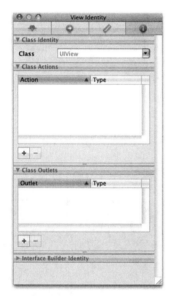

FIGURE C-9

You invoke the Identity Inspector window by choosing Tools ⇨ Identity Inspector.

LIBRARY

The Library (Tools ⇨ Library) contains a set of views that you can use for building the user interface of your iPhone applications. Figure C-10 shows the Library with its partial set of views shown.

FIGURE C-10

You can configure the Library to display its views in different modes (see also Figure C-11):

➤ Icons

➤ Icons and Labels (which is the mode shown in Figure C-10)

➤ Icons and Descriptions

Figure C-12 shows the Library displayed in the Icons and Descriptions mode.

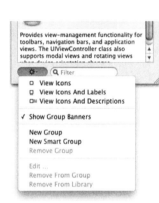

FIGURE C-11   **FIGURE C-12**

OUTLETS AND ACTIONS

Outlets and actions are fundamental mechanisms in iPhone programming through which your code can connect to the views in your user interface (UI). When you use outlets, your code can programmatically reference the views on your UI, with actions serving as event handlers that handle the various events fired by the various views.

Although you can write code to connect actions and outlets, Interface Builder simplifies the process by allowing you to connect outlets and actions using the drag-and-drop technique.

Creating Outlets and Actions

To create an action, you can click the plus sign (+) button that appears in the Class Actions section of the Identity Inspector window (see left side of Figure C-13). Remember to include the colon (:) character at the end of the action name. This character allows the action to have an input parameter of type `id`, like this:

```
-(IBAction) myAction:(id) sender;
```

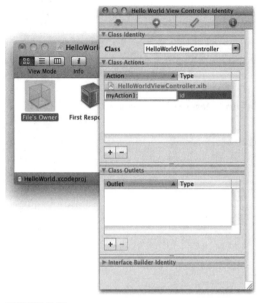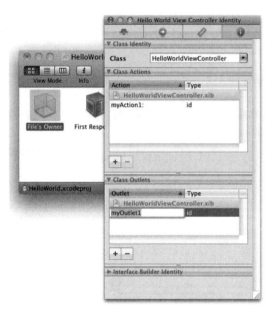

FIGURE C-13

Be sure to note that in Figure C-13 both the outlet and action are listed under the `HelloWorldViewController.xib` header. This is because the outlet and action are defined within Interface Builder.

Likewise, click the plus sign (+) button in the Class Outlets section of the Identity Inspector window to create an outlet. It is always good to specify the type for the outlet that you are defining. Using the preceding sample, if you want the outlet to connect to a `UITextField` view, you should specify the type of `myOutlet1` as `UITextField` rather than `id`.

After the outlet and action are created using Interface Builder, you still need to define them in the `.h` file, like this:

```
#import <UIKit/UIKit.h>

@interface HelloWorldViewController : UIViewController {

IBOutlet UITextField *myOutlet1;

}

-(IBAction) myAction1:(id) sender;

@end
```

 NOTE *Whether you are in Xcode or Interface Builder, be sure to save the file after you have modified it.*

Going back to the Identity Inspector window in Interface Builder, observe again that both the outlet and action are now listed under the `HelloWorldViewController.h` header (see Figure C-14). If you now try to click the plus sign (+) button again, the outlet or action will be listed under the `HelloWorldViewController.xib` header until you define them in the `.h` file.

FIGURE C-14

 NOTE *Outlets and actions defined in the* `.h` *file cannot be deleted in the Identity Inspector window by clicking the minus sign (–) button.*

Actually, a much simpler way is to define the outlets and actions directly in the `.h` files of your view controllers first. That saves you the trouble of defining them in the Identity Inspector window of the Interface Builder.

Alternately, if you do not want to manually type in the declaration of the outlets and actions in your View Controller class, you can create the outlets and actions in the Identity Inspector window, select the File's Owner item, and then choose File ➪ Write Class Files. Doing so causes Interface Builder to generate the code for the outlets and actions that you have added in the Identity Inspector window. When you use this option, Interface Builder first asks whether you want to replace or merge with the View Controller files (if they are already present). Replacing the files will cause the existing files to be replaced — and all the changes you have made to the file will be gone. Hence, this is not the recommended option. Merging the files will allow you to select the segments of code that you want to merge into your existing files. This is the safer option.

Take note that for code generated by Interface Builder, the outlets will not be exposed as properties. You must manually add the code to expose the properties using the `@property` keyword and the `@synthesize` keyword to generate the getters and setters for the properties.

 NOTE *In general, it is always easier to define the outlets and actions manually rather than have Interface Builder do it for you.*

Connecting Outlets and Actions

To connect the outlets and actions to the views, you have two options, both which are discussed in the following sections.

Method 1

For connecting outlets, Control-click and drag the File's Owner item to the view to which you want to connect (see Figure C-15).

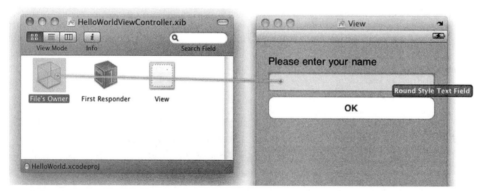

FIGURE C-15

When you release the mouse button, a list appears from which you can select the correct outlet. When defining your outlets (in the Identity Inspector window, or in code), remember that you can specify the type of view your outlet is referring to. When you release the mouse button, Interface Builder lists only the outlets that match the type of view you have selected. For example, if you defined `myOutlet1` as `UIButton` and you Control-click and drag the File's Owner item to the Text Field view on the View window, the `myOutlet1` will not appear in the list of outlets.

For connecting actions, Control-click and drag the view to the File's Owner item in the `.xib` window (see Figure C-16).

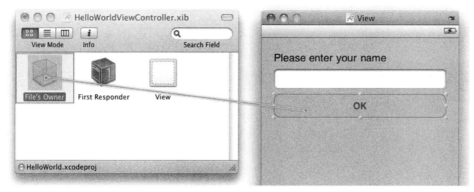

FIGURE C-16

When you release the mouse button, a list appears from which you can select the correct action.

When you have connected the outlets and actions, a good practice is to view all the connections in the File's Owner item by right-clicking it. Figure C-17 shows that the File's Owner item is connected to the Text Field view through the myOutlet1 outlet, and the Button's Touch Up Inside event is connected to the myAction1: action.

FIGURE C-17

How does the Button know that it is the Touch Up Inside event (and not other events) that should be connected to the myAction1: action when you Control-click and drag the Button to the File's Owner item? Well, the Touch Up Inside event is such a commonly used event that it is the default event selected when you perform a Control-click and drag action. What if you want to connect other events other than the default event? The second method shows you how.

Method 2

An alternative method for connecting outlets is to right-click the File's Owner item and connect the outlet to the view directly (see Figure C-18).

FIGURE C-18

For connecting actions, you can connect the relevant action with the views to which you want to connect (see Figure C-19). When you release the mouse button, the list of available events appears, and you can select the event you want.

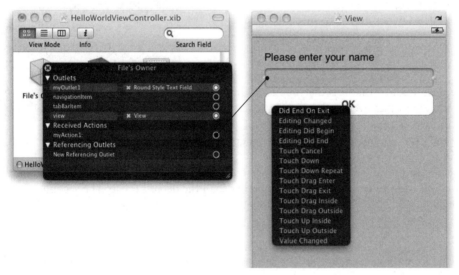

FIGURE C-19

Alternatively, you can right-click the view in question and connect the relevant events to the File's Owner item (see Figure C-20). When you release the mouse button, a list of actions is shown. Select the action to which you want to connect.

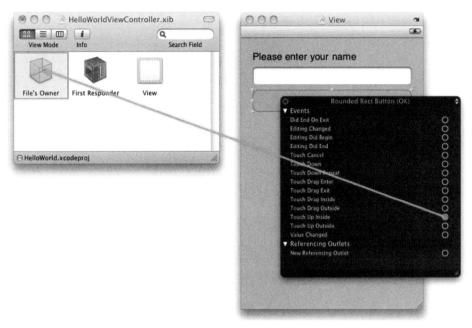

FIGURE C-20

SUMMARY

In this appendix, you had a quick overview of how to use Interface Builder to build the user interface of your iPhone application. The section on outlets and actions discussed the different ways in which you can connect outlets and actions to the views in your application.

Crash Course in Objective-C

Objective-C is an object-oriented programming language used by Apple primarily for programming Mac OS X and iPhone applications. It is an extension to the standard ANSI C language and hence it should be an easy language to pick up if you are already familiar with the C programming language. This appendix assumes that you already have some background in C programming and focuses on the object-oriented aspects of the language. If you are coming from a Java or .NET background, many of the concepts should be familiar to you; you just have to understand the syntax of Objective-C and in particular pay attention to the section on memory management.

Objective-C source code files are contained in two types of files:

➤ .h — header files

➤ .m — implementation files

For the discussions that follow, assume that you have created a View-based Application project using Xcode and added an empty class named SomeClass to your project.

DIRECTIVES

If you observe the content of the SomeClass.h file, you will notice that at the top of the file is an #import statement:

```
#import <Foundation/Foundation.h>

@interface SomeClass : NSObject {

}

@end
```

The `#import` statement is known as a *preprocessor directive*. In C and C++, you use the `#include` preprocessor directive to include a file's content with the current source. In Objective-C, you use the `#import` statement to do the same, except that the compiler ensures that the file is included at most only once. To import a header file from one of the frameworks, you specify the header filename using angle brackets (<>) in the `#import` statement. To import a header file from within your project, you use the " and " characters, as in the case of the `SomeClass.m` file:

```
#import "SomeClass.h"

@implementation SomeClass


@end
```

CLASSES

In Objective-C, you will spend a lot of time dealing with classes and objects. Hence it is important that you understand how classes are declared and defined in Objective-C.

@interface

To declare a class, you use the `@interface` compiler directive, like this:

```
@interface SomeClass : NSObject {

}
```

This is done in the header file (`.h`) and the class declaration contains no implementation. The preceding code declares a class named `SomeClass`, and this class inherits from the base class named `NSObject`.

> **NOTE** While you typically put your code declaration in an `.h` file, you can also put it inside an `.m` if need be. This is usually done for small projects.

> **NOTE** `NSObject` is the root class of most Objective-C classes. It defines the basic interface of a class and contains methods common to all classes that inherit from it. `NSObject` also provides the standard memory management and initialization framework used by most objects in Objective-C as well as reflection and type operations.

In a typical View Controller class, the class inherits from the `UIViewController` class, such as in the following:

```
@interface HelloWorldViewController : UIViewController {


}
```

@implementation

To implement a class declared in the header file, you use the `@implementation` compiler directive, like this:

```
#import "SomeClass.h"

@implementation SomeClass

@end
```

This is done in a separate file from the header file. In Objective-C, you define your class in an `.m` file. Note that the class definition ends with the `@end` compiler directive.

 NOTE *As mentioned earlier, you can also put your declaration inside an* `.m` *file. Hence, in your* `.m` *file you would then have both the* `@interface` *and* `@implementation` *directives.*

@class

If your class references another class defined in another file, you need to import the header file of that file before you can use it. Consider the following example where you have defined two classes — `SomeClass` and `AnotherClass`. If you are using an instance of the `AnotherClass` from within `SomeClass`, you need to import the `AnotherClass.h` file, as in the following code snippet:

```
//---SomeClass.h---
#import <Foundation/Foundation.h>
#import "AnotherClass.h"

@interface SomeClass : NSObject {
    //---an object from AnotherClass---
    AnotherClass *anotherClass;
}

@end

//---AnotherClass.h---
#import <Foundation/Foundation.h>
```

```
#import "SomeClass.h"

@interface AnotherClass : NSObject {

}

@end
```

However, if within `AnotherClass` you want to create an instance of `SomeClass`, you will not be able to simply import `SomeClass.h` in `AnotherClass`, like this:

```
//---SomeClass.h---
#import <Foundation/Foundation.h>
#import "AnotherClass.h"

@interface SomeClass : NSObject {
    AnotherClass *anotherClass;
}

@end

//---AnotherClass.h---
#import <Foundation/Foundation.h>
#import "SomeClass.h" //---cannot simply import here---

@interface AnotherClass : NSObject {
    SomeClass *someClass;  //---using an instance of SomeClass---
}

@end
```

Doing so results in circular inclusion. To prevent that, Objective-C uses the `@class` compiler directive as a forward declaration to inform the compiler that the class you specified is a valid class. You usually use the `@class` compiler directive in the header file, and in the implementation file you can use the `@import` compiler directive to tell the compiler more about the content of the class that you are using.

Using the `@class` compiler directive, the program now looks like this:

```
//---SomeClass.h---
#import <Foundation/Foundation.h>
@class AnotherClass;  //---forward declaration---

@interface SomeClass : NSObject {
    AnotherClass *anotherClass;
}

@end

//---AnotherClass.h---
#import <Foundation/Foundation.h>
```

```
@class SomeClass;       //---forward declaration---

@interface AnotherClass : NSObject {
    SomeClass *someClass;
}

@end
```

 NOTE *Another notable reason to use forward declaration where possible is that it will reduce your compile times because the compiler does not need to traverse as many included header files and their includes, etc.*

Class Instantiation

To create an instance of a class, you typically use the `alloc` keyword (more on this in the Memory Management section) to allocate memory for the object and then return it to a variable of the class type:

```
SomeClass *someClass = [SomeClass alloc];
```

In Objective-C, you need to prefix an object name with the * character when you declare an object. If you are declaring a variable of primitive type (such as `float`, `int`, `CGRect`, `NSInteger`, and so on), the * character is not required. Here are some examples:

```
CGRect frame;    //---CGRect is a structure---
int number;      //---int is a primitive type---
NSString *str    //---NSString is a class
```

Besides specifying the returning class type, you can also use the `id` type, like this:

```
id someClass = [SomeClass alloc];
id str;
```

The `id` type means that the variable can refer to any type of objects and hence the * is implicitly implied.

Fields

Fields are the data members of objects. For example, the following code shows that `SomeClass` has three fields — anotherClass, rate, and name:

```
#import <Foundation/Foundation.h>
@class AnotherClass;

@interface SomeClass : NSObject {
    AnotherClass *anotherClass;
    float rate;
    NSString *name;
}

@end
```

Access Privileges

By default, the access privilege of all fields is @protected. However, the access privilege can also be @public or @private. The following list shows the various access privileges:

➤ @private — visible only to the class that declares it

➤ @public — visible to all classes

➤ @protected — visible only to the class that declares it as well as to inheriting classes

Using the example shown in the previous section, if you now try to access the fields in SomeClass from another class, such as in AnotherClass, you will not be able to see them:

```
SomeClass *someClass = [SomeClass alloc];
someClass->rate = 5;                   //---rate is declared protected---
someClass->name = @"Wei-Meng Lee";   //---name is declared protected---
```

> **NOTE** *Observe that to access the fields in a class directly, you use the ->*
> *operator.*

To make the rate and name visible outside the class, modify the SomeClass.h file by adding the @public compiler directive:

```
#import <Foundation/Foundation.h>
@class AnotherClass;

@interface SomeClass : NSObject {
    AnotherClass *anotherClass;
@public
    float rate;
@public
    NSString *name;
}

@end
```

The following two statements would now be valid:

```
someClass->rate = 5;                   //---rate is declared protected---
someClass->name = @"Wei-Meng Lee";   //---name is declared protected---
```

Although you can access the fields directly, doing so goes against the design principles of object-oriented programming's rule of encapsulation. A better way is to encapsulate the two fields you want to expose in properties. Refer to the "Properties" section later in this appendix.

Methods

Methods are functions that are defined in a class. Objective-C supports two types of methods — instance methods and class methods.

Instance methods can be called only using an instance of the class. Instance methods are prefixed with the minus sign (-) character.

Class methods can be invoked directly using the class name and do not need an instance of the class in order to work. Class methods are prefixed with the plus sign (+) character.

 NOTE *In some programming languages, such as C# and Java, class methods are known as static methods.*

The following code sample shows `SomeClass` with three instance methods and one class method declared:

```
#import <Foundation/Foundation.h>
@class AnotherClass;

@interface SomeClass : NSObject {
    AnotherClass *anotherClass;
    float rate;
    NSString *name;
}

//---instance methods---
-(void) doSomething;
-(void) doSomething:(NSString *) str;
-(void) doSomething:(NSString *) str withAnotherPara:(float) value;

//---class method---
+(void) alsoDoSomething;

@end
```

The following shows the implementation of the methods that were declared in the header file:

```
#import "SomeClass.h"

@implementation SomeClass

-(void) doSomething {
    //---implementation here---
}
-(void) doSomething:(NSString *) str {
    //---implementation here---
}
-(void) doSomething:(NSString *) str withAnotherPara:(float) value {
    //---implementation here---
}
```

```
+(void) alsoDoSomething {
    //---implementation here---
}

@end
```

To invoke the three instance methods, you first need to create an instance of the class and then call them using the instance created:

```
SomeClass *someClass = [SomeClass alloc];
[someClass doSomething];
[someClass doSomething:@"some text"];
[someClass doSomething:@"some text" withAnotherPara:9.0f];
```

Class methods can be called directly using the class name, as the following shows:

```
[SomeClass alsoDoSomething];
```

In general, you create instance methods when you need to perform some actions that are related to the particular instance of the class (that is, the object). For example, suppose you defined a class that represents the information of an employee. You may expose an instance method that allows you to calculate the overtime wage of an employee. In this case, you use an instance method because the calculation involves data specific to a particular employee object.

Class methods, on the other hand, are commonly used for defining helper methods. For example, you might have a class method called `GetOvertimeRate:` that returns the rates for working overtime. As all employees get the same rate for working overtime (assuming this is the case for your company), then there is no need to create instance methods and thus a class method will suffice.

The next section shows how to call methods with a varying number of parameters.

Message Sending (Calling Methods)

In Objective-C, you use the following syntax to call a method:

```
[object method];
```

Strictly speaking, in Objective-C you do not call a method; you send a message to an object. The message to be passed to an object is resolved during runtime and is not enforced at compile time. This is why the compiler does not stop you from running your program even though you may have misspelled the name of a method. It does try to warn you that the target object may not respond to your message, though, because the target object will simply ignore the message. Figure D-1 shows the warning by the compiler when one of the parameters for the `UIAlertView`'s initializer is misspelled (the `cancelButtonsTitle:` should be `cancelButtonTitle:`).

 NOTE *For the ease of understanding, I use the more conventional term of "calling a method" to refer to Objective-C's message sending mechanism.*

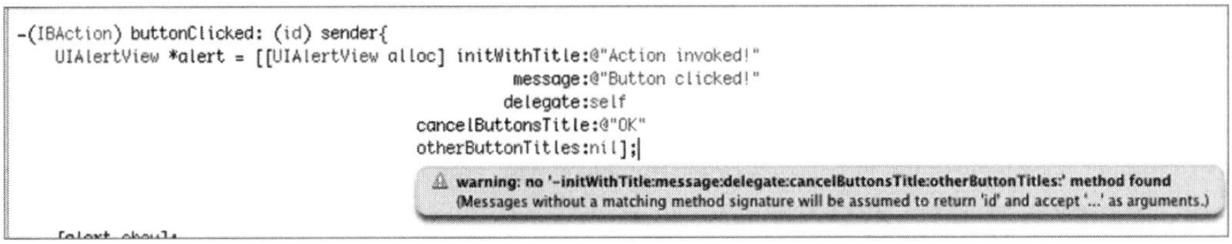

FIGURE D-1

Using the example from the previous section, the doSomething method has no parameter:

```
-(void) doSomething {
    //---implementation here---
}
```

Therefore, you can call it like this:

```
[someClass doSomething];
```

If a method has one or more inputs, you call it using the following syntax:

```
[object method:input1];                          //---one input---
[object method:input1 andSecondInput:input2];   //---two inputs---
```

The interesting thing about Objective-C is the way you call a method with multiple inputs. Using the earlier example:

```
-(void) doSomething:(NSString *) str withAnotherPara:(float) value {
    //---implementation here---
}
```

The name of the preceding method is doSomething:withAnotherPara:.

It is important to note the names of methods and to differentiate those that have parameters from those that do not. For example, doSomething refers to a method with no parameter, whereas doSomething: refers to a method with one parameter, and doSomething:withAnotherPara: refers to a method with two parameters. The presence or absence of colons in a method name dictates which method is invoked during runtime. This is important when passing method names as arguments, particularly when using the @selector (discussed in the Selectors section) notation to pass them to a delegate or notification event.

Method calls can also be nested, as the following example shows:

```
NSString *str = [[NSString alloc] initWithString:@"Hello World"];
```

Here, you first call the alloc class method of the NSString class and then call the initWithString: method of the returning result from the alloc method, which is of type id, a generic C type that Objective-C uses for an arbitrary object.

In general, you should not nest more than three levels because anything more than that makes the code difficult to read.

Properties

Properties allow you to expose your fields in your class so that you can control how values are set or returned. In the earlier example (in the Access Privileges section), you saw that you can directly access the fields of a class using the --> operator. However, this is not the ideal way and you should ideally expose your fields as properties.

Prior to Objective-C 2.0, programmers had to declare methods to make the fields accessible to other classes, like this:

```
#import <Foundation/Foundation.h>
@class AnotherClass;

@interface SomeClass : NSObject {
    AnotherClass *anotherClass;
    float rate;
    NSString *name;
}

//---expose the rate field---
-(float) rate;                      //---get the value of rate---
-(void) setRate:(float) value;      //---set the value of rate

//---expose the name field---
-(NSString *) name;                 //---get the value of name---
-(void) setName:(NSString *) value; //---set the value of name---

@end
```

These methods are known as *getters* and *setters* (or sometimes better known as *accessors* and *mutators*). The implementation of these methods may look like this:

```
#import "SomeClass.h"

@implementation SomeClass

-(float) rate {
    return rate;
}

-(void) setRate:(float) value {
    rate = value;
}

-(NSString *) name {
    return name;
}

-(void) setName:(NSString *) value {
    [value retain];
    [name release];
    name = value;
}

@end
```

To set the value of these properties, you need to call the methods prefixed with the `set` keyword:

```
SomeClass *sc = [[SomeClass alloc] init];
[sc setRate:5.0f];
[sc setName:@"Wei-Meng Lee"];
```

Alternatively, you can use the dot notation introduced in Objective-C 2.0:

```
SomeClass *sc = [[SomeClass alloc] init];
sc.rate = 5;
sc.name = @"Wei-Meng Lee";
```

To obtain the values of properties, you can either call the methods directly or use the dot notation in Objective-C 2.0:

```
NSLog([sc name]);  //---call the method---
NSLog(sc.name);    //---dot notation
```

To make a property read only, simply remove the method prefixed with the `set` keyword.

Notice that within the `setName:` method, you have various statements using the `retain` and `release` keywords. These keywords relate to memory management in Objective-C; you learn more about them in the "Memory Management" section, later in this appendix.

In Objective-C 2.0, you don't need to define getters and setters in order to expose fields as properties. You can do so via the `@property` and `@synthesize` compiler directives. Using the same example, you can use the `@property` to expose the `rate` and `name` fields as properties, like this:

```
#import <Foundation/Foundation.h>
@class AnotherClass;

@interface SomeClass : NSObject {
    AnotherClass *anotherClass;
    float rate;
    NSString *name;
}

@property float rate;
@property (retain, nonatomic) NSString *name;

@end
```

The first `@property` statement defines `rate` to be a property. The second statement defines `name` as a property as well, but it also specifies the behavior of this property. In this case, it indicates the behavior as `retain` and `nonatomic`, which you learn more about in the section on memory management later in this appendix. In particular, `nonatomic` means that the property is not accessed in a thread-safe manner. This is alright if you are not writing multi-threaded applications. Most of the time, you will use the `retain` and `nonatomic` combination when declaring properties.

In the implementation file, rather than define the getter and setter methods, you can simply use the @ synthesize keyword to get the compiler to automatically generate the getters and setters for you:

```
#import "SomeClass.h"

@implementation SomeClass
@synthesize rate, name;

@end
```

As shown, you can combine several properties using a single @synthesize keyword. However, you can also separate them into individual statements:

```
@synthesize rate;
@synthesize name;
```

You can now use your properties as usual:

```
//---setting using setRate---
[sc setRate:5.0f];
[sc setName:@"Wei-Meng Lee"];

//---setting using dot notation---
sc.rate = 5;
sc.name = @"Wei-Meng Lee";

//---getting---
NSLog([sc name]); //---using the name method
NSLog(sc .ame);   //---dot notation
```

To make a property read only, use the readonly keyword. The following statement makes the name property read only:

```
@property (readonly) NSString *name;
```

Initializers

When you create an instance of a class, you often initialize it at the same time. For example, in the earlier example (in the Class Instantiation section), you had this statement:

```
SomeClass *sc = [[SomeClass alloc] init];
```

The alloc keyword allocates memory for the object, and when an object is returned, the init method is called on the object to initialize the object. Recall that in SomeClass, you do not define a method named init. So where does the init method come from? It is actually defined in the NSObject class, which is the base class of most classes in Objective-C. The init method is known as an initializer.

If you want to create additional initializers, you can define methods that begin with the init word. (The use of the init word is more of a norm than a hard-and-fast rule.)

```
#import <Foundation/Foundation.h>
@class AnotherClass;

@interface SomeClass : NSObject {
    AnotherClass *anotherClass;
    float rate;
    NSString *name;
}

-(void) doSomething;
-(void) doSomething:(NSString *) str;
-(void) doSomething:(NSString *) str withAnotherPara:(float) value;
+(void) alsoDoSomething;

- (id)initWithName:(NSString *) n;
- (id)initWithName:(NSString *) n andRate:(float) r;

@property float rate;
@property (retain, nonatomic) NSString *name;

@end
```

The preceding example contains two additional initializers: initWithName: and initWithName:andRate:. You can provide the implementations for the two initializers as follows:

```
#import "SomeClass.h"
@implementation SomeClass
@synthesize rate, name;

- (id)initWithName:(NSString *) n
{
    return [self initWithName:n andRate:0.0f];
}

- (id)initWithName:(NSString *) n andRate:(float) r
{
    if (self = [super init]) {
        self.name = n;
        self.rate = r;
    }
    return self;
}

-(void) doSomething {
}

-(void) doSomething:(NSString *) str {
}

-(void) doSomething:(NSString *) str withAnotherPara:(float) value {
}

+(void) alsoDoSomething {
}

@end
```

Note that in the `initWithName:andRate:` initializer implementation, you first call the `init` initializer of the `super` (base) class so that its base class is properly initialized, which is necessary before you can initialize the current class:

```
- (id)initWithName:(NSString *) n andRate:(float) r
{
    if (self = [super init]) {
        //...
        //...
    }
    return self;
}
```

The rule for defining an initializer is simple: If a class is initialized properly, it should return a reference to `self` (hence the `id` type). If it fails, it should return `nil`.

For the `initWithName:` initializer implementation, notice that it calls the `initWithName:andRate:` initializer:

```
- (id)initWithName:(NSString *) n
{
    return [self initWithName:n andRate:0.0f];
}
```

In general, if you have multiple initializers, each with different parameters, you should chain them by ensuring that they all call a single initializer that performs the call to the super class's `init` initializer. In Objective-C, the initializer that performs the call to the super class's `init` initializer is called the *designated initializer.*

 NOTE *As a general guide, the designated initializer should be the one with the greatest number of parameters.*

To use the initializers, you can now call them during instantiation time:

```
SomeClass *sc1 = [[SomeClass alloc] initWithName:@"Wei-Meng Lee" andRate:35];
SomeClass *sc2 = [[SomeClass alloc] initWithName:@"Wei-Meng Lee"];
```

MEMORY MANAGEMENT

Memory management in Objective-C programming (especially for iPhone) is a very important topic that every iPhone developer needs to be aware of. As do all other popular languages, Objective-C supports garbage collection, which helps to remove unused objects when they go out of scope and hence releases memory that can be reused. However, because of the severe overhead involved in implementing garbage collection, the iPhone does not support garbage collection. This leaves you, the developer, to manually allocate and de-allocate the memory of objects when they are no longer needed.

This section discusses the various aspects of memory management on the iPhone.

Reference Counting

To help you allocate and de-allocate memory for objects, the iPhone OS uses a scheme known as *reference counting* to keep track of objects to determine whether they are still needed or can be disposed of. Reference counting basically uses a counter for each object, and as each object is created, the count increases by 1. When an object is released, the count decreases by 1. When the count reaches 0, the memory associated with the object is reclaimed by the OS.

In Objective-C, a few important keywords are associated with memory management. The following sections take a look at each of them.

alloc

The `alloc` keyword allocates memory for an object that you are creating. You have seen it in almost all exercises in this book. An example is as follows:

```
NSString *str = [[NSString alloc] initWithString:@"Hello"];
```

In this example, you are creating an `NSString` object and instantiating it with a default string. When the object is created, the reference count of that object is 1. Because you are the one creating it, the object belongs to you, and it is your responsibility to release the memory when you are done with it.

 NOTE *See the "release" section for information on how to release an object.*

So how do you know when an object is owned, and by whom? Consider the following example:

```
NSString *str = [[NSString alloc] initWithString:@"Hello"];
NSString *str2 = str;
```

In this example, you use the `alloc` keyword for `str`, so you own `str`. Therefore, you need to release it when you no longer need it. However, `str2` is simply pointing to `str`, so you do not own `str2`, meaning that you need not release `str2` when you are done using it.

new

Besides using the `alloc` keyword to allocate memory for an object, you can also use the `new` keyword, like this:

```
NSString *str = [NSString new];
```

The `new` keyword is functionally equivalent to

```
NSString *str = [[NSString alloc] init];
```

As with the `alloc` keyword, using the `new` keyword makes you the owner of the object, so you need to release it when you are done with it.

retain

The `retain` keyword increases the reference count of an object by 1. Consider the previous example:

```
NSString *str = [[NSString alloc] initWithString:@"Hello"];
NSString *str2 = str;
```

In that example, you do not own `str2` because you do not use the `alloc` keyword on the object. When `str` is released, the `str2` will no longer be valid.

 NOTE *How do you release* `str2`, *then? Well, it is autoreleased. See the "Convenience Method and Autorelease" section for more information.*

If you want to make sure that `str2` is available even if `str` is released, you need to use the `retain` keyword:

```
NSString *str = [[NSString alloc] initWithString:@"Hello"];
NSString *str2 = str;
[str2 retain];
[str release];
```

In the preceding case, the reference count for `str` is now 2. When you release `str`, `str2` will still be valid. When you are done with `str2`, you need to release it manually.

 NOTE *As a general rule, if you own an object (using* `alloc` *or* retain*), you need to release it.*

release

When you are done with an object, you need to manually release it by using the `release` keyword:

```
NSString *str = [[NSString alloc] initWithString:@"Hello"];

//...do what you want with the object...

[str release];
```

When you use the `release` keyword on an object, it causes the reference count of that object to decrease by 1. When the reference count reaches 0, the memory used by the object is released.

One important aspect to keep in mind when using the `release` keyword is that you cannot release an object that is not owned by you. For example, consider the example used in the previous section:

```
NSString *str = [[NSString alloc] initWithString:@"Hello"];
NSString *str2 = str;
[str release];
[str2 release];   //---this is not OK as you do not own str2---
```

Attempting to release `str2` will result in a runtime error because you cannot release an object not owned by you. However, if you use the `retain` keyword to gain ownership of an object, you do need to use the `release` keyword:

```
NSString *str = [[NSString alloc] initWithString:@"Hello"];
NSString *str2 = str;
[str2 retain];
[str release];
[str2 release];   //---this is now OK as you now own str2---
```

Recall earlier that in the section on properties, you defined the `setName:` method, where you set the value of the `name` field:

```
-(void) setName:(NSString *) value {
    [value retain];
    [name release];
    name = value;
}
```

Notice that you first had to retain the `value` object, followed by releasing the `name` object and then finally assigning the `value` object to `name`. Why do you need to do that as opposed to the following?

```
-(void) setName:(NSString *) value {
    name = value;
}
```

Well, if you were using garbage collection, the preceding statement would be valid. However, because iPhone OS does not support garbage collection, the preceding statement will cause the original object referenced by the `name` object to be lost, thereby causing a memory leak. To prevent that leak, you first retain the `value` object to indicate that you wish to gain ownership of it; then you release the original object referenced by `name`. Finally, assign `value` to `name`:

```
[value retain];
[name release];
name = value;
```

UNDERSTANDING REFERENCE COUNTING USING AN ANALOGY

When you think of memory management using reference counting, it is always good to use a real-life analogy to put things into perspective.

Image a room in the library that you can reserve for studying purposes. Initially, the room is empty and hence the lights are off. When you reserve the room, the librarian increases a counter to indicate the number of persons using the room. This is similar to creating an object using the `alloc` keyword.

When you leave the room, the librarian decreases the counter, and if the counter is now 0, this means that the room is no longer being used and the lights can thus be switched off. This is similar to using the `release` keyword to release an object.

There may be times where you have booked the room and are the only one in the room (hence, the counter is 1) until a friend of yours comes along. He may simply come and visit you and therefore doesn't register with the librarian. Hence, the counter does not increase. Because he is just visiting you and hasn't booked the room, he has no rights to decide whether the lights should be switched off. This is similar to assigning an object to another variable without using the `alloc` keyword. In this case, if you leave the room (release), the lights will be switched off and your friend will have to leave.

Consider another situation in which you are using the room and another person also booked the room and shares it with you. In this case, the counter is now 2. If you leave the room, the counter goes down to 1, but the lights are still on because another person is in the room. This situation is similar when you create an object and assign it to another variable that uses the `retain` keyword. In such a situation, the object is released only when both objects release it.

Convenience Method and Autorelease

So far, you learned that all objects created using the `alloc` or `new` keywords are owned by you. Consider the following case:

```
NSString *str = [NSString stringWithFormat:@"%d", 4];
```

In this statement, do you own the `str` object? The answer is no, you don't. This is because the object is created using one of the *convenience methods* — static methods that are used for allocating and initializing objects directly. In the preceding case, you create an object but you do not own it. Because you do not own it, you cannot release it manually. In fact, objects created using this method are known as *autorelease* objects. All autorelease objects are temporary objects and are added to an *autorelease pool*. When the current method exits, all the objects contained within it are released. Autorelease objects are useful for cases in which you simply want to use some temporary variables and do not want to burden yourself with allocations and de-allocations.

The key difference between an object created using the `alloc` (or `new`) keyword and one created using a convenience method is that of ownership, as the following example shows:

```
NSString *str1 = [[NSString alloc] initWithFormat:@"%d", 4];
[str1 release]; //---this is ok because you own str1---

NSString *str2 = [NSString stringWithFormat:@"%d", 4];
[str2 release]; //---this is not ok because you don't own str2---
//---str2 will be removed automatically when the autorelease pool is activated---
```

If you want to take ownership of an object when using a convenience method, you can do so using the `retain` keyword:

```
NSString *str2 = [[NSString stringWithFormat:@"%d", 4] retain];
```

To release the object, you can use either the `autorelease` or `release` keyword. You learned earlier that the `release` keyword immediately decreases the reference count by 1 and that the object is immediately de-allocated from memory when the reference count reaches 0. In contrast, the `autorelease` keyword promises to decrease the reference count by 1, not *immediately*, but sometime later. It is like saying, "Well, I still need the object now, but later on I can let it go." The following code makes it clear:

```
NSString *str = [[NSString stringWithFormat:@"%d", 4] retain];
[str autorelease];  //you don't own it anymore; still available
NSlog(str);         //still accessible for now
```

 NOTE *After you have autoreleased an object, do not release it anymore.*

Note that the statement

```
NSString *str2 = [NSString stringWithFormat:@"%d", 4];
```

has the same effect as

```
NSString *str2 = @"4";
```

Although autorelease objects seem to make your life simple by automatically releasing objects that are no longer needed, you have to be careful when using them. Consider the following example:

```
for (int i=0; i<=99999; i++){
    NSString *str = [NSString stringWithFormat:@"%d", i];
    //...
    //...
}
```

You are creating an `NSString` object for each iteration of the loop. Because the objects are not released until the function exits, you may well run out of memory before the autorelease pool can kick in to release the objects.

One way to solve this dilemma is to use an autorelease pool, as discussed in the next section.

> **REFERENCE COUNTING: THE ANALOGY CONTINUES**
>
> Continuing with our analogy of the room in the library, imagine that you are about
> to sign out with the librarian when you realize that you have left your books in
> the room. You tell the librarian that you are done with the room and want to sign
> out now, but because you left your books in the room, you tell the librarian not to
> switch off the lights yet so that you can go back to get the books. At a later time,
> the librarian can switch off the lights at his or her own choosing. This is the behav-
> ior of autoreleased objects.

Autorelease Pools

All autorelease objects are temporary objects and are added to an *autorelease pool*. When the
current method exits, all the objects contained within it are released. However, sometimes you want
to control how the autorelease pool is emptied, rather than wait for it to be called by the OS. To do
so, you can create an instance of the NSAutoreleasePool class, like this:

```
for (int i=0; i<=99999; i++){
    NSAutoreleasePool *pool = [[NSAutoreleasePool alloc] init];
    NSString *str1 = [NSString stringWithFormat:@"%d", i];
    NSString *str2 = [NSString stringWithFormat:@"%d", i];
    NSString *str3 = [NSString stringWithFormat:@"%d", i];
    //...
    //...
    [pool release];
}
```

In this example, for each iteration of the loop, an NSAutoreleasePool object is created, and all the
autorelease objects created within the loop — str1, str2, and str3 — go into it. At the end of each
iteration, the NSAutoreleasePool object is released so that all the objects contained within it are
automatically released. This ensures that you have at most three autorelease objects in memory at
any one time.

dealloc

You have learned that by using the alloc or the new keyword, you own the object that you have
created. You have also seen how to release the objects you own using the release or autorelease
keyword. So when is a good time for you to release them?

As a rule of thumb, you should release the objects as soon as you are done with them. So if you
created an object in a method, you should release it before you exit the method. For properties,
recall that you can use the @property compiler directive together with the retain keyword:

```
@property (retain, nonatomic) NSString *name;
```

Because the values of the property will be retained, it is important that you free it before you exit the application. A good place to do so is in the `dealloc` method of a class (such as a View Controller):

```
-(void) dealloc {
    [self.name release];    //---release the name property---
    [super dealloc];
}
```

The `dealloc` method of a class is fired whenever the reference count of its object reaches 0. Consider the following example:

```
SomeClass *sc1 = [[SomeClass alloc] initWithName:@"Wei-Meng Lee" andRate:35];
//...do something here…
[sc1 release];   //---reference count goes to 0; dealloc will be called---
```

The preceding example shows that when the reference count of `sc1` goes to 0 (when the `release` statement is called), the `dealloc` method defined within the class will be called. If you do not define this method in the class, its implementation in the base class will be called.

Memory Management Tips

Memory management is a tricky issue in iPhone programming. Although there are tools that you can use to test for memory leaks, this section presents some simple things you can do to detect memory problems that might affect your application.

First, ensure that you implement the `didReceiveMemoryWarning` method in your View Controller:

```
- (void)didReceiveMemoryWarning {
    //---insert code here to free unused objects---
    [super didReceiveMemoryWarning];
}
```

The `didReceiveMemoryWarning` method will be called whenever your iPhone runs out of memory. You should insert code in this method so that you can free resources/objects that you do not need.

In addition, you should also handle the `applicationDidReceiveMemoryWarning:` method in your application delegate:

```
- (void)applicationDidReceiveMemoryWarning:(UIApplication *)application
{
    //---insert code here to free unused objects---
    [[ImageCache sharedImageCache] removeAllImagesInMemory];
}
```

In this method, you should stop all memory-intensive activities, such as audio and video playback. You should also remove all images cached in memory.

PROTOCOLS

In Objective-C, a *protocol* declares a programmatic interface that any class can choose to implement. A protocol declares a set of methods, and an adopting class may choose to implement one or more of its declared methods. The class that defines the protocol is expected to call the methods in the protocols that are implemented by the adopting class.

The easiest way to understand protocols is to examine the UIAlertView class. As you have experienced in the various chapters in this book, you can simply use the UIAlertView class by creating an instance of it and then calling its show method:

```
UIAlertView *alert = [[UIAlertView alloc]
                        initWithTitle:@"Hello"
                        message:@"This is an alert view"
                        delegate:self
                        cancelButtonTitle:@"OK"
                        otherButtonTitles:nil];
    [alert show];
```

The preceding code displays an alert view with one button — OK. Tapping the OK button automatically dismisses the alert view. If you want to display additional buttons, you can set the otherButtonTitles: parameter like this:

```
UIAlertView *alert = [[UIAlertView alloc]
                        initWithTitle:@"Hello"
                        message:@"This is an alert view"
                        delegate:self
                        cancelButtonTitle:@"OK"
                        otherButtonTitles:@"Option 1", @"Option 2", nil];
```

The alert view now displays three buttons — OK, Option 1, and Option 2. But how do you know which button was tapped by the user? You can determine this by handling the relevant method(s) that will be fired by the alert view when the buttons are clicked. This set of methods is defined by the UIAlertViewDelegate protocol. This protocol defines the following methods:

- ➤ alertView:clickedButtonAtIndex:

- ➤ willPresentAlertView:

- ➤ didPresentAlertView:

- ➤ alertView:willDismissWithButtonIndex:

- ➤ alertView:didDismissWithButtonIndex:

- ➤ alertViewCancel:

If you want to implement any of the methods in the `UIAlertViewDelegate` protocol, you need to ensure that your class, in this case the View Controller, conforms to this protocol. A class conforms to a protocol using angle brackets (<>), like this:

```
@interface UsingViewsViewController : UIViewController
<UIAlertViewDelegate> {  //---this class conforms to the UIAlertViewDelegate
                         // protocol---
    //...
}
```

> **NOTE** To conform to more than one delegate, separate the protocols with commas, such as <UIAlertViewDelegate, UITableViewDataSource>.

After the class conforms to a protocol, you can implement the method in your class:

```
- (void)alertView:(UIAlertView *)alertView
clickedButtonAtIndex:(NSInteger)buttonIndex {

    NSLog([NSString stringWithFormat:@"%d", buttonIndex]);

}
```

Delegate

In Objective-C, a delegate is just an object that has been assigned by another object as the object responsible for handling events. Consider the case of the `UIAlertView` example that you have seen previously:

```
UIAlertView *alert = [[UIAlertView alloc]
                        initWithTitle:@"Hello"
                        message:@"This is an alert view"
                        delegate:self
                        cancelButtonTitle:@"OK"
                        otherButtonTitles:nil];
```

The initializer of the `UIAlertView` class includes a parameter called the `delegate`. Setting this parameter to `self` means that the current object is responsible for handling all the events fired by this instance of the `UIAlertView` class. If you don't need to handle events fired by this instance, you can simply set it to `nil`:

```
UIAlertView *alert = [[UIAlertView alloc]
                        initWithTitle:@"Hello"
                        message:@"This is an alert view"
                        delegate:nil
                        cancelButtonTitle:@"OK"
                        otherButtonTitles:nil];
```

If you have multiple buttons on the alert view and want to know which button was tapped, you need to handle the methods defined in the UIAlertViewDelegate protocol. You can either implement it in the same class in which the UIAlertView class was instantiated (as shown in the previous section), or create a new class to implement the method, like this:

```
//---SomeClass.m---
@implementation SomeClass

- (void)alertView:(UIAlertView *)alertView
clickedButtonAtIndex:(NSInteger)buttonIndex {

    NSLog([NSString stringWithFormat:@"%d", buttonIndex]);

}

@end
```

To ensure that the alert view knows where to look for the method, create an instance of SomeClass and then set it as the delegate:

```
SomeClass *myDelegate = [[SomeClass alloc] init];

UIAlertView *alert = [[UIAlertView alloc]
                        initWithTitle:@"Hello"
                        message:@"This is an alert view"
                        delegate:myDelegate
                        cancelButtonTitle:@"OK"
                        otherButtonTitles:@"Option 1", @"Option 2", nil];
[alert show];
```

SELECTORS

In Objective-C, a selector is the name used to select a method to execute for an object. It is used to identify a method. You have seen the use of a selector in some of the chapters in this book. Here is one of them:

```
//---create a Button view---
CGRect frame = CGRectMake(10, 50, 300, 50);
UIButton *button = [UIButton buttonWithType:UIButtonTypeRoundedRect];
button.frame = frame;
[button setTitle:@"Click Me, Please!" forState:UIControlStateNormal];
button.backgroundColor = [UIColor clearColor];
[button addTarget:self action:@selector(buttonClicked:)
        forControlEvents:UIControlEventTouchUpInside];
```

The preceding code shows that you are dynamically creating a UIButton object. In order to handle the event (for example, the Touch Up Inside event) raised by the button, you need to call the addTarget:action:forControlEvents: method of the UIButton class:

```
[button addTarget:self action:@selector(buttonClicked:)
        forControlEvents:UIControlEventTouchUpInside];
```

The `action:` parameter takes in an argument of type `SEL` (selector). In the preceding code, you pass in the name of the method that you have defined — `buttonClicked:` — which is defined within the class:

```
-(IBAction) buttonClicked: (id) sender{
    //...
}
```

Alternatively, you can create an object of type `SEL` and then instantiate it by using the `NSSelectorFromString` function (which takes in a string containing the method name):

```
NSString *nameOfMethod = @"buttonClicked:";
SEL methodName = NSSelectorFromString(nameOfMethod);
```

The call to the `addTarget:action:forControlEvents:` method now looks like this:

```
[button addTarget:self action:methodName
forControlEvents:UIControlEventTouchUpInside];
```

 NOTE *When naming a selector, be sure to specify the full name of the method. For example, if a method name has one or more parameters, you need to add a ":" in the sector, such as:*

```
NSString *nameOfMethod = @"someMethod:withPara1:andPara2:";
```

 NOTE *Because Objective-C is an extension of C, it is common to see C functions interspersed throughout your Objective-C application. C functions use the parentheses () to pass in arguments for parameters.*

CATEGORIES

A category in Objective-C allows you to add methods to an existing class without the need to subclass it. You can also use a category to override the implementation of an existing class.

 NOTE *In some languages (such as C#), a category is known as a an extension method.*

As an example, imagine that you want to test whether a string contains a valid email address. You can add an `isEmail` method to the `NSString` class so that you can call the `isEmail` method on any `NSString` instance, like this:

```
NSString *email = @"weimenglee@gmail.com";
if ([email isEmail])
  {
      //...
  }
```

To do so, you can simply create a new class file and code it as follows:

```
//---utils.h---
#import <Foundation/Foundation.h>

//---NSString is the class you are extending---
@interface NSString (stringUtils)

//---the method you are adding to the NSString class---
- (BOOL) isEmail;

@end
```

Basically, it looks the same as declaring a new class except that it does not inherit from any other class. The `stringUtils` is a name that identifies the category you are adding, and you can use any name you want.

Next, you need to implement the method(s) you are adding:

```
//---utils.m---
#import "Utils.h"
@implementation NSString (Utilities)

- (BOOL) isEmail
{
    NSString *emailRegEx =
        @"(?:[a-z0-9!#$%\\&'*+/=?\\^_`{|}~-]+(?:\\.[a-z0-9!#$%\\&'*+/=?\\^_`{|}"
        @"~-]+)*|\"(?:[\\x01-\\x08\\x0b\\x0c\\x0e-\\x1f\\x21\\x23-\\x5b\\x5d-\\"
        @"x7f]|\\\\[\\x01-\\x09\\x0b\\x0c\\x0e-\\x7f])*\")@(?:(?:[a-z0-9](?:[a-"
        @"z0-9-]*[a-z0-9])?\\.)+[a-z0-9](?:[a-z0-9-]*[a-z0-9])?|\\[(?:(?:25[0-5"
        @"]|2[0-4][0-9]|[01]?[0-9][0-9]?)\\.){3}(?:25[0-5]|2[0-4][0-9]|[01]?[0-"
        @"9][0-9]?|[a-z0-9-]*[a-z0-9]:(?:[\\x01-\\x08\\x0b\\x0c\\x0e-\\x1f\\x21"
        @"-\\x5a\\x53-\\x7f]|\\\\[\\x01-\\x09\\x0b\\x0c\\x0e-\\x7f])+)\\])";

NSPredicate *regExPredicate = [NSPredicate
                              predicateWithFormat:@"SELF MATCHES %@",
                              emailRegEx];

    return [regExPredicate evaluateWithObject:self];
}

@end
```

NOTE *The code for validating an email address using regular expression is adapted from* http://cocoawithlove.com/2009/06/ verifying-that-string-is-email-address.html.

You can then test for the validity of an email address using the newly added method:

```
NSString *email = @"weimenglee@gmail.com";
if ([email isEmail])
    NSLog(@"Valid email");
else
    NSLog(@"Invalid email");
```

SUMMARY

In this appendix, you had an overview of the Objective-C language. Although it did not offer comprehensive coverage of the language, it presented sufficient information for you to get started in iPhone programming.

Testing on an Actual iPhone or iPod Touch

Although the iPhone Simulator is a very handy tool that allows you to test your iPhone applications without needing an actual device, nothing beats testing on a real device. This is especially true when you are ready to roll out your applications to the world — you must ensure that it works correctly on real devices. In addition, if your application requires access to hardware features on an iPhone/iPod Touch, such as the accelerometer and GPS, you need to test it on a real device — the iPhone Simulator is simply not adequate.

This appendix walks through the steps you need to take to test your iPhone applications on a real device, be it iPhone or iPod Touch.

SIGN UP FOR THE IPHONE DEVELOPER PROGRAM

The first step toward testing your applications on a real device is to sign up for the iPhone Developer Program at `http://developer.apple.com/iphone/program/`. Two programs are available: Standard and Enterprise. For most developers wanting to release applications on the App Store, the Standard program, which costs $99, is sufficient. Check out `http://developer.apple.com/iphone/program/apply.html` to learn more about the differences between the Standard and Enterprise programs.

If you just want to test your application on your actual iPhone/iPod Touch, sign up for the Standard program.

START YOUR XCODE

To test your iPhone applications on your device, you need to obtain an iPhone Development Certificate from the iPhone Developer Program Portal. The following sections walk you through the necessary steps from obtaining your certificate to deploying your applications onto the device.

First, obtain the 40-character identifier that uniquely identifies your iPhone/iPod Touch. To do so, connect your device to your Mac and start Xcode. Choose Window ⟹ Organizer to launch the Organizer application. Figure E-1 shows the Organizer application displaying the identifier of my iPhone. Copy the identifier you obtain and save it somewhere. You will need this identifier later on.

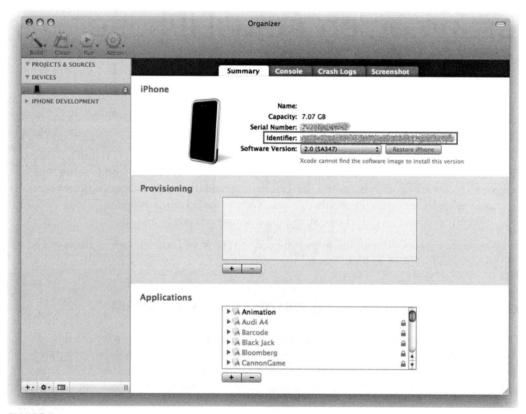

FIGURE E-1

GENERATING A CERTIFICATE SIGNING REQUEST

To request a development certificate from Apple, you need to generate a Certificate Signing Request. You can do this using the Keychain Access application located in the `Applications/Utilities/` folder (see Figure E-2).

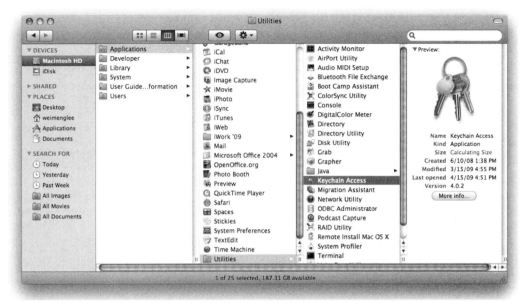

FIGURE E-2

In the Keychain Access application, choose Keychain Access ⇨ Certificate Assistant and select Request a Certificate From a Certificate Authority (see Figure E-3).

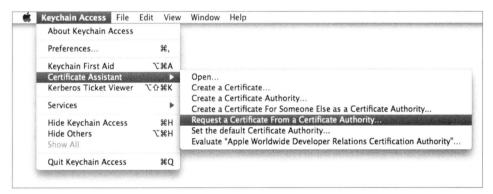

FIGURE E-3

In the Certificate Assistant window (see Figure E-4), enter your email address, select the Saved to Disk radio button, and select the Let Me Specify Key Pair Information check box. Click Continue.

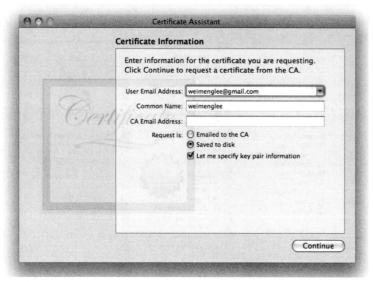

FIGURE E-4

Choose a key size of 2048 bits and choose the RSA algorithm (see Figure E-5). Click Continue.

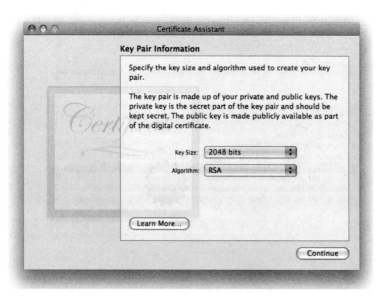

FIGURE E-5

You are asked to save the request to a file. Use the default name suggested and click Save (see Figure E-6).

FIGURE E-6

LOGGING IN TO THE IPHONE DEVELOPER PROGRAM PORTAL

After you have generated the Certificate Signing Request, you need to log in to Apple's iPhone Dev Center (see Figure E-7). Click the iPhone Developer Program Portal link on the right of the page. Remember, you need to pay $99 to have access to this page.

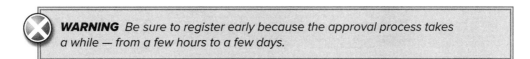

WARNING *Be sure to register early because the approval process takes a while — from a few hours to a few days.*

FIGURE E-7

On the iPhone Developer Program Portal page, click the Launch Assistant button (see Figure E-8) to walk you through the process of provisioning your iPhone and generating the development certificate.

FIGURE E-8

You should see the welcome page. Click Continue.

First, you are asked to create an App ID (see Figure E-9). An *App ID* is a series of characters used to uniquely identify an application (or applications) on your iPhone. Enter a friendly name to describe this App ID (to be generated by Apple). Click Continue.

FIGURE E-9

The next screen allows you to provide a description of your iPhone/iPod Touch. You need to provide the device ID that you obtained earlier (see Figure E-10). Click Continue.

FIGURE E-10

You are now ready to submit the Certificate Signing Request to Apple (see Figure E-11). The instructions on the screen show you the steps that you have performed earlier. Click Continue.

FIGURE E-11

In this screen, click the Choose File button to select the Certificate Signing Request file that you created earlier. After you have selected the file, click Continue.

Provide a description for your Provisioning Profile (see Figure E-12). A Provisioning Profile is generated so that you can download it at a later stage and install it on your device. Click Generate.

FIGURE E-12

A Provisioning Profile is generated (see Figure E-13). Click Continue when it's finished.

FIGURE E-13

You can download the generated Provisioning Profile onto your Mac by clicking the Download Now button (see Figure E-14). Next, click Continue.

FIGURE E-14

Drag and drop the downloaded Provisioning Profile (which, by default, is saved in the Downloads folder of your Mac) onto Xcode (located in the Dock). Doing so installs the Provisioning Profile onto your connected iPhone or iPod Touch. Click Continue (see Figure E-15).

FIGURE E-15

You can verify that the Provisioning Profile is installed correctly on your device by going to the Organizer application and viewing the Provisioning section (see Figure E-16).

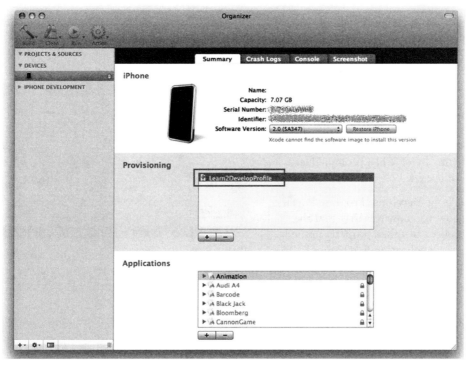

FIGURE E-16

Back in the iPhone Developer Program Portal, you are now ready to download and install the Development Certificate onto your iPhone or iPod Touch. Click the Download Now button (see Figure E-17) to download the Development Certificate to your Mac. Click Continue.

FIGURE E-17

In the Downloads folder of your Mac, double-click the `developer_identity.cer` file that you have just downloaded to install it into a keychain on your Mac. When prompted (see Figure E-18), click OK.

Back in the iPhone Developer Program Portal, it will now show you how to verify that the certificate has been installed properly in the Keychain Access application (see Figure E-19). Click Continue.

FIGURE E-18

FIGURE E-19

In the Keychain Access application, select the `login` keychain and look for the certificate named `iPhone Developer: your name` (see Figure E-20). If you can see it, your certificate is installed correctly.

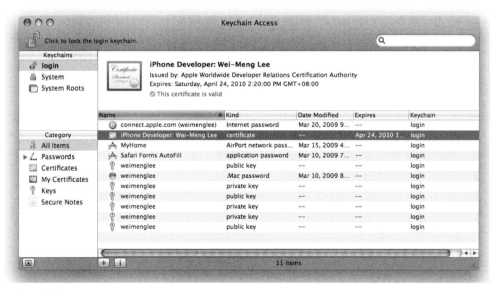

FIGURE E-20

You are now almost ready to deploy your iPhone application onto your iPhone or iPod Touch. Click Continue (see Figure E-21).

FIGURE E-21

Click Done to dismiss the dialog.

In Xcode, look for the Active SDK item. If this item is not already on the toolbar, choose View ➪ Customize Toolbar and add it to the toolbar. Then, under Active SDK, select the OS version number of the device that is currently connected to your Mac. In my case, my iPhone is running the older iPhone OS 2.0, so I selected `iPhone Device (2.0)` (see Figure E-22).

FIGURE E-22

Press Command-R to run the application. You are prompted for permission to access the certificate saved in your keychain. Click Allow (or Always Allow) to proceed with the signing (see Figure E-23).

FIGURE E-23

Your application will now be deployed to the device. You can see its progress in the Summary tab of the Organizer application (see Figure E-24).

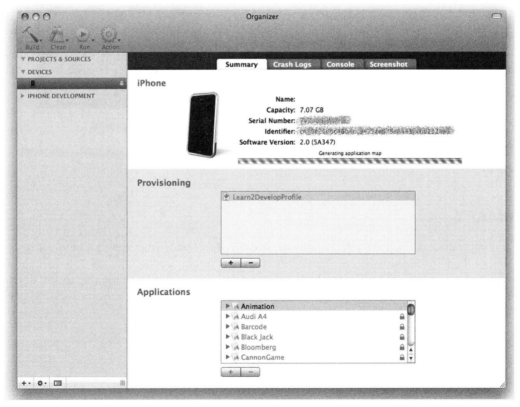

FIGURE E-24

After the application is deployed onto your device, it will be launched automatically. You can capture screenshots of your device by clicking the Screenshot tab of the Organizer application (see Figure E-25).

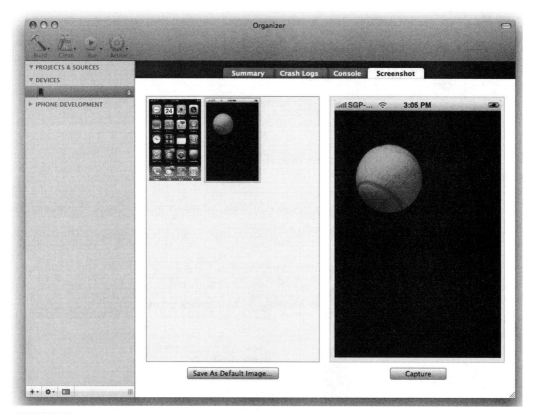

FIGURE E-25

SUMMARY

In this appendix, you have seen the various steps required to deploy your application to your iPhone or iPod Touch. Although the number of steps may seem intimidating, it is actually quite a straightforward process. The iPhone Developer program allows you to provision up to 100 devices for testing purposes. After a device is provisioned, you can use the development certificate to deploy your applications onto it.

INDEX

INDEX

iPhone SDK *(continued)*
  frameworks, 16–17, 21
  installation, 4–5
  licensing agreements, 4–5
iPhone Simulator, 4, 6, 8–12, 21
  applications
    deploying, 28
    uninstalling, 11–12
  as emulator, 9
  features, 10
    not available, 10
  gestures, 10
  limitations, 21
  Xcode, 8
IsSecure key, 272

J

JavaScript, 20

K

Key key, 269
keyboard, 115
  applications, integration, 115
  automatically display at view load, 127
  characters entered, 117
  detection, 127–138
  dismissing, 119–121, 122–126
  Email Address, 118
  height in pixels, 128
  hidden, 116
  hidden/visible notification, 128
  languages, 115, 117
  Number Pad, 118
    setting to, 121–127
  Phone Pad, 118
  Return key, 119, 138
  Search Bar, 253
  shortcuts, Interface Builder, 442
  Text Input Traits, 117–118
  TextField view, 116
  types, 117
keyboardBounds, 135
keyboardWillHide: method, 137
Keychain Access application, 482–485
keys
  IsSecure, 272
  Key, 269
  Title, 269
  Type, 269
  Values, 272

L

Landscape mode, 19, 31
  Tab Bar applications, 196–198
languages, 115, 117
launching Xcode, 421
Library folder, 303–307
Library (Interface Builder), 444–445
Library window
  Controllers, 76
  Data Views, 76
  Inputs and Values, 76
  views, 76
  Windows, Views & Bars, 76
linking actions to views, 173–175
List View, 189
listOfMovies array, 255
listOfMovies object, 231
Load Settings Values, 273
loadView method, 97
location
  coordinates, obtaining, 390–394
  GPS receiver, 390
  locationManager:didFailWithError event, 393

W

X